# CHINA CROSS TALK

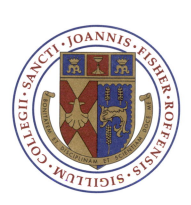

Lavery Library

St. John Fisher
College
Rochester, New York

# CHINA CROSS TALK

The American Debate over
China Policy since Normalization

## A READER

*Edited by*
Scott Kennedy

ROWMAN & LITTLEFIELD PUBLISHERS, INC.
*Lanham • Boulder • New York • Oxford*

ROWMAN & LITTLEFIELD PUBLISHERS, INC.

Published in the United States of America
by Rowman & Littlefield Publishers, Inc.
A Member of the Rowman & Littlefield Publishing Group
4720 Boston Way, Lanham, Maryland 20706
www.rowmanlittlefield.com

PO Box 317
Oxford
OX2 9RU, UK

British Library Cataloguing in Publication Information Available

**Library of Congress Cataloging-in-Publication Data**

China cross talk : the American debate over China policy since normalization : a reader /
    edited by Scott Kennedy.
        p. cm.
    Includes bibliographical references and index.
    ISBN 0-7425-1785-3 (cloth : alk. paper) — ISBN 0-7425-1786-1 (pbk. : alk. paper)
    1. United States—Foreign relations—China—Sources. 2. China—Foreign
relations—United States—Sources. 3. United States—Foreign relations—
1945–1989—Sources. 4. United States—Foreign relations—1989—Sources. I.
Kennedy, Scott, 1967–
    E183.8.C5 C469 2002
    327.73051'09'045—dc21                                          2002012833

Printed in the United States of America

⊗™ The paper used in this publication meets the minimum requirements of
American National Standard for Information Sciences—Permanence
of Paper for Printed Library Materials, ANSI/Z39.48-1992.

To my family,
my closest and dearest interlocutors on China policy

# Contents

# Foreword

In the three decades since President Richard Nixon began the U.S. opening to China, American debates about China have been among the most contentious policy debates in this country. Over the years, the debate's participants have changed and the issues have evolved, but the central question has remained the same: How should the United States approach this very complex and important nation?

The primary argument has been between advocates of engagement and those who are more skeptical of engagement's benefits. Should the United States establish normal diplomatic relations with China? Should it offer China the same terms of trade granted to most other nations? Should America defend Taiwan in case of Chinese attack? Should it sanction China for human rights abuses or the proliferation of nuclear or missile technology? These are some of the key questions that have sparked heated debate among U.S. policymakers, China analysts, and the American people. The China debate continues today, and it is only likely to intensify as China becomes increasingly assertive on the world stage.

American policy toward China is unusually complex because America has many common interests with China as well as many interests that diverge. The common interests include protecting peace and stability in Asia, combating international terrorism, and boosting trade and investment between the two nations. Cooperation between the United States and China is clearly conducive to the advancement of these interests. Yet China and the United States differ markedly in their approaches to other issues, such as political enfranchisement, human rights, the proliferation of nuclear or missile technology, and Taiwan. There is not a consensus about how the United States can best promote its interests on these sensitive issues, which provide the fuel for much debate and disagreement.

The advocates of engagement believe that the United States can have the greatest influence on China by increasing Chinese access to foreign goods, information, and people and by integrating China into international political and economic structures. They maintain that greater economic freedom and prosperity in China will, over time, lead to greater political freedom and respect for human rights. They also assert that closer ties with China will reduce the chance that a major war between the United States and China—a frightening prospect—will occur.

The advocates of a tougher approach to China counter that the United States should not do business with a government that oppresses its people and violates fundamental civil liberties and human rights. They argue that the United States should pressure China to reform by withholding a normal trade relationship and strongly condemning abusive Chinese policies. Some of them believe that an armed conflict between the United States and China is inevitable and that America should not trade with China, invest in it, or take other actions that might build up Chinese power.

One of the interesting aspects of the China debate is its unusual political breakdown in the United States. Disagreements on China do not correspond to typical partisan divides. In the U.S. Congress, for instance, a bipartisan coalition of moderate Democrats and Republicans generally backs engagement with China, while many Democratic liberals and Republican conservatives are critical of engagement for a variety of reasons. Some commentators and policymakers on the right argue for a hard-line policy toward China because of their strong ideological antipathy to communism and concerns about religious freedom and national security. They are frequently joined in China debates by labor leaders, human rights activists, and others on the left who want the United States to stand up for worker protections, civil liberties, and other freedoms. The China debate sometimes makes for strange bedfellows indeed.

In the executive branch, however, there tends to be more continuity in the approach toward China. Every U.S. president since Nixon has advanced a general policy of engagement with China, though no president has found a completely satisfactory China policy. Some presidents have come into office promising to get tough with China but quickly determined that U.S. interests in a range of areas are best served by a cooperative rather than a confrontational relationship.

To many Americans, China is a mysterious and puzzling country. Scholars of China and U.S. policymakers therefore have an important responsibility to help the American people understand China and the U.S.–China relationship. This book's wide-ranging collection of articles, speeches, and documents on U.S.–China relations reflects the diversity and intensity of the China debate over the past 25 years. The selections illustrate how far the U.S.–China relationship has come since the 1970s and how much further it has to go. They should be of interest to scholars, policymakers, and all Americans interested in understanding the relationship's many dimensions and dilemmas.

The U.S.–China relationship is today the most difficult bilateral relationship for the United States and one of the most important bilateral relationships for the world. So many major issues in the 21st century—international security, the world economy, the global environment, and human welfare—will depend in part on the evolution of U.S.–China relations. The raging debates encapsulated in this valuable book remind us that we have a great deal at stake in China and that it is imperative that America get China policy right.

Lee H. Hamilton

# Introduction

If we treat China as an enemy now, we are guaranteeing ourselves an enemy.[1]

The [Clinton] Administration believes that if we don't treat China as an enemy, it won't become one. Those who recommend a tougher approach, those who call for containing China's ambitions, are usually accused of creating a self-fulfilling prophecy. But what if the prophesy has already been fulfilled?[2]

Let me begin with an admission: You are going to agree with at most half of the views expressed in this book, and you are likely to find the remaining views misguided or unreasonable. While it is difficult enough to admit this on the very first page to a reader who may have not yet made it to the cash register or "proceeded to checkout," it even may be more difficult to predict when you will nod your head in agreement or shake your head in disgust. What is certain is that you will be provoked, pushed, and prodded at every turn, and perhaps persuaded to change your mind about what you consider to be the most appropriate American policies toward China.

In the early years of the Cold War, the United States and the People's Republic of China (PRC) were bitter enemies. Their soldiers fought against each other in Korea and almost came to blows over the tiny islands of Quemoy and Matsu, trade and investment were halted, and inflammatory denunciations were leveled at the other side practically every day. They could not even stand to officially recognize the other's existence. For a variety of reasons international and domestic, the confrontation ebbed in the early 1970s, highlighted by President Nixon's visit to China in 1972 and culminated with the formal establishment of diplomatic relations in 1979. Over the following decades, ties broadened at the official and unofficial levels, such that exchanges of goods, ideas, and people have today reached unprecedented proportions. Yet since 1989, the official relationship has been marked by a growing level of mutual suspicion and distrust. Periods of stability interspersed with crises have become the norm.[3]

At almost every turn, there has been vigorous debate about what policies the United States should adopt toward China. During the 1940s, the debate centered around whether the United States should continue to support Chiang Kai-shek's Kuomintang party, switch horses to the seemingly more popular Communists, or push for a multiparty coalition that gave a seat to all sides. In the next decade, Americans argued about whether the Communist bloc was monolithic and how to exploit or create fissures between the PRC and the Soviets. It was in the 1960s that support gradually emerged for some sort of rapprochement with China, but there was no consensus as many argued that the containment policy should be maintained. During the first two decades of the Cold War, these debates occurred primarily within the confines of government. Some journalists and scholars penned vivid and dramatic accounts about China and offered some policy suggestions, but their contributions were limited and intermittent, partly a result of the McCarthy-era witch hunts that raised doubts about the loyalty of China specialists in and out of government.[4] Only in the mid-1960s did academics begin to proactively involve themselves in the policy debate by publishing articles, testifying before Congress, and establishing policy-related organizations. The vast majority of those with a potential interest in China—pecuniary or otherwise—were not well organized and had little weight in Washington, the obvious exception being the old China (Taiwan) lobby.[5]

As fascinating and significant as the discussion over China policy was during the height of the Cold War, *China Cross Talk* is dedicated to providing a window into the debate as it has unfolded since President Carter's address to the nation on the evening of Friday, December 15, 1978, when he announced that the United States and the People's Republic would establish formal diplomatic relations and that the United States simultaneously would downgrade its relations with Taiwan. This focus is in part because this period represents a new historic chapter in the relationship of almost a quarter century when all aspects of ties—security, economics, and human rights—found their way onto the agenda, but it is also because over the following 20-plus years, the debate over American foreign policy, including that toward China, has become a more public affair. Not only have government officials spoken more often on the record about China, but, more important, they have been joined by a phalanx of additional actors: academic experts on various aspects of China and on global security and economic affairs; lobbyists representing the interests of business, the environment, human rights, and other governments; and newspaper and magazine editors, columnists, and reporters, the last often with extended experience reporting from China. The "policy community" has expanded, and so have the dynamics of policymaking. To some, this transformation has resulted in a cacophony of voices that makes it harder for the government to pursue consistent policies in the broader national interest. For others, the debate has become more democratic and hence is an inherently positive development. Regardless of the spin one puts on the change, it is clear change is here to stay.

The selections that make up the core of the present volume touch on the entire spectrum of policy issues, from what general approach the United States should adopt toward China to how it should be tailored to the various aspects of relations. The contours of what constitutes the "American" debate are somewhat ambiguous. While most selections here are by Americans, the guiding principle was to include important views expressed openly to the American government and to the American public that have had an appreciable effect on the U.S. policy discussion.[6] As such, the selections reflect a rich assortment of statements by American presidents, speeches by members of the House and Senate, testimony before congressional committees by experts and interest group representatives, magazine articles, newspaper editorials and commentaries, and even some cartoons.

There have been a variety of analyses of the American debate since normalization. As useful as these are to the policy community, students, and the broader public, such treatments have had two qualities. They have necessarily been summaries of the various views expressed, and most have been confined to a relatively short period of the debate, with the majority focusing on the period since 1989.[7] The present volume complements these efforts by allowing the participants in the debate to speak for themselves without any intervening translation provided by a second party. More important, the entries span a 23-year period. Readers can see not only how different sides have debated each other on a given issue at a given moment but also how arguments have evolved over time and how some participants have argued with themselves as their own views have changed. Thus, unlike retrospective histories, *China Cross Talk* is firsthand intellectual history.

This book is defined as much by what it contains as by what it leaves out. The selections are not about general American (and Western) perceptions of China. Nor are they dispassionate histories detailing actual American policy, the state of relations, or the internal debate within the U.S. government.[8] Rather, all the selections in this volume are polemics, if not in tone then in their advocacy of specific policy agendas based on their subjective interpretation of American interests and other factors. And finally, and most regrettably, this volume gives limited attention to Chinese perspectives on the relationship in general or on American policy. Officials of the PRC have on occasion penned letters to the editor, and Chinese scholars have published some articles in American periodicals, but the PRC citizens who have had a far more appreciable effect on the American discussion have been dissidents, two of whom are included among the main selections. The debate within China over the relationship has become increasingly complex—and quite worthy of attention by Americans—but is properly the subject of another book.[9] To compensate for this shortcoming, we have included response essays written specifically for this volume by two prominent PRC scholars, Wu Xinbo and Zhu Feng, who historically have held differing perspectives on U.S.–China relations.[10]

With an understanding of the parameters of the present volume, a few words should be offered about the parameters of the debate itself. Since the mid-1990s in the United States, the policy options on China usually have been portrayed as a choice between engagement and containment. There also has emerged a stream of intermediate options that use parts of these two terms: "constrainment," "congagement," and "conditional engagement" are the three most popular. However, this spectrum is illogical since engagement and containment are not polar opposites; the term "engagement" without a modifier simply means interaction, whereas "containment" implies a confrontational stance toward one's opponent. Policy alternatives, in fact, have varied according to how much one thinks the United States ought to accommodate China. At one end is the notion that the United States ought to use all means at its disposal to check China, whether it be on Taiwan or human rights. The most radical form of this view is a policy of rollback, which posits that U.S. interests can be served only by the replacement of the Communist government. One step toward the middle is the option of using cooperative tools, not outright confrontation, to make China accommodate U.S. interests. The next point on the spectrum also stresses cooperative relations but countenances American steps to accommodate Chinese interests as well. The final point on the continuum represents a one-sided American accommodation of China's preferences.

Given this wide array of possibilities, the question then becomes, Why might people sit at different points along this spectrum? The differences in policy preferences, between those who favor the United States taking a hard line versus those who are more accommodating, are based on varying assessments of five issues, all of which are found among this book's selections. The first concerns China's power. There has been substantial disagreement over China's present and projected military capabilities relative to the United States and its East Asian neighbors. Those more worried about China believe it has already modernized its military and will most likely make even greater strides in the future, leaving China stronger than its neighbors. More skeptical observers focus on the continued weaknesses of China's military, the likely slow pace of progress in the future, and China's inability to complete certain missions (e.g., conquer Taiwan), particularly given the relative strength and commitment of the United States to the region.

The second source of disagreement has been conflicting assessments of China's foreign policy intentions. Some believe China is a status quo power. Although Taiwan and islands in the South China Sea are exceptions, they believe that the stress China places on economic modernization tempers its irredentist ambitions. Alternatively, others see China as interested in becoming the dominant power in East Asia or even challenging the United States for global preeminence. Relatedly, they believe that unification with Taiwan is so important to Beijing that China would risk further economic development and ties with the West to achieve this goal. Many who fit in the latter camp focus on how China's growing military prowess necessarily translates into making it a dissatisfied power and/or how China is driven to reclaim its past glory as the Middle Kingdom, when other states on its periphery and afar paid tribute to China and kowtowed before the emperor.[11]

The third area of contention involves varying judgments of China's domestic political and economic situations. On the political side, opinions have ranged from those believing that China has undergone a great deal of political liberalization even without formal democratization to the view that China has remained totalitarian despite economic reforms. On the economic side, views have been just as spread apart, from the belief that China has become a market economy to the position that China has adopted Japan's mercantilist policies that radically limit foreign companies' abilities to gain a foothold and make a profit in China.

Fourth, observers have disagreed about the extent to which China is able to help the United States achieve its other foreign policy goals. During the Cold War, the main issue was whether China was a useful counterweight to the Soviets. From the 1990s on, the issue has been whether China could positively influence the behavior of rogue states, such as North Korea, and assist in addressing transnational issues that have security implications, such as environmental degradation, international crime, and terrorism. The more useful one sees China, the more likely one is to suggest relatively more cooperative policies.

The last source of disagreement shaping policy preferences toward China concerns whether liberal means can effectively shape China's behavior. From the perspective of international relations theory, liberals believe that states can be pacified in three ways. The first is democratization, on the assumption that democracies fight less because their citizens, who generally oppose war, can use democratic institutions to keep their governments from being aggressive. Such internal checks make war between democracies especially unlikely. The second is to promote the development of a market economy and international commercial linkages. The hope is that such ties create domestic interests against conflict with those with which the country interacts. And the third liberal tool is integrating a country into international formal arrangements in trade, security, and human rights, on the grounds that integration forces the country to make commitments to others based on international law and also gives it a stake in making the system work. Participants to the China policy discussion have differed sharply over whether these tools work. Realists typically challenge each tool and hold that states pursue their interests regardless of their domestic political system, economic engagement may very well strengthen a potential opponent, and states may manipulate international regimes to their advantage.

As important as the last source of disagreement is, all five have affected observers' policy suggestions. Not only have American liberals and realists disagreed, but realists have differed as well because of divergent assessments of the other four factors, a situation akin to American policy debates over Japan.[12] Thus, while some realists have not strayed from seeing the need to balance power against power, others have argued that the United States has no choice but to resort to liberal means to deal with China.[13]

With a sense of the range of options and the possible reasons for choosing different ones, what then are the actual trends in the debate over China policy? Over the past two decades, there have consistently been views that cross much of the spectrum outlined previously. What has changed has been the balance of opinion, with the weight of support shifting from a more to a less accommodating posture. The 1980s was generally an era of good feeling and the years since ones of increased suspicion. Selections for this volume are grouped into six time periods, each of which is bracketed by a key event that pushed the policy world to reassess its options. Dividing lines include crises (the 1981–1982 row over U.S. arms sales to Taiwan, June 4, and the 1996 Taiwan Straits standoff) and the start of new U.S. administrations (Clinton in 1993 and Bush in 2001).

One group of commentators whose opinions have not changed tremendously is editorial cartoonists. Their art may only rarely have an appreciable direct effect on policy, but cartoons have both reflected and shaped broader public opinion. Although there are exceptions, the vast majority of American cartoonists who have commented about China and American policy over the past 20 years have portrayed China as being totalitarian and expansionist and the American government as so beholden to economic interests that it has not sufficiently contested China's behavior on human rights or security affairs. While many might label such views simplistic and encouraging of outdated stereotypes, just as many believe that cartoonists powerfully cut to the heart of the moral dilemmas of America's China policy. Thus, given their controversial and visible place in the American conversation, examples of their work are contained at several points in the text.

The rise of opinion calling for a tougher approach to China is most clearly seen in the discussions over human rights and security issues. The dividing line in the human rights debate is a single day: June 4, 1989. Prior to that day, the human rights policy options ranged from ignoring the issue altogether to publicly criticizing China about its record. The day after June 4, the spectrum shifted; the old hard-line position of condemnation became the conciliatory position, and the new tough approach urged wide-sweeping sanctions.

President Bush decried the massacre, which would have made him appear as a hard-liner during most of the 1980s. But because he opposed the harshest sanction against China, revoking MFN (most-favored-nation status), he was labeled an accommodationist. This new spectrum has remained intact since. Those who see China moving in the right direction want to further encourage it with cooperative methods, while those who think that China is regressing or, in fact, has never progressed continue to advocate pressure, even though MFN as a tool has been effectively taken off the table.

The balance of views regarding security has moved in the same direction but much more gradually. Key moments prompting this shift have been the 1989 massacre and the collapse of communism in central and eastern Europe over the next two years; new estimates in the early 1990s that China had one of the world's largest economies in purchasing power parity terms; Chinese military exercises near Taiwan in 1995 and 1996; China's popular reaction to the U.S. bombing of its embassy in Belgrade in May 1999; the release of the Cox Report a few weeks later, which charged China with stealing U.S. nuclear weapons secrets; and China's detention of American military officers following the plane collision over the South China Sea in April 2001. The discussion has moved from the pros and cons of military cooperation in the 1970s and 1980s, including military sales, to China's conformity or lack thereof to various proliferation regimes in the late 1980s to debates about the extent of China's military power and how to counter or channel it in a favorable direction since the mid-1990s. Disagreements over antiproliferation policy have remained important (even more so after the September 11 terrorist attacks), but the topic of greatest concern in recent years has been how China exercises its own military power, not the extent to which it has aided that of others. In the 1980s, few saw China as an imminent or potential threat to the United States. Since the mid-1990s, expressions of fear about China have become commonplace.[14]

Although the dominant trend in the debate has been in a hard-line direction, there is an extremely important exception: presidents. Those occupying the White House over the past three decades, as a rule, have been far more critical and hard-line toward China as candidates than as occupants of the White House. President Clinton's shift was perhaps the most memorable. He lambasted George Bush for cozying up to the "Butchers of Beijing" during the 1992 campaign. Once in the White House, he started with a strategy based on pressure but then shifted back toward policies reminiscent of Bush's. Even President George Bush started as a China hawk. He lambasted President Carter for the terms on which normalization was agreed, the key issue to Bush being the lack of commitment toward Taiwan's security. It was not until early in the Reagan administration that Bush (and Reagan) stressed the importance of relations with China. George W. Bush has shown similar signs of retreat from a purely confrontational approach. It should be remembered, though, that since

President Nixon, all presidents have adopted policies toward China that have combined elements of cooperation and contention.

An important question is why presidents "go soft" on China or, to put it another way, become prudent. Perhaps it is because China has changed in the interim, and although a president's philosophy remained constant, China has moved enough in his direction to warrant policy revisions. An alternative possibility is that the president's view of China, not China itself, has changed from the perspective of his new position, where he must balance multiple priorities and take an overall approach. A third option is that presidents are political animals who simply follow the politically expedient path: there are potentially more votes to be won (e.g., from organized labor) by criticizing China and looking tough on defense than by appearing conciliatory during the campaign, but there are few penalties for violating this stance once in office. The last possible reason explaining presidents' "about face" is policy failure: presidents try hardline approaches but then, when they fail, move toward the middle.[15] As Deng Xiaoping was wont to say, perhaps "practice is the sole criterion of truth."

The presidential shifts may reflect a common destination for several administrations, but the tacking to and fro like a boat sailing into the wind also indicates the growing level of discord among experts, interest groups, and pundits. The relative consensus of the 1980s was replaced by polarization in the 1990s, to the point where opposing sides have had difficulty agreeing over first principles. They alternatively deride the other as "alarmists" and "panda huggers." Classic, but by no means critical, examples of such polarization are the widely divergent opinions offered up by the amateur book reviews that often accompany the advertisements for books sold through the on-line retailer Amazon.com. In *Same Bed, Different Dreams* (2001), David M. Lampton stressed how important good U.S.–China relations are to American interests. One reviewer from Oregon praised the book: "Lampton writes from a perspective unencumbered by the black and white thinking that often dominates both our domestic politics and other popular books on the subject. I found it a fascinating insider's look at a relationship that will continue to be rewarding, challenging, and very important to the world political scene." But another reader from Asia disagreed, countering, "Lampton is completely predictable. He is an apologist and seeks to justify each dreadful Chinese action against human rights with the promise of US jobs." If Bill Gertz's *China Threat* (2000) is any indication, reviews of books calling for a tougher approach on China have received similarly divergent appraisals. One East Coast reviewer gushed, "*The China Threat* by Bill Gertz is not so much informative regarding China's views towards the United States (they have always been obvious) but it is very much so regarding the previous two administrations' willingness to go blind on the subject of China." Gertz's book evoked a very different reaction from a West Coast reader, who wrote. "Facts? Rational Thought? Psh, who needs it. This is a book that started with a conclusion, and then built the arguments around it."[16] That so many books on China policy are simultaneously embraced and scorned shows that the reading public is just as divided as the specialists.

Another sign of this polarization has been the growing tendency to question the motives of one's policy opponents. Advocates and critics alike have been accused of holding their positions not because of their inherent merits but because advocacy for or adoption of certain policies supposedly benefits themselves. Few participants have gone unscathed. The Pentagon has been accused of creating a China threat so as to increase its budgets and the business community of downplaying human rights abuses and overplaying the benefits of trade because of their financial stake in China.[17] President Clinton was similarly accused by some of moderating his position on China because of campaign contributions from both domestic and foreign sources.

Not surprisingly, China specialists have not been immune to such attacks, either. From the 1950s to the early 1970s, many government and academic experts who favored cooperative ties with China were accused of being Communist sympathizers.[18] From the mid-1970s on, as China moved away from class struggle and focused on modernization, those deeply involved with China have been accused of simply being pro-Chinese. At first, the criticism was one of intellectual weakness: China specialists had a predisposition toward China, and their travels and research there only confirmed such biases. As one commentator put it, "We have a full stable of academics and other well-wishers who are not only willing, but anxious, to believe all the best about that society with which we have what they perceive to be a special relationship. They go for a guided-tour of the PRC and come back singing praises, more than faintly reminiscent of the early euphoria about the Soviet Union in the days of Lincoln Steffens."[19] In the wake of Tiananmen, Senator Paul Sarbanes (D-MD) accused President George Bush of "clientitis," that is, of favoring policies that are in China's interests because of his long association with the country.[20] More recently, added to this charge has been the criticism that China specialists have limited their criticisms of the Chinese regime and defended the importance of good ties in order to maintain their own access to the country. This purportedly has been true of former government officials, such as Henry Kissinger, who have developed lucrative consulting businesses involving China and of scholars who need to conduct field research in China.[21] These charges have grown in saliency after the Chinese government arrested several ethnic Chinese, some of whom were American permanent residents or citizens, for supposedly leaking state secrets. Two goals of this clampdown appear to have been to dissuade ethnic Chinese and other scholars from engaging in potentially politically sensitive research and to intimidate then into softening their criticism of China.[22]

Those accused of allowing their potential conflict of interest to affect their judgment have rarely directly responded to such criticisms in writing. Hence, the one defense of the intentions of those who argue for a nonconfrontational approach to China included in this volume is by William F. Buckley Jr., someone who has not regularly weighed in on China policy. Most often, participants defend their positions on their merits. They might argue that this is because their views are the product of lengthy consideration and analysis and that they do not want to legitimize attacks on their character. Their critics would say that such silence is because the conflicts of interests are so obvious that they are indefensible. Regardless of these charges' merits, it appears that this aspect of the debate will endure until the polarization on actual policy advice subsides.

The final aspect of the debate over China policy deserving mention is its surprisingly theatrical character. The back-and-forth between opposing views is in some ways reminiscent of the Chinese performance art of "cross talk" (*xiangsheng*). Originating in the Song Dynasty (960–1279), cross talk is somewhat akin to Abbott and Costello's "Who's on first?" routine. There are typically two performers, a wise man and a fool. Their lyrical conversation incites the audience's laughter because the play on words and ambiguous contexts inevitably result in mutual misunderstanding. Their dialogues are often repetitious and rarely conclude with either party satisfied.[23]

I am not suggesting that the American China policy debate has been farcical, but it has exhibited other characteristics reminiscent of cross-talk performances. The policy discussion has also been somewhat repetitious, as old arguments have been recycled and applied to new circumstances. By the late 1990s, even the participants themselves had qualities of actors in a prescripted play. This was most evident in the annual debates over MFN, in which congressional hearings were stagelike dramas featuring stereotypical characters: the multinational business executive with a growing stake in the China market, the apparel manufacturer threatened by Chinese imports, the human rights activist with new details of imprisonment and torture, the dissident with policy advice rooted in his or her own suffering, the objective expert dispensing dispassionate wisdom, and, finally, members of Congress alternatively showing their displeasure at the administration's appeasement or support for the administration's balanced approach.

Sitting in the audience, one could easily become frustrated. One would hope in vain for a clear ending in which one side triumphed over the other, but this has never been the case. At least since the normalization of relations—and likely long before—proponents and opponents of developing strong relations with the People's Republic have argued past each other as much as at each other, often not directly addressing the other side's main points.[24] And opponents have looked at the same events, facts, or statements and drawn diametrically opposed conclusions about their significance. A cynic might say that the performers recognize these weaknesses and continue onward because it is the theater of the debate itself that gives them their raison d'être.

However, a more positive interpretation certainly can be made. Most grati-fying is that there has been a spirited public debate at all. It has provided out-side observers with a clear indication of the various policy options, their ratio-nales, their likelihood of being adopted, and post hoc assessments of their effectiveness. All of this has been available to the public. As complex as the pol-icy process in China has become, the vast majority of deliberations have been inaccessible to the average Chinese. In addition, this observer's contact with participants who hold opposing views suggests that policy disagreements in the American debate have been genuine and borne out of research, experience, and reflection. There has been no casting director; instead, the various actors to this drama have been self-selected, an indication that they have held their views prior to assuming their roles.

So, if you missed the performance the first time around or if you want to catch it again, consider *China Cross Talk* your ticket to a restaging of the debate's most memorable scenes. Which characters you determine are the wise men and women and which the fools is entirely up to you. Enjoy the show.

## NOTES

1. Joseph S. Nye Jr., "The Case against Containment: Treat China like an Enemy and That's What It Will Be," *Global Beat,* June 22, 1998, at www.nyu.edu/globalbeat.

2. Robert Kagan, "China's No. 1 Enemy," *New York Times,* May 11, 1999.

3. The secondary literature on American–Chinese relations during the 20th century is voluminous. The best general introduction, which concludes with a detailed biblio-graphic essay, is Warren I. Cohen, *America's Response to China: A History of Sino–American Relations* (4th ed.) (New York: Columbia University Press, 2000). The most up-to-date review of the state of historiography on 20th-century U.S.–East Asian relations is Warren I. Cohen (ed.), *Pacific Passage: The Study of American–East Asian Relations on the Eve of the Twenty-first Century* (New York: Columbia University Press, 1996). A very informative collection of retrospective interviews with American officials is contained in Nancy Bernkopf Tucker (ed.), *China Confidential: American Diplomats and Sino–American Relations, 1945–1996* (New York: Columbia University Press, 2001).

4. On the role of the government's "China Hands," see Paul Gordon Lauren (ed.), *The China Hands' Legacy: Ethics and Diplomacy* (Boulder, CO: Westview Press, 1987). Examples of nongovernmental voices during this period are Theodore H. White and Annalee Jacoby, *Thunder Out of China* (New York: William Sloane Associates, 1946), and John K. Fairbank, "China: Time for a Policy," *Atlantic Monthly,* April 1957.

5. The most prominent of these organizations, the National Committee on United States–China Relations, was created in 1966. Scholarly voices encouraging rapproche-ment include Robert Blum, *The United States and China in World Affairs*, ed. A. Doak Barnett (New York: McGraw-Hill, 1966); A. M. Halpern (ed.), *Policies toward China: Views from Six Continents* (New York: McGraw-Hill, 1966); John King Fairbank, *China: The People's Middle Kingdom and the USA* (Cambridge, MA: Belknap Press of Harvard

University Press, 1967); and A. Doak Barnett and Edwin O. Reischauer (eds.), *The United States and China: The Next Decade* (New York: Praeger, 1970). Academic opinion even more critical of U.S. policy to date is reflected in Edward Friedman and Mark Selden (eds.), *America's Asia: Dissenting Essays in Asian-American Relations* (New York: Pantheon Books, 1971). Defenses of containment and not recognizing the PRC include William Steuart McBirnie, *Red China's Secret Plans for Destroying America* (Upland, CA: Prisoners Bible Broadcast, 1965), and American Council on World Freedom, *Red China and Its American Friends: A Report on the Red China Lobby* (Washington, DC: American Council on World Freedom, 1971). On the China lobby, see Stanley D. Bachrack, *The Committee of One Million: "China Lobby" Politics, 1953–1971* (New York: Columbia University Press, 1976).

6. The one exception among the written selections of material not originally intended for an American audience is the 1998 article by Gerald Segal from the British periodical *New Statesman*, which was chosen because it is a more concise statement of an article Segal published in an American policy journal, "Does China Matter?" *Foreign Affairs*, Vol. 78, No. 5 (September/October 1999), pp. 24–36. Also, two editorial cartoons from the 1980s first appeared in the Hong Kong–based *Far Eastern Economic Review*, a magazine widely read by American East Asia experts and in the mid-1980s purchased by Dow Jones Incorporated.

7. Three useful analyses of the debate are Denny Roy, "The 'China' Threat Issue," *Asian Survey*, Vol. 36, No. 8 (August 1996), pp. 758–771; June Teufel Dreyer, "State of the Field Report: Research on the Chinese Military," *AccessAsia Review*, Vol. 1, No. 1 (August 1997), at www.nbr.org/publications/review; and Owen Harries, "A Year of Debating China," *The National Interest*, No. 58 (Winter 1999/2000), pp. 141–147.

8. On American and Western perceptions of China, see Harold Isaacs, *Scratches on Our Minds: American Views of China and India* (3rd ed.) (Armonk, NY: M E Sharpe, 1980); Richard Madsen, *China and the America Dream: A Moral Inquiry* (Berkeley: University of California Press, 1995); Jonathan D. Spence, *The Chan's Great Continent: China in Western Minds* (New York: Norton, 1998); Colin Mackerras, *Western Images of China* (rev. ed.) (Oxford: Oxford University Press, 1999); Rupert Hodder, *In China's Image: Chinese Self-Perception in Western Thought* (New York: St. Martin's Press, 2000); and Jeffrey N. Wasserstrom, "Big Bad China and the Good Chinese: An American Fairy Tale," in Timothy B. Weston and Lionel M. Jensen (eds.), *China beyond the Headlines* (Lanham, MD: Rowman & Littlefield, 2000), pp. 13–35. Several very good histories on U.S.–China relations that provide insight into the internal policy debates are Harry Harding, *A Fragile Relationship: The United States and China since 1972* (Washington, DC: Brookings Institution, 1992); James Mann, *About Face: A History of America's Curious Relationship with China, from Nixon to Clinton* (New York: Vintage, 1998); Patrick Tyler, *A Great Wall: Six Presidents and China: An Investigative History* (New York: PublicAffairs, 1999); and David M. Lampton, *Same Bed, Different Dreams: Managing U.S.–China Relations, 1989–2000* (Berkeley: University of California Press, 2001).

9. On Chinese views in general, see David L. Shambaugh, *Beautiful Imperialists: China Perceives America, 1972–1990* (Princeton, NJ: Princeton University Press, 1991); Phillip C. Saunders, "China's America Watchers: Changing Attitudes towards the United

States," *The China Quarterly,* No. 161 (March 2000), pp. 41–65; Michael Pillsbury, *China Debates the Future Security Environment* (Washington, DC: National Defense University Press, 2000); Bates Gill and James Reilly, "Sovereignty, Intervention and Peacekeeping: The View from Beijing," *Survival,* Vol. 42, No. 3 (Autumn 2000), pp. 41–59; Yong Deng and Fei-Ling Wang (eds.), *In the Eyes of the Dragon: China Views the World* (Lanham, MD: Rowman & Littlefield, 1999); Geremie R. Barme, "To Screw Foreigners Is Patriotic: China's Avant-Garde Nationalists," *China Journal,* No. 34 (July 1995), pp. 209–234; and Tong Lam, "Identity and Diversity: The Complexities and Contradictions of Chinese Nationalism," in Weston and Jensen, *China beyond the Headlines,* pp. 147–170.

10. Zhu Feng has been more liberal and suggested more conciliatory Chinese policies toward the United States than Wu Xinbo. Wu has also stressed the importance of good U.S.–China relations, but he has called for the United States to make greater compromises. On Zhu Feng, see "Powell Visit May Further Ties," *China Daily,* July 28, 2001; Philip P. Pan, "Beijing Open to Talks on U.S. Plan; Missile Defense Deal May Be Considered," *Washington Post,* September 5, 2001, p. A14; and Mary Kwang, "Chance for Better China–U.S. Ties," *The Straits Times* (Singapore), September 25, 2001, p. 14. On Wu Xinbo, see his "The United States: An Enlightened Superpower in an Ideal World? A Chinese Perspective," *Washington Quarterly,* Vol. 24, No. 3 (Summer 2001), pp. 63–71. More conservative than Wu and not included here is the view that questions the overriding importance of a good relationship and counsels China to "say no" to the United States. See Zhang Xiaobo and Song Qiang, "China Can Say No to America," *New Perspectives Quarterly,* Vol. 13, No. 4 (Fall 1996), pp. 55–56.

11. Such a view of China's imperial-era foreign relations is not unanimously held. Some historians argue that Chinese foreign policy, while steeped in ritual, often involved negotiation and compromise with other peoples and that China was open to trade and cultural influences. The best general overview that takes this perspective is Warren I. Cohen, *East Asia at the Center: Four Thousand Years of Engagement with the World* (New York: Columbia University Press, 2000). On the role of ritual in particular, see James L. Hevia, *Cherishing Men from Afar: Qing Guest Ritual and the Macartney Embassy of 1793* (Durham, NC: Duke University Press, 1995). The more traditional interpretation of Chinese imperial foreign relations can be found in John King Fairbank and Merle Goldman, *China: A New History* (Cambridge, MA: Harvard University Press, 1998).

12. Mike M. Mochizuki, "American and Japanese Strategic Debates: The Need for a New Synthesis," in Mike M. Mochizuki (ed.), *Toward a True Alliance: Restructuring U.S.–Japan Security Relations* (Washington, DC: Brookings Institution Press, 1007), pp. 43–82.

13. One realist put it this way: "As with all too many of the problems of security in East Asia, we may begin with a realist diagnosis but be forced into banking on liberal solutions, simply because the costs of controlling the balance of power may be too high." Richard Betts, "Wealth, Power, and Instability: East Asia and the United States after the Cold War," *International Security,* Vol. 18, No. 3 (Winter 1993–94), p. 55.

14. According to Rielly, the percentage of Americans who perceive the development of China as a world power as a "critical" threat to the United States rose from 40% in

1990 to 57% in 1994 and remained at that level in 1998. Meanwhile, the comparable percentage of American elites ("leaders") holding the same view rose from 16% in 1990 to 46% in 1994 to 56% in 1998. John E. Rielly (ed.), *American Public Opinion and U.S. Foreign Policy, 1995, 1999* (Chicago: Chicago Council on Foreign Relations), at www.ccfr.org.

15. The term "about face" is the title of at least two books on China: John Tierney Jr., *About Face: The China Decision and Its Consequences* (New Rochelle, NY: Arlington House, 1979); and James Mann, *About Face.*

16. These comments were all obtained from Amazon.com's website in July 2001.

17. One could even imagine an attack on human rights organizations that posits they overstate China's violations in order to keep themselves politically relevant and influential or that journalists and their editors hype the dangers of a strong China in order to sell more copies of their publications. The same could be said of reporters who advance their careers through uncovering "disloyal" Americans in the policy and academic communities.

18. John S. Service, *The Amerasia Papers: Some Problems in the History of U.S.–China Relations* (Berkeley: Center for Chinese Studies, University of California, 1971); John Paton Davies Jr., *Dragon by the Tail: American, British, Japanese, and Russian Encounters with China and One Another* (New York: Norton, 1972); and Gary May, *China Scapegoat: The Diplomatic Ordeal of John Carter Vincent* (Washington, DC: New Republic Books, 1979).

19. Richard Walker, "The China Question: Some Observations," in Tierney, *About Face*, pp. 187–188. For a similar criticism of China specialists, see Simon Leys, *The Burning Forest: Essays on Chinese Culture and Politics* (New York: Henry Holt, 1985), pp. 194–207. Lincoln Steffens (1866–1936) was an investigative journalist who visited the Soviet Union in 1919. After returning to the United States in 1921, he famously commented, "I have seen the future and it works." Steffens later became disillusioned with the Soviet Union, which is reflected in his memoir, *The Autobiography of Lincoln Steffens* (New York: Harcourt, Brace, 1931).

20. Senate Committee on Foreign Relations, "U.S. Policy toward China," 101st Congress, 2nd sess., February 7, 1990, p. 30.

21. Murray Hiebert, "Red Scare," *Far Eastern Economic Review,* October 12, 2000, p. 28.

22. Kathy Wilhelm, "Dear Mr. Jiang . . .," *Far Eastern Economic Review,* April 26, 2001, p. 30.

23. Although cross-talk performances typically have two performers, they can have one or several participants. When there are two, the wise man could alternatively be a host or a funny man, and the fool would then be a guest or a straight man, respectively. For an introduction to cross talk, see Cornelius C. Kubler, *Listening Comprehension in Chinese: Performing "Comic Dialogues" (shuo xiangsheng)* (New Haven, CT: Yale University Far Eastern Publications, 1995). The most famous foreign performer of cross talk in China is Mark Rowswell, who moved there in the late 1980s and uses the stage name Dashan (literally "big mountain"). His website (www.dashan.com) provides exam-

ples of his performances. See also Ian Johnson, "Warn Regis Philbin: You Can't Get Rich Being on T.V. in China," *Wall Street Journal*, February 22, 2000, p. A1.

24. Michael G. Barnhart has also used the cross-talk analogy to highlight similar problems in the global human rights debate. See his "Getting Beyond Cross-Talk: Why Persisting Disagreements Are Philosophically Nonfatal," in Lynda S. Bell, Andrew J. Nathan, and Ilan Peleg (eds.), *Negotiating Culture and Human Rights* (New York: Columbia University Press, 2001), pp. 45–67.

# Acknowledgments

This volume owes its existence to many people and organizations. First and foremost are the authors and copyright holders of the selections reprinted here. Without their gracious permission, *China Cross Talk* would not have been possible. For reasons of space, many extremely well-written and representative pieces could not be included here. They are listed in the Further Reading section at the end of the book. To give readers context about the authors, at the end of each selection I have included their affiliations at the time they made their contributions or their most recent affiliations if they did not hold formal positions at the time. For several, I have also listed some of their positions both before and since the contributions were made. In the excerpted congressional hearings, this book follows the custom of the original transcripts by identifying all participants in House hearings by their gender titles and official participants in Senate hearings by their honorific titles.

I am also grateful to Lee Hamilton, Wu Xinbo, and Zhu Feng for their contributions; they each provide a helpful context in which to place the reprinted selections. Numerous individuals offered ideas, information, and encouragement at several stages in the book's creation. They include, but are not limited to, Warren I. Cohen, Nicholas Cullather, Bruce Dickson, Banning Garrett, Bates Gill, Harry Harding, Karen Kennedy, Mary Beth Kennedy, Peter Kennedy, Jason Kindopp, Cornelius C. Kubler, Anthony Kuhn, David M. Lampton, Winston Lord, Michael O'Hanlon, David Shambaugh, Sherry Syence, Arthur Waldron, Jeff Wasserstrom, and Margaret Yan. Indiana University's East Asian Studies Center and the Department of East Asian Languages and Cultures provided valuable financial support.

A special thanks is expressed to Gyung-Ho Jeong, an energetic Indiana University graduate student in political science who tracked down hundreds of potential articles, books, speeches, congressional hearing transcripts, and editorial cartoons. Without his able assistance, this book would have taken far longer to produce. I also am indebted to my editors at Rowman & Littlefield. Susan McEachern brought the idea for a reader on the growing American worries over China to my attention in the weeks after the April 2001 plane collision and allowed that idea to grow in new directions. She has provided wise counsel at every turn. And during production, Erin McKindley expertly melded a diverse bunch of selections into an aesthetically pleasing and easy-to-read text.

Finally, I thank my family, to whom *China Cross Talk* is dedicated. The profound relationships several of them have had with Asia is largely what brought me to China in the first place. Since then, China and American policy toward that country have been a staple of conversation with my entire family. These freewheeling exchanges, which mirror the variety of views in the pages that follow, provided the genuine inspiration for this book.

# PART I

# TOWARD FULL NORMALIZATION (1978–1983)

This December 1978 cartoon highlights China's large population and the importance of informal news sources even for major events. Reprinted by permission from Cartoonists & Writers Syndicate.

# Switching Ties: Recognizing Reality?

*In the days and months following President Carter's announcement that the United States and China would establish diplomatic relations, his administration received some praise, but it was also attacked from many quarters. Critics charged the administration did not sufficiently consult with Congress and that it abandoned the Republic of China on Taiwan. Several members of Congress filed suit against the president in court, and in the spring of 1979, Congress passed the Taiwan Relations Act (TRA), which required the United States to continue to provide weapons to Taiwan to ensure its defense.*

## Diplomatic Relations between the United States and the People's Republic of China, Address to the Nation

### *Jimmy Carter*

I would like to read a joint communiqué which is being simultaneously issued in Peking at this very moment by the leaders of the People's Republic of China.

#### JOINT COMMUNIQUÉ ON THE ESTABLISHMENT OF DIPLOMTIC RELATIONS BETWEEN THE UNITED STATES OF AMERICA AND THE PEOPLE'S REPUBLIC OF CHINA JANUARY 1, 1979

*The United States of America and the People's Republic of China have agreed to recognize each other and to establish diplomatic relations as of January 1, 1979.*

*The United States of America recognizes the Government of the People's Republic of China as the sole legal Government of China. Within this context, the people of the United States will maintain cultural, commercial, and other unofficial relations with the people of Taiwan.*

*The United States of America and the People's Republic of China reaffirm the principles agreed on by the two sides in the Shanghai Communiqué and emphasize once again that:*

- *Both wish to reduce the danger of international military conflict.*
- *Neither should seek hegemony in the Asia-Pacific region or in any other region of the world and each is opposed to efforts by any other country or group of countries to establish such hegemony.*
- *Neither is prepared to negotiate on behalf of any third party or to enter into agreements or understandings with the other directed at other states.*
- *The Government of the United States of America acknowledges the Chinese position that there is but one China and Taiwan is part of China.*
- *Both believe that normalization of Sino-American relations is not only in the interest of the Chinese and American peoples but also contributes to the cause of peace in Asia and the world.*

*The United States of America and the People's Republic of China will exchange Ambassadors and establish Embassies on March 1, 1979.*

Yesterday, our country and the People's Republic of China reached this final historic agreement. On January 1, 1979, a little more than 2 weeks from now, our two Governments will implement full normalization of diplomatic relations.

As a nation of gifted people who comprise about one-fourth of the total population of the Earth, China plays, already, an important role in world affairs, a role that can only grow more important in the years ahead.

We do not undertake this important step for transient tactical or expedient reasons. In recognizing the People's Republic of China, that it is the single Government of China, we are recognizing simple reality. But far more is involved in this decision than just the recognition of a fact.

Before the estrangement of recent decades, the American and the Chinese people had a long history of friendship. We've already begun to rebuild some of those previous ties. Now our rapidly expanding relationship requires the kind of structure that only full diplomatic relations will make possible.

The change that I'm announcing tonight will be of great long-term benefit to the peoples of both our country and China—and, I believe, to all the peoples of the world. Normalization—and the expanded commercial and cultural relations that it will bring—will contribute to the well-being of our own Nation, to our own national interest, and it will also enhance the stability of Asia. These more positive relations with China can beneficially affect the world in which we live and the world in which our children will live.

We have already begun to inform our allies and other nations and the Members of the Congress of the details of our intended action. But I wish also tonight to convey a special message to the people of Taiwan—I have already communicated with the leaders in Taiwan—with whom the American people have had and will have extensive, close, and friendly relations. This is important between our two peoples.

As the United States asserted in the Shanghai Communiqué of 1972, issued on President Nixon's historic visit, we will continue to have an interest in the peaceful resolution of the Taiwan issue. I have paid special attention to ensuring that normalization of relations between our country and the People's Republic will not jeopardize the well-being of the people of Taiwan. The people of our country will maintain our current commercial, cultural, trade, and other relations with Taiwan through nongovernmental means. Many other countries in the world are already successfully doing this.

These decisions and these actions open a new and important chapter in our country's history and also in world affairs.

To strengthen and to expedite the benefits of this new relationship between China and the United States, I am pleased to announce that Vice Premier Teng has accepted my invitation and will visit Washington at the end of January. His visit will give our Governments the opportunity to consult with each other on global issues and to begin working together to enhance the cause of world peace.

These events are the final result of long and serious negotiations begun by President Nixon in 1972, and continued under the leadership of President Ford. The results bear witness to the steady, determined, bipartisan effort of our own country to build a world in which peace will be the goal and the responsibility of all nations.

The normalization of relations between the United States and China has no other purpose than this: the advancement of peace. It is in this spirit, at this season of peace, that I take special pride in sharing this good news with you tonight.

## NOTES

Jimmy Carter, "Diplomatic Relations between the United States and the People's Republic of China, Address to the Nation," December 15, 1978, *Weekly Compilation of Presidential Documents*, Vol. 14, No. 50, pp. 2264–2266.

Jimmy Carter, 39th president of the United States (1977–1981)

The Twain Meet

This December 1978 cartoon suggests that Taiwan was a casualty of the U.S.–P.R.C. rapprochement. Reprinted by permission from the *New York Times*.

# Our Deal with Peking—All Cost, No Benefit

## *George Bush*

The airwaves are filled now with glad tidings from the White House, proclaiming that President Carter's China initiative has brought us much closer to peace on earth, good will to man.

How joyous it would be if that were true, but, unfortunately, nearly every Christmas story has its grinch—and this one is no exception.

The tragic fact is that the price our government has paid in recognizing the People's Republic of China has not only diminished American credibility in the world but has also darkened the prospects for peace. And I would venture that in the privacy of the Great Hall [of the People], the Chinese are acutely aware of that.

Let me explain by first introducing a bit of history. When I arrived in Peking in 1974 as the U.S. representative there, the Nixon and Kissinger trips and the Shanghai Communiqué were already on record. The United States was committed to eventual recognition of the People's Republic.

Moreover, ordinary Chinese citizens were intensely emotional in their desire for reunification with Taiwan. I remember in the early days how Chinese workmen refused to hang a map of Asia on my office wall because it showed Taiwan in a different color from the mainland. Not long thereafter, at sporting games that drew provincial teams from all over the mainland, the stands exploded with cheers when the announcer identified one squad as "our brothers from Taiwan." Government propaganda reflected much the same sentiment.

Yet, in private conversations the rulers of the People's Republic took a very different view. They were committed, of course, to the "liberation" of Taiwan, but that was always a distinctly secondary issue. "You have time; there is no hurry," they said over and over again.

When President Ford, Secretary Kissinger and I met with chairman Mao Tse-tung [Mao Zedong] in October 1975, he repeated that settlement of the Taiwan question might take the United States and China "one year, ten years, or even a hundred years" to achieve. He clearly expected to die before it happened, and he was equally clear that if the United States wanted more time to modify opinion at home, that was readily acceptable.

What concerned Mao far more than the Taiwan question—and has since preoccupied his successors—was the gathering strength of the Soviet Union. The leaders in Peking are terrified that one day they may be encircled by a Soviet empire, eager to gobble them up. Forty-five Russian divisions are already poised on their northern border, and in recent months their security has deteriorated along their southern rim as well.

To the Chinese, the key to peace is for the United States and its western allies to act as a firm, reliable counterweight to Soviet pressures. Only if the United States remains a credible world power—one that honors its commitments and lives up to its responsibilities—are they themselves secure.

## BREAKING A TREATY WITHOUT CAUSE

Here, then, is the situation that Jimmy Carter found when he entered the Oval Office:

On one hand, Peking was transfixed with the idea that the Soviet Union sought "hegemony" in many parts of the globe and was already convinced that the West was growing "soft."

On the other hand, while continuing to pay lip service to "normalization" of relations with the United States, the Chinese quietly accepted the fact that the two sides were deadlocked on that issue. For several years, Peking had insisted on three preconditions before there could be "normalization": The United States had to abrogate its mutual defense treaty with Taiwan, had to withdraw troops there, and had to withdraw recognition from Taiwan, acknowledging Peking as the sole, legitimate government of China. The United States had consistently balked at those terms, insisting that it would not formally recognize Peking until there was a firm, explicit commitment to settle the Taiwanese issue peacefully. And there the negotiations were stuck.

Because of the importance of the Russian threat, however, the questions of full "normalization" and of Taiwan were never a major barrier to progress on commercial and strategic issues. China and the United States had entered a de facto political relationship that had two great virtues: It permitted both sides to begin working harmoniously together, and it also allowed the United States to maintain the integrity of its commitment to Taiwan. In an imperfect world, that was a major accomplishment.

It was in this context that President Carter's Dec. 15 announcement was such a bombshell.

The immediate question was not whether we should recognize Peking. Many Americans now agree that a close, working relationship between Washington and Peking should advance the cause of peace and world trade. Personally, I have long felt that in spite of the totalitarian nature of the Chinese government, it was in our own national interest to improve relations with Peking.

But the critical question was the terms on which the recognition was negotiated. Incredibly, it turns out that the United States has now accepted all three of Peking's original demands—and has capitulated on its own demand for a guarantee on Taiwan, abandoning a faithful friend in the process. For the first time in our history, a peacetime American government has renounced a treaty with an ally without cause or benefit.

## A FIGLEAF FOR RETREAT

By the administration's own admission, it never received—or even asked for— specific assurances from Peking about a peaceful solution to the Taiwanese question. In Peking's eyes, the Taiwanese matter continues to be strictly an internal issue, and in its constitution the "liberation" of Taiwan remains an unchallenged goal.

In response, the administration argues that the mainland will wink at future U.S. arms sales to the Taiwanese. But in the same breath, administration officials say *sotto voce* that those sales will be "restrained."

The administration also argues that Peking has neither the capability nor the incentive to conquer Taiwan. But any student of Chinese history—remembering that during the Cultural Revolution, only 10 years ago, some of today's Chinese leaders were driven down Peking streets with sticks—can properly ask: Who knows with certainty what lies ahead? It is true that armed conquest by the mainland does not seem imminent, but because of unilateral action by the United States the 17 million people of Taiwan are now hostage to the changing whims of the Peking leadership.

The terms that the Carter administration has accepted, and even trumpeted, are the same terms that have been available for the past seven years. But they were always refused before because we knew—just as the Chinese knew—that in the absence of sufficient guarantees, they were but a figleaf for an abject American retreat.

The terrible truth is that the United States now stands exposed to the world as a nation willing to betray a friend—even when there is no apparent gain.

There is, of course, room for reasonable men to disagree about the benefits that might now accrue to China and the United States in trade and investment. Contrary to administration claims, however, I believe the gains that are likely to occur undoubtedly would have occurred anyway under our existing relationship.

Over the past year and a half, before these negotiations had even begun, the Chinese were ardently seeking western technology and our sales to China were rising dramatically. Over the past four months the commercial pace has accelerated, and many American companies have begun making serious plans for trading with the mainland and investing there. But it has always been apparent in the commercial field that China needs us more than we need them. Indeed, it was precisely China's growing eagerness for trade that gave the United States greater leverage in our diplomatic bargaining than we had ever had before— leverage that we carelessly tossed aside.

## MORALITY AND STRATEGY

At its heart, however, the China question is not one of trade and technology but of fundamental morality and international strategy.

As sociologist Peter Berger wrote earlier this year, "If there is one universal, indeed primeval principle of morality, it is that one must not deliver one's friends to their enemies." Berger was writing of refugees fleeing from Vietnam in their small, makeshift dinghies. "These boats," he said, "bear a message. It is a simple and ugly message. *Here is what happens to those who put their trust in the United States of America.*"

For President Carter, who professes a strong belief in Christian ethics, it should be a tormenting thought that by his hand, the United States has put an entire people adrift in a cruel, hostile sea—and for scarcely any purpose.

The moral question is closely linked to the strategic issue that is causing perhaps even greater consternation in many chanceries of the world.

Throughout the postwar period America's credibility—joined with America's military might—has been the glue that has held together the non-communist world. Justifiably, both friend and foe alike are now asking, however, whether the United States can still be counted on to keep its word. Increasingly in recent years the United States has staked out a clear, unequivocal position, has invited others to join us, and then, as counterpressures have built up, has suddenly, inexplicably buckled.

In Africa, we committed ourselves to support the forces of moderation. But when black moderates in Rhodesia arranged with Prime Minister Ian Smith for the transfer of power and free elections, we threw in our lot with Marxist radicals.

In recent negotiations in the Middle East, the Israelis announced that they were prepared to accept a final plan drafted with American help. But when

Egypt raised the ante, we modified our position to accept the new Egyptian proposals, and when the Israelis refused to go along, we publicly kicked them in the shins.

In Europe, President Carter convinced our German and French allies that we would build a neutron bomb, and Helmut Schmidt courageously supported him. But then, in the face of a Soviet propaganda campaign, the administration knuckled under and shelved the project. Even now, as contradictory signals emanate from Washington, our NATO allies wonder whether the United States will honor its pledge to raise defense expenditures by about 3 percent a year.

In Iran, the Carter administration placed considerable pressure on the shah to accelerate his liberalization program—sometimes, according to reports, against his better judgment. But when trouble broke out, our government disappeared over the hill. The world recognizes, even if we do not, that the United States could have been demonstrative in its support for the shah, issuing firmer statements, engaging in naval deployments, and responding with something more than timidity when the Russians warned us to stay out of it.

To friends of the United States, who have been chilled by these recent events and by our posture on SALT, the mindless abandonment of Taiwan thus comes at a particularly inopportune time. Why now? And why would the president act so unilaterally, without consulting with the Congress, especially after the Senate had insisted by a unanimous 94-to-0 vote upon such consultations? Unfortunately, there are no easy answers.

Understandably, Peking has been prominent among those worried about America's deteriorating position in the world. It has been particularly dismayed about Cuban intervention in Ethiopia, the major Soviet role in Afghanistan (a neighbor to both China and Iran), the pro-Soviet coup in South Yemen, as well as the hesitant U.S. response to Soviet claims with regard to a role in Iran. Indeed, this area of the world—including Southern Asia, the Persian Gulf and the Indian Ocean—is just as important strategically to the Chinese as to the United States.

The ultimate irony, then, of this "normalization" is that China, whose primary interest lies in a strong, steadfast American presence in the world, has now seen just how easily we can be pushed around. The Chinese realize that we have given all and gained nothing, and while they engage in self-congratulations, they know in their hearts that by our actions, we have also made the world a more dangerous place than it was only a few weeks ago.

## NOTES

George Bush, "Our Deal with Peking—All Cost, No Benefit," *Washington Post*, December 24, 1978, p. D1. Reprinted by permission from the Office of George Bush.

George Bush, Republican nominee for president; former U.S. representative to the United Nations; director of the Central Intelligence Agency; U.S. representative to Peking; vice president of the United States (1981–1989); and 41st president of the United States (1989–1993)

# Chinese Realities

## *Charles W. Yost*

It is disappointing that George Bush, an able chief of our liaison mission in Peking and an excellent ambassador to the United Nations when the People's Republic was first seated there, should have seen fit, in the *Post's* Outlook section Dec. 24, to drag out several shop-worn red herrings about U.S.–China relations.

Bush says that the United States, by normalizing relations with the People's Republic and cutting diplomatic ties with Taiwan, has "abandoned a faithful friend" and "diminished American credibility in the world." With all due respect, those remarks raise more questions about Bush's credibility than about America's.

The United States continued to recognize the Nationalists on Taiwan and the government of China for nearly 30 years after they had fled the mainland and their effective rule had been confined to some 17 million out of a total of more than 800 million Chinese. Whether that was faithfulness, myopia or domestic politics I leave to the reader to judge.

In any case, once Richard Nixon, in the Shanghai Communiqué of 1972, had formally accepted the fact that "there is but one China and that Taiwan is part of China," and had declared his intention to normalize relations with the People's Republic, any logical rationale for diplomatic relations and a defense treaty with Taiwan disappeared.

Henry Kissinger has repeatedly said that, had it not been for Watergate, the process of normalization would have been completed during Nixon's second term. There is little likelihood that it could have been completed at that time, when Chairman Mao Tse-tung was still alive and Teng Hsiao-ping's [Deng Xiaoping's] pragmatic posture had not yet prevailed, on any better terms than President Carter obtained. Very probably the terms would have been less satisfactory.

As to "American credibility in the world," I can testify, as one who dealt for many years at the United Nations with the question of Chinese representation, that our credibility is much more likely to be enhanced than diminished by our recognition of the facts of life in East Asia. Our European allies have been urging us for years to establish normal relations with China. Japan did so several years ago.

Bush correctly points out that the primary Chinese preoccupation at this time is building barriers against "hegemonism," that is, what they perceive as the "Russian threat." They themselves would hardly have sought a relationship with the United States that they thought would undermine U.S. "credibility" vis-à-vis the Soviet Union. Obviously, they believed it would have the contrary effect. Most people would agree with them.

In East Asia in particular, U.S. "credibility" is likely to be enhanced by the establishment, after so many years of mistrust and misunderstanding, of a stabler, more normal and more constructive relationship with the principal power on the mainland. It seems fair to judge, for example, that the small non-Communist countries on China's periphery—South Korea, Thailand, the Philippines—will henceforth be more, rather than less secure.

As to the future of Taiwan itself, the Chinese position is that this is an internal matter and that they will make no formal commitment in regard to it. Nevertheless, Vice Chairman Teng has recently assured a group of visiting congressmen that China has no intention of using force against Taiwan and that its autonomous economic relations with the United States and the rest of the world will not be affected by normalization of U.S.–China relations. Peking has, moreover, in recent days made a number of amicable moves in regard to Taiwan, suggesting a policy of reconcilation and gradualism rather than force or threat of force.

Of course, policies and leaders can change. However, there are two durable, inhibiting factors. First, China does not now have and will not soon have the military capability to launch an amphibious assault on Taiwan. Second, any attempt to launch or threaten such an assault would obviously shatter both the valuable political relationship and the mutually profitable economic association with the United States, Japan and Western Europe that Chairman Hua Kuo-feng [Hua Guofeng] and Teng are promoting in pursuit of Chinese security and modernization. It seems most unlikely they would risk the benefits they are seeking by such a course to seize an objective they expect, as Bush points out, to fall into their laps in any case in "one year, ten years, or even a hundred years."

The situation on Taiwan depends primarily on the Taiwanese. If they wish to preserve their autonomy, they will—with their booming economy and foreign trade—be able to do so. If they wish to draw closer to the rest of China, they have the option. The choice in any near future will be theirs.

## NOTES

Charles W. Yost, "Chinese Realities," *Washington Post,* January 10, 1979, p. A15.

Charles W. Yost, former U.S. ambassador to Laos (1955), Syria (1957), and Morocco (1958–1961) and U.S. representative to the United Nations (1969–1971)

# 2

# Economic Normalization: Benefits and Dangers

*One of the steps following the establishment of diplomatic relations was to create the legal foundation for greater commercial ties. In 1974, the U.S. Congress passed the Jackson–Vanik amendment. The amendment removed most-favored-nation (MFN) status—the standard tariff rate for imports applied to the goods from the vast majority of a country's trading partners—for any nonmarket country that did not permit freedom of emigration for its citizens. The substantially higher non-MFN tariff rates essentially halted trade. The law was originally passed in order to pressure the Soviets to allow Jews to emigrate from the Soviet Union, but its restrictions were applied to all Communist countries. The president was authorized to waive the amendment's restrictions through an executive order if he could certify to Congress that a country covered by the amendment allowed its citizens to freely emigrate. Congress then could uphold or revoke the president's waiver. If Congress did not act, the president's waiver would be implemented automatically. Many issues raised during the initial consideration of MFN status for China in the 1979 hearings excerpted here surfaced again in the 1990s. In 1980, China followed Romania (1975) and Hungary (1978) to become the third Communist country to be granted MFN by the United States.*

## Agreement on Trade Relations between the United States and the People's Republic of China

*Senate testimony by Henry M. Jackson, Adlai E. Stevenson III, Warren Christopher, Cord Hansen-Sturm, Amy Young-Anawaty, and F. A. Meister*

**Senator Jackson** [*witness*]: I wish to express my appreciation for this opportunity to testify before your committee in strong support of the trade agreement between the United States and the People's Republic of China, which includes a provision for giving China most-favored-nation treatment and opening the way to the granting of credits.

This United States–China Trade Agreement lays the foundation for the expansion of trade and financial ties between our two countries, with major mutual benefits. China's pursuit of a long-term modernization program calls for ongoing high levels of imported capital goods and technology, and China's leaders are counting on placing substantial orders with firms in this country.

As many of us in the Congress see it, the United States has a significant stake in the continued existence of a strong, independent China. We share with China a common interest in key strategic areas. China's leaders explicitly recognize shared security interests with us, with Japan, and with our NATO allies in Europe. In fact, the People's Republic is playing a central role in the geopolitical balance of power in the world, including the struggle to deter Soviet aggression and expansionism in critical areas of tension. Efforts to aid China in its drive to become a modern industrial state, and to work with her where our strategic and bilateral concerns run parallel are in American as well as Chinese interests.

A basic difficulty in getting this trade agreement before the Congress in timely fashion has been the position of top administration officials favoring a policy of "even-handed treatment" of Russia and China. In fact, we find that administration officers—notably in the State and Commerce Departments—have not finally shaken themselves free of this misguided view.

According to this notion, if we give the benefits of MFN and credits to China, we must also give them to the Soviet Union. If China is in conformity with our law and the Soviets not in conformity, then it is argued, efforts must be made to interpret the law to accommodate the country that has chosen not to conform. In the present case, the country that has chosen not to conform is the Soviet Union and the law in question is section 402 of the Trade Act of 1974.

In fact, China and the Soviet Union are two very different countries at different stages of development, with different interests and ambitions, different associates and allies, and different relations with this country. They should be treated on separate tracks and, in our own national interest, they cannot be treated alike.

I have been told that this basic position was stated to the Chinese leaders by Vice President Mondale during his August visit to the People's Republic. I am fully aware, however, that the administration is not all of one mind on this matter.

As my colleagues know, section 402 of the Trade Act of 1974, the Jackson-Vanik amendment, prohibits the extension of most-favored-nation treatment and official credits, credit guarantees, or investment guarantees, to any non-market economy country which restricts the right of its citizens to emigrate freely. The President, however, may waive these prohibitions with respect to a particular country if he reports to the Congress that: one, he has determined that such [a] waiver will substantially promote the objective of free emigration, and two, he has received assurances that the emigration practices of that country will henceforth lead substantially to the achievement of the objective of free emigration.

The President has determined that these requirements have been met by the People's Republic of China, and he has issued an Executive order waiving the application of section 402 (A) and (B).

I am pleased to see that the President has based his case for MFN to China both on official assurances regarding future emigration practices provided by Chinese leaders in diplomatic exchanges, and on official assurances publicly stated by senior Chinese leaders.

Administration spokesmen have informed us that before the trade agreement was signed this year on July 7, top U.S. Embassy officers discussed Chinese emigration policy and practice with the Ministry of Foreign Affairs in Beijing in light of the legal requirements of the Jackson-Vanik amendment.

The Chinese were fully apprised of these requirements, including the requirement that assurances regarding future emigration practices be given, and at that time senior Chinese officials provided the assurances the law requires. We are informed that there is a written record of these official exchanges which administration officials should certainly make available to this committee before it votes on Senate Concurrent Resolution 47.

On several recent occasions Chinese leaders have publicly given assurances regarding their government's future policies on emigration.

For example: in a Washington, D.C., speech before the National Association of Chinese-Americans and Overseas Chinese in the U.S.A. on January 30 of this year, Vice Premier Deng Xiaoping said:

> Many of you may have relatives living on the mainland of China and wish that they may come over for a family reunion, and others may wish to go back to China to visit their relatives. This is quite natural and understandable. The Chinese Government will treat legitimate wishes favorably and with sympathy and will adopt effective measures to satisfy these wishes. You may rest assured on this score.

. . . Mr. Chairman, of all the individual liberties contained in the UN Declaration of Human Rights, none is more fundamental than the right to emigrate. We in the Congress have particularly emphasized that right because it is the touchstone of all human rights. And in this effort we have international law on our side. As cosponsor with you of the Jackson-Vanik amendment, I believe, we—and the vast multitude of supporters of the Jackson-Vanik amendment—can take satisfaction from the way our amendment is encouraging greater respect for freer emigration.

In closing, let me just say that I appear here today to urge this committee and the Senate to move expeditiously to pass Senate Concurrent Resolution 47, the resolution to approve this promising agreement on trade with the People's Republic of China. . . .

**Senator Stevenson** [*witness*]: The normalization of relations between the United States and the People's Republic of China offers potentially important economic opportunities for the United States. I support MFN and official credits for the People's Republic of China, but to grant these benefits to the People's Republic of China and not the U.S.S.R. risks a further deterioration of already strained relations with the Soviet Union.

Such a break with past policy implies that MFN is some act of grace to be bestowed by the United States on China as a reward for good behavior. Our policy has been to proceed cautiously and even-handedly with respect to both the Communist superpowers. There is no reason for breaking with that policy.

The perceptions of our intentions are the realities in a world little understanding the nuances of American politics. To be perceived as playing favorites between China and the Soviet Union, whatever the intentions, risks making the United States a participant in the conflict between these Communist powers and with no assurance that either our political or economic interests will be served.

Indeed, whatever economic benefits are gained in China will be more than offset by losses in the larger Soviet market and elsewhere in a world that already looks upon the United States as an unreliable supplier of goods and credits. . . .

The basis in the Trade Act for determining eligibility for MFN and Eximbank credits is confined to nonmarket economy countries and their policy on emigration. Section 402 of the act—the Jackson-Vanik amendment—prohibits the extension of MFN and credits to nonmarket countries that restrict free emigration.

By implication we are indifferent to the emigration policies of other nations and the policies of the nonmarket nations on other subjects. In its historical content, section 402 implies that if the Soviet Union permits the release of a sufficient number of Jews, its actions in the Middle East, or East Africa or Cuba are of relative unimportance—at least insofar as trade goes.

To proceed along the lines proposed, the United States must conclude that the People's Republic of China has satisfied the requirement for "assurances" of free emigration with unpublicized statements by unidentified officials and others about family reunion, not free emigrations, and the sarcastic question of the Deputy Premier, "How many millions do you want?"

The Soviet Union is now permitting emigration of Soviet Jews at the annual rate of about 50,000, but it gives no such assurances. No great power will suffer the indignity of granting the required "assurances" as a price for trade. To find that Chinese assurances satisfy the law, the United States must bend it to its convenience at risk of being held to account by courts which attach more importance to the laws demands. Thus, the ignominy falls not on the People's Republic of China or U.S.S.R. They voice their contempt for this law. It falls on the United States. Failing to change our law, we ignore it.

Those who engage in selective moralizing forget the Chinese land reform of the 1950's and the excesses of the cultural revolution of the 1960's while remembering Stalin's reign of terror, or else their concerns have little to do with human rights including emigration.

This law reflects the caprice of congressional politics in foreign policy. The United States did not complain about the suppression of human rights in the Soviet Union until that nation had begun to respect them. The United States itself severely limits the entry of refugees.

It protests the failure of Vietnam to stop emigration. Great Britain is urging the People's Republic of China to stop the flow of refugees to Hong Kong. The United States does not want the People's Republic of China to let its people emigrate freely to Hong Kong. Hong Kong is already overwhelmed. The United States wants assurances of free emigration in order to comply with a law it cannot change. It wants free emigration in selected cases only.

United States policy on East-West trade lacks coherence; it also lacks integrity. . . .

Unlike my friend, Senator Jackson, I urge the committee to move slowly. The Congress should consider this agreement with some deliberation and take time to reconstruct an evenhanded policy that enables the executive branch to move ahead with the Soviet Union and the People's Republic of China.

In the interim there is no reason to neglect our economic and political interests in Eastern Europe which are ill-served by a policy which effectively prevents U.S. trade to the benefit of our competitors, and insures the continued subservience of those nations to the U.S.S.R. . . .

**Mr. Christopher** [*witness*]: Mr. Chairman and members of the committee, the establishment of diplomatic relations with the PRC on January 1 opens a new era for United States–China relations based on equality, mutual interest, and respect. However, diplomatic relations alone do not automatically insure the development of a normal and mutually beneficial relationship. Thus, our task is clear: We must find new ways to build a new relationship in tangible and practical ways.

Barriers to trade pose one hindrance to a useful relationship with the People's Republic of China. The trade agreement you have before you, by reducing these barriers and creating incentives to trade, will go a long way toward cementing the bonds between China and the United States.

Nondiscriminatory treatment, credits, insurance, a favorable investment climate, and business facilitation are the lifeblood of trade. Without them, trade with China would wither. With them, we can forge the stable and constructive ties with China that we seek, and that will guide us into the 1980's and beyond.

Our new ties with China are of fundamental importance to the United States and to the prospects for a peaceful and prosperous world. We want to encourage China to play a constructive and stabilization role in Asia. We want to see a prosperous China, a China that can feed and fuel itself.

Failure to approve this agreement would unfortunately be viewed as a sign that the United States is not interested in moving toward such a constructive, mutually beneficial relationship with the Chinese. It is in our interest for China's next generation of leaders to look back in 1990 upon the relationship we are now building with a sense of satisfaction and to view the United States as a reliable partner in development. . . .

We have examined China's emigration record. We have studied their public statements made by their officials, and we have had discussions with the Chinese on their emigration policy. Based upon all of these factors, we are confident, as the President has reported, that the requirements of section 402 of the Trade Act have been satisfied.

In closing, I seek your support and urge that you give this agreement speedy approval. . . .

**Senator Danforth** [*committee member*]: Is it the position of the administration that trade policy should be used as a means of enforcing human rights policy?

**Mr. Christopher**: Senator, in a very limited number of circumstances, I think it might be justified. I think that the Congress took a strong action with respect to coffee exports from Uganda as an example of a situation where human rights considerations played a role in trade policy.

There are a number of other statutes which we try to faithfully carry out which prevent certain kinds of trade, or trade facilitation, in countries which are gross and consistent violators of human rights standards.

But I think that that is not a weapon of first choice, but is a sanction that should be used carefully and sparingly.

**Senator Danforth**: It certainly is not used evenly, is it?

**Mr. Christopher**: Senator, the world is certainly not even in that regard. I hope our policy is coherent, if it does not always seem consistent.

**Senator Bradley** [*committee member*]: Mr. Christopher, what are the broader goals, if any, that the administration hopes to achieve by increasing commercial relations with the People's Republic of China?

**Mr. Christopher**: Well, I suppose the most important goal is our concept, Senator Bradley, that trade is a civilizing and important foreign policy tool in and of itself. The relations that are created between countries when their businessmen have interchange are valuable in creating a relationship between the two countries.

Second, there is no question that trade with China offers a new outlet for our industries, gives us an opportunity to improve our balance-of-payments picture, gives us a new and gigantic market, at least a potentially gigantic market.

Third, we have a stake in China being a successful power in its part of the world and in its ability to defend itself. I think we look forward to the modernization of China because we think that improvement in their economy and their commitment to improve the living standards of their people are desirable things form the standpoint of stability and world peace.

Those are the things that come first to mind.

**Senator Bradley**: Do you feel that increased trade will affect the political system of China in any way?

**Mr. Christopher**: In the long term, I think increased trade does have positive effects. I am a great believer in the fact that other countries are influenced when they come into contact with our system and our people.

I do not mean they are going to change from an autocratic Communist society overnight because they meet 100 U.S. businessmen. I think it is good for the United States and I think it is good for the world when countries which have been as isolated as China come into contact with our society and our civilization and the way we live. . . .

**Mr. Hansen-Sturm** [*witness*]: . . . The membership of the National Foreign Trade Council which was founded in 1914, comprises a broad cross section of U.S. companies engaged in all major fields of international trade and investment including manufacturers, banks and services.

The National Foreign Trade Council welcomes the conclusion of an Agreement of Trade Relations between the United States of America and the People's Republic of China. It regards the signing of such Agreement on July 7th as an essential factor in the normalization of commercial relations between the two countries.

The council urges approval of this agreement. . . .

The council also welcomes the procedures agreed upon in this agreement to facilitate and promote trade between the two countries, exchange of information, the settlement of disputes, and the protection of patents, trademarks and copyrights.

We hope that the implementation of this agreement will lead to the availability of export-import credits to finance export sales, thus making American companies more competitive with Japanese and West European industries where comparable institutions assist their exporters in the financing of large sales. There is growing evidence that U.S. firms are unable to secure domestic financing for such sales.

There is a wide gap between current restrictive trade policies of the United States, vis-à-vis the PRC, and those of other leading industrial countries; they extend MFN and export credits in trade relations with the PRC. Consequently, the United States is at a trading disadvantage.

If the United States is to reduce the trade deficit, it is essential that the flow of exports of U.S. goods and services be increased. In our opinion, this agreement will open up a substantial new market for exports of U.S. goods and services at a time when continued trade deficits have made export expansion a necessity. . . .

**Ms. Young-Anawaty** [*witness*]: . . . In prior testimony, the Law Group has urged suspending trade benefits accorded to Romania until that country improved its record of observing the human rights of its Hungarian minority. This position is based on our belief that the actions of the Romanian Government breach the spirit of United States human rights policy as embodied in the Jackson-Vanik amendment.

Today, our message is different. Today we concur with the administration that nondiscriminatory treatment for the People's Republic of China would be desirable and beneficial for both the United States and China. We urge the Senate, however, to proceed with caution in granting most-favored-nation trading status to China until assurances have been received that China's observance of human rights comports with international norms.

The United States often has used its trade relationships to accomplish foreign policy objectives: witness the trade embargoes imposed upon Cuba, Rhodesia, Uganda and more recently the oil embargo with Iran.

In enacting the Jackson-Vanik amendment the Congress has sought to withhold beneficial trade relations until it has evidence of increased respect for human rights and in particular the freedom to emigrate, within Eastern bloc countries.

We wish to emphasize the fact that the United States is still in a position to use special trade relations as a bargaining device to ensure respect for human rights. Clearly, the time to insist on respect for human rights in China as a quid pro quo for trade benefits is before the bargain is sealed and the trade agreement is implemented.

The reason for our concern is that so little is really known about the situation of human rights in China. Although the President in his letter to the Congress suggests that he has received assurances from senior Chinese officials with regard to freer emigration and the reunification of families, these assurances as yet lack specificity.

Assistant Secretary of State for Human Rights, Patricia Derian, in a speech before the American Branch of the International Law Association on November 10th, remarked that our relations with China were so new that the

United States simply did not have enough indicators to be able to judge China's adherence to international human rights norms.

We do know that on 29 September 1972 the People's Republic of China stated in a letter to the United Nations Secretary-General that all human rights treaties signed and ratified by the government of Taiwan would not be recognized until they were examined by the government in Beijing.

As of August 1979, China has not officially recognized any of those agreements. Surely, at a minimum, the stipulation could be made that the present government honor international human rights obligations and consider, as the United States currently is considering, ratification of those international human rights treaties already signed.

Although the United States has no clear picture of the human rights situation in China, news reports have given some indication of their precarious state. While from May to September, news accounts touted the new surge of liberalization in China as evidenced in demonstrations, attacks on the government in the Chinese press and the famous poster appearing on "democracy wall," recent setbacks appear to undermine those gains.

Human rights violations as reported in Amnesty International's 1978 report on "Political Imprisonment in the People's Republic of China," as well as reports of the infamous torture prison at Qin Cheng and most recently the closed trial of dissident leader Wei Jingsheng raise serious questions about China's commitment to human rights.

In conclusion, while we essentially favor trade connections with China, we urge the Senate to seek assurances that such trade relations do not compromise United States human rights policy. Although China's emigration practice may be exemplary, as shown by Deng Xiaoping's statement that Beijing would allow ten million people to leave the country at any time, the adequacy of its overall human rights record is far from apparent.

We believe the Jackson-Vanik amendment, although focused on free emigration, was designed by Congress to be a window through which the United States could view its trading partners' regard for human rights. As Congressman Vanik, one of the architects of the Jackson-Vanik amendment, stated in hearings before the House Subcommittee on Trade last July 9, "The Jackson-Vanik amendment covers the whole spectrum of human rights."

Establishing a new trade relationship with China thus presents the United States with a singular opportunity clearly to signal an even-handed policy free from arbitrary distinctions and applicable to all our trading partners.

To articulate that policy specifically, it is that the U.S. does not target only certain human rights violators or certain human rights violations, but demands adherence to minimum international human rights standards by all those who seek trade concessions with the United States.

We hope the Senate will see the political wisdom of seizing this opportunity to make this statement. . . .

**Mr. Meister** [*witness, prepared statement*]: The American Footwear Industries Association, whose member firms account for approximately 90 percent of domestic non-rubber footwear production and a substantial number of suppliers to the industry, asks you to consider, in your deliberations on the granting of Most-Favored-Nation (MFN) status to the People's Republic of China, the potentially serious impact that this will have on import-sensitive industries such as footwear and other leather products.

This Committee, the Congress and the Administration have recognized that the domestic non-rubber footwear industry is possibly the most import-impacted industry in the United States. There have been two unanimous findings of injury by the International Trade Commission. In fact, it was this Committee that initiated the second injury case before the ITC.

Yet, despite these comprehensive and legitimate injury findings, we continue to be wracked by excessive footwear imports. We suffer from a 53 percent import-penetration ratio. In 1979, 56 million more pairs of non-rubber footwear will be imported than in 1976—the base year for the import relief program.

In fact, the Administration's limited import control program of Orderly Marketing Agreements (OMA's) with Taiwan and Korea has proven to be a dramatic failure, since footwear imports from all other countries have been permitted to surge. For example, in 1979, while Korea and Taiwan will be down only 54 million pairs, or 27 percent, from 1976 levels, other countries of the world are projected to be up by 110 million pairs or 64.4 percent. . . .

The Administration and the Congress have recognized that labor-intensive industries are threatened severely by the likely emergence of the People's Republic of China as a major exporter, indeed an overwhelming exporter, of labor-intensive products. Specifically, the U.S. Government already has taken strong unilateral actions to control China's textile exports to the United States. We support this strong action, but our industry firmly believes that consistent public policy requires a similar policy of import controls for the domestic non-rubber footwear industry. Our case is at least as compelling as that of the textile industry—we, too, are labor-intensive, have been found twice to be seriously harmed by imports, and suffer from declining domestic production and employment.

With imports at an all-time high, domestic production at an all-time low, and a totally ineffective Administration control program, we now face the frightening specter of China. The People's Republic of China clearly has a potential of unparalleled dimension to flood our market with footwear.

We ask this committee, in its deliberations on MFN status for China, to take appropriate steps to ensure that the U.S. Government adopt an equally tough stance on footwear imports from China as it has done with textiles. If this committee ignores the serious threat posed by China to our already beleaguered industry, our very survival will be at stake. . . .

## NOTES

Senate Committee on Finance Subcommittee on International Trade, "Agreement on Trade Relations between the United States and the People's Republic of China," 96th Congress, 1st sess., November 15, 1979. Testimony by Henry M. Jackson, Adlai E. Stevenson III, Warren Christopher, Cord Hansen-Sturm, Amy Young-Anawaty, and F. A. Meister.

Henry M. Jackson, senator (D-WA); Adlai E. Stevenson III, senator (D-IL); Warren Christopher, deputy secretary of state during the Carter administration (1977–1981) and secretary of state during the Clinton administration (1993–1997); Cord Hansen-Sturm, chairman, China Committee, National Foreign Trade Council, Inc.; Amy Young-Anawaty, executive director, International Human Rights Law Group; F. A. Meister, president and chief executive officer, American Footwear Industries Association

# 3

# Playing the China Card?

*Besides expanding commercial links, the United States and China also took steps to improve their military relationship. Beginning in 1973, a few officials in the Nixon and Ford administrations argued that security ties would make China a more valuable counterweight against the Soviets. The decision to move forward on strategic relations gained momentum in the Carter administration, at which point some dual-use technologies were allowed to be sold to China. The policy was advanced when the Reagan administration decided to permit sales of military hardware, a step that was announced at the conclusion of the trip to China of Secretary of State Alexander Haig Jr. in June 1981. Although the vast majority of experts and media criticized this step, military sales grew to over $100 million by 1989 before being suspended following the June 4 massacre.*

## The New Era in East Asia

### *House testimony by John H. Holdridge*

**Mr. Holdridge** [*witness, prepared statement*]: I am pleased to have been invited here today to try to answer your questions about U.S. policy toward the People's Republic of China and Taiwan. . . .

To begin, let me review our strategic interests in a sound, healthy relationship with China:

Our security and that of Japan, South Korea and our ASEAN friends have been demonstrably enhanced by the growth of close U.S.–China ties. We gain very positive benefits both in the Asian and in the general balance of forces.

In the Taiwan Strait, tensions are at an all time low.

China is supportive of our global and regional efforts to strengthen our defense posture and alliance structure against expansionism by the Soviets and their proxies.

Throughout most of the Third World we no longer compete with the Chinese as rivals. Instead our policies are often complementary.

In short, the U.S.–China relationship is a major component in our global and regional security policies. . . .

The starting point for the administration's policy toward China can be found in President Reagan's statement of last August 25 [1980], that our China relationship is global and strategic and one that we should develop and strengthen in the years ahead. In this context, we undertook an extensive policy review to assess our China relationship on the premise that China is not our adversary, but a friendly, developing country with which, without being allied, we share important strategic interests.

We decided to liberalize further our export controls over dual use technology sales to China and, perhaps more importantly, to implement the new procedures effectively.

We are considering possible legislative changes to amend U.S. laws which treat China as a member of the Soviet bloc. We intend to work closely with the Congress on this.

We concluded that we should revise the regulations on international traffic in arms to permit the licensing of commercial sales to China on a case-by-case basis.

Our export control policy toward China is designed to strengthen our economic involvement in China's modernization by raising the level of technology that will be routinely approved for sale to China. Our interest in a successfully modernizing China is clear. Only the interests of our adversaries would be served by a weak China that had failed to modernize or a China that, in its frustration, had turned away from moderation and cooperation with the West.

Our export controls for China should reflect its role as a friendly, nonadversary state, clearly differentiating China from the Soviet bloc and minimizing the regulatory burden on U.S. companies. We want to help U.S. companies employ their technology edge fully and gain greater opportunities in the China market. Participating in China's economic development benefits business and strengthens bilateral ties. We want to have China look to us as a trusted supplier. Shackling U.S. business would not only cost us money but cause us to miss a unique opportunity to build a viable relationship with a quarter of the world's population.

Some statutes remain on the books which inhibit the expansion of our relations with China. Some of these laws were enacted to protect against the difficulties arising from interaction between market and non-market economies and should be viewed in this context.

Nevertheless, a number of these statues prohibit cooperation with China by the U.S. Government or private industry due to Beijing's earlier association with the Soviet bloc. As Secretary Haig informed the Chinese during his recent trip to Beijing, the Reagan Administration is currently reviewing such legislation and will seek appropriate congressional action to end past discrimination no longer consistent with our present strategic relationship. . . .

The steady development of our relations with China over the last several years, as well as our evolving strategic cooperation, make it inappropriate for us to maintain the tight controls on munitions exports to China that we do on such exports to adversaries. A flat prohibition on sales to China, a friendly country, chiefly benefits its opportunistic and aggressive neighbor. This decision is not a decision to sell any specific weapons systems [or] military technology; it will merely enable Beijing to make requests to purchase from U.S. commercial sources any items on the U.S. munitions list, including weapons. We are by no means committed to approving such requests, but only to considering them, on a case-by-case basis, just as we do for all other friendly nations.

We do not expect this to lead to a sudden or uncontrolled surge of U.S. weapons sales to China. First of all, our own intentions are to move slowly, with appropriate caution and to ensure that any weapons are only defensive in character. The Secretary made clear in Beijing that as far as defense exports are concerned, we intend to proceed in a gradual and careful way, bearing fully in mind the concerns of and, as appropriate, consulting the Congress, our friends and allies. Thus, we are not seeking to press arms on China or to move recklessly.

Secondly, we do not believe the Chinese will come forward with massive requests. There are budgetary and foreign exchange constraints and practical difficulties in integrating the most sophisticated technology into their own systems.

Neither we nor the Chinese seek an alliance or an otherwise dramatically expanded security relationship. While they view our willingness to consider military equipment transfers as one measure of our intent to pursue a long-term strategic association with them, they also recognize that we still treat them in a different fashion from our close allies, particularly in the sharing of sensitive technology. For us, the critically important thing is that we are now willing, for the first time, to deal with China in this area similarly to the way we deal with other friendly nations—in the Middle East, Latin America, Africa and Asia. . . .

We see these initiatives as natural developments in the positive evolution of our relations with China over the last decade. We intend to implement these policies in a measured, controlled manner, reflective of third country interests. We do not see a closer relationship with China as directed against the interests of any other country. Instead, we perceive an historic opportunity to build constructive, friendly relations with a country which is a future world power occupying a strategic position in the Asia-Pacific region and on the Eurasian landmass. Our long-term objective is to enhance greatly the stability of the region by strengthening U.S.–China ties.

As I have indicated, this in no way means that we will ignore Taiwan. We want to continue to improve the substance of our unofficial relations with the people of Taiwan. On his trip, the Secretary told the Chinese that we would continue to manage these relations—as we have since normalization—on the basis of the joint communiqué. As we have consistently stated, our own law establishes a basis for the continuation of these unofficial relations. It is clear that we have certain differences over Taiwan, which of course include the sale of defensive arms. We listened to Chinese views and we made our views known. I think both sides came away from these meetings with a greater awareness of the other's sensitivities over Taiwan.

Both the Chinese and we realize that for the foreseeable future the political significance of the steps we have taken will far outweigh the immediate military and economic consequences. These are, however, very important gestures aimed at consolidating a long-term relationship in which we will hope to be able to continue to engage our Chinese friends in a positive foreign policy dialogue—particularly in Asia—and to build a network of reinforcing ties which, while leaving us free to pursue internal and foreign policy goals independently, will nonetheless ensure cooperative and friendly U.S.–China relations well into the 21st century.

## NOTES

House Committee on Foreign Affairs Subcommittee on Asian and Pacific Affairs, "The New Era in East Asia," 97th Congress, 1st sess., July 16, 1981. Testimony by John H. Holdridge.

John H. Holdridge, assistant secretary of state for East Asian and Pacific affairs

# Misreading China

## David M. Lampton

Weapons sales, although often intended to bolster a country's strategic influence in a particular area, may precipitate more foreign policy problems than they solve. The Reagan administration's June 1981 decision to consider authorizing weapons sales to China on a case-by-case basis exemplifies this predicament. This decision is deficient on several grounds. It will not favorably influence Soviet behavior, contribute to stability in the Far East, or make the U.S. relationship with Beijing more durable. And it needlessly relinquishes useful initiative in U.S. foreign policy.

Reagan's decision carries President Carter's China arms policy to its logical conclusion. To a considerable extent, the Reagan administration intends its new China connection to be a by-product of Soviet–U.S. competition. Moreover, it hopes that arms sales to China will make continuing U.S. arm sales to Taiwan more palatable to Beijing. Over Beijing's protests, the United States would like to try to buy the acquiescence of both Beijing and Taipei to the U.S. relationship with the other by selling arms to both.

Yet each weapons sale becomes the justification for the subsequent sale of additional equipment, but provides no guarantee of better relations or greater security. For example, Washington softened its termination of the U.S.–Taiwan security treaty through an announcement of arm sales to Taiwan in early 1980. Three weeks later, the Department of Defense announced that it would consider issuing export licenses for military support equipment to China. Beijing's anger at possible future U.S. weapons sales to Taipei brought about the June 1981 relaxation in U.S. arms policy toward China. It is time to consider the risks and consequences of such an approach.

U.S. arms sales to China have two purposes: to solidify American ties to China and to deter adventurous Soviet behavior. Unfortunately, the two objectives are inconsistent. Weapons sales to China will discourage Soviet aggression only if Moscow knows that such sales will not occur if it exercises restraint. In the absence of such American assurances, the Soviets will inevitably draw the most ominous conclusions. Yet Beijing opposes holding arms transfers to China hostage to the vagaries of Soviet behavior. The Chinese want weapons sales linked solely to the status of their relationship with the United States. In short, what the Chinese want runs counter to the requirements of successful deterrence. For deterrence to succeed, the United States must link sales to Soviet behavior; for Sino–U.S. relations to prosper, it cannot. Consequently, weapons sales to China under present conditions will not discourage Soviet adventurism around the globe, but may even precipitate it.

U.S. arms sales to China will also affect arms control policy. West German chancellor Helmut Schmidt already has expressed his concern about possible U.S. arms sales to China. He sees these sales as another indication that Washington has not accorded arms control negotiations sufficient importance. To insure allied cooperation in theater nuclear force (TNF) modernization in Western Europe, the United States must take seriously West European admonitions to try to negotiate an appropriate TNF arms control treaty with the Soviets. But America will not inspire confidence among its allies with a gratuitous, largely symbolic slap at Moscow. Selling arms to Beijing can be viewed as just such a slap.

Beijing's own defense policies have hardly kept pace with its strident international alarms about Soviet aspirations for global hegemony. While encouraging the West and Japan to strengthen their defenses, China has cut its defense budget twice in the last two years, most recently by an estimated 22 per cent. This reduction brings reported defense spending down to $11 billion, although other important defense expenditures are scattered throughout the Chinese budget. In addition, the Chinese are reducing the People's Liberation Army (PLA) by at least 800,000 persons and are converting a sizable chunk of defense industry to civilian production. Civilian goods currently make up half the total output of Chinese defense plants. Although no one knows precisely the cost of modernizing the PLA so that it could halt a conventional Soviet attack, current estimates range from $41–63 billion for weapons alone.

These defense cuts are justified given China's domestic economic situation. The reductions, however, do raise questions regarding the seriousness of Beijing's commitment to defense modernization. It is now unclear what role Chinese leaders expect the United States to play in their military modernization effort. Does China expect, and should America provide, weapons coproduction agreements, government subsidized weapons sales, and military aid in the near future? And will Washington's budding military relationship with Beijing serve U.S. interests in Asia?

. . . Reagan's approach to China should give greater weight to Japan and its interests. On April 24, 1981, Walter Stoessel, Jr., under secretary of state for political affairs, declared that "our relationship with Japan is . . . the cornerstone of our policy in Asia. . . ." Less than a week later, John Holdridge, assistant secretary of state for East Asian and Pacific affairs, said: "Strategic relations with China are of overriding vital significance." The administration had not defined its Asian priorities when it took its China initiative. Such inconsistency unsettles both Tokyo and Beijing.

Japan's foreign policy pivots around three axes: the U.S.–Japanese security relationship, the need to maintain assured access to raw materials and markets, and the desire to coexist peacefully with the Soviet Union. Japan is not overly concerned about the possibility of limited American weapons sales to China, viewing them as simply a crude, naïve, and ultimately futile U.S. attempt to bludgeon the Soviets. Yet Tokyo is concerned that a Sino-Soviet arms race ultimately could force it to re-arm at levels that would create tremendous internal political friction. In addition, it sees nothing to gain and much to lose from participation in an explicitly anti-Soviet relationship with Beijing and Washington, even though Japan agreed to language known to be offensive to Moscow in its 1978 peace treaty with China. Greater militarization of the Far East could imperil Japan's resource life line.

Expanded Chinese military capabilities may also profoundly affect India. New Delhi has unresolved territorial disputes with Beijing, and the two states have twice fought over these areas. Although both sides tried to improve relations during Chinese Foreign Minister Huang Hua's June 1981 visit to India, strengthening ties will require a protracted effort. In addition, China staunchly supports Pakistan, India's primary enemy. Enhanced Chinese military capabilities, along with the recently proposed $3.2 billion U.S. aid package to Pakistan, may drive New Delhi even closer to Moscow. The Soviet Union's recent shipment of advanced fighter aircraft to India may be an indication of stronger Soviet-Indian ties.

Yet India and the United States share an important trade relationship, New Delhi maintains more than 1 million men under arms, and India juts out into one of the world's most important sea lanes. To alienate India, militarize the subcontinent, or drive India into increased dependence upon the Soviet Union would not serve U.S. interests.

Before supplying Beijing with weapons, the United States should consider that China has territorial disputes with six neighboring states in addition to India—the Soviet Union, Japan, Korea, the Philippines, Malaysia, and Vietnam. Control of potentially vast offshore energy and mineral resources plays a role in disputes with most of the coastal states. Beijing already has contested all South Korean, Japanese, and Vietnamese efforts to extract petroleum resources in disputed shelf areas without China's consent. Peaceful mechanisms for resolving these competing claims are needed. It is unwise for the United States to increase China's military capabilities when ownership of these resources is still undetermined.

U.S. military sales to China may at some point adversely affect the security of Taiwan. There is no guarantee that China's current moderate policies regarding Taiwan will endure. Recent media attacks on past Chinese leaders who surrendered Taiwan to Japan in the 1895 Treaty of Shimonoseki signal that leaders who compromise on Taiwan are subject to charges of national betrayal.

Articles appearing in China and in Hong Kong's leftist press ominously declare that were Taiwan to acquire nuclear weapons, link up with Moscow, refuse peaceful negotiations with Beijing for a long time, or proclaim independence from a unified China, Beijing would then be compelled to respond with force. Even as he was named party chairman at the Communist Party Central Committee's Sixth Plenary Session in mid-1981, Hu Yaobang reaffirmed his support for a unified China: "We have never knuckled under to any pressure from any foreign power. . . . We are resolved to strive together with the people of the whole country, not least including those in Taiwan, for its return and for the sacred cause of the complete reunification of our motherland."

Furthermore, arms sales to China make it difficult for the United State to avoid additional sales to Taiwan, an occurrence that could wreck carefully nurtured U.S.–Chinese ties. Taiwan's newly appointed representative of the Coordination Council for North American Affairs, Ts'ai Wei-p'ing, has indicated that his first priority is to ask the United States for a "sufficient supply of arms." Were the United States to supply China with arms, Taiwan's assessment of what was sufficient for its own defense would undoubtedly rise. . . .

# NOTES

David M. Lampton, "Misreading China," *Foreign Policy*, No. 45 (Winter 1981–1982), pp. 103–114. Reprinted by permission from David M. Lampton.

David M. Lampton, professor of political science at Ohio State University; president of the National Committee on U.S.–China Relations (1988–1997); currently director of China studies at the Johns Hopkins University School of Advanced International Studies

# 4

# Managing Taiwan

*The commitments made in the 1979 Taiwan Relations Act (TRA) soon became a key bone of contention between the United States and the PRC, the latter of which had hoped that the break of the defense treaty between the United States and Taiwan would mean an end to the military relationship as well. Adding fuel to the fire, candidate Ronald Reagan in 1980 stated that he believed the TRA meant the United States and Taiwan had an "official" relationship, which signified a potential challenge to the original terms of U.S.–PRC normalization. In the summer of 1982, the United States and China announced an agreement, discussed in the selections in this chapter, in which the United States pledged to gradually reduce its weapons sales to Taiwan as long as the PRC maintained its policy of seeking peaceful unification. To reassure Taiwan, the United States simultaneously privately promised Taiwan's leadership that the United States would not: 1) set a date for termination of arms sales to Taiwan; 2) alter the terms of the TRA; 3) consult with China in advance before making decisions about U.S. arms sales to Taiwan; 4) mediate between Taiwan and China; 5) alter its position about the sovereignty of Taiwan, namely, that the question was one to be decided peacefully by the Chinese themselves and would not pressure Taiwan to enter into negotiations with China; and 6) formally recognize Chinese sovereignty over Taiwan.*

## Statement on Relations with China and Taiwan

### Ronald Reagan

. . . We now maintain full and friendly diplomatic relations with China. This relationship began only three years ago, and it is one we should develop and strengthen in the years ahead.

It's a delicate relationship, and the Reagan-Bush administration will handle it with care and respect with due regard for our own vital interests in the world generally and in the Pacific section specifically.

China and the United States have a common interest in maintaining peace so that our nations can grow and prosper. Our two-way trade has now reached approximately $3½ billion annually, and China's program of modernization depends in a major way on Western and United States technology.

Along with many other nations, we and China share a deep concern about the pace and scale of the Soviet military buildup. Chinese leaders agree with Japanese leaders that the United States must be a strong and vigorous defender of the peace, and they specifically favor us bolstering our defense and our alliances.

It is quite clear that we do not, however, see eye-to-eye on Taiwan, and, thus, this is an appropriate time for me to state our position on this subject.

I intend that U.S. relations with Taiwan will develop in accordance with the law of our land, the Taiwan Relations Act. This legislation is the product of our democratic process and is designed to remedy the defects of the totally inadequate legislation proposed by Jimmy Carter. By accepting China's three conditions for normalization, Jimmy Carter made concessions that Presidents Nixon and Ford steadfastly refused to make.

I was, and am, critical of his decision, because I believe he made concessions that were not necessary and not in our national interest.

I felt that a condition of normalization, by itself a sound policy choice, should have been the retention of a liaison office on Taiwan of equivalent status to the one which we had earlier established in Peking.

With a persistent and principled negotiating position, I believe that normalization could ultimately have been achieved on that basis. But that is behind us now. My present concern is to safeguard the interests of the United States and to enforce the law of the land.

It was the timely action of the Congress, reflecting the strong support of the American people for Taiwan, that forced the changes in the inadequate bill which Mr. Carter proposed. Clearly the Congress was unwilling to buy the Carter plan which it believed would have jeopardized Taiwan's security.

This act, designed by Congress to provide adequate safeguard for Taiwan's security and well-being, also provides the official basis for our relations with our longtime friend and ally. It declares our official policy to be one of maintaining peace and promoting extensive close and friendly relations between the United States and the 17 million people on Taiwan, as well as the 1 billion people of the China mainland.

It specifies that our official policy considers any effort to determine the future of Taiwan by other than peaceful means a threat to peace and of grave concern to the United States. And most important, it spells out our policy of providing defensive weapons to Taiwan and mandates the United States to maintain the means to resist any resort to force or other forms of coercion which threaten the security of the social or economic system of Taiwan. . . .

I would not pretend, as Carter does, that the relationship we now have with Taiwan, enacted by our Congress, is not official. I am satisfied that this act provides an official and adequate basis for safeguarding our relationship with Taiwan. And I pledge to enforce it. . . .

## NOTES

Ronald Reagan, "Statement on Relations with China and Taiwan," August 25, 1980.

Ronald Reagan, Republican candidate for president; former governor of California; and 40th president of the United States (1981–1989)

# United States–China Joint Communiqué on United States Arms Sales to Taiwan

1. In the Joint Communiqué on the Establishment of Diplomatic Relations on January 1, 1979, issued by the Government of the United States of America and the Government of the People's Republic of China, the United States of America recognized the Government of the People's Republic of China as the sole legal government of China, and it acknowledged the Chinese position that there is but one China and Taiwan is part of China. Within that context, the two sides agreed that the people of the United States would continue to maintain cultural, commercial, and other unofficial relations with the people of Taiwan. On this basis, relations between the United States and China were normalized.

2. The question of United States arms sales to Taiwan was not settled in the course of negotiations between the two countries on establishing diplomatic relations. The two sides held differing positions, and the Chinese side stated that it would raise the issue again following normalization. Recognizing that this issue would seriously hamper the development of United States–China relations, they have held further discussions on it, during and since the meetings between President Ronald Reagan and Premier Zhao Ziyang and between Secretary of State Alexander M. Haig, Jr., and Vice Premier and Foreign Minister Huang Hua in October, 1981.

3. Respect for each other's sovereignty and territorial integrity and non-interference in each other's internal affairs constitute the fundamental principles guiding United States–China relations. These principles were confirmed in

the Shanghai Communiqué of February 28, 1972, and reaffirmed in the Joint Communiqué on the Establishment of Diplomatic Relations which came into effect on January 1, 1979. Both sides emphatically state these principles continue to govern all aspects of their relations.

4. The Chinese government reiterates that the question of Taiwan is China's internal affair. The Message to Compatriots in Taiwan issued by China on January 1, 1979, promulgated a fundamental policy of striving for peaceful reunification of the Motherland. The Nine-Point Proposal put forward by China on September 30, 1981, represented a further major effort under this fundamental policy to strive for a peaceful solution to the Taiwan question.

5. The United States Government attaches great importance to its relations with China, and reiterates that it has no intention of infringing on Chinese sovereignty and territorial integrity, or interfering in China's internal affairs, or pursing a policy of "Two Chinas" or "one China, one Taiwan." The United States Government understands and appreciates the Chinese policy of striving for a peaceful resolution of the Taiwan question as indicated in China's Message to Compatriots in Taiwan issued on January 1, 1979, and the Nine-Point Proposal put forward by China on September 30, 1981. The new situation which has emerged with regard to the Taiwan question also provides favorable conditions for the settlement of United States–China differences over the question of United States arms sales to Taiwan.

6. Having in mind the foregoing statement of both sides, the United States Government states that it does not seek to carry out a long-term policy of arms sales to Taiwan, that its arms sales to Taiwan will not exceed, either in qualitative or in quantitative terms, the level of those supplied in recent years since the establishment of diplomatic relations between the United States and China, and that it intends to reduce gradually its sales of arms to Taiwan, leading over a period of time to a final resolution. In so stating, the United States acknowledges China's consistent position regarding the thorough settlement of this issue.

7. In order to bring about, over a period of time, a final settlement of the question of United States arms sales to Taiwan, which is an issue rooted in history, the two governments will make every effort to adopt measures and create conditions conductive to the thorough settlement of this issue.

8. The development of United States–China relations is not only in the interests of the two peoples but also conducive to peace and stability in the world. The two sides are determined, on the principle of equality and mutual benefit, to strengthen their ties in the economic, cultural, educational, scientific, technological and other fields and make strong, joint efforts for the continued development of relations between the governments and peoples of the United States and China.

9. In order to bring about the healthy development of United States–China relations, maintain world peace and oppose aggression and expansion, the two governments reaffirm the principles agreed on by the two sides in the Shanghai Communiqué and Joint Communiqué on the Establishment of Diplomatic Relations. The two sides will maintain contact and hold appropriate consultations on bilateral and international issues of common interest.

## NOTE

"United States–China Joint Communiqué on United States Arms Sales to Taiwan," August 17, 1982, *Weekly Compilation of Presidential Documents*, Vol. 18, No. 33, pp. 1039–1040.

# U.S. Policy toward China and Taiwan

## Senate testimony by Claiborne Pell, John Glenn, S. I. Hayakawa, and John H. Holdridge

**Senator Pell** [*committee member*]: . . . [A]t first blush the joint China–United States communiqué seems fair. However, on further examination I find myself very concerned with the interests of the native Taiwanese, some 16 million people out of a total Taiwan population of 18 million, or pretty close to 90 percent of the people. Too often our discussions of China-Taiwan policy assume that the hopes, dreams, and aspirations of the native Taiwanese are shared by the mainland Chinese authorities in power on both sides of the Taiwan strait. In fact, nothing could be further from the truth.

The evidence of this is the martial law that has remained in effect in Taiwan for over 30 years. The results of this are apparent when you talk to native Taiwanese without any chaperones or advisers around. And I think we should bear in mind the old idea of self-determination. We fought World War I with that as one of our goals. We have forgotten it in many places since.

I believe that given a free choice, the Taiwanese would opt for a separate identity—a free and independent Taiwan. Unfortunately, I conclude after having read the communiqué and examining it more carefully and noting the inherent contradiction between "peaceful reunification," mainland China's position, and "peaceful resolution," our hope, that it could make it more difficult, if not eliminate the possibility altogether, for the people on Taiwan to choose a free, independent democratic government. And when I say independent I mean independent of mainland China.

I hope I am wrong but if not, I believe we cannot stand by and condone PRC pressures on Taiwan to bend to its desires. This must be a choice freely made not by the Government on Taiwan governing by martial law, but by the people of Taiwan. . . .

**Senator Glenn** [*committee member*]: . . . Along with the chairman and other members of the committee I helped draft the legislation which became known as the TRA [Taiwan Relations Act]; so we, better than most perhaps, know what we intended to accomplish in that act. And I can tell you that in my considered judgment the communiqué announced today does undermine the spirit and intent of the TRA.

Three years ago the executive branch appeared before this committee arguing that the United States intended to sell arms to Taiwan indefinitely, but that this need not be mentioned in the legislation we were considering at that time, the Taiwan Relations Act. Administration spokesmen went further and indicated that the President might, in fact, veto a bill that contained specific arms sales assurances for Taiwan. I am glad to say that Congress failed to blink in that confrontation.

In President Reagan's words 2 years ago, the Congress was clearly unwilling to buy the Carter plan which it believed would have jeopardized Taiwan's security. . . .

The legislative history demonstrates beyond a doubt that the intent of this passage was to insure that arms sales decisions, albeit prudent and cautious, would be made in Washington, not in Peking or Taipei.

Now, because we anticipated the PRC would pressure us to end or limit Taiwan arms sales, we provided in the act a framework for the executive branch to resist such pressures. Without these written assurances and confidence that the President would faithfully carry out the TRA, I seriously doubt that the Congress would have been prepared to go along with normalization and the PRC demand that we terminate the Mutual Defense Treaty with Taiwan.

The communiqué announced today discards that very carefully crafted framework, the heart of the TRA, in favor of an arms sales formulation negotiated under Chinese threats of a retrogression of United States–PRC relations.

. . . I should also note in passing that President Reagan's concessions came just 2 years after candidate Reagan pledged that he "would not impose restrictions which are not required by the Taiwan Relations Act and which contravene its spirit and purpose." . . .

**Senator Hayakawa** [*committee member*]: . . . The unveiling of the latest joint communiqué between the United States and the PRC leaves much to be desired. As a semantic purist I am somewhat disturbed by the lack of clarity in the language. I am afraid unless one looks very closely at the whole document and what is said and what is not said, it appears as though the United States is turning its back on the people of Taiwan. However, I believe there is enough ambiguity so that no one need take any offense.

The wonderful thing about language is its ability to mean whatever we may want it to mean. As a psychologist I recognized that what we have here is a situation not uncommon in human affairs: a totally ambiguous situation. In one sense Taiwan and China are one country because they both say so. Taiwan says China is one country, and the PRC says China is one country. But in another sense they are not one country.

There are many ambiguities in everyday life with which one lives. Often we condemn them as hypocrisies, but life always puts us into situations in which we have to live with these hypocrisies and endure them, hoping that some day a consistent or rational point of view can prevail, perhaps even with a solution which is not yet thought of.

If you look at the present situation between Taiwan and China where they are making totally inconsistent and incompatible assertions about each other the PRC is saying that Taiwan is really one of our provinces, and we have complete authority over Taiwan, so that if you, the United States, sell them arms, you interfere in our internal affairs. But we go ahead and sell Taiwan arms, and the PRC does not start a war over it. They do nothing more than make a big squawk and accept what is essentially an illogical situation.

I think that we will have to live with this ambiguity for some time to come. Insofar as any of us on any side of this problem insist we be perfectly logical about it, we will perpetrate some awful injustice on somebody. The only way to guarantee a minimum of justice for perhaps a few decades to come is to accept this ambiguity, to accept this, shall we say, hypocrisy on all sides.

It seems to me that this joint communiqué is just another one of the necessary ways of enduring this illogic, and even though it has been called another temporary palliative, it may have positive, permanent consequences insofar as it places the burden on the PRC to resolve their differences with Taiwan only through peaceful means; and that we have asked them to underline, and they have. . . .

**Ambassador Holdridge** [*witness*]: . . . As we went into these negotiations, we had two things in mind, our historic obligations to the people of Taiwan and our important and growing relations with the People's Republic of China. Throughout the entire period of our discussions with Beijing, we were guided by these dual considerations. It is a fundamental national interest of the United States to preserve and advance its strategic relations with China. At the same time we have, as you said, obligations to old friends and we will not turn our backs on them. . . .

Let me turn to this morning's communiqué. It reaffirms the fundamental principles which have guided United States–Chinese relations since the inception of the normalization process over 10 years ago. This reaffirmation is significant. It illustrates the strength and durability of these principles. On this foundation the United States established relations with China which have been economically beneficial to us and which have greatly enhanced our vital strategic interests.

At the same time, we have maintained and strengthened our commercial and cultural relations with the people of Taiwan. We have achieved these important goals without impairing the security of the people of Taiwan, and indeed, because of these improved relations between China and the United States, Taiwan has never been more secure.

The communiqué also addresses an issue which was not resolved at the time of normalization of relations, the question of U.S. arms sales to Taiwan. During discussions leading to normalization, China demanded that arms sales be terminated. We refused. China agreed to proceed with normalization despite this disagreement but reserved the right to raise this issue again.

. . . I believe it is well known that the normalization negotiations almost foundered on this whole question of continued U.S. arms sales to Taiwan, and it was only at the last minute by, I would say, a very statesmanlike decision on the part of the leadership of the People's Republic of China that the decision was made to go ahead, but it really was touch and go.

When China agreed to proceed with normalization despite disagreement on arms sales to Taiwan, it reserved the right to raise the issue again. When it did so last year, we agreed to engage in discussions to determine whether an understanding could be reached. The alternative to our agreeing to hold such discussions would clearly have been the beginning of a process of deterioration in our relations, deterioration that could have been irresponsible had we allowed such a process to start.

. . . [O]ur foreign policy objective was to preserve a valuable relationship which otherwise might well have and probably would have undergone a serious and possibly fatal deterioration. We undertook these discussions, therefore, with the hope that a formula could be found which would permit the continued growth of our relations with China, but also with the firm resolve that there were principles regarding the security of Taiwan which could not be compromised.

Those principles embodied in the Taiwan Relations Act commit the United States to sell to Taiwan arms necessary to maintain a sufficient self-defense capability. Aware of our consistent and firm opposition to the use of force against Taiwan, the Chinese during these discussions, and I mean the most recent ones, agreed to state in very strong terms their policy of pursuing a peaceful resolution of the Taiwan issue, and eventually came to describe this policy as "fundamental."

The Chinese insisted, however, that we agree to the ultimate termination of arms sales. We refused because the level of our arms sales must be determined by the needs of Taiwan, and we could not agree to a termination date as the Chinese demanded which might impair our ability to meet those needs. At the same time, we recognized that China's peaceful policy bore directly on the defense needs of Taiwan. So long as the policy continued, the threat to Taiwan would be diminished.

As I have noted, assurances of such continuity were provided when the Chinese began to describe their peaceful policy on the resolution of the Taiwan question as, as I have said, "fundamental," which contains the connotation of unchanging and long term. Let me say this again: which contains the connotation of unchanging and long term. We were thus able to consider a policy under which we would limit our arms sales to the levels reached in recent years and would anticipate a gradual reduction of the level of arms sales. . . .

We should keep in mind that what we have here is not a treaty or an agreement but a statement of future U.S. policy. We fully intend to implement this policy in accordance with our understanding of it. I hope I have made that point abundantly clear in my remarks today. I can further assure you that, having participated closely in the negotiations, I am confident the Chinese are fully cognizant of that understanding. . . .

**Senator Pell**: Mr. Secretary. I was struck in your statement by two expressions. You mentioned that any policy we have is in the context of our historic obligation to the people of Taiwan. I like that phrase "people of Taiwan." And then you said the solution would be worked out by the Chinese themselves. By "Chinese" you presumably mean mainland China and the Government of Taiwan. But when you talk about a historic obligation to the people of Taiwan, were you thinking of the 2 million from mainland China or the 16 million Taiwanese who were there prior to their arrival?

**Ambassador Holdridge**: When we talk about the people of Taiwan, Senator Pell, we are talking about the totality.

**Senator Pell**: That totality, as you know, a small minority has controlled through marital law for the last 30 years, but you feel they should be considered as one ball of wax?

**Ambassador Holdridge**: We do, indeed.

**Senator Pell**: Have we told the Chinese at any time in the American view nothing in the communiqué precludes American support for a separate, independent Taiwan in the event that the people of Taiwan determine one day that is their wish?

**Ambassador Holdridge**: As I said, Senator Pell, the only position we take in this matter is that the resolution of the Taiwan question should be by the Chinese people themselves. Our only responsibility with respect to this situation is that this resolution be by peaceful means.

**Senator Pell**: So our emphasis is on peaceful means.

**Ambassador Holdridge**: Peaceful means, yes. And we do not take any position on the ultimate outcome.

**Senator Pell**: But we would have no objection if one day the Taiwanese exercised their numerical majority—not exercised but exploited their numerical majority and decided they wanted to be free and independent. We would not interfere with that.

**Ambassador Holdridge**: That is a hypothetical question, Senator Pell.

**Senator Pell**: It would not be if there were an election. [Laughter.]

**Ambassador Holdridge**: We do not see any trends in that direction at this time. . . .

**Senator Glenn**: What does "gradually reduce" mean? Does that mean 1 year, 10 years? Will it be starting immediately? How do you define it?

**Ambassador Holdridge**: We will not operate on the assumption that we will delay in this whole process. We have come to an agreement—not an agreement but an understanding with the PRC, and I think they expect us to carry out in good faith as we expect them to carry out in good faith the commitment to carry out a fundamental policy of working toward the peaceful resolution of the Taiwan question, so there is an obligation on both sides.

**Senator Glenn**: That does not answer my question. Is it 1 year, 20 years?

**Ambassador Holdridge**: There is no time frame established in this document.

**Senator Glenn**: What do the Chinese expect? What does the PRC expect?

**Ambassador Holdridge**: I have no idea what the Chinese expect. This is something we will have to work out over an historical period of time. . . .

**Senator Glenn**: . . . [F]undamental policies can become un-fundamental policies right away, and if the arms balance has been allowed to become a negative balance for Taiwan over a period of years, you cannot make it up in the same time that you could change a "fundamental policy." . . .

## NOTES

Senate Committee on Foreign Relations, "U.S. Policy toward China and Taiwan," 97th Congress, 2nd sess., August 17, 1982. Testimony by Claiborne Pell, John Glenn, S. I. Hayakawa, and John H. Holdridge.

Claiborne Pell, senator (D-RI); John Glenn, senator (D-Ohio); S. I. Hayakawa, senator (R-CA); John H. Holdridge, assistant secretary of state for East Asian and Pacific affairs

# 5

# Human Rights Strategies

*China's human rights situation during the Mao era and early Deng years was not well understood in the early 1980s. Amnesty International wrote its first report on China only in 1978, and Human Rights Watch's Asia division would not be founded until 1985. The following hearing demonstrates that in the early 1980s, the government and experts were still discussing whether the United States was justified in making human rights in other countries a legitimate issue and, if so, how to effectively promote those rights without sacrificing other goals.*

## Reconciling Human Rights and
## U.S. Security Interests in Asia

### House testimony by Robert Barnett, Andrew J. Nathan, and Kenneth Lieberthal

**Mr. Barnett** [*witness*]: . . . When I was first approached to present views to you on human rights in China, I disclaimed adequate qualification, but said that I would, of course, be willing to come before you, if asked.

A little later, I received the written invitation which contains the 12 difficult questions which you are putting to our witnesses. My reaction to them was that no one anywhere could do them justice.

However, there they were, and I will try to respond to them without much elaboration or qualification. . . .

#### HEARING ON CHINA SUBCOMMITTEE QUESTIONS

. . .

(4) Is there anything that could be done to advance the cause of human rights that the U.S. Government is not now doing? If so, what? If not, why not? Do you think educational and cultural exchanges help? Legal

training? Is China such a violator of human rights that it should not be eligible for aid?

(5) Would people in China be hospitable to democracy and legal due process? Some experts contend that given China's Legalist-Confucian culture and tradition that institutions protecting individual human rights, competitive elections, an untrammeled free press, etc. are alien to the Chinese or at least not matters of high significance. These people say that Chinese stress the group and nation, hierarchy, harmony and respect for authority. How do you evaluate these claims?

(6) Some authorities believe that a democratic China would create anarchy; China would fall apart and lose its national unity and purpose. Do you agree or disagree? Why? Are there any good reasons why ruling groups in China cannot move further or faster in a democratic direction?

(7) Some argue that for foreigners to advocate human rights in China only will hurt the cause of human rights in China by making human rights look like a foreign imposition. These people say a proud and nationalistic people such as the Chinese will resent and reject attempts by foreigners to interfere in Chinese domestic matters and that therefore, for good pragmatic reasons, the U.S. should stay out. How do you weigh these claims which have also been made for South Korea and other countries?

(8) How would you evaluate the 1981 State Department Human Rights Report on China? What positive or negative purposes are served by such reporting requirements?

(9) How important a priority should the promotion of human rights in China be for American foreign policy?

(10) The argument is made that America's strategic ties to China are so vital that the U.S. Government should not harm its relations with the PRC by pressing issues of human rights concern. Do you agree? Please explain.

. . .

**Mr. Barnett**: Question 4: China should be eligible for what is bound to be quite limited foreign aid if it wants it, and if we wish to extend it, without regard to allegations of behavior by Chinese authorities toward Chinese people. This is Peking's business.

If the United States wants to advance the cause of human rights, the most effective method for doing so is by example. How the United States handles the economic and social problems of its own people, especially our minorities, and how it assures safety in the streets and offers opportunity for creative self-fulfillment by its people is noticed everywhere in the world.

The United States was perhaps the most widely admired country in the world during its Great Depression, largely because of the daring and compassion of its welfare programs.

Educational and cultural exchanges should enrich both of our societies, and make it widely possible to understand much better what are our real strengths and weaknesses.

Lacking these exchanges we, on our side, had totally inadequate comprehension of the tragedy of China's Cultural Revolution.

Question 5: China, for thousands of years, has been conscious that the legitimacy of authority—the Mandate of Heaven—was ultimately tested by the welfare of the people. Moral precepts guided administration of the law.

Confucian historians rendered moral judgment, dynasty after dynasty, on government administration at the imperial, provincial, and local levels.

China's Confucian legalist, philosophic, and legal inheritance, however, never dealt with individual human rights.

This inheritance, as such, does not show a Chinese incapacity to assimilate our notions of democracy and legal due process. However, given both opportunity and incentive to adopt them, even Chinese in Taiwan, when professing commitment to democracy, refer to something quite different from American democracy.

Out of the recently adjourned People's Congress has come much evidence of the intent of China's leaders to respect law, encourage greater personal freedom, and accept the value of dissent.

But talk of rectification—for which I read that is, purges—suggests that these goals will be pursued in ways alien to ours.

Question 6: Some Americans beheld Mao, particularly during the Cultural Revolution, as presiding over an egalitarian society unmatched in all history.

Some called this populism a pure expression of democracy. However, we now know that most Chinese themselves viewed that period differently and welcomed, when it occurred, Deng's overthrow of the Gang of Four and reduction of China toward more free and democratic processes than before.

Few Americans truly understand all the hidden factors that have made possible that transformation. What is particularly difficult to understand is how China, whether under Mao or in transition to Deng's guiding authority, escaped anarchy.

What we do know, however, is that its dynamics was entirely Chinese.

Question 7: Foreign advocacy of human rights in China would not improve the cause. It would be either irrelevant, or marginally harmful.

Question 8: The 1981 State Department Human Rights Report on China was, I think a fair and conscientious effort to comply with prescribed reporting requirements. The report suffered, however, from stress on anecdote.

It could not cast much light on the moral dilemmas of a leadership which recognizes that its legitimacy depends on wisely guiding the behavior of 1 billion Chinese, occupying an area almost exactly the size of the United States, facing forbidding challenges of day-to-day survival.

Question 9: A high priority should be accorded to study of China but, while strengthening political ties and understanding, cooperating on projects of mutual interest, and increasing exchanges of goods and persons, we should not accord priority to promoting human rights, as such, in China.

Question 10: In conversations with China about strategic interests which we may share, we should not press human rights issues, unless we are prepared to invite Chinese views on our management of such matters in the United States.

Our traditions and systems differ, and we should respect the differences, even when the Chinese differences might offend us. . . .

**Mr. Nathan** [*witness*]: . . . The key point that I want to make is that I believe we can and should promote human rights vigorously even in those societies such as China where our conceptions of human rights are not fully shared.

I would like to present four reasons for my believing this.

First of all, China does criticize the American political system very freely in its press which, as you know, is party and government controlled.

I do not see any reason for us to be reticent about commenting forcefully on their political system. I certainly do not think there is any cultural imperialism or interference in internal affairs involved when Americans speak out on politics in other countries.

Second, although there are important differences between American and Chinese values, nonetheless, American democracy enjoys great prestige among the Chinese people, and I think we would lose this prestige if we don't speak up in defense of Chinese citizens who exercise legitimate freedoms of speech, for example, and other rights.

Third, international attention often forces governments to be more respectful of human rights. It produces results, sometimes only because they want to avoid embarrassment, but also sometimes because when foreign commentators draw attention to a particular case, then the government in that country takes another look and finds out that even their own values have been contravened by the way that case was handled by somebody in that society.

Fourth, I believe that increased international communication about rights issues by virtue of—in this case—of our making, bringing attention to cases that concern us helps to educate or persuade people and leaders in other countries over a very, very slow and long and contentious process which may be frustrating, but I think that history shows that these ideals are attractive and can to some extent spread.

. . . Some people argue that American pressure for rights would destabilize China. My answer to this is that I think the Chinese political system is far too stable to be affected by anything that the United States may do in the realm of human rights.

Of course, there are other things we could do that might destabilize even the most stable country, but not in this area, I don't think so.

I believe too that greater openness and freedom within China would actually enhance the political stability of that country, even though it would produce a superficial picture of greater—what may appear to be greater conflict.

Another argument that sometimes is made is that American pressure for human rights would undermine China's more moderate leaders. I do not share this view either, although I do think that the elite political struggle in China may be affected by American behavior.

I think that that struggle is so complicated and is affected by so many factors, both internal and external, that it is basically hopeless to think that by withholding our comment on human rights issues, we can somehow assure the success of the moderate leaders, or that that would be even an important factor. . . .

Third, it has been argued that our pressure on rights issues might drive China into the arms of the Soviet Union. Here my thought is that such cooperation as exists between China and the United States is not really based upon shared political views or cultural friendship, even though we often hear about friendship, but based upon a parallelism of strategic interests, and in my view a certain amount—in fact a considerable degree—of rapprochement with the Soviet Union is likely to be in China's interest and is likely to take place regardless of what we say about human rights in China.

So I do not see any compelling political reasons or realpolitik reasons why the American Government or citizens should be afraid to say whatever we may think about human rights in China. . . .

**Mr. Lieberthal** [*witness*]: . . . I want to summarize my statement rather than read it in full. . . .

First, given China's very different historical and philosophical tradition, is it appropriate for us to judge the PRC by our own set of values? The American and Chinese cultural traditions do differ dramatically and in ways that are pertinent to human rights issues. Thus, for example, the Chinese lack a background for appreciating democracy, the rule of law, and freedom of speech.

Democracy makes assumptions about equality, conflict, and choice that are not widely held in China. The Chinese believe since any system of law can be abused it is the quality of the leaders rather than the quality of the laws that determines the virtue of the systems; and full freedom of speech presumes a natural separation between the government and the people that the Chinese do not endorse.

This different philosophical tradition, however, does not mean that Chinese do not value highly some of the things that we call human rights. There now appears, for example, to be widespread demand in China for greater security against arbitrary search and seizure, for less intrusion of politics into daily life, for more freedom of travel and residence, and for greater freedom for various forms of traditional religious practice, among other things.

We should, therefore, be sensitive to the fact that while some of our human rights concerns are widely shared in China, others derive from such a different philosophical tradition they seem strange, alien, and possibly subversive. At the same time though, we must not make the error of believing that none of our concerns are shared by large numbers of Chinese.

The second issue: Can Peking adopt a more forthcoming position toward human rights and still retain the power to rule a country of China's size and complexity? I believe a loosening up in China would have a beneficial impact upon their system. Chinese leaders traditionally have felt that to rule China requires a strong hand. They are loathe, however, to take on the risk of social upheaval. In any case, the conservatives, military, police, and party bureaucracies are so strong I feel it would be impossible politically even for Deng Xiaoping to change significantly China's human rights posture.

Third, does our policy appear to be interfering in Peking's internal affairs? The concerns we have bypass the governments in China and elsewhere, but the Chinese are particularly sensitive to issues of sovereignty, and the driving force of their revolution was to stop other countries' interference in their domestic affairs. Thus the chances of Peking's adopting a sharply negative response to issues we raise are substantial.

Finally, do we in any case have enough leverage with China to affect its domestic human rights policies? Overall we have very little leverage with any country of continental size, especially in that country's domestic policy. While we can get some Chinese co-operation in areas where they require specific American inputs—such as in passing laws necessary for U.S. participation in offshore oil cooperation—we do not have similar leverage over general domestic issues such as human rights treatment.

In view of the above answers to those four objections, what should the United States do? I think our policy must be sensitive to three basic realities. First, China's human rights policy is not going to improve dramatically no matter what we do. Indeed, probably the best we can hope for is a situation roughly akin to that now prevailing in the Soviet Union, where citizens are allowed to be cynical and apolitical and to have somewhat diverse living styles so long as they do not engage in prolonged, open opposition to the government, in which case they will be silenced by the police.

Second, China's current overall development strategy has already significantly improved the human rights situation there through the adoption of policies that are based on the need to appeal to peasants and intellectuals and by toning down the ferocity of political struggle.

Last, the United States is closely identified with this new economic development strategy in the minds of leading Chinese. Any significant worsening of United States–Chinese relations, therefore, can weaken the momentum behind this strategy, almost certainly to the detriment of the human rights situation in the PRC.

In view of these realities, the United States has, I believe, only three available approaches if our goal is to further human rights in China as much as possible without triggering a counterproductive response in Peking.

First, we should work to keep United States–Chinese relations on an even keel so as to bolster the people in China whose program is most compatible with our human rights concerns. This does not mean that we should yield to each new Chinese demand. It does mean that we should avoid the type of careless rhetoric that has so harmed United States–Chinese relations over the past 1 to 2 years. Overall, I feel that our academic and cultural exchanges with China play a positive role in this area. To repeat, though, missteps in relations generally harm the cause of human rights in the PRC.

Second, the United States should keep human rights on the world agenda through our international speeches in forums and through our own examples at home. The Chinese are sensitive to international prestige and thus they will feel pressure if other countries begin to recognize the validity of human rights concerns. Admittedly this is a long-term, indirect, and frustrating strategy, but more direct public approaches, such as the annual "State Department Country Report on Human Rights in China" are at best ineffective and at worse offensive to Peking and counterproductive.

Finally, the United States should raise directly and privately with Peking human rights issues that the United States finds particularly egregious and that stem directly from PRC government policy. Such issues may include excessively harsh punishments meted out to dissidents, persecution of religious leaders, and so forth. The United States can assert these actions draw down China's reservoir of good will in America. I personally believe, however, that works like Fox Butterfield's book, *Alive in the Bitter Sea*, have so taken the bloom off the Chinese rose in the United States that the U.S. Government will not, in reality, find itself seriously hemmed in by aroused American public opinion. Privacy is important for any such representation to Peking to be effective. More public postures such as congressional resolutions are likely to be ineffective or counterproductive.

## NOTES

House Committee on Foreign Affairs Subcommittees on Asia and Pacific Affairs and Human Rights and International Organizations, "Reconciling Human Rights and U.S. Security Interests in Asia," 97th Congress, 2nd sess., September 29, 1982. Testimony by Robert Barnett, Andrew J. Nathan, and Kenneth Lieberthal.

Robert Barnett, former deputy assistant secretary of state for East Asian and Pacific affairs; Andrew J. Nathan, professor of political science, Columbia University; Kenneth Lieberthal, professor of Chinese politics, Swathmore College and later professor, University of Michigan; National Security Council staff member during the Clinton administration (1998–2000)

- PART II -

# THE GOLDEN YEARS (1984–1988)

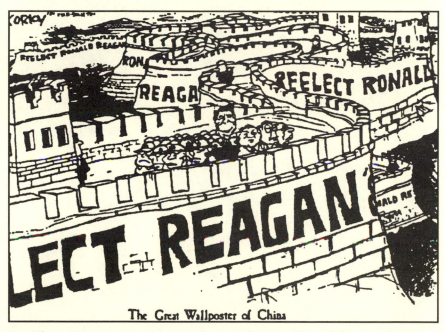

President Reagan was extremely popular in China following his April 1984 visit there. Reprinted by permission from Corky Trinidad.

# 6

# A Growing Relationship

*After at least temporarily resolving their differences over Taiwan in 1982, the tone of the relationship between the United States and China remarkably improved. President Reagan's April 1984 visit to China symbolized the transformation of ties that occurred since the 1960s. The image of a reformist China that would be a close partner, if not ally, to the United States was widely shared. A few voices, though, did caution that a stronger China was not necessarily in U.S. interests.*

## United States–China Relations

### House testimony by A. Doak Barnett, Donald Zagoria, and Gerald Solomon

**Mr. Barnett** [*witness, prepared statement*]: . . . U.S. policy toward China since the early 1970s has been a remarkable success story in many respects. The contrast between Sino-American relations today and the situation that prevailed in the 1950s and 1960s is striking.

For more than two decades, from 1949 until 1971, the United States and China were locked in hostile confrontation. We fought one war with Chinese in Korea, waged another by proxy in Vietnam (against what American leaders at the time perceived to be Chinese-backed Communist expansionism in Southeast Asia), and confronted the Chinese in a series of crises in other areas on China's periphery. We poured large resources into a policy designed to build up military forces and alliances aimed at isolating and containing China. The direct costs to the United States of conflict and confrontation with China, in terms of both men and money, were high, and the effects of U.S.–China hostility on East Asia were very destabilizing. The United States and China competed against each other's influence throughout the region, and the prevailing atmosphere was characterized by tension and uncertainty, punctuated by periodic military clashes.

In the twelve years since the dramatic shift of policy in 1971–72, engi-
neered on the U.S. side by President Richard Nixon and Henry Kissinger, and
on the Chinese side by Chairman Mao Zedong and Premier Zhou Enlai, the
situation has fundamentally changed in many important respects. Instead of
confronting each other with implacable hostility, the United States and China
have gradually expanded mutually beneficial bilateral relations, have searched
for common ground in dealing with numerous international problems, region-
ally and globally, and have pursued policies toward many countries and areas,
especially within the East Asian region, that are mutually supportive, tacitly if
not explicitly.

The transformation of our bilateral relations in the past twelve years has
been extraordinary. Until 1971–72, there were virtually no contacts between
us, except for the generally sterile ambassadorial-level talks held at Geneva
and Warsaw. Since then, very extensive, and still growing, relationships have
developed between our governments and societies. Not only do our top leaders meet periodically, and our diplomats deal with each other on a continuous
basis, working relations based on more than twenty official agreements have
been established between numerous American government agencies and
their counterparts in China, and cooperative programs have been started in a
wide range of fields. Three bilateral commissions, dealing with science and
technology, trade and commerce, and general economic cooperation, have
been established to promote broader ties. Trade has grown much faster than
anyone predicted a decade ago, and, although the level is still relatively low
compared to that of trade with our major commercial partners, it already is
significant from the perspective of U.S. exporters of agricultural products and
technology, and it is even more important from the Chinese point of view.
American corporations, particularly in the energy field, are becoming
involved in a big way, and on a long-term basis, in China, especially in offshore oil development, creating a new convergence of economic interests of
major long-run importance. Scientific and cultural ties, some official but on
the U.S. side mainly non-official, have expanded remarkably. A very large
number of American educational and research institutions now have very
close ties with comparable institutions in China. The number of American
scholars and students in China is still fairly small. However, Chinese studying
in the United States now total over 10,000—more than the peak number of
Chinese who studied in the Soviet Union in the 1950s. In effect, the United
States is helping China to train a new generation of specialists and scientific
and economic leaders. More broadly, other contacts, and the general flow of
people between our two countries, have grown from virtually nothing to a
firmly impressive level. Hundreds of Chinese delegations of many sorts have
visited the United States, and tens of thousands of American tourists now visit
China every year.

Today, moreover, instead of the across-the-board opposition to each other's policies that characterized our relations in earlier years, there is an important convergence of interests and parallelism in our policies toward many areas and issues. We both see the Soviet Union's military buildup in East Asia as the principal potential threat to our security interests and stability in the region. We agree that there is a need for a strong counter-weight to check and deter Soviet pressures, and, although our policies even toward Moscow are by no means identical, we both see an important parallelism in our views about the security problems posed by Soviet military power, and each of us recognizes that the other contributes to a balance of power that serves our respective interests. We both now view good relations with the Japanese as essential to stability in the region, and instead of competing to weaken each other's influence there, we both favor closer ties among Americans, Chinese, and Japanese. In Korea, while Washington and Beijing back competing regimes in the South and North, both of us now place high priority on the need to prevent military conflict on the peninsula. In Southeast Asia we both are strongly supportive of the ASEAN nations and, although our interests in this area, as in many others, are different in some respects, we both oppose Vietnam's domination of Kampuchea and Hanoi's close alignment with Moscow. In South Asia, we both oppose Soviet domination of Afghanistan and are supportive of Pakistan's efforts to cope with the problems and dangers that the Soviet invasion of Afghanistan pose in that region.

In sum, the establishment of friendly and expanding ties between the United States and China has been more rapid, and has gone farther in many respects, than even the greatest optimists would have believed possible twelve year ago, and the benefits to the United States as well as to China have been enormous.

Yet, there is no basis for complacency on our part about the future. Despite the progress that has been made, U.S.–China relations are still fragile, and unstable, in important respects. Even in the brief twelve years since the initial opening in the early 1970s, there have been some periods of serious strain, and major ups and downs, in our relationship. Moreover, while it is important to recognize the parallelism in some of our positions and policies, it would be naïve to overlook, or to underestimate, the difficulties posed by major continuing differences. Our relationship is complicated by some very difficult problems. Most important are the differences over the Taiwan issue. In addition, despite the fact that we hold common views on many international problems, we differ on many others, and even though we share some important strategic interests, there still are important differences in our broad strategic outlooks.

Other problems in our relationship derive from differences in our values, our political systems, our economies, and our societies, and from the fact that foreign policy decisions in our two countries are influenced by very different domestic forces.

The task facing both Washington and Beijing in the period ahead is to work steadily not only to expand mutually beneficial bilateral ties and broaden areas of international cooperation, but also to try to reduce our differences and manage the most difficult problems in our relationship so as to avoid major political crises or setbacks. The goal, in short, should be the achievement of a more stable relationship—one that can be sustained over the long run. This will not be achievable unless each side is very sensitive to the concerns of the other. Managing our problems successfully will also require that leaders in each country avoid unrealistic expectations about what can be expected from the other. Mismanagement of the inevitable problems in the relationship by either or both sides could well result in retrogression; this was what occurred during 1981–82 when China came close to downgrading our diplomatic ties, and it could happen again. . . .

. . . [T]he record of ups and downs during the past twelve years indicates that there is little basis for complacency about the future. That record highlights several important facts: first, that while U.S.-China relations are extremely important to both countries, they are also very complicated and in some respects still fragile and unstable; second, that while the potential for broadening, strengthening, and stabilizing ties gives cause for optimism, realism demands that we recognize that serious problems will continue to complicate our relationships and accept that there are limits to what our expectations should be; and third, that continued strengthening of our ties will only be possible if leaders in both countries show restraint in dealing with the unavoidable problems that will unquestionably continue to arise in our relations and be prepared to make the necessary compromises to prevent our differences from creating new crises. . . .

**Mr. Zagoria** [*witness*]: . . . [I]t seems to me that the gradual rapprochement between the United States and China has been the most important new political factor in the Far East during the 1970's. The committee asks whether this United States-Chinese relationship should be seen largely in terms of a global balance of power or in terms of the regional balance of power, and I would say it should be seen in terms of both.

The global benefit is that a cooperative United States–People's Republic of China relationship enhances deterrence of Soviet adventurism everywhere by forcing the Soviets to contemplate the danger of overextension in several theaters of combat at once. Like the United States, the Soviet Union is concerned about the prospect of having major forces pinned down in one theater when conflict in another theater erupts. Thus, fear of conflict with China in Asia is bound to influence Soviet thinking about potential adventures in Europe, Southwest Asia, or elsewhere.

In particular, China serves as a crucial counterweight to the expansion of Soviet power in Asia. The People's Republic of China helps to restrain North Korean adventurism against South Korea; it helps to shore up Thailand against Vietnam; Pakistan against Moscow. It seeks to eject the Soviets from Afghanistan and the Vietnamese from Kampuchea, and in general, seeks improved relation with all of the non-Communist states in the region because of its overriding concern with Soviet and Vietnamese expansion.

To be sure, there are important differences between the Chinese and American positions on Korea and Indochina, but on the decisive issue, containing Soviet expansion, there is a common position.

Finally, a cooperative United States–Chinese relationship seems to me to be an important element in the Pacific success story of American foreign policy in recent years. Pacific Asia is the most economically dynamic region of the world, one of the most stable, one of the few in which there are viable regional institutions, as evidenced by talk of the new Pacific community, one of the few regions of the world where it is very hard to develop a scenario for war.

Much of this stability and prosperity is related to the new chapter in Chinese-American relations, as Professor Barnett has suggested.

For those who say that the People's Republic is not so important to the United States, and not such an important power, I would say this: By conservative estimates, by the year 2000, China will have a GNP of approximately $1 trillion. It will have an extremely potent nuclear force. It will play a very substantial geostrategic role in a world where United States–Soviet competition will remain the decisive competition and it will play an even greater role in Asia than it does now. . . .

**Mr. Solomon** [*committee member*]: First, . . . let me commend . . . you gentlemen for your testimony. . . . I don't want you to think because I smiled or laughed at something that you said earlier that I did not respect you. I do.

I was particularly glad to hear that you think that President Reagan is pragmatic and not a right-wing nut of some kind, as some people think. Although I would take exception with the statement that there is little difference between former President Jimmy Carter and President Reagan. I, for one, was somewhat concerned when the latest communiqué was entered into between this country and the People's Republic of China. I met with the President personally shortly after that to let him know of my concerns. I can assure everyone in this room that in spite of that communiqué, the so-called Shanghai II communiqué, that President Reagan has said the Taiwan Relations Act is the law of the land, which he or any other President must abide by.

Let me further assure everybody here that we in the Congress intend to keep it that way. It will not be diminished in any way, not even over a period of time.

Someone also made the point that the People's Republic of China was conservative in borrowing or increasing its national debt and that is easy to understand, particularly when I think the median income in the PRC is something like $300; that is median and certainly not the low income. When you pay your people slave wages like that, it is easy not to borrow money, I suppose.

I am particularly concerned because of the imports coming into this country, including clothing, software, wood products, and other imports that are produced by those $300-a-year-or-less wages. When you compare that to Taiwan, where the median income is somewhere around $2,400, you see a considerable difference. Even more so in the United States, where the median income is over $10,000. When people that work in the clothing industry in New York City or up in the Adirondack Mountains, where I come from, where they produce folding chairs, wood products, are losing their jobs because of the imports being brought into this country at about half what it actually cost to produce them in the United States it is a deplorable thing. I'm tired of seeing people in areas like I represent who don't have a chance of getting jobs or being put out of work because of imports like this. . . .

So, Mr. Zagoria, I would just ask you the question: You painted a rather glowing picture of Communist China in your earlier presentation, even though you rebutted some of that, which is why I sort of laughed later on in answer to some of [committee member] Mr. Dymally's questions. But you left with me the impression that Communist China is no longer a threat, either to the United States, as far as our security and the future security of this nation is concerned, and they are not a threat to any other nation, not even Taiwan. I would just ask you: Is that correct? Are they a threat to the United States possibly in the future? Are they a threat to any other nation or are they a threat to Taiwan at some future time?

**Mr. Zagoria**: I think that China may well be a threat for our grandchildren. It is certainly too weak now to be a threat to the United States or to the Soviet Union or to most of its neighbors in Asia and it is primarily preoccupied, and will be, in my opinion, for the next several decades, with internal economic development.

What happens in 20 or 30 years from now, once China becomes much stronger, is something that no one can really predict. A lot will depend on what happens in the intervening 20 or 30 years. I can imagine many different possibilities: some more favorable to the West; some much less favorable to the West. . . .

I am rather cautiously optimistic about the future of China for a number of reasons. One, it seems to me that the Leninist development strategy that the Chinese got stuck with as a result of their alliance with Russia in the 1950's has been thoroughly discredited throughout much of the world. It doesn't work very well.

The Chinese are doing economic reforms; the East Europeans are doing them; the Russians themselves are beginning to do them. Communist countries are increasingly driven toward economic reforms by the failure of the orthodox Soviet Communist system.

In addition, inside China, that Leninist model has been discredited by the heritage of Russian imperialism against China. Also, those reforms are working. The past 5 years have been fairly successful, the most successful in the past 10 or 15 years, economically speaking.

Also, China will be able to look upon non-Communist systems in Asia as a reference model. For a variety of reasons, it seems to me that there is some possibility to believe that over the longer term, China may prove to be more flexible in making the changes and in making adjustments than the Soviet Union and indeed, over the longer run, if the Chinese and the Hungarian reforms toward a more liberal kind of communism work, I think eventually the Soviets themselves may be driven in this direction.

So, I think we are witnessing the beginning of a rather historic transition in China that could have very profound consequences, not least of all on the Soviet Union itself.

**Mr. Solomon**: I thank you, Mr. Zagoria, and I think what you have done is to confirm just about my entire position of needing to proceed with caution. . . .

I think it can all be summed up by saying that, in Korea, I think we proved our point once and for all that we are not an aggressive nation. If we ever were an aggressive nation, we would have crossed that Yalu River. We would have gone into China and would have become an aggressive nation. We didn't do it because we are Americans. This is the United States of America.

Last, I will just say concerning the threat to our grandchildren, that I am a young grandfather with a grandchild and I think that is the whole crux of this thing here today. . . .

**Mr. Solarz** [*committee chair*]: Do either of you see any prospect whatsoever for the eventual establishment of a political system in China which would be based on the principles of political pluralism? Do you even see the possibility for the eventual establishment of a political system in China, based on the domination of the Communist Party, but where, within the framework of that party, one has a genuine measure of internal democracy, say like what we have in Mexico, or do you think that even that is virtually inconceivable?

**Mr. Barnett**: Frankly, I am a pessimist on that score. I think I can envisage liberalization within the framework of an authoritarian society going further than it has so far, but real pluralism or democracy, à la Mexico, in my judgment is very unlikely. The problems are too great; the size of the country is too great; the traditions do not support it. Now, people can argue that if, over time, there are, rising living standards, higher literacy, and gradual liberalization, maybe at some point there is going to be a qualitative change.

But I tend to be pessimistic, Congressman.

**Mr. Solarz**: Mr. Zagoria.

**Mr. Zagoria**: It depends on degrees here. We are not going to see an end to a one-party system, but I think there already is the beginning for greater pluralism and diversity in the society and in the economy. I could imagine that gradually expanding within the framework of a one-party system. . . .

## NOTES

House Committee on Foreign Affairs Subcommittees on Asian and Pacific Affairs and on International Economic Policy and Trade, "United States–China Relations," 98th Congress, 2nd sess., April 3, 1984. Testimony by A. Doak Barnett, Donald Zagoria, and Gerald Solomon.

A. Doak Barnett, director of China studies, Johns Hopkins University School of Advanced International Studies, former professor, Columbia University (1961–1969) and senior fellow, Brookings Institution (1969–1982); Donald Zagoria, professor of government, Hunter College and Graduate Center, City University of New York; Gerald Solomon, congressman (R-NY)

# Toast at a Welcoming Banquet Hosted by Premier Zhao Ziyang of China in Beijing

### Ronald Reagan

Premier Zhao, ladies and gentlemen, since we arrived yesterday, the graciousness with which we have been received has been truly heartwarming. A Chinese proverb best describes my feeling: "When the visitor arrives, it is as if returning home."

Having already known Premier Zhao, one of the purposes of my visit was to make new friends. But I find, especially after meeting President Li [Xiannian] and General Secretary Hu [Yaobang], that instead of making friends, I am among friends.

Mr. Premier, this has been a stimulating day. Much was accomplished, not the least of which was the renewal of the personal rapport we established during your memorable visit to the United States [in January 1984]. Your visit permitted you to judge for yourself the intentions of the American people. I hope the good will you experienced, just as I enjoyed from your people today, confirmed to you that our citizens want our countries to work in harmony.

The American and Chinese Governments have responded to that wish in a series of formal communiqués which set forth the fundamental principles of our relationship—the 1972 Shanghai communiqué, the January 1, 1979, com-

**This cartoon depicting President Reagan during his April 1984 visit to China captures how far he had moved over the course of his first term from supporting Taiwan (the Republic of China) to stressing good ties with mainland China (the People's Republic). Reprinted by permission from Morgan Chua and the *Far Eastern Economic Review*.**

muniqué establishing diplomatic relations, and the August 17, 1982, communiqué negotiated by my administration.

Mr. Premier, by any accounting the cooperation between China and the United States already has been a boon to our people. We have both gained. In the last few years, two-way trade has taken off. There has been a veritable explosion of student, science, business, and tourist exchanges between our peoples. Joint business ventures which profit all concerned are multiplying.

We would be less than candid if we minimized the significance of the benefits we each receive from our good relations. Standing together, we can expand the trade and commercial ties that increase the quality of life in both countries. Standing together, we can further peace and security. Great nations, if adversaries, cannot draw from each other's strength.

The commitment to stand as friends has been made. The promise is solid. The challenges that remain, however, will take both patience and mutual understanding. I have suggested and, with your permission say again this evening: Let us use as our guide the principle of *hujing huhui*—mutual respect, mutual benefit. This principle has within it both dignity and fairness.

Another source from which to draw is our knowledge of each other, a well of familiarity which increases in depth with every passing day.

We are each working hard to learn more about the delicate and detailed workings of the other's system—ours with its complex legal procedures based on the separation of powers, and yours with its own intricate patterns. Insights into why and how decisions are made can help both of us appreciate our agreements and accept in good faith our disagreements.

From what we see, Premier Zhao, my countrymen are enthused by what is happening in China. Your modernization program, an ambitious undertaking, makes our future relationship even more promising. You are striving to quadruple your production by the year 2000, and the eyes of the world are watching as you progress on this peaceful and productive course. The American people wish you success and offer you our cooperation in this great endeavor.

Americans, more than others, admire those who set great goals and strive to improve their lot. When that first American merchant ship set sail for China 200 years ago, our Forefathers were citizens of a weak republic living in an unexplored and undeveloped land. We Americans are proud of our accomplishments in these last 200 years, just as you are rightfully proud of the enormous contributions Chinese civilization has made to mankind.

As China moves forward to modernize and develop it economy, the United States is eager to join in a cooperative effort to share the American capabilities that helped turn our country from a vast wilderness into an industrial giant. Those American capabilities flow from the creative enterprise our society encourages. Our progress is based on what we have found to work. If it did not work, the American people, who are pragmatic by nature, would likely have abandoned it long ago.

China today, I understand, is taking its own practical approach. By increasing incentives and decentralizing decision-making, you are promoting innovation, creativity, and a better ability to adapt to local conditions. The responsibility system in agriculture has spurred increases in food production throughout China, and the special economic zones are providing dramatic examples of how incentives can raise productivity and offer bountiful opportunities for a better life.

In your drive for modernization, you have our best wishes. If you ask our advice, we can only answer with truth as we see it. But let me assure you, we want you to succeed. Having 1 billion people—nearly a quarter of mankind—healthy, well fed, clothed, and housed, educated, and given the opportunity for a higher standard of living, is in the interest of good and decent people everywhere. It is certainly in the interest of the American people, who wish to trade and be friends with the Chinese people.

Premier Zhao, as we're all well aware, our cooperation is based on more than simply the desire to improve our economies. Today the peace of the world is threatened by a major power that is focusing its resources and energies not on economic progress but, instead, on military power.

The shift in military might of the last decade has made trust and friendship between us even more vital. I know it is your desire, and that of the United States as well, that peace be preserved. We seek to better the quality of life of our people, and that can be done only in a peaceful environment. War is the great destroyer of all the hopes of mankind.

To preserve the peace and protect our own sovereignty and independence, we stand together in opposing expansionism and hegemony. We stand together in support of the independence of Afghanistan and Kampuchea. Both of us seek to promote peace and reconciliation through dialog between South and North on the Korean Peninsula. Both of us seek the early independence of Namibia and an end to outside interference in the affairs of southern Africa. Although our prescriptions for getting there are quite different, we share a common desire for a resolution of the turmoil in the Middle East and Central America. Both of us seek an end to the use of chemical weapons and agree on the necessity of reducing nuclear arms.

A strong China, dedicated to peace, clearly is in the best interest of international stability and in the best interest of the United States. A robust and enduring friendship will bolster the security of both our countries without compromising the independence of either. It will be the trust between us that will keep us and the world at peace. In this, let us be of the same mind. And as a saying from "The Book of Changes" goes, "If two people are of the same mind, their sharpness can cut through metal."

It is the hope and prayer of the American people that someday there will no longer be a need for our nation to use any of its resources to produce weapons of any kind. The Chinese and American people are now showing the world by our example that there is a better way than hatred and violence.

Many of us in this room have seen much history in our lifetime. My own lifetime spans one-third of the history of the American Republic. Over the many years that God has permitted me to live, I have observed the changing nature of the relationship between our two countries.

At times, our feelings toward each other were hostile and negative. Today, we have the opportunity to keep our countries on a path of genuine good will that will reap rewards for generations to come. Let us not shy from the task. It will not be easy; yet, let us move forward so that someday when the young people of our countries reach a ripe old age, they will look back, and there will be no memory of a time when there was anything else but friendship and good feelings between the Chinese and American people. That is a gift we can give to them.

In our shared spirit of friendship, peace, and cooperation, I am delighted to note that both President Li and General Secretary Hu have accepted our invitation to visit the United States. We look forward to reciprocating the warm hospitality that we've been shown in your beautiful country.

And in the same spirit, permit me, Premier Zhao, to propose a toast. To your health, Mr. Premier, to the health of President and Mrs. Li who so graciously acted as our hosts yesterday, to the health of Chairman Deng [Xiaoping], General Secretary Hu, and the other distinguished Chinese citizens it is my privilege to meet this week, and to the friendship and cooperation between our two countries.

## NOTES

Ronald Reagan, "Toast at a Welcoming Banquet Hosted by Premier Zhao Ziyang of China in Beijing," April 27, 1984, *Weekly Compilation of Presidential Documents,* Vol. 20, No. 18, pp. 602–605.

Ronald Reagan, 40th president of the United States (1981–1989) and former governor of California

# The United States and China in
# the New Balance of Power

## Thomas W. Robinson

By mid-1985, the United States and China had experienced a decade and a half of progressively improving relations. The two countries had first agreed on the necessity to face, "in parallel," the common threat from the Soviet Union. They had gone on to work out the political basis for restoring their own diplomatic relations, agreeing on how to remove, temporarily, the Taiwan issue as the principal impediment before them. They had then worked out a series of economic, technological and cultural agreements to place on firm footing their reciprocal needs for trade, investment, technology transfer, educational training and mutual cultural cooperation.

They had begun to work out details of a security arrangement, including the sale and transfer of military technology and broad, if still diffuse, agreement for maintaining the peace in Asian hot spots, like Korea, cooperating in the support of groups actively opposed to Soviet imperialism, like the Afghans, and opposing the regional expansion of states allied with Moscow, like Vietnam. Finally, they had cemented their ties by a continuing series of state visits: four American Presidents visited China and three top post-Maoist leaders came to the United States.

Much of this opening out of relations—state-to-state and "people-to-people"—was based on solid and rational national interests and on the changing character of the domestic situations in the two countries. For the United States, the period represented the chance to end the long years of estrangement that began with the establishment of Communist rule in Beijing in 1950 [*sic*]: to utilize Chinese power in the great global contest of power against the Soviet Union; to draw China out into the American-led world of industrial and cultural interdependence so that China could never again slip back into dangerous isolationism; and to play an important role in the pace and direction of Chinese modernization once that country had definitely decided to undergo the several revolutions under that rubric. For China, the 15 years provided an opportunity to add a portion of American military power to its own against the possibility of Soviet attack; to move ahead in its quest to recover Taiwan, which only the United States could arrange; to find out from America what the modern world had become since China voluntarily left the international system in 1966; and to gain access to American and other Western markets and the associated technology, capital, and institutions that are vital to the success of China's modernization. . . .

Part of the newly emerging equation is the length to which Beijing will go in restoring ties with Moscow—even if only for economic development purposes—and whether that will contribute, at each step along the way, to exacerbating American–Soviet military competition. At some point, voices will surely be raised in Washington asking what the United States is obtaining, in the security realm, for all its costly transfers to China of American economic, technological and educational largess. The answer may be positive—that the game is still worth the candle—so long as the Chinese are not foolish enough to flaunt their newly restored ties with the Soviet Union and so long as their public attitude toward the Americans continues to be positive.

Given the quarter century of Sino–Soviet discord, few expect anything close to the restoration of security ties between Beijing and Moscow. Rather, it seems likely that China will continue to lean toward the United States in the strategic triangle, at least enough to continue the defense insurance policy that America has written in China's regard and to keep up the flow of goodies from the United States. Still, there are disturbing signs and trends that American policymakers will have to consider. First, and perhaps foremost, is the political situation in the two countries.

In Beijing, the first post-Mao succession appears to be imminent if China's de facto leader, Deng Xiaoping, goes through with his promise to accompany his old generation colleagues into retirement following the Chinese Communist party's September, 1985, conference. Although Deng could still wield power from behind the scenes, much as he has in the decade since Chairman Mao Zedong's death, it will be much harder to do so in view of the onrush of "younger" successors coming into office and Deng's own advanced age. The central political question for China will remain open until his successors are firmly in office and have conclusively demonstrated their own policy direction. . . .

Even in the United States, it is possible that domestic political changes could greatly affect Washington's China policy. Domestic political issues, like protectionism and abortion, could spill over into foreign policy. Human rights issues, always a factor in American foreign policy, could affect relations with China. Congressional and presidential elections could catch up China-related problems, like Taiwan, spy revelations, or the transfer of too sophisticated technology. The American people might tire of the media saturation of television specials and series on China, and a mood swing of public opinion might result. If the United States becomes involved in a military conflict, say in the Persian Gulf, and China attempts to take advantage of temporary America inattention to Asia to advance its cause vis-à-vis Taiwan, a swift turnaround of both public opinion and policy could occur. While these possibilities might seem far-fetched in mid-1985, the course of American foreign relations clearly indicates that, as in China, domestic developments in the United States heavily influence attitudes and policies toward other countries.

. . . To the extent that by the turn of the century China is successful in becoming the strong and powerful state that Prime Minister Zhou Enlai forecast at the beginning of the modernization drive, to the same extent Beijing will find new interests, farther from its boundaries. The expansion of interests and therefore the degree of involvement commensurate with national power are what imperialism is all about. And a state that, relatively suddenly, appears on the regional or even the global scene upsets the balance of power ("other things being equal") and is always called an imperialist by the others. So it was with Britian, France, Germany, the United States, and Russia in their time and so it will be with China during the last part of the twentieth and the first portion of the twenty-first century.

It is only a question of how China will use its newfound power. Aside from Taiwan, the country has few territorial ambitions—some islands in the South China Sea, a few hundred square miles of disputed mountains and river islands on the Sino–Soviet border, perhaps in the very long run Mongolia. It is more important to make sure that every power equilibrium in the three regions surrounding China be formed with Chinese participation, and that no change be made without Beijing's consent. This means including China in any settlement of the Kampuchean question (for that would determine the balance in southeast Asia), the Afghan–Pakistani–Indian imbroglio (which would do the same for the South Asian balance), and the Korean question (Korea being the center of power politics in northeast Asia). Already in the mid-1980's there were signs of Chinese interest in each of these issues. Such signs will multiply henceforth. Of even greater importance, perhaps, is the acceptance of a Chinese element at the level of global politics, i.e., the strategic triangle. Beijing wants it known that no future American–Soviet agreement or arrangement can be made or made to last without Chinese participation. That is what Beijing's pronouncements about the various superpower arms control negotiations are all about, and that is why they will also escalate in number and tone.

Finally, China clearly desires an area of the world that it can call its own, not in the sense of a sphere of influence—although Southeast Asia will eventually become that—but a geographic area and a group of nations that will look to China as its natural leader. The only candidate is, of course, the third world. And much of Chinese diplomatic activity is already being devoted to currying favor with those states (for example, the Group of 77s, the "South," and the Organization of Petroleum Exporting Countries).

In sum, then, China has already started down the road of imperialism and will try to cover a fair distance before the century is out. And it is in the business of acquiring the means for making the journey successful. It has already done a reasonable job in the military sphere and is seeking from the Americans and others transfer of the requisite military technology, sample hardware, and techniques to complete the process of military modernization. Not only is it upgrading the training and the equipment of the ground forces, but it is also laying in the necessary investments for a global nuclear force (both land- and sea-based, if not yet air), and for power projection across the high seas.

Further, China possesses the potential for rapid expansion of other important elements of power. Even in the mid-1980's, its economic development is converting it into a strong trading nation and it will soon make its weight felt in international economic institutions. It utilizes foreign aid, technological assistance and military sales and transfers as instruments of policy. It has a strong cultural policy, what with its attractive cuisine and arts, and a natural audience among the Sino-oriented states of Asia and the overseas Chinese communities throughout the globe.

Perhaps most important, Beijing is adept at playing the diplomatic game, having learned the art of alliance-alignment making and breaking through long years of schooling during the Chinese Communist party's pre-1949 struggle for power and during the quarter century of a diplomacy of movement and confrontation within the Sino-Soviet-American triangle. Beijing possesses a distinctive and successful negotiating style, a corps of trained foreign service officers, and a growing base of experience in its research institutes and scholars. All the domestic elements supporting a strategy of expanding influence, therefore, are either in place, abuilding, or on the drawing boards. The process will take time, but "good" results should eventuate.

It follows that, in any stocktaking of the American–Chinese relations of the mid-1980's, the cooperative gains to both sides have largely been made and the danger of conversion into a zero-sum game is increasing. But that is not likely to happen, at least in an extreme form, for a number of reasons, both internal and external. Internally, there is still room for the further expansion of various American–Chinese ties. Trade should rise to new heights as the Chinese economic expansion accelerates. American technology transfer to China is still in its initial stages, with military and nuclear technology transfers yet to begin. Educational contacts are burgeoning, as are scientific exchanges. Chinese leaders know that the Soviet military threat is unlikely to diminish in the absolute sense and may even increase; the American insurance policy is thus still necessary, however unfortunate that may be for Beijing's freedom of foreign policy maneuver. China needs the United States to introduce it further to the world of complex interdependence. And if Taiwan is ever to be taken, it will have to be with Washington's cooperation. Many of these same statements can be repeated on the American side—in terms of trade, defense, education and international cooperation. America needs China as much as Beijing needs Washington.

Externally, the outlines of a very interesting set of changes in the Asian and global balances of power are beginning to take shape. Essentially, the balance at both levels is shifting, and not merely in response to China's new drive for influence. In Asia, other states are also becoming conscious of the foreign policy uses of their new power. . . .

. . . [T]he requisites for a stable balance of power in Asia are present, even when viewed from the comparatively early stage of the mid-1980's.

At the global level, much the same will prove to be true. First, a China taking part in the strategic triangle will still, in all probability, be a junior partner, given the growth potential left in the United States and the Soviet Union. Second, the triangle will itself be subject to pressure from outside, as first Japan and—to be sure, considerably later—India and perhaps Brazil or a united West Europe—change its shape to a quadrilateral. China's influence, great though it may be, will be comparatively restricted. Third, China will be subject to the same panoply of global influences that affect other nations. These include population explosion, pollution and other environmental problems, nuclear proliferation, a general diffusion of power, and the many revolutions attendant on modernization. These will tend to keep China, as all others, in a reactive state, so strong and so unknown will be their effects.

Finally, there will be the very interdependence of the rapidly modernizing globe. China will have to participate in such an interdependent community, for to attempt to insulate the country from the outside world would consign China perpetually to the role of the latecomer and the outsider.

A balance of power in Asia (and globally) will serve to hem in Beijing's expansionist tendencies. It is true that a new balance will have to be dynamic and will be composed of forces present only in outline form in the mid-1980's. It is also true that, with the best of intentions and a plenitude of the requisite means of power, those in charge of constructing a new balance could fail at their tasks. But all the elements are already in place. The role of the United States is to assist China's entry into the modern world economically and to encourage Beijing to play a responsible role in the new balance of power. A China and a United States in a national interest-centered partnership could become the central elements in a new structure of power that could benefit themselves and many other states and peoples. If, on the other hand, China chooses to threaten the balance of power, the United States will still be able to resume its historic role as the balancer in Asia, adding its own power to those who might feel Chinese pressure.

## NOTES

Thomas W. Robinson, "The United States and China in the New Balance of Power," *Current History,* September 1985, pp. 241–244, 281. Reprinted with permission from *Current History* magazine (September 1985). © 1985, Current History, Inc.

Thomas W. Robinson, professor of international relations, Georgetown University

# The China Connection

## A. James Gregor

. . . Since the inception of the Chinese Communist Party, "imperialism" has been the touchstone of its domestic and foreign policy. During the revolutionary struggle, their presumed relationship to "imperialism" determined the lot of the Chinese population. Beijing's official foreign policy has always been "anti-imperialist." Nonetheless, the PRC has, at various times, had relations with traditional monarchies, sheikhdoms, military juntas, and overtly anticommunist regimes. For the theoreticians in Beijing, such flexibility is part of historical and revolutionary "dialectics." Revolutionary struggle requires the flexibility that permits collaboration with those with whom one has a common interest, however temporary, in order to mobilize resistance against one's principal adversary. These tactical accommodations are dictated by the peculiarities of any given situation. As long as the United States was the principal adversary of "proletarian China," Beijing made common cause with a variety of political regimes—so long as those regimes were prepared to oppose U.S. imperialism.

When the Soviet Union became "social imperialist" and replaced the United States as the principal adversary of Communist China, the United

States became a potential member of a prospective "united front" against Moscow's hegemonic intentions. Now that the Soviet Union appears prepared to negotiate some kind of settlement with the PRC, and the United States seems disposed to serve as a counterweight to Soviet military forces in East Asia, Beijing apparently has opted for foreign policy "independence." It seeks an alliance with the "progressive forces" in the Third World to accelerate the collapse of all forms of imperialism and hegemony and to facilitate the advent of world communism, anticipated by the philosophers of dynastic China as the "Great Harmony" of Confucius.

What all this seems to indicate is that Beijing's relations with imperialist and hegemonic powers will be cautious and manipulative. Many of the interests Beijing shares with such powers are transient. In judging where its interest lie, Beijing will, in the last analysis, keep its own counsel—which is not at all surprising. Sovereign nations have been doing just that since time immemorial.

It should be borne in mind, however, that the national and revolutionary interests of the People's Republic of China are not often compatible with the national and foreign policy interests of the United States. Consequently, relations between the two nations should be conducted on the basis of cautious cost accounting. A reasonable assessment should be made of both potential benefits and anticipated costs. Principles of strict reciprocity should govern bilateral trade, and the U.S. national interest should determine whether technology transfers to the PRC should continue. Unfortunately, such an assessment is not easy to make. There is considerable evidence that suggests that U.S. policymakers have been influenced by judgments of academics and media professionals that could most charitably be characterized as sinocentric.

Allen Whiting has identified as "unduly sinocentric" the notion that the PRC might either divert Soviet forces in East Asia from their anti-Western pursuits or free them for just such use. The PRC is incapable of accomplishing either. The People's Republic of China will remain a regional military power. Unlike Japan, it lacks virtually all the qualities necessary to enable it to serve as a swing-weight between the United States and the Soviet Union.[1]

Americans tend to overlook the fact that Beijing has the potential for working considerable mischief among the East Asian allies of the United States. As we have seen, Beijing has used force in the South China Sea to secure what it considers the "sovereign territory of the motherland." It has threatened violence against the Japanese in the dispute over the Senkaku Islands in the Asian continental shelf. Its claims in the South China Sea also conflict with those of the Philippines, Indonesia, Malaysia, Brunei, and Vietnam, not to mention the Republic of China on Taiwan. Beijing's insistence that all the maritime territory of the region constitutes part of the PRC "may foreshadow military action there once the PLA acquires the capability. . . . Strengthening Beijing's ability to pursue its territorial claims . . . in the

South China Sea is antithetical to [the United States'] larger interests, whatever [the] particular problems [of the U.S.] with Vietnam, Laos, and Kampuchea may be. . . . In short, the American judgment that a strong China will serve the cause of peace and stability in Asia is not shared by all [U.S.] allies and friends there."[2]

Beijing's insistence upon the "reunification" of Taiwan with the regime on the mainland threatens to destabilize a region critical to the defense of East Asia. Beijing's continued formal support of North Korea's demands on South Korea complicates the planning necessary for the strategic defense of Japan. Any nonpeaceful change on the Korean peninsula that would reduce the U.S. presence there would make the defense of the West Pacific far more difficult.

As for economic relations between the United States and the PRC, it appears that neither nation will be vital to the other for the remainder of this century. Beijing has diversified its export markets and utilizes various suppliers; consequently, U.S. trade, technology, investments, and loans—although convenient and useful—are not essential to the PRC's ongoing development. United States trade with, and investment in, the People's Republic of China will remain marginal. A number of U.S.-based international corporations will probably enjoy substantial profit from their relations with the PRC, but it is doubtful whether Communist China will make any real contribution to the material well-being of Americans in general. In fact, Americans have underwritten, with their tax dollars, at least part of the economic and political reconstruction now going on in the People's Republic of China. U.S. government appropriations constitute about 25 percent of all capital loans made available to the PRC by the World Bank and the International Monetary Fund and about 25 percent of the grants and financial assistance made available to the PRC by United Nations agencies. U.S. government guarantees for export-import transactions and relief from tariff duties—Washington's designation of the PRC as a most-favored nation, and the benefits that derive from the relaxation of restrictions on technology transfers to the PRC—have all contributed to Communist China's welfare and were made possible, directly or indirectly, by U.S. taxpayers.

Relations between the United States and the People's Republic of China have probably reached a stage at which a general review of those relations would be salutary. How much is the United States prepared to invest in the rehabilitation of the neo-Stalinist political system that prevails in the People's Republic of China? What are the real benefits—strategic, economic, and political—that Washington can reasonably expect from its "China connection"? In order to obtain those benefits, will the United States have to mortgage the interests of the noncommunist nations of Asia?

In the mid-1980s, it has become evident to a great many Americans that the United States does not have a principled China policy. Washington seems simply to have made ad hoc responses to issues and opportunities as they have arisen, and relations between Washington and Beijing have simply "developed." As relations between the two countries developed, constituencies formed in the United States, composed of individuals who benefited from those relations. Military men found themselves associating with their counterparts in the People's Liberation Army; academics became involved in exchange programs; businessmen became increasingly enthusiastic about the prospect of access to the "world's single largest market"; and farmers began to profit from the sale of wheat and soybeans.

What seems to have been lost in all this is the general interest. It is unlikely that "enhanced" strategic cooperation with the PRC—possibly to the detriment of long-standing U.S. relations with allies in East Asia—will serve the security interests of the United States, however much it might serve the interest of some constituency in the military. It is equally unlikely that most Americans will find it in their ultimate best interests to support the perpetuation of a Marxist-Leninist bureaucracy and agree to the rehabilitation of a neo-Stalinist China with capital and technology transfers, however much U.S. business interests might profit from such cooperation.

The United States has sought to foster the establishment and maintenance of pluralistic societies and open-market systems in East Asia and throughout the world. The People's Republic of China may seem dedicated to "reform," but it is most unlikely that the Chinese Communist Party will ever surrender its bureaucratic control of China—or abandon its legitimating commitment to "Marxism-Leninism–Mao Zedong Thought." The leadership in Beijing might modify its political creed, but it is not likely that the ensconced bureaucracy will surrender its privileges in the pursuit of "bourgeois democracy" or capitalism.

In the last analysis, the future of Asia and the best interests of the United States depend not on the cultivation of relations with the People's Republic of China, but on Washington's success in balancing its relations with the PRC and with those nations with which Americans share more in terms of political and economic modalities and security interests. Ultimately, Japan, the Republic of Korea, the Republic of China on Taiwan, the Republic of the Philippines, Malaysia, Singapore, Thailand, and Indonesia will have a more determinate influence on the future of East Asia than will the People's Republic of China. In that sense, maintenance of the "China connection" may ultimately prove to be of secondary importance to the West Pacific policy of the United States.

## NOTES

A. James Gregor, *The China Connection: U.S. Policy and the People's Republic of China* (Stanford, CA: Hoover Institution Press, 1986), pp. 211–214. Reprinted with the

A. James Gregor, professor of political science, University of California, Berkeley

1. See Allen S. Whiting, "Sino-American Relations: The Decade Ahead," *Orbis*, 26, no. 3 (Fall 1982): 697–719.

2. Ibid., pp. 705, 706, 707.

# 7

# The Benefits and Dangers
# of Nuclear Cooperation

*Prodded by American industry, in the mid-1980s the Reagan administration strongly advocated the sale of civilian nuclear reactors and equipment to China. However, the Nonproliferation Act passed by Congress in 1978 required the president to guarantee that such sales would not contribute to proliferation. Although China became a member of the International Atomic Energy Agency (IAEA) in 1984, it had yet to sign the 1968 Nuclear Non-Proliferation Treaty (NPT). Thus, the Reagan administration had to defend its position based on informal pledges made by China. Despite the ensuing criticism, permission for such transfers was granted; however, no sales were ever consummated.*

## Proposed Nuclear Cooperation Agreement with the People's Republic of China

### House testimony by Kenneth L. Adelman

**Mr. Adelman** [*witness, prepared statement*]: I am pleased to appear before this distinguished Committee today to discuss the peaceful nuclear cooperation agreement between the United States and China, the first agreement with a nuclear weapon state since the Nuclear Non-Proliferation Act.

Before addressing how this agreement advances important non-proliferation interests, I should place it into the broad picture of enhanced U.S.–Chinese consultation on arms control. This type of consultation followed on the heels of the President's April 1984 visit to China. Soon thereafter, in the summer of 1984, I led a delegation of American officials to Beijing to concentrate on arms control. The Chinese reciprocated by having their arms control experts come here just last month.

Non-proliferation has been a key topic in these discussions with the Chinese. I explained to the Chinese that non-proliferation is one of the highest U.S. priorities; as well as the one area of arms control which has been perhaps the most successful. This agreement continues that record.

This Committee has, of course, already received ACDA's Nuclear Proliferation Assessment Statement on the agreement, which we provided to the President prior to his approval of the agreement. The prime question before you now—as before the President on July 23—is: "Does this new agreement contribute to U.S. non-proliferation efforts?" I believe the answer is a resounding "Yes." Why? Because our agreement with China helps ensure that they are part of the non-proliferation solution, rather that part of the problem.

During the 1960's and 1970's, China rejected non-proliferation norms. They actually portrayed proliferation in a favorable light by openly declaring that the spread of nuclear weapons around the globe would diminish the power of the United States and the Soviet Union and enhance the opportunities for revolution. China denied that a world of more nuclear weapon states would enhance the risk of nuclear war.

China also undertook no international legal obligations, and had no policy, to require safeguards and other controls on its nuclear exports. This naturally quickened our concerns about Chinese actions that could help other countries acquire nuclear explosives. Clearly, herein lay the potential for great harm to global non-proliferation efforts, in both word and deed. And, needless to tell this Committee, words are exceedingly important in this realm. They affect the strength of the international norms and standard upon which non-proliferation ultimately rests.

Against this background the United States opened talks on peaceful nuclear cooperation with China, first in 1981 and then more intensively in 1983, with ACDA participating in all stages of the negotiation.

After two years of negotiations, an agreement was initialed during President Reagan's visit to China. It then became necessary to engage in further discussions with China to clarify matters related to implementation of its nuclear policies. We did not want to proceed until we were completely satisfied. We were willing to wait as long as need be. These discussions concluded successfully at the end of June.

Over these past two years, the Chinese government has taken a number of important non-proliferation steps. First, it made a pledge that it does "not engage in nuclear proliferation" nor does it "help other countries develop nuclear weapons." The substance of this pledge has been reaffirmed several times by Chinese officials both abroad and within China. In fact, China's Sixth National People's Congress made this policy a directive to all agencies of that large and complex government. As such, it constitutes a historic and positive change in China's policies. It helps bolster rather than break down those critical norms and standards that comprise the non-proliferation regime.

Second, in January 1984, China joined the over 100 members of the International Atomic Energy Agency (IAEA), which plays such a critical role in international non-proliferation efforts. This was a necessary step in China's evolution toward acceptance of the basic norms of nuclear supply.

Third, China adopted a policy of requiring IAEA safeguards on its nuclear exports to non-nuclear weapons states. This, too, was a big plus. Not only could a supplier that did not accept this basic norm directly contribute to spreading uncontrolled nuclear equipment and material to potential nuclear weapon states; it could also undermine the consensus of supplier countries that has been painstakingly constructed over the past decade.

Fourth, during our hours and hours of discussions, the Chinese have made it clear that they will implement their policies in a manner consistent with the basic non-proliferation practices we and others support so vigorously.

In the short span of two years, China has embraced non-proliferation policies and practices, which it had eschewed so vociferously for a quarter of a century. This clearly is a turnabout of historic significance in our efforts to prevent the spread of nuclear weapons. The Chinese are to be applauded for such a change of course.

We can take a measure of pride in this as well. For I believe that the lengthy discussions by the United States and other supplier nations with China, combined with the prospect of agreements for peaceful nuclear cooperation, contributed heavily to these Chinese actions.

We will, of course, watch Chinese practices closely to satisfy ourselves that China's actions are consistent with its words, with our expectations, and with our policies and laws. The Chinese know that. They know that nuclear cooperation with us rests on their strict adherence to basic non-proliferation practices discussed and clarified at such great length. The agreement before you rests on that foundation. It could rest on no other.

As presented in ACDA's Nuclear Proliferation Assessment Statement, all statutory requirements for such agreements have been fully met. Two issues that were subject to protracted negotiations are worth mentioning.

The agreement before you contains a provision for "mutually acceptable arrangements for exchanges of information and visits" in connection with transfers under its terms. This was done to help ensure that all the agreement's provisions will be scrupulously honored. The specifics of visits and information exchanges will be worked out with the Chinese before any licenses are issued for nuclear exports. They will permit visits by U.S. personnel to sites in China wherever our material or equipment, subject to this agreement, is located.

The second issue concerns the right of prior approval over reprocessing of spent fuel subject to the agreement.

The agreement notes that neither party contemplates reprocessing such material. In fact, activities of this kind are not likely to become an issue in China for at least 15 years. While the language dealing with this issue does differ from that in other agreements, it is clear that China cannot reprocess without U.S. approval.

Other aspects of our Assessment Statement can be fully explained in response to your questions. Let me just add now that U.S. interests are fully protected. This agreement includes many written guarantees and controls to ensure that material, equipment, or technology supplied by the United States will not be misused.

If they are misused, or if China's non-proliferation policies do not live up to their pledges and to our expectations, we have clear recourse. We hope and expect that this agreement will lead to significant peaceful nuclear commerce with China—otherwise the President would not have sent it to you—but the agreement is only an umbrella agreement. That is, it permits but does not require the export of any nuclear items. Thus, if Chinese behavior ever became inconsistent with our understandings, we would suspend the licensing of exports. The Chinese know that.

To conclude: China's recent non-proliferation steps are and will be critical to our mission of bolstering vital non-proliferation norms and standards. Our long talks with the Chinese, as well as the prospects of civil nuclear cooperation with the U.S. and other suppliers, contributed to these major improvements in China's non-proliferation policies. Further, as I said, the agreement will enhance our efforts to cooperate to strengthen non-proliferation norms and actions.

Thus, I believe this agreement is fully in U.S. national interests. I trust that, after a thorough consideration of all the issues, you and the whole Congress will agree.

## NOTES

House Committee on Foreign Affairs, "Proposed Nuclear Cooperation Agreement with the People's Republic of China," 99th Congress, 1st sess., July 13, 1985. Testimony by Kenneth L. Adelman.

Kenneth L. Adelman, director, Arms Control and Disarmament Agency during the Reagan administration

# Carrying Friendship Too Far

## Editors of The New Republic

The Ayatollah Khomeini and Muammar al-Qaddafi are probably the heads of state whom the world would least like to see with their fingers poised at the

**In the late 1980s concern mounted over Chinese weapons prolif-
eration. Reprinted by permission from Morgan Chua and the *Far
Eastern Economic Review*.**

nuclear button. Neither man has the bomb but both are scheming to get their
hands on the technology. If they succeed, it may well be thanks to the reckless
nuclear export policy of the People's Republic of China—and perhaps even to
the reckless export policy of the Reagan administration. In the name of Sino-
American rapprochement, we are about to embark on a 30-year Agreement for
Nuclear Cooperation with the most egregious proliferator in the history of the
atomic age.

The most likely setting for nuclear war is not the Black Hills of Dakota or
Siberia or even Europe, but the Third World. Clearly, then, our best means of
averting nuclear holocaust lies in preventing the spread of atomic weapons to
smaller, less responsible countries. Yet the Reagan administration's proposed

agreement with China is not the first time an American president transcended our outspoken verbal commitment to nonproliferation for financial and geopolitical gains. In 1980 President Carter waived the Nuclear Nonproliferation Act in order to provide India with nuclear fuel deliveries, and three years later Reagan circumvented the same statute by designating France as a surrogate supplier. Now we seem on the verge of an even greater folly.

A number of considerations have converged to produce the China agreement. One prime impetus has been the woes of the American nuclear power industry, which hasn't sold a single reactor in the United States since 1975. China's budding energy program, with its call for six foreign-supplied reactors by the year 2000, offers Westinghouse and its cohorts a potential seven-billion-dollar market. Also working in favor of the agreement is the current frustration over the trade deficit. Few in Congress can resist the lure of a possible ten-figure sale. Perhaps most important, the administration sees the agreement as a way to secure further strategic ties to China.

No one doubts that selling nuclear power reactors to China would serve all of these valid goals. But almost everybody who has carefully examined the text of this agreement recognizes that it is poorly worded and courts catastrophe. At the moment five countries—the U.S., USSR, Britain, France, and China—admit to possessing nuclear weapons. Two others, India and Israel, are widely suspected of having joined the club. Three of the five weapons states and 125 non-weapons states have signed the Nuclear Nonproliferation Treaty, which includes a list of procedures for verifying the strictly peaceful use of any nuclear export to a non-weapons state.

China has persistently refused to ratify the Nonproliferation Treaty or to follow its recommended safeguards. Until just last year, China's official pronouncements actually declared that nuclear proliferation was a worthwhile enterprise serving to erode U.S.–Soviet nuclear hegemony. "So long as the imperialists refuse to ban nuclear weapons," the Chinese government once declared, "the greater the number of socialist countries possessing them, the better the guarantee of world peace." With this policy China established itself as the National Rifle Association of nuclear matters. Since 1980 U.S. intelligence sources have reported several Chinese shipments of nuclear materials to Argentina, India, and South Africa, whose nuclear ambitions are well established.

China's most egregious breach of the nonproliferation ethic is its collaboration with the nuclear program of neighboring Pakistan. In exchange for permission to study Pakistan's enrichment techniques, the Chinese reportedly have provided design information on a bomb already successfully tested in China. Intelligence documents indicate that Chinese technological assistance since at least 1980 has brought Pakistan within two years of possessing its own small nuclear arsenal. And since Libya's oil revenues have helped support the

Pakistani program, the CIA fears that Pakistan may be obliged to share its technology with Qaddafi.

Supporters of the agreement acknowledge China's poor nuclear record. But they insist that Beijing's behavior has changed. In 1983 [*sic*] China signed on as a member of the International Atomic Energy Agency, ending a 30-year boycott. In January 1984 Premier Zhao Ziyang declared before a White House audience, "We do not engage in nuclear proliferation ourselves, nor do we help other countries develop nuclear weapons."

America's 1978 Nonproliferation Act sensibly requires more than just amiable after-dinner words. The law demands a "guaranty" of safeguards on U.S. nuclear shipments to any country as well as American consent to any retransfer of technology or enrichment or reprocessing of fuel supplied by us. The guarantee is essential because any of these procedures can lead to the distillation of nuclear explosive materials.

The agreement with China, however, provides no safeguarding mechanism other than "mutually acceptable arrangements for exchanges of information and visits" to be clarified at some point in the future through "diplomatic channels." If China decides to enrich or reprocess U.S.-supplied nuclear fuel, we are required "to consider such activities favorably" while holding "consultations to agree on mutually acceptable arrangements."

Despite these glaring loopholes, Kenneth Adelman, the director of the Arms Control and Disarmament Agency, has asserted that the nebulous "exchanges of information and visits" clause is "adequate to provide confidence against the misuse of any items subject to the proposed agreement." Similarly, in lieu of formal consent rights over retransfer, enrichment, or reprocessing, Adelman accepted China's private pledge that it has "no plan to undertake reprocessing of spent fuel from power reactors for at least 15 years." Adelman also claims that "the prospect of the proposed agreement played an important role in bringing about this evolving attitude [toward nonproliferation] on the part of China." The logic seems to be: what we can't get the Chinese to concede publicly, we can expect them to concede privately on the basis of their newfound commitment to nonproliferation. Contrary to the available evidence, Reagan officials insist that an admittedly tainted trading partner is inching toward reform and that our surest means of encouraging this process is through further commercial involvement. This sounds like "constructive engagement" with South Africa.

As with the putative reforms of the Botha regime, China's purported spiritual rebirth is at best a tenuous, begrudging concession, at worst a calculated charade. For starters, despite Zhao's White House dinner toast, there's good reason to believe that China's fundamental attitude toward the merits of proliferation hasn't changed. In July 1985, long after Chinese envoys had begun to project a more conciliatory tone to their American audiences, Vice Chairman Zhou Peiyuan of the Chinese People's Political Consultative Conference told the Brazilian press that Third World nations should develop nuclear energy technology "if they feel the need to have it for peaceful purposes" as a means of "breaking the monopoly of the two superpowers: the Soviet Union and the United States." According to a CIA translation of the Brazilian report, Zhou defended China's initial atomic explosion "as a way of breaking the nuclear monopoly." This sort of talk purposely muddles the vital distinction between nuclear power and nuclear destructive power in the hope of breaking a U.S.–Soviet "monopoly."

Nor are current Chinese nuclear export practices much different from those of the past. After the initialing of the agreement in April 1984, the State Department was forced to reopen negotiations with the Chinese to clarify their commitment to nonproliferation. It seems that after Chinese negotiators had renounced assistance to "outlaw" state—those with secret, weapons-oriented nuclear development programs—Chinese technicians were discovered at Pakistan's top secret nuclear facility. By July of this year, U.S. intelligence had satisfied itself that the Chinese were gone from Pakistan, and Reagan signed the agreement. But since then reports have surfaced in the intelligence community that China has continued its nuclear exports to South Africa and Argentina and, even more disturbing, that it has engaged an Iranian envoy in serious discussions over the export of sensitive nuclear technology once the U.S. cooperation pact is secured. China has held meetings with Iranian representatives in both Beijing and Tehran to discuss terms for the sale of nuclear-capable surface-to-surface missiles. Agence France-Presse reported on October 23 that the talks were "progressing rapidly."

Since the inauguration of the International Atomic Energy Agency two decades ago, every nuclear power agreement signed by the U.S. has contained a safeguards requirement. Yet in his official assessment of the China deal, ACDA director Adelman pleaded that "the United States did seek Chinese acceptance of IAEA safeguards on U.S. supply under the agreement, but the Chinese adamantly refused." Why cave in to China's refusal? The argument is that since China is a nuclear weapons state, IAEA safeguards aren't strictly required by law. This is true. It's also true that the "exchange of information and visits" provision isn't much of a safeguard in any sense of the word. Obviously the U.S. negotiators were willing to sacrifice the spirit of American nonproliferation law as long as the appearance of legality was maintained. They made such concessions because, as the language of the final document illustrates, proliferation was the least of their concerns.

The State Department and its allies insist that the negotiators made no such concessions. They argue that despite the text of the agreement, they have obtained private assurances from the Chinese that Beijing will cooperate with unwritten American expectations. In particular the chief American negotiator, Special Ambassador Richard T. Kennedy, has prepared a classified "Summary of Discussions," in which he asserts that the Chinese have provided further pledges to reform their nuclear export policies. Touting these unwritten, unofficial assurances, he claims that the China pact would not compromise our vigilance against the spread of nuclear weapons. A number of representatives believe he is bluffing.

Fortunately there is a way to call the bluff. Senators John Glenn and Bill Roth, along with their colleagues in the House, have introduced measures to clarify the ambiguous passages of the agreement. The Glenn-Roth bill simply articulates the State Department's professed interpretations of these passages as official U.S. policy and requires the president to certify that the Chinese accept these interpretations before the licensing of any nuclear exports. It mandates specific safeguards and frees us from any obligation to yield to China's discretion. It requires China to issue a "written, detailed statement of its non-proliferation policies," and reaffirms our understanding that the agreement is subject to U.S. export laws. Since the bill does no more than bind both countries publicly to the commitments purportedly secured in private by the State Department, there is no apparent reason to oppose it.

The real threat of the Glenn-Roth proposal is not, as the State Department claims, that it will "gut the agreement" but that, quite the contrary, it will put guts into it. It may, as some officials protest, demand a degree of strictness to which the Chinese will never submit. These officials may be right. If so, the world is better off without this deal.

## NOTE

Editorial, "Carrying Friendship Too Far," *The New Republic,* November 25, 1985, pp. 7–9. Reprinted by permission of *The New Republic,* © 1985, The New Republic, Inc.

# PART III

# IN THE WAKE OF TIANANMEN (1989–1992)

**Lambert Der's cartoon suggesting the dashed hopes for democracy in China appeared soon after June 4, 1989. Reprinted by permission from Lambert Der.**

# 8

# The Initial Response to June 4

*June 4, 1989, was a watershed moment not only in the People's Republic but in China's relations with the rest of the world, particularly with the United States. The sense of optimism felt in the United States in the mid-1980s vanished instantly. President Bush, originally a critic of the terms of normalization, turned into one of the most forceful advocates for maintaining stable relations with Beijing despite the tragedy. He and others who supported his stance were severely criticized.*

## The President's News Conference

### George Bush

**The President**: During the past few days, elements of the Chinese Army have been brutally suppressing popular and peaceful demonstrations in China. There has been widespread and continuing violence, many casualties, and many deaths. And we deplore the decision to use force, and I now call on the Chinese leadership publicly, as I have in private channels, to avoid violence and to return to their previous policy of restraint.

The demonstrators in Tiananmen Square were advocating basic human rights, including the freedom of expression, freedom of the press, freedom of association. These are goals we support around the world. These are freedoms that are enshrined in both the U.S. Constitution and the Chinese Constitution. Throughout the world we stand with those who seek greater freedom and democracy. This is the strongly felt view of my administration, of our Congress, and most important, of the American people.

In recent weeks, we've urged mutual restraint, nonviolence, and dialog. Instead, there has been a violent and bloody attack on the demonstrators. The United States cannot condone the violent attacks and cannot ignore the consequences for our relationship with China, which has been built on a foundation of broad support by the American people. This is not the time for an emotional response, but for a reasoned, careful action that takes into account both our long-term interests and recognition of a complex internal situation in China.

There clearly is turmoil within the ranks of the political leadership, as well as the People's Liberation Army. And now is the time to look beyond the moment to important and enduring aspects of this vital relationship for the United States. Indeed, the budding of democracy which we have seen in recent weeks owes much to the relationship we have developed since 1972. And it's important at this time to act in a way that will encourage the further development and deepening of the positive elements of that relationship and the process of democratization. It would be a tragedy for all if China were to pull back to its pre-1972 era of isolation and repression.

Mindful of these complexities, and yet of the necessity to strongly and clearly express our condemnation of the events of recent days, I am ordering the following actions: Suspension of all government-to-government sales and commercial exports of weapons, suspension of visits between U.S. and Chinese military leaders, sympathetic review of requests by Chinese students in the United Sates to extend their stay, and the offer of humanitarian and medical assistance through the Red Cross to those injured during the assault, and review of other aspects of our bilateral relationship as events in China continue to unfold.

The process of democratization of Communist societies will not be a smooth one, and we must react to setbacks in a way which stimulates rather than stifles progress to open and representative systems. . . .

**Q**: Yes, Mr. President. You have said the genie of democracy cannot be put back in the bottle in China. You said that, however, before the actions of the past weekend. Do you still believe that? And are there further steps that the United States could take, such as economic sanctions, to further democracy in China?

**The President**: Yes, I still believe that. I believe the forces of democracy are so powerful, and when you see them as recently as this morning—a single student standing in front of a tank, and then, I might add, seeing the tank driver exercise restraint—I am convinced that the forces of democracy are going to overcome these unfortunate events in Tiananmen Square.

On the commercial side, I don't want to hurt the Chinese people. I happen to believe that the commercial contacts have led, in essence, to this quest for more freedom. I think as people have commercial incentive, whether it's in China or in other totalitarian systems, the move to democracy becomes more inexorable. So what we've done is suspended certain things on the military side, and my concern is with those in the military who are using force. And yet when I see some exercising restraint and see the big divisions that exist inside the PLA [People's Liberation Army], I think we need to move along the lines I've outlined here. I think that it's important to keep saying to those elements in the Chinese military, "Restraint: Continue to show the restraint that many of you have shown." And I understand there are deep divisions inside the army. So this is, we're putting the emphasis on that side of it. . . .

**Q**: Mr. President, you spoke of the need for the U.S. to maintain relations with China. But given the brutality of the attacks over the last couple of days, can the U.S. ever return to business as usual with the current regime?

**The President**: I don't want to see a total break in this relationship, and I will not encourage a total break in the relationship. This relationship is, when you see these kids struggling for democracy and freedom, this would be a bad time for the United States to withdraw and pull back and leave them to the devices of a leadership that might decide to crack down further. Some have suggested I take the Ambassador out. In my view, that would be 180 degrees wrong. Our Ambassador provides one of the best listening posts we have in China. He is thoroughly experienced. And so let others make proposals that in my view don't make much sense. I want to see us stay involved and continue to work for restraint and for human rights and for democracy. And then down the road, we have enormous commonality of interests with China, but it will not be the same under a brutal and repressive regime.

So I stop short of suggesting that what we ought to do is break relations with China, and I would like to encourage them to continue their change. . . .

**Q**: Will you, Mr. President, be able to accommodate the calls from Congress for tougher sanctions? Many lawmakers felt you were slow to condemn or criticize the violence in China before now, and many are pushing for much tougher action on the part of this country.

**The President**: I've told you what I'm going to do. I'm the President. I set the foreign policy objectives and actions taken by the executive branch. I think they know, most of them in Congress, that I have not only a keen personal interest in China, but that I understand it reasonably well. I will just reiterate to the leaders this afternoon my conviction that this is not a time for anything other than a prudent, reasoned response. And it is a time to assert over and over again our commitment to democracy, emphasize the strength that we give to democracy in situations of this nature. And I come back to the frontline question here: I do think this change is inexorable. It may go a couple of steps forward and then take a step back, but it is on the move. The genie will not be put back in the bottle. And so I am trying to take steps that will encourage a peaceful change, and yet recognize the fact that China does have great pride in its own history. And my recommendations are based on my knowledge of Chinese history.

So, I would argue with those who want to do something more flamboyant, because I happen to feel that this relationship is vital to the United States of America, and so is our adherence to democracy and our encouragement for those who are willing to hold high the banner of democracy. So we found, I think, a prudent path here. . . .

## NOTES

George Bush, "The President's News Conference," June 5, 1989, *Weekly Compilation of Presidential Documents,* Vol. 25, No. 23, pp. 839–843.

George Bush, 41st president of the United States (1989–1993); former U.S. representative to the United Nations; director of the Central Intelligence Agency; U.S. representative to Peking; and vice president of the United States (1981–1989)

# Human Rights and Political Developments in China

## House testimony by Michel Oksenberg

**Mr. Oksenberg** [*witness, prepared statement*]: . . . A political crisis now exists in China. Beijing is under martial law. Believing they had lost control of their capital city, in early June, the leaders of China callously ordered heavily armed forces to penetrate and occupy the center of Beijing, and in the inevitable resulting turmoil, untold thousands of unarmed civilians and soldiers were killed and wounded. In subsequent days, the leaders have unleashed the instruments of totalitarian rule in the major cities.

There is much about the current situation that is unknown: exactly who at the top is in charge of what, how the army feels about all of this, what the attitudes of provincial officials are, and most importantly what the populace is thinking. But amongst the many uncertainties, three conclusions are unmistakable: first, there has been a massive failure of governance in China; second, the leaders of China are once again attempting to force their people into an ideological straightjacket; and third, the leaders of China have done immeasurable damage to their stature in world affairs.

All this poses a challenge to American foreign policy. The challenge affects both our principles and our national interests. The challenge to fundamental American values is clear. The leaders have terminated a ten-year record of gradual and halting improvements in their respect for human rights and in establishment of a legal system. Recognizing the human rights abuses in China, we welcomed the progress and based our approach on encouraging and nurturing positive trends. Now we must ask: How should we react to a deteriorating situation?

. . . Until this spring, the leaders of China were seen around the world as responsible, balanced, credible individuals. Some exceptions existed, such as over their handling of Tibet or their reaction to earlier student demonstrations. But they were basically respected for their judgment; their words counted. In a few days, through their precipitous and violent deeds, they lost much of their international standing. International norms of behavior demand that we exhibit disdain toward leaders who order an army to fire upon their own people when other courses of action are available to them.

The result is evident. In revulsion, the rest of the world has disengaged somewhat from China. . . .

Let the reason for this global retreat or withdrawal from China be clearly understood. It is not the product of a conspiracy led by the United States. It is not due to a coordinated policy of Western governments. It is not the result of the improvement of Sino-Soviet relations. It is not attributable to hostile Western journalists filing distorted dispatches from China. It is not the consequence of a plot by a small number of Chinese intellectuals. It does not stem from students failing to leave the square at the right time. Nor is it the outcome of a struggle for power, in which one defiant leader—Zho Ziyang—stimulated a mass movement that otherwise would have been handled deftly. These are the reasons that the leaders of China offer for their debacle. And I suspect that the leaders believe their own explanation. They are unprepared to accept the real reasons for their domestic and foreign plight: their own lapse of judgment; their isolation; their tragic failure to understand and respond to the profound social and intellectual changes caused by their own economic reforms and openness to the outside world; and their lack of concern for the worldwide reaction to the violent suppression of the demonstrations. . . .

Our interests with respect to China are discernible and extensive, however. Let me enumerate them:

- We expect China to help maintain stability in East Asia and to contribute to the global balance-of-power. This means we count on China to retain a realistic sense of Soviet foreign policy, to help sustain peace on the Korean peninsula, to demonstrate patience and seek a peaceful evolution of the Taiwan issue, to abide by its agreement with Britain over the future of Hong Kong, to assist in a solution of the Cambodian problem that will bring peace and independence to that tragic land, to abide by its commitment not to engage in nuclear proliferation, to refrain from destabilizing but lucrative arms sales in the Middle East, and to support arms control measures where China's interests are involved. This is a long list indeed. China's generally constructive position on these issues has been quite helpful in the past decade. A return to previous postures would complicate our foreign policy considerably. But we cannot take Chinese cooperation for granted; it requires nurturing, consultation, and mutual understanding.

- We also need Chinese cooperation in addressing problems that transcend national boundaries: dealing with the greenhouse and ozone effects, controlling communicable diseases, preventing the growth and marketing of narcotics, halting illegal population migration across national boundaries, limiting population increases, raising enough food, and so on. . . .
- We also have an interest in a humanely governed China and in a China committed to policies of economic and political reform. This is not dictated solely by sentimental, moralistic or humanitarian concerns. Rather, China can neither play a responsible role in world affairs nor address the problems of global interdependence unless it has a unified, effective government. And its government cannot be effective unless it enjoys the support and trust of its people. . . .
- Finally, we have a commercial interest in China. We seek a share of China's growing market, as China secures access to our markets. . . .

In short, we have major strategic interests with China. It is a great power that sets it apart from, for example, Bulgaria, Czechoslovakia, or Romania. It is a nuclear power. And it is a nation with which we are unprepared to sustain an adversarial or animosity ridden relationship. Our strategy toward China since 1971 has been to draw it out of its isolation and to integrate it in the international community. Underlying this strategy was the recognition that the burden of keeping China poor, weak, and isolated in world affairs—our strategy of the previous twenty years—had proven too costly. Our calculus was that by building strong links to China strategically, intellectually, commercially, and even militarily in this early state in its rise, we would reduce the chances of China's becoming a disruptive, expansionist power as it grew stronger militarily. Our expectation was that a forthcoming posture toward China would prompt its leaders gradually to accept and abide by international standards of behavior.

That is why a vigorous response to the events of May and June is necessary. Not since 1975–76 has the government of China been as scornful of internationally accepted codes of conduct, and it is important to remind the leaders of China that when they depart from the norms of the international community, a severe price is paid. . . .

I believe for the most part that the response has been appropriately tough to date. I particularly approve the suspension of weapons sales, the delay in issuance of concessional interest rate loans to China by the United States and our allies, the delay in processing new World Bank loans, the postponement of the GATT negotiations, and the postponement of any further relaxation of export controls. . . .

I believe no more should be done at this time, though if human rights abuses persist, emigration is restricted, or China's international behavior becomes irresponsible, it may be necessary to apply further sanctions—such as withdrawal of MFN status or tightening export control restrictions. I am not averse to applying additional sanctions out of principle. I simply think prudence dictates seeing whether what we have already done will be sufficient. Prudence also dictates holding further, damaging moves in reserve, in case the situation continues to deteriorate.

I also do not believe—as some might argue—the events of May–June invalidate our strategy of engaging China in the world community. To the contrary, the clash between modernizers and conservatives proved so intense because our strategy was working. . . .

What considerations should therefore govern our approach to China at this point? Here is the list that I would keep in mind:

- Let our expressions of moral indignation recognize that most of the Chinese officials who receive our statements probably share our grief and dismay toward the tragedy. Too many of our pronouncements are self-righteous and do not acknowledge that our sentiments are felt by many Chinese as well. Human life and dignity are as precious to Chinese as they are to Americans.

- Let us not inadvertently drive the leaders of China into isolation or evoke their strong inclinations toward xenophobia and nativism. Excessive rhetoric on our part or application of the harshest economic sanctions available to us could return us to an adversarial relationship with China.

- Let us not so weaken our ties with China that, if a similar abandonment of reform policies were to occur in the Soviet Union, the natural and only course for Moscow and Beijing would be to forge a close relationship. It is important that we continue to engage in dialogue with the Chinese and consult with them on matters of mutual concern.

- Let us not become entwined once again in a Chinese civil war. A number of Chinese intellectuals and students, for totally understandable reasons, seek to overthrow their government and wish to enlist us in their cause. Even as we sympathize with their plight and give them refuge in our midst, as we must, let us recognize that their interests and ours do not coincide.

- Let us therefore retain a balanced posture, mindful of both interest and principle. Let us not be governed by the emotion of the moment but keep in mind—as President Bush has sought to do—our longer term strategy, pursued by five Presidents, of seeking to integrate China into the international community.

- But let the leaders of China confront the consequences of their actions. Deny them the opportunity to blame China's intensifying economic difficulties on Western actions. Let the burden rest on the leaders for their inability to confront inflation, deficits, unemployment, and problems in agricultural and energy production.
- Keep the United States in step with Western Europe and Japan. Do not depart from our allies, and do not become a special target of Chinese animosity. The Japanese position is particularly crucial. Historically, we know the price to be paid when our China policy departs dramatically from that of Japan.
- Do not undertake measures that do more harm to the people of China than to its government. Let us remember the target and whose mind we are seeking to change. And let us not do more damage to ourselves than to the Chinese government. I put withdrawal of MFN status [and] of Commodity Credit Corporation financing in this category.
- Maintain scholarly communications with China. Sending our scholars to China, if serious research is possible, will help us better understand that country, and continuing to welcome their scholars here will position us well when normalcy returns.
- Finally, let us preserve our flexibility. We wish to respond with alacrity should the situation improve. Writing President Bush's sanctions into law may not give him the flexibility he will need in the conduct of our China policy.

All of these injunctions point in one direction. The Administration appropriately has imposed numerous punishing economic sanctions. The time has come to wait and watch, to test and probe for signs of improvement, to be prepared to apply additional sanctions, and to preserve flexibility. There is much about the current situation that dictates prudence, caution, and balance. We are fortunate to have a President that understand the situation, and he merits bipartisan support—not pressure—from the Congress. . . .

## NOTES

Committee on Foreign Affairs Subcommittees on Human Rights and International Organizations, on Asian and Pacific Affairs, and on International Economic Policy and Trade, "Human Rights and Political Developments in China," 101st Congress, 1st sess., July 19, 1989. Testimony by Michel Oksenberg.

Michel Oksenberg, Center for Chinese Studies, University of Michigan (1973–1991); former National Security Council staff member during the Carter administration; and professor at Stanford University (1995–2001)

# Sanctions or Subdued Relations:
# The International Response to the 1989 Massacre

## James D. Seymour

What is the international community to do when a government's domestic behavior is utterly offensive and in violation of established international norms? To respond by committing an act of war is clearly out of the question. Are there any suitable lesser punishments? The question is particularly vexing when, as in the case of China and the United States, the nations of the antagonistic governments have strong emotional attachments to each other.

Relations between the United States and the People's Republic of China (PRC) divide easily and sharply into two periods, and are defined largely by American conservatives' attitudes toward China. (Liberals have been consistently ambivalent toward the PRC, and have had little impact on American policies toward the country.) The two eras are demarcated by Henry Kissinger's secret visit to China in 1971. Before that year, there was little in the way of a political relationship between the two countries, and virtually no economic relationship. The United States did make occasional propagandistic reference to the undemocratic nature of the Chinese system, but both subjective and short-term strategic considerations always have been much more weighty considerations. Thus, Secretary of State James Baker was making something of an understatement when he said that although he deeply regretted the executions of protesters, human rights "is not the only principle which determines our foreign policy."[1] Lacking here is a sense that long-run American interests depend on the friendship of the Chinese *people*. The example of South Korea suggests that if America is seen as backing a repressive regime, the anti-Americanism that is engendered could last much longer that the repressive regime itself. China once exemplified this anti-Americanism.

The 1950s and 1960s were what can be called a period of total sanctions against China. American conservatives felt betrayed by a China that did not appreciate the many years of support for Chiang Kai-shek's Republic, and they had equally irrational fears of the Sino-Soviet and the Sino-Vietnamese alliance. Whatever the intended effect of the sanctions, they were not only ineffective, they were counterproductive and helped drive the country into the arms of the Soviet Union.

In terms of human rights, the late 1960s and early 1970s comprised the worst period in Chinese history. Although political violence did seem on the decline in 1971, for the people who had been brutalized and imprisoned, there was still no hint of restoration of rights. The fact that the shift in U.S.

policy toward China came in 1971 when extreme human rights abuses continued, demonstrates how little Washington cared about the question of democracy.

The promise that a more open China would be a more humane and free one seemed to be borne out—until 1989. Then came the slaughters, first in Lhasa, and then in Beijing, Chengdu, Xian, Lanzhou, and elsewhere. The reaction of the Bush administration was measured: the United States "cannot ignore the consequences for our relationship with China." The president, who fancies himself a China expert, tried to display enough anger to appease the Congress, which was being prodded by human rights organizations and Chinese exiles to impose heavy sanctions. However, he was reserved enough not to produce unnecessary headlines.

Bush cancelled the sales of weapons to China, and suspensed direct contact between senior U.S. and Chinese officials. However, the decision to allow the sale of dual-use items such as satellites and airliners (which are often used to shuttle troops to martial-law areas) reduced the significance of these steps.

The American response was no more tepid that that of some other countries. Japan was slow to criticize the massacre and only briefly cut off economic assistance to China. Other countries (albeit those with less clout), such as Australia, Canada, France, Great Britain, and Sweden, were willing to make greater sacrifices. For example, France, which had been one of the first Western countries to establish diplomatic relations with the PRC, now became a particularly hospitable haven for dissident exiles. Only time will tell whether the attitude of Paris or Washington is more farsighted.

Certainly, in the short run, Bush's caution has gained nothing. The Chinese authorities, who claim not to care at all about sanctions, seem upset with the United States for three general reasons. First, Americans are held at least partially responsible for the anti-government movement. Second, the United States and other countries have been assailed for extending the visas of students from China. Finally, Beijing does not like the way the media portrayed the turmoil. The Voice of America (VOA) reporting has come under particularly heavy criticism. As a result concrete measures were taken, such as jamming VOA, postponing the start of the Peace Corps program in China and cancelling plans for Fulbright scholars to teach there. The cancellation of the Fulbright scholars' stay is a rare example of China failing to encourage the continuation of cultural exchanges which, in general, are going forward.

Should more in the way of economic sanctions have been imposed? First it must be said that no great claim can be made for sanctions against foreign governments. About half the time they do not work at all, and the other half the results are difficult to measure. Still, sanctions enable one to do *something* when no good alternatives are available. This at least satisfies the home demand for a political response. And in the case of China, where modernizers place great stress on economic relations with the United States, economic sanctions would touch a particularly sensitive nerve.

Sanction will probably be less damaging to China's economy than will the purely risk versus reward decisions of Westerners not to increase activities there. International and Japanese banks have cut lending in the belief that, because of the unrest and stalled economic reforms, the PRC is a poor credit risk. Likewise, China's grain imports and textile exports seem in jeopardy. Tourists and investors are shying away from China. The resulting decline in the country's hard currency reserves makes it difficult to buy foreign products.

Still, the sanctions may be suitable in the face of serious human rights violations. The type and timing of sanctions against China can be judged according to the following criteria:

(1) *The importance of trade in specific areas to Chinese leaders.* Yang Shangkun, author of the massacre, sorely needs military equipment and technology. At this moment, gun sales to the United States are doing well. Sanctions against the gun trade would be effective, especially since they primarily would hurt China's offending military-industrial complex. As for commerce in general, Mao Zedong proved that China can survive without international trade. However, such commerce now accounts for almost 20 percent of China's gross national product.

(2) *The hardship inflicted on the public.* In the case of China, a grain embargo would be inappropriate since the general population would be adversely affected. But a halt in the sale of airplanes to China would target the military without harming the Chinese people as a whole.

(3) *The political implications of non-economic relations.* In the cases of athletic and cultural exchanges, the value of the exchanges in keeping China open must be weighed against the luster they add to the regime.

(4) *The strength of the statement about unacceptable government behavior.* There is little point in imposing sanctions if they are accompanied by an apologetic chorus from prominent members of the ruling party.

(5) *Multilateral support.* There must be participation by nearly all of China's trading partners for economic sanctions to be effective. So far sanctions against arm sales and military or high-level contacts have received international support. Broad-spectrum commercial sanctions, however, would not receive international approval, thereby hurting China less than the country imposing such sanctions.

(6) *Support in the sanctioning country to sustain the sanctions until the human rights situation improves.* Sanctions accomplish nothing if they are backed away from before there is any improvement. Furthermore, ineffective sanctions hand the offending government a propaganda victory.

In measuring the value of sanctions one must take a long-range view. Their imposition stands primarily as a warning that the international community will extract a price from future irresponsible rulers who engage in serious human rights violations. The price is as much symbolic as monetary. As we have noted, the real economic impact comes not from sanctions but from the chilling effect that the overall situation has on business. Thus, in the final analysis, the value of sanctions lies in the moral stance taken and the signal sent. Furthermore, it would probably be a mistake to declare that sanctions have produced a victory when improvements do occur. Most of the credit for improved conditions should go to the reformers within the country.

Just as important as the sanctions themselves is the rhetoric that accompanies them. If the Bush administration is to be faulted for its handling of the Chinese situation, it should not be criticized primarily because of the specific sanctions it imposed, since people are bound to differ on precisely what sanctions are appropriate. Rather, the problem lies in pulling punches. Not only were the sanctions diluted through over-interpretation, but the month after it was declared that there would be no high-level diplomatic contacts, Secretary of State James Baker, at his request, met with Foreign Minister Qian Qichen. The signals suggested that priority was being given not to opposing butchery but to maintaining "the relationship." The implication is that it is most important to maintain ties with the ruling Chinese group, even at the expense of the relationship with the Chinese people, who, May events made clear, do not support their leaders. The U.S. government committed the same error in the 1940s and 1950s when it backed the discredited Chiang Kai-shek regime—a mistake for which the West paid a price for decades.

To be sure, the signals seem to have been strong enough to outrage conservatives in Beijing. Readers of China's press are asked to believe that the United States has been trying to subvert and overthrow China's economic and political order. On July 9, 1989, *People's Daily* accused the United States of "wanton interference in China's internal affairs" and attempting "subversion through peaceful evolution." Conservatives would like to continue the economic relationship, but they want little cultural and no political impact from the "bourgeois liberal" West.

The regime's attitude may seem odd in view of Washington's actual hands-off attitude. It can be accounted for by the Chinese leaders' frustration in dealing with their own people and need to blame their problems on someone else. Ironically, the diatribes in China's press may reduce the likelihood of long-term anti-Americanism among the Chinese public. At any rate, it is clear that the present leaders have chosen not to be our friends, and the U.S. public figures who have thought to the contrary engage in wishful thinking.

Few wars ever settle matters of principle, but World War II was an exception. Primarily as a result of international revulsion over the Holocaust, the

THE INITIAL RESPONSE TO JUNE 4

principle was established that governments do not have absolute sovereignty, and there are international limits to the abuses which they are permitted to commit against their own citizens. Nothing is more important than upholding that principle, which was established after such a terrible sacrifice. After the 1989 China massacre, many governments rose to the occasion, though the United States and Japan were not among them. But it must be borne in mind that the problem is not primarily one of relations among states. Rather, the fundamental issue is between tyranny and humanity.

In a more immediate sense, the problem is between the Chinese authorities and the Chinese people. The Chinese Communist Party has lost much of its legitimacy; knowledgeable people overwhelmingly support the goals and means of the Tiananmen workers and students. According to one poll of Beijing residents, only 1 percent found the protesting students' demands unreasonable. In this situation, Washington must choose sides wisely, if at all. Although some argue that geostrategic interests require our maintaining good relations with China's rulers, this view springs from the needs of a bipolarity which no longer exists. Indeed, given China's close relations with the Khmer Rouge, they hardly make an attractive ally, whereas the Soviet Union is becoming increasingly easier for us to get along with. The thinking of American opinion makers does not seem to be changing with the times. Spokesmen for business interests, including such organizations as the U.S.–China Business Council and the more broadly-focused National Committee on U.S.–China Relations, seem reluctant to take a strong and consistent stand in favor of political liberalization and human rights.[2] Even more damaging to long-term Sino-American relations are such individuals as Henry Kissinger and Alexander Haig, who have steadfastly stood by the most repressive elements in the Chinese government.

It surely would be helpful if American liberals reclaimed a voice in the matter. Sino-American relations are too important to be subject to erratic swings at the hands of American conservatives. The latter have made their belated contributions; the Sino-American economic relationship has grown phenomenally. However, the political relationship has been awkward. The conservatives in Washington and the conservatives in Beijing have had an odd symbiotic relationship, but public opinion, especially the opinion of intellectuals in both countries, increasingly has been operating on a different wavelength from that of the leaderships. For the first time, the American public views the Soviet Union more favorably that China. If Washington would place itself more clearly on the side of political reforms, that would render the present Beijing leadership "odd man out," which is the way it should be.

Sanctions and moral posturing may not be as effective as we and the Chinese people might like. Still, it would be foolish for Western countries, through unrestricted trade and business-as-usual diplomacy, to slow down the process of dynastic decline. This would only delay the return to China of the politics of decency.

## NOTES

James D. Seymour, "Sanctions or Subdued Relations: The International Response to the 1989 Massacre," *The Fletcher Forum of International Relations,* Vol. 14, No. 1 (Winter 1990), pp. 55–61. Reprinted by permission from *The Fletcher Forum of World Affairs.*

James D. Seymour, senior research scholar, East Asian Institute, Columbia University

1. *Wall Street Journal,* 30 June 1989, 15.

2. The U.S.–China Business Council issued a statement deploring the "violent suppression and wanton killing . . . and apparent turning away from . . . economic liberalization," but chairman Roger Sullivan opposed sanctions. See *The China Business Review,* July 1989, 9. See also, David M. Lampton and Roger Sullivan, "The Price China Has Paid," *Christian Science Monitor,* 10 July 1989, in which the authors argue that China has paid enough of a price for the mistakes of its leaders, and that the West's response should be minimal. The National Committee did issue a statement highly critical of the crackdown, but appeared to soften its message in statements aimed at China. See interview with Chairman David M. Lampton in the pro-Communist *Wehui Bao* (Hong Kong), 4 September 1989, 2; and FBIS, 5 September 1989, 4–6. Lampton told the author that *Wenhui Bao* highly distorted the interview in its published version.

# The Caricature of Deng as a Tyrant Is Unfair

## Henry Kissinger

Both the U.S. Senate and the House of Representatives have, after extraordinarily cursory debate, voted overwhelmingly to impose sanctions against China going well beyond the measures already taken by President Bush. Such a lopsided vote in direct opposition to a popular president with considerable experience in Chinese affairs is remarkable.

The vote was also unprecedented. I cannot recall sanctions invoked by either the president or Congress against a major country in reaction to events entirely within its domestic jurisdiction. The case of South Africa concerned a peripheral player on the international scene. The only comparable precedent—the Jackson-Vanik Amendment designed to spur Jewish emigration from the U.S.S.R.—backfired. And it only withheld additional benefits as do the congressional sanctions against China. Moreover, Congress established no criteria for eventually lifting the China sanctions.

To avoid any misunderstanding, let me summarize my own views regarding the events around Tiananmen Square. No government in the world would have tolerated having the main square of its capital occupied for eight weeks by tens of thousands of demonstrators who blocked the authorities from approaching the area in front of the main government building. In China a demonstration of impotence in the capital would unleash the lurking regionalism and warlordism in the provinces. A crackdown was therefore inevitable. But its brutality was shocking, and even more so the trials and Stalinist-style propaganda that followed.

Nevertheless, China remains too important for America's national security to risk the relationship on the emotions of the moment. The United States needs China as a possible counterweight to Soviet aspirations in Asia, and needs China also to remain relevant in Japanese eyes as a key shaper of Asian events. China needs the United States as a counterweight to perceived ambitions from the Soviet Union and Japan. In return China will exercise a moderating influence in Southeast Asia and Korea and not challenge America in other areas of the world. These realities have not been altered by events around Tiananmen. Should this reciprocity evaporate, Soviet policy would gain in flexibility and Japan would doubt the Asian role of the United States. America's position in the rest of Asia—especially in Korea—could become uncomfortable indeed.

Anyone familiar with the history and attitudes of China will therefore share the reluctance of President Bush—who is after all a humane and compassionate man—to launch the United States on a course both dangerous and undefinable.

At least two questions need to be addressed:

(a) Why should the United States Congress challenge a relationship that has enjoyed bipartisan support for nearly two decades?
(b) What is to be achieved by the course advocated by the congressional majority?

The passions result in part from the impact of television coverage. The media described events accurately enough, but television could not—in the nature of the medium—supply the historical or political context (Ted Koppel's special being an important exception).

But what happened in Beijing was not a simple morality play. The conflict grew intractable because serious individuals were in conflict over important issues. What began as a student protest for greater popular participation in government fused with the intraparty struggle of factions headed by the deposed general secretary, Zhao Ziyang, against groups surrounding senior Chinese leader Deng Xiaoping over the pace of economic reform and the need for political change. I have known Zhao Ziyang for nearly a decade. He is an attractive human being and a dedicated reformer who in his last conversation with me outlined a program of price reform which was both indispensable as a move to market economics and politically risky because it was bound to raise prices.

But I also know Deng as a reformer and a good friend of the United States. I remember him during a visit of mine to Beijing in 1975 when he stood up against the Gang of Four on behalf of ties to America—a warning to those who now claim China has no place to go regardless of sanctions. Though I have never discussed it with him, I suspect that President Bush's perceptions are heavily influenced by the same experience.

Thus in my view the caricature of Deng in American discussions as a tyrant despoiling Chinese youth is unfair. For the past decade and a half, Deng has been the driving forces behind Chinese reform. He introduced aspects of market economics and sought to institute a more predictable judicial system. His tragedy is that he has been too successful in the economic field and too hesitant in the political area. He has been too committed to communism to be prepared to face the fact that free-market economies cannot be instituted by a totalitarian Communist Party; but he was also too committed to progress to abandon a course bound to undermine one-party rule.

In a similar dilemma, President Mikhail S. Gorbachev of the Soviet Union has sought to construct a power base outside the Communist hierarchy, specifically in the Supreme Soviet. By contrast, Deng, a survivor of the Long March, sought to forestall the decline of Communist power by reforming it. He tried to subject every party member to review, and when that failed, he restricted the Communist Party hierarchy to essentially conceptual tasks.

Neither course worked. The weeding out of 30 million party members aborted because it had to be administered by the very people who needed to be removed. The reduction of the role of the Communist Party created a vacuum, especially after Deng moved Zhao from the prime minister's position to the office of general secretary of the Communist Party to replace Hu Yaobang.

As a result, Zhao Ziyang's reform program, which in the best circumstances would have been difficult to implement, foundered. Trapped between a government he no longer controlled and a Communist Party indifferent to his policies, Zhao Ziyang appealed to groups beyond his normal Communist reform constituency. In early May, two weeks into the student upheaval, Zhao contradicted Deng before the Asian Development Bank when he stated that the student protest was not a serious matter. Two weeks later when welcoming Gorbachev, Zhao stressed on television that Deng was making all the key decisions. This was generally interpreted as an attempt to place all the blame on Deng.

By then certainly it was apparent that the protesters had obtained support from organs beyond the capacity of student groups. Ten of thousands of protesters would not have survived day after day in the main square of the capital without food, elementary sanitation and medical care. Almost all reporters agreed on the excellence of their communication. Access to the main square of the capital was no longer controlled by the government.

None of this detracts from the fact that most of the grievances of the protesters were real. At the same time, the government in Beijing was unlikely to preside supinely over its own demise. For two centuries the overwhelming problem of China's domestic politics has been the maintenance of national unity. In the Chinese perception, ever since the Opium Wars of the 1840s, foreigners have systematically nurtured Chinese disunity to despoil the country. At my first meeting with Prime Minister Chou En-Lai [Zhou Enlai] on my secret trip to China in 1971, he expressed—to my amazement—his conviction that Japan, the United States and the Soviet Union all had as their ultimate aim the division of China.

No doubt Deng and his associates saw the demonstrations in Tiananmen Square as a threat not only to their own rule but to the cohesion and ultimately the independence of China. They remembered that during the Cultural Revolution, the student Red Guards created by Mao ultimately spawned so many competing groups under the same banner that the army had to be called on to rescue coherence from these autonomous satrapies. If the government could not control the main square of the capital, its ability to govern the rest of China would quickly erode.

I support the appeals for moderation of the summit meeting of the democracies as well as the measures President Bush has already taken to express his concern. But what would be the goal of going further in a situation of such complexity? Would it be to punish Beijing for past actions now irrevocable? Would it be to promote what the United States might regard as the reform faction? Does the United States really want to commit itself to overthrowing the government of China?

Punishing a country for past actions is bound to backfire. To go further than the steps the president has already taken would be to court a demonstration of impotence. Sooner or later the punitive sanctions will fail, if only because the Chinese government cannot undo its past actions, and geopolitical realities will dictate a rapprochement between the United States and China. By then, however, an essential element of American foreign policy could be in tatters.

It has been argued that the United States must bring pressure on the government in Beijing lest it antagonize the emerging forces in China. But does the United States know enough even to identify these forces or to understand how to help them? Would the success of the students in Beijing have brought democracy or civil war? The anniversary year of the French Revolution should remind us that the course and outcome of revolutions cannot be deduced from the proclamations of its creators. Within the last decade the Iranian revolution consumed its democratic spokesmen.

U.S.–Chinese relations prospered during the passage from Mao to Hua [Guofeng] to Deng despite their bitter antagonisms, because America stayed aloof from the impenetrable thicket of Chinese domestic politics. It was perceived by all contenders as committed to the eternal Chinese goals of territorial integrity and the well-being of its people.

Such an attitude is all the more important now because Chinese change did not end with the events on Tiananmen Square. I believe Deng's statement that he remains committed to economic reform. This has, after all, been the theme of his long life and the cause of his personal suffering. The hesitation of eight weeks before the crackdown, the efforts by even Li Peng to meet with student leaders, the visit of Zhao Ziyang and Li Peng to the hunger strikers in the hospital demonstrate the reluctance of the Chinese leadership to take measures likely to undermine the international prestige so laboriously accumulated over the past decade and a half.

The Chinese leaders must realize, or their successors will learn, that economic reform is impossible without the educated groups that supplied some of the fervor of the Beijing upheaval and of the workers who furnished much of the muscle. Thus, as so often in Chinese history, the rhythm of Chinese life and of Chinese common sense is likely to produce some practical solution. It would therefore be extraordinarily unwise for the United States to disengage from China at a moment of such fluidity or to adopt policies likely to be interpreted in Beijing as attempts to overthrow the government.

Advocates of additional sanctions claim that China's interest in American help is so great no sanction would jeopardize the relationship. That could be a dangerous illusion. If the Chinese leadership concludes—albeit reluctantly—that the outside pressure to which America is supposed to be the counterweight is overbalanced by America's interventions in China's domestic affairs or even by the inability of the executive and Congress to develop a coherent policy, it could invoke Chinese xenophobia as a defense against perceived American intervention in its domestic affairs.

The challenge of China thus goes beyond the events at Tiananmen Square. And President Bush's refusal to let himself be stampeded will in the long run serve America's national security as well as the values America cherishes.

## NOTES

Henry Kissinger, "The Caricature of Deng as a Tyrant Is Unfair," *Washington Post*, August 1, 1989, p. A21. Reprinted by permission from Henry Kissinger. © Tribune Media Services, Inc. All rights reserved. Reprinted with permission.

Henry Kissinger, head of Kissinger Associates, an international consulting firm; former national security adviser during the Nixon administration and secretary of state in the Nixon and Ford administrations

A play on the Batman and Robin duo, known for their anticrime heroics, this cartoon ridicules President Bush's response to the suppression of the 1989 demonstrations. Reprinted by permission from Chuck Ayers and *Akron Beacon-Journal.*

## Kissinger's Kowtow

*Stephen J. Solarz*

In the days when China still had emperors, anyone who approached the Dragon Throne was required to abase himself and kowtow before the sovereign. Now Henry Kissinger, even before his forthcoming visit to the Middle Kingdom, has kowtowed to China's latter-day emperor through the op-ed page of *The Washington Post.*

Kissinger, whose article argued that "no government in the world would have tolerated having the main square of its capital occupied for eight weeks" and that "a crackdown was therefore inevitable," appears to believe that China's leaders were justified in crushing the democracy movement and that our strategic interests with Beijing are far too important to make an issue of human rights. True to form, he appeals for a policy of amoral Realpolitik by erecting the straw man of a hysterical Congress that, according to him, went way overboard in its response to the Tiananmen Massacre. Yet what did Congress really do? It did not impose a comprehensive trade embargo, revoke China's most-favored nation tariff status, suspend its textile quota, eliminate its eligibility for

Export-Import Bank financing or reduce the sophistication of the American dual-use technology China is privileged to receive.

Congress did codify the suspension that President George Bush had already imposed on the transfer of military items and on the multilateral liberalization of China's access to dual-use technology. It also prohibited the sale of crime-control equipment such as cattle prods and suspended U.S. government-funded risk insurance and feasibility studies. Furthermore, contrary to Kissinger's patently false statement that Congress "established no criteria for eventually lifting the China sanctions," the legislation provided for presidential waivers on human rights or national security grounds.

Kissinger, who now defends the president's policy as a way of criticizing Congress, neglects to mention that he opposed a suspension of military cooperation with China before the president's decision to freeze all arms sales. Unlike the president and Congress (who approved the legislation he condemns by a vote of 418 to 0), he apparently saw nothing wrong with continuing to sell arms to a "People's Liberation Army" that engaged in the brutal slaughter of people it was supposed to protect.

The actions of Congress did not reflect a mere spasm of emotion. Indeed, its motivation was precisely the same as the president's: to demonstrate that the United States cannot do business as usual with a government that relies on indiscriminate violence and sweeping repression. Obviously, Kissinger still fails to understand that America's relations with other countries—particularly a Communist country like China—must rest on a solid foundation of public opinion. When the Chinese government resorts to the wanton violation of human rights, it will inevitably pay a price with the American public and its elected representatives.

Kissinger grudgingly acknowledges that "most of the grievances of the protesters were real." Would that he had asserted that Beijing's citizens were justified in voicing those grievances, and that a significant segment of Chinese officialdom agreed on the urgent necessity of political reform. Would that he had admitted that the party could have solved the crisis by accepting the people's reasonable demands. Would that he had recognized that the demonstrations had almost ended by June 3rd, and that the army's resort to violence was a deliberate effort to intimidate the populace into submission. By evoking all the paranoid reasons why Deng Xiaoping and his henchmen believed repression was necessary, however, Kissinger justifies their actions.

There is no question that the United States' relationship with China is geopolitically important. Yet most American policy-makers have come to realize, particularly in the context of Mikhail Gorbachev's "new thinking," that Beijing is no longer quite the counterweight against Moscow that Kissinger thought it was in the early 1970s. True, China has played a constructive role in Asia in recent years. But it does so in pursuit of its own national interest, not for the purpose of pleasing the United States, and it will continue to do so on that basis.

Instead of offering an apologia for repression, thereby confirming the prejudices of his Chinese interlocutors, Kissinger could better use his time in Beijing explaining to Deng and his colleagues why China will continue to suffer international opprobrium until they demonstrate genuine respect for the human rights of their own people. It would also be helpful if, after reaffirming America's recognition of China's continued geopolitical significance, he called on them to end martial law, release political prisoners, end the executions and get on with a serious program of political reform.

## NOTES

Stephen J. Solarz, "Kissinger's Kowtow," *Washington Post*, August 6, 1989, p. B7. Reprinted by permission from Stephen J. Solarz.

Stephen J. Solarz, congressman (D-NY) and chairman of the House Foreign Affairs Subcommittee on Asian and Pacific Affairs

# The Missions

*One of the most controversial moves President Bush made was sending two officials, National Security Adviser Brent Scowcroft and Deputy Secretary of State Lawrence Eagleburger, to Beijing to privately meet with Chinese leaders twice in 1989, first in July and then in December. Such moves seemed to contravene the administration's own ban on high-level contacts announced that June. The second meeting was made public on December 9, only after Scowcroft and Eagleburger arrived in Beijing. The July visit was not revealed to the public until December 19, after Ambassador Lord wrote the following op-ed, which was only in response to the second visit. Secretary Eagleburger's February 1990 testimony, which appears next, was in defense of both missions.*

## Misguided Mission

### Winston Lord

Since the June massacre in Beijing, Americans have hoisted two banners. One proclaims "sustain indignation"; the other, "preserve bilateral relations."

These principles are not mutually exclusive. Indeed the United States had struck the right balance between condemnation and connection until Gen. Scowcroft's pilgrimage. That mission both erased any pretense of official indignation and weakened the true foundations of Sino-American relations.

The administration's justifications are not persuasive:

Don't isolate the Chinese leaders. It is they, fearing their own people, who have isolated themselves. Their fixation is with power. Censure may not budge them—although the sharp world reaction to executions may have limited the numbers. But international acquiescence surely reinforces their view that crushing their populace elicits only fleeting outcries, no lasting repercussions.

Directly convey American outrage. In the Middle Kingdom, dispatching a high-level delegation speaks much louder than any words. Furthermore Scowcroft's public toast expressed as much outrage for the administration's critics as for the perpetrators of the massacre. Judging by the official backgrounding, his private remarks blamed Congress for all the furor. Whatever mild reproaches he may have transmitted were screened out by their media; the Chinese people were treated only to friendly smiles and exchanges.

Maintain contact on international issues. Senior officials gain access and carry weight. The Chinese reaffirmation that they won't ship intermediate missiles to volatile areas, though recycled, is important; so too is dialogue on Cambodia and Korea. But there are alternative channels unburdened by the awful symbolism of the Scowcroft voyage, such as our ambassadors and high-level meetings in international forums. In any event the Chinese pursue a hardheaded, independent foreign policy based on national interests, not spite over levels of contact.

Weigh the Soviet factor. While the geopolitical dimension of Sino-American ties remains important, it has evolved from a de facto alliance against the Soviets to the more nuanced realm of multipolar balance. Beijing needs to worry more about fast-moving U.S.–Soviet relations than Washington does about Sino-Soviet relations. Today on top of abiding historical, geopolitical and economic limits to Sino-Soviet rapprochement, add Gorbachev's heresies at home and in Eastern Europe. Their contagion poses a much greater threat to China's leaders than Western "bourgeois liberalization."

The administration forfeited moral reproof to seek improved bilateral ties. But even on its own terms the Scowcroft mission was severely misguided for the long run. Consider each of the key audiences.

The only group pleased by the visit, the predominant hard-liners in Beijing, will be gone in a few years. They have reinforced their power with images of business as usual. They take satisfaction that once again the foreigner pays tribute. Gratitude is not esteem.

The closet moderates in and out of government will form the core of leadership with whom we will deal in the future. Far from strengthening their hand, the administration has robbed them of the argument that Chinese repression and xenophobia entail costs. Japan, Europe and others will feel free to follow the Scowcroft trail.

The despair, disillusionment and anger of other Chinese is widespread. Only the tiny percentage in Western countries understand that the administration's posture does not reflect the American mainstream. The rest must conclude that the blood around Tiananmen Square has truly been scrubbed away.

The trek to Beijing has shattered the broad consensus in America. For 20 years five presidents of both parties had pursued a balanced policy which garnered overwhelming bipartisan support. Now this secure base is rudely shaken by passionate debate. A backlash may well produce heavier sanctions than those the administration already opposes.

One does not shore up the long-term foundations for Sino-American relations by appearing weak to China's leaders and callous to the Chinese and American people. One does not earn respect abroad by reversing field within months and practicing double standards. One cannot maintain a balanced approach at home by submerging our values and disdaining congressional and public opinion.

The damage done by the mission was compounded by its egregious style. Clinking glasses on worldwide television, Gen. Scowcroft lined up the administration with the Beijing regime against the Chinese and American people: "In both our societies there are voices of those who seek to redirect or frustrate our cooperation. We both must take bold measures to overcome these negative forces."

Two days later, in Berlin, Secretary of State James Baker pronounced: "In their peaceful urgent multitude the peoples of Eastern Europe have held up a mirror to the West and have reflected the enduring power of our own best values . . . true stability requires governments with legitimacy, governments that are based on the consent of the governed."

Let us hope that the administration would hold to these eloquent sentiments longer than six months if there were slaughters in the Tiananmen Squares of Eastern Europe or the Soviet Republics. The Scowcroft mission sends precisely the wrong signals to Gorbachev. Both the Chinese and Eastern European demonstrations have been massive, broadly based and entirely nonviolent. The main difference is that the Chinese people made very modest demands for dialogue with their leadership, while the Eastern Europeans have made very radical demands for the overthrow of theirs.

To be sure, the administration would react strongly over a sustained period to any massacre of innocents in Europe—and Gorbachev probably knows this. That is precisely the point. What we have here is not just a double standard but cultural, if not racial, bias—however unintentional and unconscious. Are we to believe that Chinese are not like Europeans, that they never had freedom and cannot afford it now because China would be ungovernable and "stability" is crucial to economic reform?

For years critics complained of a double standard in human rights, one for the Soviet Union, another for China. But there were two legitimate reasons for a more muted approach toward Beijing. First, Chinese society, with glaring exceptions, was generally moving in the right direction while the pre-Gorbachev Soviet Union was not. Second, China posed no threat to the United States and proved helpful on many international issues while the Soviet Union was expanding its arsenals and engaging in adventurism.

With many of these premises now overturned, it is time to shelve the double standard.

The president knew the trip would unleash a huge domestic storm, but acted boldly to stem a downward spiral in Sino-American relations. He is gambling that Beijing will make major concessions before Congress reconvenes. We can anticipate some positive moves, but we should not let Beijing or Washington inflate the significance of cosmetic gestures.

Instead Beijing should:

- Acknowledge that last spring was a tragedy for patriots, not only for soldiers;
- Grant amnesty to demonstrators, not conduct witchhunts;
- Free countless dissidents in jail, not just two in an embassy;
- Remove fears, not just martial law;
- Let in VOA broadcasts, not just an additional broadcaster;
- Welcome without onerous conditions journalists, scholars and Peace Corps volunteers, not just computers and cash;
- Cease intimidation of foreigners and invective against America.

This agenda in not utopian. It merely calls for the status quo ante June.

The regime is unlikely to move significantly on such fronts. If it does, I, for one, would be delighted to modify my verdict on the Scowcroft mission.

In foreign policy there is frequent tension between the imperatives of strategy and morality, between preserving peace and promoting human rights. Happily for the policy-maker these pursuits are often mutually reinforcing, with no difficult tradeoffs. What better example than the glorious panorama of Eastern Europe. Could there possibly be a more profound contribution to peace on the European continent than the realizing of long-suppressed aspirations? In a few short months, enemy armies have dissolved, warning times have multiplied, and a formidable buffer zone has emerged.

The new agenda for American diplomacy thus features the encouragement of freedom in societies moving toward post-Communism. This pursuit dramatically strengthens the prospects for peace as well. Meanwhile the octogenarians in the Forbidden City are in a time warp, finding common cause with the likes of Honecker and Ceausescu, Castro and Kim, while the Chinese people hunger for rights being grasped by peoples on the other side of the globe.

The administration, which strives skillfully to keep up with the times in Europe, was trapped in its own time warp when it launched Gen. Scowcroft. We can hope that Chinese actions in coming weeks will ease these sufferings of the people and thereby Washington's plight. But realistically it will take new leaders for China to catch up with history.

Until that time when we can fully resume cooperation with China, we should restore a measured approach. The choice is not solely between isolation and approbation. Let us conduct necessary business with the Beijing authorities in workmanlike fashion, not with fawning emissaries. Let us calibrate our actions with theirs. Let us maintain productive links where possible with progressive Chinese forces. Above all, to serve American interests as well as values, let us align ourselves with China's future.

## NOTES

Winston Lord, "Misguided Mission," *Washington Post,* December 19, 1989, p. A23. Reprinted by permission from Winston Lord.

Winston Lord, former U.S. ambassador to China (1985–1989); staff member of the National Security Council during the Nixon administration (1969–1973); and assistant secretary of state for Asian and Pacific affairs during the Clinton administration (1993–1997)

# United States Policy toward China

## House testimony by Lawrence S. Eagleburger

### THE FIRST TRIP TO BEIJING

**Mr. Eagleburger** [*witness, prepared statement*]: . . . The secret trip that General Scowcroft and I made to Beijing last July was intended precisely to convey an undiluted message from the President to the Chinese leadership about America's horror over Tiananmen. As we all know only too well, messages delivered below the level of the top leaders often get softened or altered on the way up the chain of command. Moreover, actions taken in the glare of publicity often engender public posturing, in which saving "face" becomes more important than a sober consideration of the issues.

Accordingly, the President decided to send a quiet mission directly to China's leader. Our purpose was to convey to the Chinese, without ambiguity, a clear sense of the reaction in this country, beginning with that of the President, to what had happened. We firmly communicated that the United States does not condone the appalling violence used to suppress the peaceful demonstrations, nor do we condone the repression that has followed. I can tell you that our July visit was neither easy nor pleasant.

I have heard some say that the first trip may have stiffened the spines of China's leaders and delayed the day of relaxation. I do not believe that. I believe that the first trip demonstrated the seriousness of American purpose, made clear the stakes involved in a worsening of our relations, and, ultimately, provided an incentive for a return to the path of reform.

A few months after the trip, the President had to decide whether to sign the Pelosi bill, a well-intentioned and broadly supported legislative act that sought to provide ironclad protections for Chinese students in this country from being forced to return to their homeland. Obviously, the easy and popular choice for the President would have been to sign the bill into law.

But there were other considerations. The President could take administrative action that would accomplish all of the objectives of the Pelosi bill, yet reduce the likelihood of retaliation by the Chinese against exchange programs with the United States.

Accordingly, the President issued a directive that included the substantive measures in the Pelosi bill—and more. Indeed, some of the protections under the President's directive, such as the authorization for employment in this country, are actually broader that those in the Pelosi bill.

The subsequent debate over whether to override the President's veto demonstrated that this was not a popular decision. Yet, the sustaining of that veto in the Senate should assure us not only that the Chinese students and scholars in this country may remain here, but that the door will still be open for more to come. Thus, the process of exchange so vital to strengthening the forces of reform in China will continue.

## THE SECOND TRIP TO BEIJING

In December, the President decided that it was time for a bold move to try to begin a process leading to better conditions in China and better U.S.–China relations. Having heard over and over again that it was up to the United States to "unite the knot" in our relations, we noted that, after visits to China by former President Nixon and former Secretary of State Kissinger, China's spokesmen had begun to join us in talking of both side taking steps to improve relations, a subtle but distinct signal.

### A. Our Message to the Chinese

The President decided to act. Again, he ordered Brent Scowcroft and me to be his special emissaries to the Chinese leadership. Again, our mission was to deliver an undiluted message of the need for China to take steps to improve our relations. We also briefed the Chinese on the Malta Summit, in accordance with our general practice of consulting with them after our summits with the Soviets.

The President knew that he would be taking this action in the face of popular opposition and at substantial political risk. But it was a risk he was willing to take because of his experience over the years in dealing with China and the Chinese, because of his personal acquaintance with many of China's leaders, and because of his judgment that it just might begin a process which would lead to improvements in the lot of the Chinese people. All the talk of clinking glasses, surprise announcements, and warm toasts misses the point. The Chinese leadership needed to know how they could improve their relations with the United States, and we told them.

## B. The Results

The first thing that needs to be said about assessing the results of that second trip is that it is far too early to come to conclusions. Again, the goal was not a specific result, but to give impetus to a process of interaction, where each side would address the other's concerns and establish the basis for resolving our differences. That process has only just begun.

Steps have been taken. They represent movement in a direction I believe most Americans recognize as favorable. Nonetheless, much more needs to be done.

In bilateral U.S.–China relations, Beijing has agreed to resume discussions on the Fulbright program of scholarly exchanges. Beijing has also agreed to receive Peace Corps volunteers for the first time. Even before Tiananmen, the agreement to receive those volunteers was a difficult and sensitive matter for the Chinese. We see movement today as a symbolically important step to deepen relations at the grass roots level.

Beijing has also accredited a resident correspondent from the Voice of America. You all know that U.S. reporters were expelled last year. This step to renew VOA's presence in Beijing is welcome.

More broadly, China's foreign ministry spokesman issued a statement that China would not sell medium-range ballistic missiles to any Middle East countries, and denied plans that China would sell M-9 missiles to Syria. This statement, and the related denial, went beyond previous Chinese pronouncements on the subject and addressed specific U.S. concerns. The Chinese statements are positive, but we will remain vigilant on the issue of missile sales, especially to unstable regions of the world.

Internally, too, there has been guarded, cautious, even grudging movement in a direction we see as right for the people of China, as well as right for U.S. interest. Early last month, China lifted the martial law regime imposed in Beijing last May. Many observers regard this action by the Chinese as "cosmetic." We wish it had been far less ambiguous than it was. But it is, nonetheless, an achievement of some significance. The process of reducing tensions has to begin somewhere, and I do not believe we should give the back of our hand to what was evidently a difficult Chinese decision to begin to respond to foreign and domestic calls for moderation. We should seek to build on it, to urge that it be made less "cosmetic," and not reject it and risk providing a pretext for darker forces to block China's movement toward positive reforms.

On January 18, Beijing took another step by releasing 573 detainees. We wish that detailed information about these cases had been provided for the world to examine, for it would have greatly increased the impact of this act of leniency. Naturally, we will press for the fullest possible accounting of all those detained and sentenced since the Tiananmen events, and for further acts of leniency and amnesty by the authorities. Nevertheless, the act of releasing hundreds of people may be the beginning of efforts at reconciliation that are sorely needed in China today. . . .

## NOTES

House Committee on Foreign Affairs, "United States Policy toward China," 101st Congress, 2nd sess., February 8, 1990. Testimony by Lawrence S. Eagleburger.

Lawrence S. Eagleburger, deputy secretary of state during the Bush administration (1989–1992); acting secretary of state (1992–1993)

# MFN: Creating Linkage

*Soon after June 4, there were calls for wide-sweeping sanctions. Many in Congress latched on to the removal of China's most-favored-nation (MFN) status as the most appropriate instrument to demonstrate American outrage and push the Chinese government to improve its human rights practices. The president's annual waiver, which had been a routine affair up until then, suddenly became the focal point of policy debates. Congress voted on China's MFN (later renamed NTR [normal trade relations]) status every year between 1990 and 2001. In 2000, the U.S. Congress passed legislation that was signed by President Clinton agreeing to provide China permanent NTR status upon its entry into the World Trade Organization (WTO). China acceded to the WTO in late 2001.*

## Most-Favored-Nation Status for the People's Republic of China

### House testimony by Nancy Pelosi and Richard Solomon

**Ms. Pelosi** [*witness, prepared statement*]: Most-favored-nation status, which entitles a trading partner to the lowest tariffs offered to any country, is denied by law to nations with centralized economies unless they have policies of open emigration. Clearly, China does not meet this requirement.

I believe that, by renewing most-favored-nation status for China without a package of comprehensive sanctions, the President has missed yet another opportunity to express American indignation over the deplorable actions undertaken by the Chinese government since MFN was last renewed on May 31, 1989.

Since that time, the government has killed thousands of China's young people in Tiananmen Square, it has detained tens of thousands of Chinese and Tibetans, it has imposed de facto martial law, it has placed restrictions on student exchanges and it has begun to dismantle the economic reforms made in the 1980s.

Many members of Congress and China experts have called repeatedly on the President to send a clear and principled message of outrage to the leaders in Beijing. He has missed every opportunity to do so. He missed an opportunity by vetoing the bill to protect Chinese students; he missed an opportunity by intervening personally on the veto override; he missed another opportunity by authorizing the Scowcroft visits and the resumption of U.S. support of World Bank lending. And now, the President has renewed most-favored-nation status to China, missing yet another opportunity to send an unequivocal message of U.S. condemnation to the Chinese regime who ordered the massacre in Tiananmen Square and the ensuing repression.

It is this series of missed opportunities that provides the backdrop for our debate today. While, in itself, most-favored-nation status does not imply advocacy of a regime's policy—South Africa has most-favored-nation status—the fact that this renewal announcement follows a long list of concessions to the Chinese government, in the absence of any concessions by them, gives an appearance of U.S. willingness to ignore the economic and political repression currently occurring in China.

I have consistently said that we must examine the MFN issue within the larger framework of U.S.–China relations. First, I have repeatedly urged the administration to oppose World Bank loans, because their renewal would open the floodgates for bilateral and commercial lending, depriving us of one our most effective sanctions. Other countries are looking to the United States for leadership on this issue. The President, however, has insisted on a resumption of lending for basic human needs and has broadened this definition—turning it into a loophole through which forestry, vocational training and agricultural project loans can pass.

Second, although Congress sent the President a package of sanctions against China, he has acted to weaken most of them. Despite the ban on military cooperation, the President allowed a continuation of U.S.–Chinese cooperation at Wright-Patterson Air Force Base; the President waived the sanction against the transfer of satellite technology; he immediately resumed high-level government-to-government contacts with China by sending Scowcroft and Eagleburger to meet with Deng Xiaoping in July and later in December; and he softened the United States' position on support of World Bank loans to China, allowing basic human needs loans to go forward in February.

Given this conciliatory policy toward China, is there any wonder that Deng Xiaoping believes that he will be vindicated by the West's inaction?

Without a strengthening of U.S. sanctions, without increased funding for Voice of America, without vigorous consideration of Taiwan's entry into the

GATT; without even a strong presidential tribute to those young martyrs of democracy who died for their vision of political freedom—an extension of most-favored-nation status cannot be defended.

Like China, America is a country of diverse cultures. We are united, however, by a common principle—that government rules at the will of its citizens and that open political discourse is the greatest weapon against tyranny.

There is no longer any question that the government of China scoffs at this universal principle. The tens of thousands of demonstrators held today in Chinese and Tibetan prisons attest to this fact.

America must not allow the principle of freedom and democratic discourse to become a victim of Chinese governmental tyranny. Given the repeated failure of the President to take a principled stand and his refusal to do so now, I believe Congress should oppose most-favored-nation status to the People's Republic of China.

**Mr. Solomon** [*witness, prepared statement*]: Mr. Chairman, Members of the committee, I appreciate this opportunity to testify on behalf of the Administration on the question of China's most-favored-nation (MFN) trade status. As you know, the President this morning announced his decision to extend for another year China's MFN certification. We know that this issue is a matter of lively interest in the Congress, and I am here to lay out for you our thinking that underlies the President's judgment. . . .

The dilemmas of our current China policy bring to mind F. Scott Fitzgerald's observation that the mark of a first-rate intellect is the ability to keep two opposing ideas in one's mind and still be able to function. The foreign policy equivalent is the effort to balance the competing demands of hard-nosed national interests and our national values, aspirations and ideals. Our post-Tiananmen approach to China has been a consistent effort to preserve some essential elements of a key relationship that serves important national interests while at the same time sending a clear message that aspects of Beijing's human rights performance have been—and remain—unacceptable and preclude a fully normal relationship.

Let us be clear. This administration regards the situation in China with regard to the protection of human rights as deeply disturbing. . . .

Last year's outrageous killing of non-violent demonstrators by troops in Beijing caused the Administration and the Congress to impose a series of sanctions on China. Other democratic countries took actions in parallel with our own. Evidence of continuing repression of dissent in China now prompts a desire by many in this country to strike back—by imposing still more sanctions.

The legislatively mandated annual decision for extension of MFN now before us is thus, for some, a convenient outlet for such a punitive impulse. Some of the Chinese students in this country even argue that the U.S. should escalate sanctions to the maximum extent possible, and use MFN as a weapon to devastate the Chinese economy and deepen China's international isolation. These voices believe that the plight of their countrymen must be made much worse before the Chinese people will rise up and rectify the situation. And they calculate that the withdrawal of MFN is a sure way to create the conditions for upheaval.

We find this "worse is better" logic flawed and inappropriate as a basis for national policy. Such an approach *would* inflict suffering on the Chinese people. But *it would not*, in our view, achieve the desired goals of improving the human rights situation or encouraging a return to economic and political reform. . . .

We cannot break faith with the people who count on us by destroying the basis of commerce with China. Trade is not just a cold set of financial transactions between our two countries; it is a primary channel for contact between Americans and Chinese, for interchange of ideas and values which has contributed significantly to the progressive changes in China over the past decade. Commerce is a force for change; and as we have seen this past year in dramatic development around the globe, economic modernization and the workings of the information revolution bring with them ineluctable pressures for political reform as well.

Let me emphasize that granting MFN is in no sense an act of approval of a given country's policies. The term "most favored nation" is something of a misnomer: it merely means that normal tariff rates—rather than discriminatory tariffs—will apply to bilateral trade. It does not mean that the country in question is our most favorite nation. As Chairman Solarz has pointed out, many countries with which we have profound differences—Iraq and Syria, which have been on our terrorist list; and South Africa, against which we have broad sanctions—have retained MFN status. None of our friends and allies amongst the democratic countries are contemplating the draconian step of withdrawing China's MFN status. . . .

In summing up, I would emphasize that the President has decided in favor of extending China's MFN status because it serves clear U.S. interests: in promoting our objectives of reform, modernization, and the advancement of human rights; of maintaining productive official contacts; of protecting the interests of American business and American consumers; and in working to maintain Hong Kong's stability and future viability.

The extension does not in any way imply acquiescence to political repression and human rights violations. The measures initiated by the President in June, 1989—suspending arms exports and high-level governmental exchanges, and seeking postponement of multilateral development bank loans beyond those for basic human needs—remain essentially in place, as do the Congressional sanctions enacted in February. These measures clearly define our dealings with the current regime in Beijing as less than normal.

Reaffirming MFN shows that we know where our interests lie, and that we are on a steady course—one that recognizes the dynamics of economic and political change and the importance of the long-term relationships with the people of China that commerce can facilitate. It reflects our concern for the welfare of the millions of Chinese with whom we share a vision of the future. And finally it recognizes that we convey our concerns most effectively to the Chinese when we do so in unison with our major allies. As I have pointed out, no other ally supports eliminating MFN trade status for China, so that any U.S. action would be unilateral.

We would have liked the Chinese leadership to respond more rapidly than it has to our concerns for reconciliation and reform. I have noted the positive, if limited, steps the Chinese government has taken. The crucial point in this regard is that Beijing clearly sees no alternative to a policy of economic openness to the outside world. Mr. Chairman, I for one have faith in the dynamism of the marketplace, in the inexorable effect of economic modernization on social and political reform. We should not underestimate the power of international commerce as a force for change. So long as China is engaged economically, the very forces for reform that boiled over at Tiananmen will be in play. China cannot sail against the winds of change.

We hope that the Chinese leadership will soon build on the steps it has taken to relieve repression and address other U.S. concerns so that the American people, the Congress and the Administration can be satisfied of its intention to improve relations and return to its earlier commitment to political and economic reform. But we must avoid the temptation to be excessively punitive—especially in ways that harm our own interests.

We should not let our frustration over the slow pace of Beijing's response lead us to take unilateral actions which will harm millions in China who look to us to help keep their country open—actions which would undercut vital long-term U.S. interests. The central authorities in Beijing would not bear the brunt of MFN withdrawal. Indeed, they would try to turn it to their advantage by laying the blame for their economic problems on outsiders. It is China's economic reformers, those Chinese hoping to emigrate, Hong Kong and American business who would be the real losers.

## NOTES

House Committee on Foreign Affairs Subcommittees on Human Rights and International Organizations, Asian and Pacific Affairs, and on International Economic Policy and Trade, "Most-Favored-Nation Status for the People's Republic of China," 101st Congress, 2nd sess., May 24, 1990. Testimony by Nancy Pelosi and Richard Solomon.

Nancy Pelosi, congresswoman (D-CA); Richard Solomon, assistant secretary of state for East Asian and Pacific affairs during the Bush administration (1989–1993)

# Extending Most-Favored-Nation Status for China

## Senate testimony by Max Baucus, Morton Bahr,
## Holly J. Burkhalter, and Roger G. Sullivan

**Senator Baucus** [*committee member*]: . . . Mr. Chairman, last year we were all shocked and appalled by the brutal steps that the Chinese Government took to repress the student democracy movement. I, like you, will never forget the picture of a Chinese student singlehandedly blocking a line of tanks. I will never forget the shock and horror that we all felt when we heard the news of the slaughter in Tiananmen Square.

The question we are considering today is not whether or not we approve of China's actions. Clearly, we do not. Every Member of the Senate has condemned the actions of the Chinese Government. The question before us today is whether or not removing most-favored-nation status from China would improve the human rights situation. Sadly, in my judgment, removing most-favored-nation status from China would not increase respect for human rights in China.

In most cases, China would find new markets for the products they would otherwise export to the United States. The economic impact that might be felt would certainly not be sufficient and force China into changing its domestic policy. Quite to the contrary, economic sanctions could cause China to further withdraw from the world community. Remember, the positive changes we saw in China in the 1980s were closely linked to expanding economic ties to the West. If the economic ties to the West are broken the incentive for further progress will be gone.

I have also heard from a number of thoughtful Chinese students studying in America who argue that economic sanctions by the United States could cause further deterioration in China. In my judgment, it is the wrong time to impose economic sanctions. Sanctions now could reverse progress rather than encourage it. . . .

China retaliated against U.S. wheat exports to China in 1984 after the U.S. restricted Chinese textile exports. In all likelihood wheat, the U.S. major export to China, would again be the target of China's retaliation. Last year China was our largest export market for wheat. American wheat farmers stand to lose more than $1 billion annual sales to China if sanctions are imposed. [In s]hort, wheat farmers could once again be forced to bear the cost of foreign policy sanctions just as they did when the United States imposed a grain embargo on the Soviet Union.

I believe it would be a serious threat to repeat the mistakes we made by imposing the Soviet grain embargo. Every Member of the Senate, every

Member of the House, and the overwhelming majority of the U.S. citizens desperately want to show their disgust with the current Chinese government. We all wish there was a way to strike out to strike a blow for student protesters. But the reality is there is no easy way.

Further, I am not willing to sacrifice the interests of American farmers and businessmen and workers in a hollow show of outrage. And unfortunately, I believe withdrawing most-favored-nation status from China would be just that, a hollow show of outrage. It may make us feel better, but it would do nothing for the democracy movement in China. It might even make the situation worse. . . .

**Mr. Bahr** [*witness*]: . . . We believe President Bush's decision to continue to grant most-favored-nation trade benefits to China is a grave moral and political error. It shouts to the world and to the Chinese leadership in particular that the United States will continue with business as usual despite the existence of a brutally oppressive regime. Money was deemed more important than standing up for individual rights.

As we know, there are those who would rather wrap themselves in the debate on flag-burning rather than standing up for those values that make our country great. We believe the actions of the Chinese Government demand revocation of most-favored-nation trade status. As representatives of workers in this country we were gratified to see workers in China play a major role in the demonstrations for democracy and to note that high on their agenda was the formation of truly autonomous trade unions.

In those heady days of May and early June 1989 we received reports of independent unions being organized in many parts of that country. We now know that the formation of independent unions in China helped precipitate the brutal repression that the world witnessed. Deng Xiaoping said that these unions were symptoms of what he called the "Polish disease." No wonder then that his first target in Tiananmen Square was the tent headquarters of the Beijing union. Almost all of the union's key leaders are now in jail or have disappeared.

If the events of the last year have taught us anything, it is that the Communist authorities in China initiated economic changes not because they intended to loosen their hold on power, but to strengthen it.

It is very important to understand what "free enterprise" means in the PRC. In the southern province of Guangdong—and we heard a lot of testimony on that just a few minutes ago—which is the PRC's testing ground, foreign investors, mainly from Hong Kong, the United States and Taiwan, rushed to take advantage of an incredibly low-wage, pliant labor force. Here, the Chinese Government guaranteed that troublesome workers would not be a problem, and that bureaucratic obstacles would be swept away.

This committee should know that free enterprise in the PRC is also closely tied to China's vast forced labor gulag—a group of labor camps which could hold as many as 10 million people. These camps have been put on a profit basis in order to comply with Deng's new economic policies, and [are] required to earn hard currency. We know that they are part of the subcontracting system that feeds the region's thousands of joint ventures. They are also in the business of offering inmates to foreign companies as employees.

The time has come for Congress to address the myth that trade with China somehow promotes democracy there. On the contrary, trade with China serves to perpetuate an evil and corrupt system run by the Communist Party. Over the last several months the AFL-CIO has heard that the removal of most-favored-nation status would deal a body blow to these enterprises. This would be true and that is why removal of most-favored-nation privileges makes sense.

Another myth that we have heard is that the removal of most-favored-nation status would cause harm to the American consumer. This argument is most often presented by businessmen who may have just left Hong Kong, Korea, Taiwan or the United States to escape paying higher wages to workers, or to get around new environmental regulations in these countries.

Quite frankly, such arguments from the business community about the cost of a break in trade with China sell the American people short. The American people have spent billions of dollars to defend democracies overseas. Business should also be willing to sacrifice a bit for the cause of freedom. . . .

Finally, there is the national security argument, that we just cannot afford to anger a nation which has great influence in the world and which would cause trouble for sales . . . of missiles and other weapons. Such an argument smacks of appeasement and blackmail. In sum, all the arguments that support the status quo are based on the proposition that [the] leaders of China are honorable men with whom a bargain can be struck.

But can you really say this about men who ordered the cold blooded murder of their fellow citizens and who have systematically terrorized an entire population in Tibet? Can you say that about men who have no compunction about selling missiles—and now we hear rumors of chemical weapons—to terrorist states in the Mideast? Can you say this about men who forced sterilization of women? Can you say this about men who support the Khmer Rouge in Cambodia?

While the case is clear that China is [in] violation of Jackson-Vanik immigration requirements, the AFL-CIO also believes that Congress should deny most-favored-nation benefits to China because of its repression of human rights.

For too long the administration has treated China's rulers in a special way. In doing so, it has accepted human and labor rights violations which have been condemned in Cuba, Libya, South Africa, the Soviet Union, Nicaragua, and Chile. This double standard should end. The first step in that process should be the withdrawal of most-favored-nation trading status from China. . . .

**Ms. Burkhalter** [*witness, prepared statement*]: . . . As we observe the first anniversary of the imposition of martial law and the killing at and around Tiananmen Square, it is appropriate to evaluate the current state of human rights in China, the results of the Bush Administration's policy toward Beijing, and the advisability of further sanctions against China.

Asia Watch has been sharply critical of the Administration's China policy. The Administration's response to the events of June 3 and 4, 1989 (and subsequent repression) was far too tepid to have had the effect on Beijing of promoting respect for human rights and reversing the crackdown. Lu Jinghua, a founding member of the Beijing Workers Autonomous Federations, stated in meetings in Washington last month that she felt that international pressure exerted by trade sanctions was crucial in the long term to produce real change in China. She said that she and her worker colleagues would rather suffer the short-term pain of any economic dislocation caused by sanctions, than endure the current regime for the long term.

The original sanctions imposed by the Bush Administration, such as opposition to loans to China at the World Bank, the ban of high-level diplomatic contacts, and the suspension of commercial sales of military items have been eroded considerably. In addition to undoing his own sanctions against China, President Bush has invoked his broad waiver authority to limit the impact of sanctions required by the Congress in sanctions legislation. In December, President Bush waived the congressional ban on the export of three communications satellites to China. And in February, a congressional ban on Export-Import Bank financing was waived, and a $9.75 million loan was made to China National Offshore Oil Corp.

Nor has the Bush Administration neglected symbolic opportunities to reassure the Chinese leadership that they have United States support. The veto of the so-called "Pelosi bill" which would have extended protection to Chinese students in the U.S. and President Bush's frantic arm-twisting to prevent the Senate from overriding his veto signaled all too clearly that this Administration would go to any lengths to avoid embarrassing Beijing.

Before turning to the question of additional sanctions against China, it is worthwhile to examine just what concessions President Bush got from the Chinese leadership for his efforts. The Chinese were concerned about sanctions, and took actions clearly meant to influence the Congress. In the period preceding the first significant debate on China in the U.S. Congress (the debate on the Pelosi bill in early [1990]) the Chinese leadership announced its first human rights concession since the crackdown: the lifting of martial law in Beijing and the release of 573 detainees. Unfortunately, the prisoner releases appeared to have been a publicity stunt, as no names were released and no names provided of the tens of thousands still jailed. And the lifting of martial law was offset by a flurry of new laws and regulations which were enacted to enshrine martial law restrictions on speech, press, and assembly, and by the fact that some 40,000 PLA troops simply exchanged their uniforms for police uniforms and continued their duties in the city.

The Chinese leadership's gestures were more than outweighed by a deteriorating human rights situation throughout the year. In addition to the thousands of prisoners jailed in the aftermath of Tiananmen Square, Asia Watch has documented several dozen further arrests and trials of pro-democracy individuals that took place between October 1989 and January 1990, and has received reliable reports that many others (though names are not yet known) were arrested or tried over the same period. . . .

The Chinese have been persuaded that at least some gestures are required if they are to retain MFN for the coming year. The Congress and the Bush Administration should put China on notice that much more is required for there to be serious consideration of MFN renewal this year. The Administration should abandon private diplomacy at this point, and an aggressive public stance should replace it. The Administration did not hesitate to use very public diplomacy when it sent Brent Scowcroft and Lawrence Eagleburger to China to restore warm relations with Beijing. They should do the same today, but this time with a different message.

Congress, for its part, can do much to help by using the MFN process to obtain maximum concessions from China. Congress should strongly consider suspending MFN for a period until the Chinese implement an amnesty for political prisoners. (This is precisely the condition which the U.S. imposed on Poland following the imposition of martial law and the jailing of thousands of political prisoners.) Or Congress should enact a new set of conditions on MFN for China and require the Administration to report on Chinese performance on a number of issues, including release of political prisoners, an end to the widespread use of beatings and torture in Chinese prisons, resolution of the Fang Lizhi case, good faith participation in the U.N. peace negotiations on Cambodia, and an end to military aid to the Khmer Rouge. If by the end of [a] six or twelve month period the Chinese have not made significant, certifiable progress on these issues, MFN should be withdrawn.

In 1978 Deng Xiaoping returned to power, making the argument that those close to Mao had created a catastrophic political and economic situation through their hardline policies. He made the argument that China could only save itself if changes were made. Today, the hardliners have largely prevailed with their unique blend of economic growth with repression—"market Stalinism" and at little cost. If Li Peng and his cohorts are permitted to continue their policies with U.S. support, they will only consolidate their power within China and the 1989 democracy movement prisoners, like their 1979 Democracy Wall colleagues, will face many years in jail.

Yet inevitably another democracy movement will rise up from the ashes of Tiananmen Square. Asia Watch favors tough sanctions against China, including limits and conditions on MFN, in the hopes that the authorities will think twice about destroying the next democracy movement in China. . . .

**Mr. Sullivan** [*witness, prepared statement*]: . . . The issue of whether to extend China's Most-Favored-Nation (MFN) status for another year, as we have done every year since 1979, is a difficult one. Americans find the human rights behavior of the current Chinese regime to be abhorrent and support the limited sanctions already adopted by the U.S. Government to express our outrage. Companies find the business climate under such a regime unattractive and hope for a return to the polices of reform and openness. Beijing does not appear to be listening, so it is tempting to consider the withdrawal of MFN as a logical next step. It would certainly be a powerful sanction; indeed I can think of nothing else we might reasonably consider that would cause as much damage to the Chinese economy.

A decision to interfere with free trade in this way and to dismantle the structure of trade built up around the original extension of MFN to China ten years ago would have serious, unintended consequences. Now we may decide those unintended consequences are worth bearing, but we have to know what they are before we can make such an assessment. We need, therefore, to ask the following key questions.

First, who will be hurt? Had we asked ourselves this question in 1980 after the Soviet Union invaded Afghanistan, we would never have imposed the grain embargo, a quixotic gesture which damaged only our own farmers.

Removing MFN is not such an obviously misguided option because China would be hurt. The removal of MFN would increase the rate of duty on the top 25 dutiable imports from China from an average of 8.76 to a prohibitive 50.49%. Considering the types of products now being imported and the comments of business executives closet to the action, we estimate that the removal of MFN would mean at a minimum a 50% reduction (or $6 billion) in Chinese exports to the United States. Some of these products would find markets elsewhere, but most would not since they are produced in large part for the American or other foreign joint ventures or local factories under contract to American, Hong Kong or Taiwan firms. If the U.S. market for these low margin goods were effectively closed, many of these operations would simply move to another country or shut down.

It is impossible to quantify the damage to American consumers, importers and retailers. Importers suggest that over time they would be able to shift to alternative sources elsewhere in Asia or possibly in Eastern Europe but the short-term cost and dislocations would be considerable. Retailers, who must place their orders in March or April for delivery in time for Christmas, would sustain significant losses. Prices on toys, games, clothing and other light industrial products would go up, particularly for those American consumers who try to stretch their limited resources by shopping at K-Mart and other discount stores.

If we revoke China's MFN status, we also must assume Chinese retaliation. American exports, which last year totaled about $6 billion, would be reduced by at least one-third. If past behavior is any guide, China would designate the U.S. as a source of last resort. When they did this in 1975–1976 U.S. agricultural exports fell from 5 million tons per year to zero. In 1989 we sold over 7 million tons ($1.08 billion) of wheat, an amount equal to 20% of our total wheat exports, large quantities of fertilizers, $500 million worth of commercial aircraft, over 10% of our total forest products exports, up to one-third of our total soda ash exports and considerable quantities of mining and construction equipment. All of these products are readily available to China from other sources.

Retaliation would also deal a severe blow to American companies who have invested 10 years in trying to enter the emerging China market. For all the real difficulties companies have experienced in China, it is not a market that we should lightly cede to Asian and European competition. This is what would happen were the United States to unilaterally remove MFN from China, a drastic step no other industrialized country is even considering. Finally, among the innocent victims of removal of MFN would be the people of Hong Kong who already face a crisis of confidence over their future under Chinese rule in 1997.

The second question is would all this collateral damage be worth it? . . . I do not think so, and I hope the Congress will agree. Ask the farmers who are still living with the after effects of the 1980 grain embargo against the Soviet Union how they feel about losing their livelihood so that the country can express its outrage.

If, on the other hand, our policy goal is to bring about change in China's policies, to encourage greater respect for human dignity and a return to the policies of reform and openness to new ideas, then the costs or collateral damage of sanctions might seem more bearable. It is easy to talk about costs when someone else is going to have to bear them, but if there were any reasonable assurance that removal of MFN would lead to substantial policy change in China or the removal of the current regime, then the costs might well be considered worth it, even by the innocent victims of collateral damage: the farmers, consumers, retailers, importers, exporters, and the people of Hong Kong.

And so we come to the most fundamental question of all: would removal of MFN status work? Would it change the policies of the Chinese Government? The burden of proof ought to be on those who advocate inflicting all this pain on innocent victims, but I will suggest at least a few reasons why the removal of MFN will not bring about the kind of change we all seek in China. The first is history. We tried trade sanctions in 1950 and all they did was to isolate China and enable its government to justify even more repressive measures in the name of nationalism. It took thirty years before we could restore a normal relationship. The Soviet Union tried to bring China to its knees in 1959 by withdrawing credits and technicians, a far more powerful sanction than either our embargo of 1950 or the proposed removal of MFN since China was at that time already isolated from the rest of the world. China's response was to tighten its belt and unite its people in an anti-Soviet campaign that continued for over 25 years.

There is no convincing evidence that the MFN sanction would work, indeed it would probably make matters worse. Certainly it would play into the hands of the hard-liners. MFN does not prop up the anti-democratic, anti-reform central planners in Beijing. On the contrary MFN is what enables some vestige of a pro-reform, market-oriented sector in China to survive. Over 50% (or more than $6 billion) of China's exports to the United States are produced, not by the inefficient States enterprise under the choke-hold grip of the central planning bureaucracy, but by the very people in China who are resisting the Beijing central planners: the entrepreneurial village, private, and foreign joint ventures in South China. There were twenty million such enterprises in China in May 1989. The current leadership has shut down between two and four million of them since. What is the sense of our adopting a policy which would destroy that entire sector? The impoverishment of South China will not damage Li Peng and his colleagues; on the contrary it will remove the last major obstacle of their campaign to stamp out the reforms of the past ten years and restore what President Vaclav Havel called the totalitarian system which is "the source of nightmares."

. . . A faltering economy puts pressure on the regime to modify its policies to try to make the environment attractive enough so that foreign companies will resume bringing in badly needed capital and knowhow. But the regime faces a dilemma. As the ideologues of the current regime correctly point out, foreign trade and investment are subversive of a centrally-planned, Marxist-Leninist system. And so such a regime loses either way. If it will not reform, business dries up. If it resumes reform, the regime begins to move toward pluralism and reliance on market forces. . . .

Where will the inspiration for reform come from in China if we helped bring about the destruction of the private and semi-private sector in South China and the withdrawal of foreign investment enterprises from China? Again we would play into the hands of the hard-line ideological minority in the Chinese leadership who pay lip service to the slogans of reform and openness to the outside but who appear secretly to favor a return to a more easily managed isolation.

The weight of the evidence suggests clearly, then that revocation of China's most-favored-nation status would not change the Chinese government or its policies for the better; on the contrary it would cause greater suffering in China and in Hong Kong and probably delay any prospect for return to reform for many years. On what basis, then can we justify such a radical departure from free trade policy as the withdrawal of MFN?

I am aware that many in Congress, including some on this committee, favor attaching new human rights conditions to future MFN renewal as a compromise measure which would balance the desire to avoid the collateral damage I have outlined with the need to send a strong signal of disapproval to the Chinese leadership.

Attractive though it may be on its face, conditionality creates insurmountable problems in practice. The fundamental problem is that the Chinese leadership, by its intransigence over the past year, has already made clear that it is unlikely to make fundamental changes in internal policy to accommodate U.S. concerns. While they want economic development and trade with the West, the current leaders are even more concerned with their physical and political survival.

American companies understand this clearly. They would conclude that the Chinese would not meet any meaningful conditions that the U.S. government imposed and would make their business plans accordingly. Their Chinese partners would also likely begin making preparations for the time MFN is taken away by, among other things, dumping massive amounts of product in the U.S. market.

The economic damage to China, to Hong Kong, and to the American economy would thus be almost as great with conditional MFN as with outright withdrawal. The only difference is that American companies would have a year's notice to plan their withdrawal from the China market.

The issue would be much more difficult if the current Chinese leadership appeared capable of retaining power far into the future. Most analysts agree this is unlikely. The leadership is old and out of touch with the world and its own people. We need to look beyond this regime, keeping up the pressure for change but positioning ourselves to work effectively with a new, more flexible and reform-minded government when it emerges. This means preserving the structures which have been built up over the past ten years since the establishment of diplomatic relations and maintaining the most extensive private contacts (cultural, educational and commercial) which a xenophobic Chinese regime will permit. This is the basis on which I conclude that American interests are best served by maintaining MFN status for China without new conditions.

# NOTES

Senate Committee on Finance, "Extending Most-Favored-Nation Status for China," 101st Congress, 2nd sess., June 20, 1990. Testimony by Max Baucus, Morton Bahr, Holly J. Burkhalter, and Roger G. Sullivan.

Max Baucus, senator (D-MT); Morton Bahr, president of Communications Workers of America, AFL-CIO; Holly J. Burkhalter, Washington director of Human Rights Watch; Roger G. Sullivan, president of the United States–China Business Council

# – PART IV –

# TRYING A NEW CHINA STRATEGY (1993–1995)

Jim Berry contrasts President Clinton's apparently weak human rights policy with President Theodore Roosevelt's foreign policy, from which the phrase "speak softly and carry a big stick" became popular. Jim Berry © NEA. Reprinted by permission.

# - 11 -

# MFN: To De-Link or Not De-Link?

*During the 1992 election campaign, Democratic presidential candidate Bill Clinton made the promotion of democratization an organizing principle of his foreign policy. He chastised President Bush for being prone to "coddle dictators from Baghdad to Beijing" and said that if elected, he would condition extension of China's most-favored-nation (MFN) status on progress in human rights, market access, and proliferation. In his first two years in office, President Clinton implemented and then abandoned this policy, drawing praise and criticism at both junctures.*

## Statement on Most-Favored-Nation
## Trade Status for China

### William J. Clinton

. . . Today, Members of Congress have joined me to announce a new chapter in United States policy toward China.

China occupies an important place in our Nation's foreign policy. It is the world's most populous state, its fastest growing major economy, and a permanent member of the United Nations Security Council. Its future will do much to shape the future of Asia, our security and trade relations in the Pacific, and a host of global issues from the environment to weapons proliferation. In short, our relationship with China is of very great importance.

Unfortunately, over the past 4 years our Nation spoke with a divided voice when it came to China. Americans were outraged by the killing of prodemocracy demonstrators at Tiananmen Square in June of 1989. Congress was determined to have our Nation's stance toward China reflect our outrage. Yet twice after Congress voted to place conditions on our favorable trade rules toward

China, so-called most-favored-nation status, those conditions were vetoed. The annual battles between Congress and the Executive divided our foreign policy and weakened our approach over China.

It is time that a unified American policy recognize both the value of China and the values of America. Starting today, the United States will speak with one voice on China policy. We no longer have an executive branch policy and congressional policy. We have an American policy.

I am happy to have with me today key congressional leaders on this issue. I am also honored to be joined by representatives of the business community and several distinguished Chinese student leaders. Their presence here is a tangible symbol of the unity of our purpose. I particularly want to recognize Senate Majority Leader George Mitchell of Maine and Congresswoman Nancy Pelosi of California. Their tireless dedication to the cause of freedom in China has given voice to our collective concerns. I intend to continue working closely with Congress as we pursue our China policy.

We are here today because the American people continue to harbor profound concerns about a range of practices by China's Communist leaders. We are concerned that many activists and prodemocracy leaders, including some from Tiananmen Square, continue to languish behind prison bars in China for no crime other than exercising their consciences. We are concerned about international access to their prisons. And we are concerned by the Dalai Lama's reports of Chinese abuses against the people and culture of Tibet.

We must also address China's role in the proliferation of dangerous weapons. The Gulf war proved the danger of irresponsible sales of technologies related to weapons of mass destruction. While the world is newly determined to address the danger of such missiles, we have reason to worry that China continues to sell them.

Finally, we have concerns about our terms of trade with China. China runs an $18 billion trade surplus with the U.S., second only to Japan. In the face of this deficit, China continues practices that block American goods.

I have said before that we do not want to isolate China, given its growing importance in the global community. China today is a nation of nearly 1.2 billion people, home to 1 of every 5 people in the world. By sheer size alone, China has an important impact on the world's economy, environment, and politics. The future of China and Hong Kong is of great importance to the region and the people of America.

We take some encouragement from the economic reforms in China, reforms that by some measures place China's economy as the third largest in the world, after the United States and Japan. China's coastal provinces are an engine for reform throughout the country. The residents of Shanghai and Guangzhou are far more motivated by markets than by Marx or Mao.

We are hopeful that China's process of development and economic reform will be accompanied by greater political freedom. In some ways, this process has begun. An emerging Chinese middle class points the antennae of new televisions toward Hong Kong to pick up broadcasts of CNN. Cellular phones and fax machines carry implicit notions of freer communications. Hong Kong itself is a catalyst of democratic values, and we strongly support Governor Patten's efforts to broaden democratic rights.

The question we face today is how best to cultivate these hopeful seeds of change in China while expressing our clear disapproval of its repressive policies.

The core of this policy will be a resolute insistence upon significant progress on human rights in China. To implement this policy, I am signing today an Executive order that will have the effect of extending most-favored-nation status for China for 12 months. Whether I extend MFN next year, however, will depend upon whether China makes significant progress in improving its human right record.

The order lays out particular areas I will examine, including respect for the Universal Declaration of Human Rights and the release of citizens imprisoned for the nonviolent expression of their political beliefs, including activists imprisoned in connection with Tiananmen Square. The order includes China's protection of Tibet's religious and cultural heritage and compliance with the bilateral U.S.–China agreement on prison labor.

In addition, we will use existing statutes to address our concerns in the areas of trade and arms control.

The order I am issuing today directs the Secretary of State and other administration officials to pursue resolutely all legislative and executive actions to ensure China abides by international standards. I intend to put the full weight of the Executive behind this order. I know I have Congress's support.

Let me give you an example. The administration is now examining reports that China has shipped M–11 ballistic missiles to Pakistan. If true, such action would violate China's commitment to observe the guidelines and parameters of the Missile Technology Control Regime. Existing U.S. law provides for strict sanctions against nations that violate these guidelines. We have made our concerns on the M–11 issue known to the Chinese on numerous occasions. They understand the serious consequences of missile transfers under U.S. sanctions law. If we determine that China has in fact transferred M–11 missiles or related equipment in violation of its commitments, my administration will not hesitate to act.

My administration is committed to supporting peaceful democratic and promarket reform. I believe we will yet see these principles prevail in China. For in the past few years, we have witnessed a pivotal point in history as other Communist regimes across the map have ceded to the power of democracy and markets.

We are prepared to build a more cooperative relationship with China and wish to work with China as an active member of the international community. Through some of its actions, China has demonstrated that it wants to be a member of that community. Membership has its privileges, but also its obligations. We expect China to meet basic international standards in its treatment of its people, it sales of dangerous arms, and its foreign trade.

With one voice, the United States Government today has outlined these expectations.

## NOTES

William J. Clinton, "Statement on Most-Favored-Nation Trade Status for China," May 28, 1993, *Weekly Compilation of Presidential Documents,* Vol. 29, No. 21, pp. 981–982.

William J. Clinton, 42nd president of the United States (1993–2001)

# Chinese Checkers

## *Editors of* The Nation

The China card keeps coming up in the permanent pokergame of diplomacy, and once again an American administration is wildly misplaying it. In the lastest folly of China policy, the Clinton government seeks to apply a noble but narrow—and inherently hypocritical—standard of democratic behavior on Beijing before normal trade rights are renewed in June. Secretary of State Christopher's approach to the Chinese leaders has been hectoring, and naturally Beijing is resistant. Because the diplomatic interchanges are conducted on a public stage and played to the global media, posturing takes precedence over substantive bargaining. Clinton & Co. are perilously close to losing all their cards without accomplishing any of their objectives.

Human rights make a problematic foundation for the construction of foreign policy. However virtuous the effort, there are too many differences of definition, opportunities for dishonesty and occasions for self-delusion. It was only a few years ago that American governments even thought to make the attempt. Jimmy Carter elevated human rights to a prominent place in the conduct of international relations, but from the start his theory was contradicted by the practices of his National Security Adviser, Zbigniew Brzezinski, who insisted on making exceptions. Iran, Indonesia, South Korea and the other "Brzezinski countries"—those subimperial outposts assigned the task of insuring stability in their regions—were allowed to repress their citizens

"I TOLD THEM CANDIDLY HOW WE FELT ABOUT THEIR HUMAN RIGHTS RECORD"

**Secretary of State Warren Christopher returned from a March 1994 trip to China without any concessions from the Chinese government on human rights, which would have made it politically easier for President Clinton to end conditioning of MFN. Copyright 1994 by Herblock in *The Washington Post*.**

at will, while foreign governments more at odds with the United States were penalized.

The use of human rights as just another card in the power play of foreign policy was perfected in the Reagan/Bush years. Democracy was defined as militant anticommunisim, allowing Reagan to wage counterrevolutionary wars around the world. Struggles for economic equality and social justice were not considered worthy of the Reagan crusade.

Clinton had an opportunity to extend what Carter had tentatively begun, but in his discussion of foreign policy he preferred to concentrate on the uses of diplomacy to promote American economic "competitiveness" rather than human rights. China policy thus presented a conspicuous contradiction. On the one hand, American economic interests clearly required close and cordial relations with Beijing, to facilitate the explosive expansion of U.S. corporate investment and the growing amount of trade, now estimated at $40 billion annually. On the other hand, American public opinion of China had not recovered from the outrage of Tiananmen Square, and a variety of Clinton's critics—from the Republican right (still harboring an ancient enmity to "Red China") to the liberal/left human rights community—demanded that the Administration keep up the pressure on Beijing.

The result has been the somewhat ham-handed U.S. diplomatic demarche culminating in Christopher's humiliating visit to China, during which Beijing heatedly rejected American demands for better treatment of dissidents. By June 4, Clinton will have to certify that China has made significant progress on the rights front, or else revoke its most-favored-nation status. And because the latter outcome is unacceptable to aggressive U.S. businesses operating in China, Clinton will probably give in to Beijing, with some rhetorical salutes to disguise the defeat.

Underlying the particular trade problem with China is the fact that the United States—as the most powerful advocate of democratic diplomacy in the world—continues to apply democratic demands selectively. Clinton has no problem doing business with the most dreadful regimes if their crimes are not exposed by the press or if American opinion has not been mobilized against them. Moreover, the diplomatic strategy is undermined when whole categories of human rights are deliberately left off the negotiating table. The most egregious violations in China involve economic and social injustice. Americans are enraged when students seeking freedom of expression are repressed, but no one worries much about the hundreds of millions of Chinese workers who are locked into a system of low wages and bad working conditions unalleviated by even the possibility of popular organization for change. Indeed, U.S. business interests flourish under such a system—which is why the diplomacy of human rights makes such little progress after all.

### NOTE

Editorial, "Chinese Checkers," *The Nation,* April 4, 1994, pp. 435–436. Reprinted with permission from the April 4, 1994 issue of *The Nation*.

# How to Boost China's Free Market—and Punish the State

## Fang Lizhi and Zhao Haiching

The people of China have everything at stake in President Clinton's decision whether to renew the trade benefits that Beijing enjoys.

China's record on human rights remains dismal. By its recent crackdowns on political and religious dissidents, it has clearly indicated that it has no intention of making significant progress in human rights—the very progress the President, in his 1993 executive order, made the basis for renewing tariff privileges in the American market.

Just this week, the authorities rearrested Wei Jingsheng, the outspoken critic of the Government and a resolute advocate of democracy and human rights. His "crimes" were meeting with foreign journalists and with John Shattuck, the State Department's No. 1 rights official, and publishing articles espousing his views.

The President and Congress need not face the stark choice of total revocation of trade benefits or total abandonment of principle. A more thoughtful solution would be wise.

Mr. Clinton should revoke most-favored-nation status for products made or sold by Government-controlled enterprises, thereby pressing the regime for change. But he should not cancel them for the private sector, which needs incentives to grow.

This approach was debated and agreed upon last year by virtually all of the recognized leaders of the China democracy movement active in the U.S. It is supported by many, if not all, of our colleagues in China.

If Mr. Clinton bends to pressure from Beijing and its friends in the U.S. business community who are concerned with profits, not lives, he will give the hard-liners a green light to suppress human rights and democratic aspirations. And the hard-liners will have proved that the Administration lacks the political will to confront them further on this issue. This would set back the cause of human rights in China for years, unleash a new wave of repression and fear, and encourage the apparatchiks to stare down the U.S. on many critical issues.

The President gave the human rights movement hope with his seven-point rights agenda in the May 1993 executive order. It said that without progress by the Chinese Government, he might cancel its tariff benefits at the end of this May. He cannot now forsake the movement. Emboldened by his linking human rights with trade, the movement mustered the courage to again challenge the regime on political reform. The result? Arrests and detentions of dozens of activists for peacefully expressing themselves.

Beijing desperately needs the $30 billion trade surplus it is expected to have with America this year. If the regime believed that it would lose billions of dollars, it could have easily met the conditions that Mr. Clinton set last year, in bipartisan consultations with Congressional leaders. But the well-financed American campaign against this policy, coupled with voices in the Administration urging appeasement convinced the hard-liners that eventually the U.S. would blink.

Secretary of State Warren Christopher's recent trip to Beijing was of great importance because he demonstrated a determined effort to uphold the Clinton policy—for which he received little thanks at home—and to overcome the misperception in Beijing circles that Washington had gone soft on the rights issue.

Beware. Our own experience with the regime convinces us that before the end of May, a cynical Beijing will make limited cosmetic gestures and send a trade delegation to buy millions of dollars in U.S. products in order to keep its tariff benefits.

Some Administration officials argue that any gestures, no matter how insignificant, should be considered important. If the President heeded them, he would undermine the Administration's credibility worldwide, this would cause irreparable harm to democracy and freedom in China.

After 10 years of reform, China's economy is about half centrally planned and half free-market. The emerging market economy is heartening, even if China's idea of a free market does not mirror Western ideas of one.

For those interested in a prosperous, free China, there are ample grounds for renewing trade benefits for products of China's private-enterprise economy and for products of joint ventures with corporations in the U.S., Hong Kong, Taiwan and elsewhere.

Such benefits, after all, have long been granted to free-market economies. For those with centrally planned economies, the Jackson-Vanik amendment makes freedom of emigration a requirement for this privilege.

There is no need for an elaborate program to determine what is and is not a state enterprise. The Customs Service need not be burdened, because categories of products mainly produced by the state can be easily identified and correct tariffs imposed. If some products got through, little harm would be done: the point would be to send a message about how much America values freedom in China.

Without the annual review of most-favored-nation status, the Chinese Government's behavior in the past four years would have been far worse. Neither the annual review nor the link between rights and trade should be abandoned.

## NOTES

Fang Lizhi and Zhao Haiching, "How to Boost China's Free Market—and Punish the State," *New York Times,* April 7, 1994, p. 27.

Fang Lizhi, a leading Chinese astrophysicist and dissident, remained in the U.S. embassy for several months following the June 4 incident, then moved to the United States and continued his scientific work at the University of Arizona; Zhao Haiching, president of the National Council on Chinese Affairs

# The President's News Conference

## *William J. Clinton*

Good afternoon. Today I would like to announce a series of important decisions regarding United States policy toward China.

Our relationship with China is important to all Americans. We have significant interests in what happens there and what happens between us. China has an atomic arsenal and a vote and a veto in the U.N. Security Council. It is a major factor in Asian and global security. We share important interests, such as in a nuclear-free Korean Peninsula and in sustaining the global environment. China is also the world's fastest growing economy. Over $8 billion of United States exports to China last year supported over 150,000 American jobs.

I have received Secretary Christopher's letter recommending—as required by last year's Executive order, reporting to me the conditions in that Executive order. He has reached a conclusion with which I agree, that the Chinese did not achieve overall significant progress in all the areas outlined in the Executive order relating to human rights, even though clearly there was progress made in important areas including the resolution of all emigration cases, the establishment of a memorandum of understanding with regard to how prison labor issues would be resolved, the adherence to the Universal Declaration of Human Rights, and other issues. Nevertheless, serious human rights abuses continue in China, including the arrest and detention of those who peacefully voice their opinions and the repression of Tibet's religious and cultural traditions.

The question for us now is, given the fact that there has been some progress but that not all the requirements of the Executive order were met, how can we best advance the cause of human rights and the other profound interests the United States has in our relationship with China?

I have decided that the United States should renew most-favored-nation trading status toward China. This decision, I believe, offers us the best opportunity to lay the basis for long-term sustainable progress in human rights and for the advancement of our other interests with China. Extending MFN will avoid isolating China and instead will permit us to engage the Chinese with not only economic contacts but with cultural, educational, and other contacts and with a continuing aggressive effort in human rights, an approach that I believe will make it more likely that China will play a responsible role, both at home and abroad.

I am moving, therefore, to delink human rights from the annual extension of most-favored-nation trading status for China. That linkage has been constructive during the past year. But I believe, based on our aggressive contacts with the Chinese in the past several months, that we have reached the end of the usefulness of that policy and it is time to take a new path toward the achievement of our constant objectives. We need to place our relationship into a larger and more productive framework.

In view of the continuing human rights abuses, I am extending the sanctions imposed by the United States as a result of the events in Tiananmen Square, and I am also banning the import of munitions, principally guns and ammunition from China. I am also pursuing a new and vigorous American program to support those in China working to advance the cause of human rights and democracy. This program will include increased broadcast for Radio Free Asia and the Voice of America, increased support for nongovernmental organizations working on human rights in China, and the development with American business leaders of a voluntary set of principles for business activity in China.

I don't want to be misunderstood about this: China continues to commit very serious human rights abuses. Even as we engage the Chinese on military, political, and economic issues, we intend to stay engaged with those in China who suffer from human rights abuses. The United States must remain a champion of their liberties.

I believe the question, therefore, is not whether we continue to support human rights in China but how we can best support human rights in China and advance our other very significant issues and interests. I believe we can do it by engaging the Chinese. I believe the course I have chosen gives us the best chance of success on all fronts. We will have more contacts. We will have more trade. We will have more international cooperation. We will have more intense and constant dialogue on human rights issues. We will have that in an atmosphere which gives us the chance to see China evolve as a responsible power, ever growing not only economically but growing in political maturity so that human rights can be observed.

To those who argue that in view of China's human rights abuses we should revoke MFN status, let me ask you the same question that I have asked myself over and over these last few weeks, as I have studied this issue and consulted people of both parties who have had experience with China over many decades: Will we do more to advance the cause of human rights if China is isolated or if our nations are engaged in a growing web of political and economic cooperation and contacts? I am persuaded that the best path for advancing freedom in China is for the United States to intensify and broaden its engagement with that nation.

I think we have to see our relations with China within the broader context of our policies in the Asian-Pacific region, a region that, after all, includes our own Nation. This week, we've seen encouraging developments, progress on resolving trade frictions with the Japanese and possible progress towards stopping North Korea's nuclear program. I am determined to see that we maintain an active role in this region in both its dynamic economic growth and in its security.

In three decades and three wars during this century, Americans have fought and died in the Asian-Pacific region to advance our ideals and our security. Our destiny demands that we continue to play an active role in this region. The actions I have taken today to advance our security, to advance our prosperity, to advance our ideals I believe are the important and appropriate ones. I believe, in other words, this is in the strategic, economic, and political interests of both the United States and China, and I am confident that over the long run this decision will prove to be the correct one. . . .

## NOTES

William J. Clinton, "The President's News Conference," May 26, 1994, *Weekly Compilation of Presidential Documents,* Vol. 30, No. 21, pp. 1166–1171.

William J. Clinton, 42nd president of the United States (1993–2001)

# MFN for Red China: A Tragic Mistake

### Senate floor remarks by Jesse Helms

Mr. President, President Clinton's decision to renew most-favored-nation trading status for Communist China is another tragic chapter in the President's foreign policy failures. Despite Red China's having deliberately flaunted the conditions laid out by Mr. Clinton himself for MFN renewal—through the May 1993 Executive order—the President is discarding what he once proclaimed to be steadfast principles. And he is doing it in a shameful kowtow to China's Communist emperors.

This latest foreign policy disaster should be no surprise. From the start, Mr. Clinton's China policy has been fraught with contradiction. As a candidate, Mr. Clinton viciously attacked George Bush for "coddling the dictators in Beijing" and publicly endorsed human rights conditionality for MFN. However, once in office, President Clinton preferred Mr. Bush's soft approach—and tried to adopt it in a very flawed way. Bill Clinton's attempt to reconcile his opposing positions has resulted in the worst possible outcome, today's ineffective policy of appeasement masquerading behind a human rights façade.

The basis of my criticism of Mr. Clinton is not partisan politics. I consistently and publicly expressed my disdain for President Bush's being soft on China. I voted to override the Bush veto of legislation I cosponsored—and Congress passed—conditioning China's MFN.

I therefore welcomed President Clinton's 1992 get-tough campaign rhetoric. It was a policy change long overdue. While I had hoped that nonproliferation and fair trade conditions also would be mandatory requirements for China's MFN renewal, I nonetheless supported President Clinton's Executive order which linked human rights progress to MFN as an encouraging first step in the right direction.

But, Mr. President, it is now clear that the Executive order turned out to be nothing but a bluff—and an amateurish one at that. By elevating human rights through this defective plan to the primary MFN renewal conditions, all other concerns, including the equally important nonproliferation and unfair trade problems, have been cast aside receiving no attention at all. Assessing correctly from the beginning that despite all its human rights bluster the Clinton administration would not revoke MFN, China has balked at improving human rights and has been let off the hook on every other issue thanks to the administration itself.

Mr. President, instead of recognizing this policy to be a failure, and changing course, the Clinton administration has turned to appeasement in a desperate attempt to get something—anything—from China. Knowing the administration needs some human rights gesture to justify MFN renewal, the Chinese have been able to extort—and get—whatever they want. The administration has succumbed almost daily to this blackmail. Oh, how the Chinese Communists must enjoy seeing the United States beg and grovel. How they must enjoy yanking the U.S. chain. It is humiliating.

Recognizing that the United States accounts for 40 percent of China's exports—96 percent of which are covered by preferential MFN tariffs—and that the United States provides Beijing with its only significant hard currency, MFN is a reward that the United States bestows upon China, not the other way around. How the Chinese must be relishing the irony of it all.

Mr. President, among some of the blatant examples of appeasement, the administration has:

- Weakened nonproliferation sanctions despite China's continued nuclear testing and lack of positive action on other nonproliferation concerns;
- Failed to impose any penalties for China's gross violation of textile quotas;
- Failed to even cite—let alone penalize—China for the piracy of intellectual property rights;
- Failed to prosecute Chinese caught engaging in industrial espionage in the United States;

- Upgraded military relations and offered Chinese military experts unprecedented access to America's most sensitive defense laboratories despite China's continued, aggressive military modernization and continued sale of weapons to brutal regimes like those in Burma and Iran;
- Approved the transfer of new super computers and sensitive satellite launch technology that could be used to improve Red China's offensive, strategic nuclear missiles arsenal despite China's refusal to join the current nuclear testing moratorium or adhere to missile technology controls;
- Sanctioned Taiwan—but not mainland China—for inadequate endangered species convention enforcement;
- Insulted the democratically elected President of America's long-time friend and ally on Taiwan at the behest of the Communist Chinese ambassador in Washington;
- And insulted the U.S. Congress—the elected representatives of the American people—in an effort to placate Beijing's dictators.

What has all of this gotten the United States? Nothing. Even on human rights, the one issue on which the Clinton administration staked its entire policy, the result is failure. . . .

Yet, despite the obvious lack of significant, overall progress as called for in the President's own executive order, China's MFN is being renewed. . . .

The ramifications of this debacle go way beyond the Great Wall. Why should North Korea take seriously our threats of sanctions should they continue to refuse inspections of their nuclear facilities? It's no wonder two-bit generals in Haiti laugh at us. American credibility is being lost and I fear that the cost President Clinton will incur to regain respect is the unnecessary loss of American lives in some ill-defined military (mis)-adventure somewhere.

It is time for President Clinton to learn from mistakes and craft a more effective policy that recognizes China as the tough, Communist competitor that it is. Instead of allowing the Chinese ambassador in Washington to dictate our China policy, Foggy Bottom ought to stand up and fight for American interests. No relationship is too sensitive or fragile to be a fair relationship.

Truly successful Sino-American relations must be based on respect. Mr. President, how can the United States effectively pressure the Chinese to address satisfactorily unfair trade, nonproliferation and human rights concerns if we succumb repeatedly to Chinese blackmail and make hollow threats, like MFN revocation, for which we have no intention of carrying out? China will only start treating American interests with respect when this administration begins to act in ways that command respect. Renewing MFN under today's hypocritical standard is a poor way to start commanding respect.

# NOTES

Jesse Helms, "MFN for Red China: A Tragic Mistake," remarks on the Senate floor, June 15, 1994.

Jesse Helms, senator (R-NC)

# China's Bid for the 2000 Olympics

*In 1993, Beijing was one of five finalists competing for the right to host the 2000 summer Olympics (the other cities were Sydney, the eventual winner; Manchester; Istanbul; and Berlin). The U.S. House of Representatives passed a resolution in July urging the International Olympic Committee (IOC) to deny Beijing's bid when the IOC met to vote in late September. In the final round of voting, Sydney beat out Beijing 45 to 43. Although the congressional resolution was nonbinding and only one of the IOC's 88 voting members was from the United States, many in China blamed the United States for Beijing's loss.*

## Don't Give Olympics to China

### Charles Graybow

With China facing pressure from the Clinton administration to make progress in basic human rights in order to retain its trade benefits, and currently in the thick of a bidding war for the 2000 Summer Olympic Games, expect Beijing to continue making high profile—although largely cosmetic—goodwill gestures.

In the past several months, the Chinese government has released six dissidents who were jailed for participating in the 1989 Tiananmen Square and 1979 Democracy Wall movements, and has eased restrictions on foreign journalists. Nevertheless, President Clinton recently decided against automatically extending China's most favored nation (MFN) trade status in 1994, instead conditioning renewal next year to more substantive advances on rights issues. But despite these continuing concerns over its dismal record, Beijing is still a co-favorite to win the right to host the 2000 Games when the International Olympic Committee (IOC) votes on a site in September.

China clearly does not deserve the honor.

While at first glance the Olympics bid may appear to be separate from the weightier trade issues, in fact the Chinese leadership views both MFN renewal and securing the Games as important and complemetary steps in maintaining its power. At home, the government needs the benefits of increased trade as it moves to open up the economy and improve living standards in the hope of warding off demands for democracy. Meanwhile, it desperately seeks to land the Games as a way to boost an international image tattered by relentless human rights violations.

Coming at the onset of the millennium, the 2000 Olympics have taken on heightened symbolism. Many favor awarding the Games to China, which holds one-fifth of the world's population and has one of the fastest expanding economies, in recognition of the increasing geopolitical impact developing nations will have in the next century.

In sharp contrast to this idealistic symbolism, however, is the reality of the Chinese government's brutality. It goes far beyond the much-publicized 1989 Tiananmen Square killings, to the daily rights abuses that continue in China and especially in Tibet, which has been forcibly and illegally occupied by China for 44 years. These abuses include the jailing and torture of dissidents, the suppression of religion, and the use of prison labor in state factories.

Beijing's supporters say politics should not be mixed with sports, and that in any case, giving the Olympics to China would engage the country's leaders rather than isolate them.

The reasoning on both counts is flawed. If Beijing lands the Games, the Chinese government would use this victory as "proof" that it had been granted legitimacy by the international community. Even as it crushes internal dissent, the regime would sell itself as a model for how the Third World should deal with human rights issues. One only has to consider the way Hitler tried to use the 1936 Berlin Olympics to promote the idea of Aryan supremacy to realize the potential for turning the Games into a political spectacle.

To argue that human rights considerations only serve to "politicize" sports is a smoke screen. Moral and ethical concerns apply to sports as much as to any other human activity.

As to the second charge, that constructive engagement will lead to democratic reforms, the burden should instead be on China's rulers to first take concrete steps toward granting their citizens basic rights. Although Chinese paramount leader Deng Xiaoping now tells his people that "To get rich is a glorious thing" and has endorsed free-market ideas, there have been no accompanying political or human rights reforms.

The current substantial state-run lobbying effort underscores the importance the Chinese government attaches to landing the Games. In March, as Beijing lavishly hosted IOC delegates, armies of children cleaned the streets, the police presence was higher than usual, and vehicle use was curbed to reduce pollution and congestion.

The government also dredged up Lei Feng, the mythical army hero whose name is invariably invoked to rally the people to sacrifice for one cause or another, to inspire citizens to mobilize to land the Games. But as one Beijing-based diplomat candidly told the *Far Eastern Economic Review*, "Don't view the mass mobilization as just a means of getting the Olympics. Rather, regard the Olympics as a pretext for the mobilization." The government would then reap this nationalistic outpouring for its own political ends.

Anita DeFrantz is the lone IOC delegate from the United States. She owes Beijing a fair hearing, but one that would include a thorough consideration of human rights issues. Moreover, the entire IOC must recognize that granting Beijing the honor of hosting the Games would amount to an undeserved endorsement of China's aging autocrats, and worse, signal its citizens that their plight does not matter.

## NOTES

Charles Graybow, "Don't Give Olympics to China," *The Plain Dealer* (Cleveland, Ohio), June 21, 1993, p. 5B. Reprinted by permission from Charles Graybow.

Charles Graybow, Freedom House

# Beijing Deserves the 2000 Olympics

## Jonathan Kolatch

In September, the 94 members of the International Olympic Committee will meet in Monte Carlo to decide which of six cities will host the first Olympic Games of the next century. Beijing and Sydney are the leading candidates.

Oblivious to the historic wave of pragmatism that has swept over China since the 1989 crackdown as well as to the wishes of ordinary Chinese, Sens. Bill Bradley and Dennis DeConcini and Rep. Tom Lantos, in parallel Senate and House resolutions, are branding Beijing unsuitable as host of the Olympic Games on human rights rounds. In legislating their Olympic opposition to Beijing, the sponsors interweave dubious fact with blatant distortion.

In testimony before the Senate Commerce Committee debating his anti-Beijing bill, Bradley made the preposterous assertion that 1 million Chinese were jailed at the time of the 1990 Asian Games in Beijing. While most-favored-nation status encourages "positive developments" in China, Bradley

continued, hosting the Olympic Games curiously would not. DeConcini somehow found encouragement in the deteriorating economic and civil order in the
former Soviet states, but only bleakness in prospering China.

At no point during the skewed hearing did backers of the bill explore how
the Olympics might hasten the pace of change in China. Nor was one expert
witness called who professed any knowledge of 1993 China.

In fact, rather than rewarding despots and dictators, a vote for Beijing in
2000 will go far toward guaranteeing a continuing orderly transition from
authoritarianism to a more open China.

As a just-issued IOC report confirms, China's 2000 Olympics bid is "realistic and solid." To hold the 1990 Asian Games, Beijing built or extensively ren-
ovated 79 stadiums, gymnasiums and practice sites, in addition to constructing
extensive support facilities. In all, the Chinese spent more than $1 billion on
the Beijing Asian Games with the primary purpose of showing the world that
China is qualified to conduct the Olympics. For China, hosting the 2000
Olympics has been a national priority since 1983.

The Chinese, in their relentless Olympic-bid propaganda, claim that the
Beijing Asian Games were "a complete success." That begs for qualification. All
scheduled sporting events went off without a hitch, the technical systems
worked, media buses faithfully met all travel schedules—even with no passen-
gers to transport.

Where the Beijing Asian Games failed was in their professed aim to "raise the
spirit of the Chinese people." Starting a year before the event, the people of
Beijing were force-fed three massive enthusiasm parades, and workers nation-
wide were coerced in varying degrees into underwriting the cost of the games.
In pursuit of "exceptional order," non-Beijingers without special permits were
banned from Beijing during the games, tickets to matches were withheld from
public sale, and the stands were packed instead with orchestrated "cheerers."
Beijing was an antiseptic city during the Asian Games, without popular support.

But the Beijing of 1993 is not the Beijing of 1990. The 1989 Tiananmen
uprising, still raised here like the hiccups whenever the subject of China comes
up, is a moribund issue in China. Stimulated by the chaotic disintegration of the
Communist world, Chinese opted for order and unprecedented prosperity.

The Chinese lack freedom of expression and free elections and continue to
have limited job choice. But they enjoy freedom to acquire a passport and
travel abroad, freedom to go into private business and get rich or go bankrupt,
access to global information through proliferating satellite television, and
widely available telephones and faxes with which to share their private thoughts
uncensored. China is a country headed toward the next century, and most
Chinese appreciate this.

On a recent month-long trip to six Chinese cities, I queried dozens of people
of all strata, including many who had been adamantly opposed to the Beijing

Asian Games, about their feelings toward the 2000 Olympics. The most negative responses elicited were isolated expressions of apathy. The Chinese government, when it suits its needs, lies with conviction. But its claim that the Chinese people overwhelmingly support the 2000 Olympic Games reflects reality.

The Chinese people back the games because they offer only benefits for Beijing and China. Whether or not the $1 billion expended on the Beijing Asian Games was a wise investment, it has already underwritten much of the cost of the 2000 Olympics. China projects a surplus of $120 million for the 2000 Olympics. Richard Carrion, a banker and IOC member from Puerto Rico, who visited Beijing in March as a member of an IOC Enquiry Commission, considers Beijing's arithmetic conservative and sound.

The seven-year buildup to the 2000 Olympics will ensure a period of extended growth in a country that by the year 2000 will be on the road to having the world's largest economy. The influx of visitors will bring a continuing flow of outside influences that the Communist leadership has given up trying to filter. As the examples of South Korea, Singapore and Taiwan teach, a prosperous, more cosmopolitan China will inevitably induce a politically more moderate, more democratic China.

For those concerned about mainland intentions when Hong Kong reverts to China in 1997, the 2000 Olympics would provide an additional three-year buffer. It would be a foolish Chinese government that would risk the goodwill and financial benefits of the Olympic Games (as Moscow did in 1980 over Afghanistan) by cracking the whip in Hong Kong.

Finally, China deserves the Olympics because Asia deserves the Olympics. Europe has hosted the Summer Olympic Games 15 times, the Americas five. Asia, with 60 percent of the world's population, has hosted the games only twice. Beijing is Asia's overwhelming choice for the Olympic Games.

There are those in Congress who insist upon seeing China's bid to host the 2000 Olympics as a rusty lever with which to manipulate China's march forward according to their own priorities. Most Chinese, they should know, see the 2000 Olympics as a golden opportunity. They fail to understand why the U.S. Congress seeks to deny it to them.

## NOTES

Jonathan Kolatch, "Beijing Deserves the 2000 Olympics," *Washington Post,* July 30, 1993, p. A21. Reprinted by permission from Jonathan Kolatch.

Jonathan Kolatch, independent writer; author of *Is the Moon in China Just as Round? Sporting Life and Sundry Scenes* (Jonathan David Publishers, 1992)

- 13 -

# Dealing with a Stronger China

*In the 1990s, American experts and officials started to more seriously consider the ramifications of a stronger China for U.S. interests. This was precipitated by the collapse of the Soviet Union and economic trends in China and elsewhere. In 1992 and 1993, several sources, among them the International Monetary Fund, estimated that China had the world's second or third largest economy in terms of purchasing power parity. In addition, after three years of retrenchment, China's economy in 1992 resumed its fast rate of growth, leaving some to project that the size of China's economy would surpass that of the United States early in the first decade of the next century. Coupled with relatively slower growth in the United States and a recession in Japan, such estimates were welcomed by the business community, while those who considered the potential security implications were more concerned.*

## A Strong China: Is the United States Ready?

### Thomas L. McNaugher

East Asians don't know quite what to make of China these days. Their expanding involvement in China's rapidly growing economy is making them rich. But it is also helping to make China strong. Leaders in Beijing are already claiming broader areas and offshore islands with a new assertiveness and buying weapons from Russia capable of backing those claims with force. As one Singaporean diplomat told American researcher David Hitchcock last year, "All of Southeast Asia is scared" by the growth of China's power.

Americans too seem to be worrying more about China. Beside longstanding concern about China's arms sales to "backlash" states and its poor human rights record now stand visions of China as an "awakening dragon" preparing to assert its dominance in East Asia. Samuel Huntington writes of a Sino-centric

Confucian civilization headed for conflict with the West—a threatening China that must be contained much as the Soviet Union was during the Cold War.

How seriously should we take the notion of a "threat" from China? Alarmists would seem to be exaggerating. China's military is huge but also vastly undeveloped doctrinally and technologically. That will change if present trends continue, but recent double-digit economic growth, while striking, is probably unsustainable. At least as plausible as an "awakening dragon" is a China plagued by economic decentralization and political decay and thus unable to exploit its enormous power potential. Finally, since 1978 China's leaders have sought a stable and friendly international environment to encourage economic growth. They have solved their once-rancorous border dispute with Russia and shelved their territorial disputes with India. Far from being a threat, today's China would seem to confirm liberal claims that economic growth and interdependence encourage cooperation and conflict resolution.

Yet China's growth is indeed worth worrying about, not because it will surely continue, nor because a strong China will seek to dominate its neighbors, but because if China continues to grow it will confront the world with a change in power relationships of unprecedented size, ultimately involving the emergence of a power capable of overshadowing Japan, perhaps even the United States. In the past, large power transitions have been marked by instability and conflict. China's ties to the global economy may soften this one. But if not, China's growth is likely to threaten regional stability—a vital U.S. interest—regardless of China's intent.

China's growth is already tweaking insecurities around East Asia. And while East Asians will try to cooperate in balancing and containing China's power, lingering suspicions and an underdeveloped regional security structure obstruct such alliances. Although China is years away from posing a serious direct military threat to the United States (assuming it wants to), the destabilizing effects of its growth could easily find their way to the U.S. doorstep. . . .

## THE UNITED STATES AND A STRONG CHINA

The possibility that the United States will be pulled into regional disputes involving China suggests a compelling need to collect the fragments of U.S. China policy—the concern for trade one day, arms transfers the next, help with North Korea the next—into a more coherent whole. The difficulty of predicting China's future is no excuse for ignoring the implications of China's continued growth.

The challenge is especially great since the United States, despite its own strength, has been consistently uncomfortable with the prospect of a strong China. This was true even during the Cold War, when China helped the United States counter Soviet power. A communist power, indirectly a recent enemy in

Vietnam, and a direct threat to Taiwan, China was not the most cooperative of strategic partners. Beijing resented U.S. support to Taiwan, feared U.S. inconsistency, and was reluctant to curtail its own freedom of action by tying itself closely to the United States. After 1982 each country tended to go its own way, China to a more balanced stance between the superpowers, the United States to a more Japan-oriented anti-Soviet policy.

As the need for strategic cooperation declined, tensions in the relationship began to rise. Some had to do with China's internal behavior, notably its human rights abuses. But others—concern about the growing U.S. trade deficit with China, for example, or about China's arms sales to unsavory Middle Eastern regimes—were grounded in skepticism about the kind of international citizen China intended to be.

Even the human rights debate, so prominent after the Tiananmen crackdown in 1989, was not without strategic content. Those wishing to curtail China's most-favored-nation (MFN) trade status with the United States were saying, in effect, either that the United States should not help China grow strong or that it should help only if China's behavior met certain standards. Some continued to define those standards in terms of China's international behavior—its arms transfers and trade surplus. But even those most concerned with human rights expected a more democratic China to be better behaved internationally.

The human rights–trade link was based partly on the assumption that, with the Cold War over, China was weak and strategically unimportant; with strategic allies, after all, Washington handles human rights issues quietly and behind the scenes. Whether that assumption was true at the time (the Soviet Union's collapse actually increased China's regional power by removing a threat), it isn't now, as President Clinton's recent move to sever the link suggests. If the United States wants to deal with a growing China, it will have to refine its tools for doing so.

## CHINA AND ARMS CONTROL

Indeed, it will have to drop more than the "sledgehammer" of curtailing China's trade status. Long before they raised this threat, U.S. policymakers sought to induce China's adherence to various global arms control agreements by offering or refusing to license the export of U.S. high technology, in effect offering to help China grow strong so long as it agreed to play by established rules of "good" state behavior. The effort never worked that well and is probably outrunning its usefulness.

To be sure, China has slowly become more involved in arms control. In 1980 it sent its first delegation to the disarmament conference in Geneva, where its negotiators have become increasingly involved in shaping agreements like the

Chemical Weapons Convention and the Comprehensive Test Ban Treaty. Nor has China been completely unwilling to sign certain agreements—especially those that constrain others besides itself. Thus it signed the Outer Space Treaty in 1984 to slow a superpower "space race" that might have degraded its nuclear forces. But it has refused to negotiate nuclear arms control, since to do so might ultimately hobble its top-priority but still relatively underdeveloped nuclear weapons programs.

Problems arise for the United States in the range of agreements that lie between the easy and the unacceptable. The Non-Proliferation Treaty (NPT) and the Missile Technology Control Regime (MTCR) would cut China's lucrative sales of nuclear and missile technology and marginally curtail its ability to support old allies (Pakistan) and new friends (Iran, Syria). Here U.S. technological inducements have affected China's commitment to arms control. But they have had less effect on China's behavior. . . .

A similar pattern of halting entry and spotty compliance has marked China's acceptance of the MTCR, to which Beijing committed itself late in 1991 as part of the same high-tech deal that brought it into the NPT. China reportedly canceled prospective missile sales to Syria and Iran. But evidence of continuing Chinese missile technology exports to Pakistan forced President Clinton to invoke U.S. sanctions in August 1993.

Some would not hold Beijing responsible for illicit arms sales, arguing that the sales are often conducted by relatives of China's ruling elite, who operate beyond the control of the Foreign Ministry. Yet precisely because they are related to China's rulers, these operators could presumably be brought to heel if those rulers cared enough to do so.

At the other extreme are critics who see Beijing as a rogue state that, in the words of Senate staffer William Triplett, "has violated every nonproliferation pledge it has ever made." Yet this charge, while partially true, overlooks the distance Beijing has come—from revolutionary power opposed to arms control to a "semi-status-quo" power that has signed several arms control agreements and complies with some, if not all, of them. Unless we write cases of compliance off as deception (which some do—this is, after all a civilization for which deception is a key strategic virtue), there is more of a puzzle here than China's critics admit.

## ESTABLISHED POWER, GROWING POWER

Perhaps tensions between the United States and China on arms control are only to be expected. The established rules of international conduct, written by the strong and naturally favoring their interests, are likely to be resented by any rising power. Thus the NPT freezes nuclear inequality in place, and any nuclear arms control talks would also likely assure China's current inferiority. And the

MTCR forbids missile sales (among China's few marketable military technolo-gies) while leaving U.S. aerospace firms free to market sophisticated aircraft worldwide.

Small and weak states, destined always to be rule takers rather than rule makers, may have to accept this situation and satisfy their interests as best they can. By contrast, rising powers, especially one with China's proud past, recent growth rates, and enormous potential, have every reason to resist agreements that reflect current power relationships in hopes of negotiating from a stronger position down the road. This seems to be Beijing's approach to the Spratlys.

But the United States is too powerful and potentially dangerous to be put off. Besides, its technological inducements have been useful. And if some of the rules the United States proffers appear unfair to the Chinese, others may be growing more attractive as economic growth increases China's stake in the pre-vailing status quo. China's spotty record of compliance with arms control may reflect the ambiguities of this situation.

But cheating has also been a form of power—a risky one, but perhaps the only one available to China at its current stage of development. Take China's elicit links to Pakistan. Rather than vehemently denying accusations that it con-tinues to sell missile components to Pakistan, Beijing has instead offered to dis-cuss those sales if the United States will discuss its 1992 decision to sell F-16s to Taiwan. Evidently the Clinton administration has recently agreed to this link-age. Cheating has opened the chance for leverage over a weapons deal China staunchly opposes.

For now, U.S. officials will do no more than listen politely but then ignore China's arguments, as they have in the past. But past practice may have a lim-ited future, since the stakes in this game are changing in China's favor. Growth and global involvement are reducing China's need for U.S. technology, while the collapse of the Soviet Union has reduced the urgency of China's search for technical advance. For the United States, on the other hand, the end of the Cold War has made proliferation more worrisome than ever. It will be increas-ingly difficult to "buy" China's agreement with dribs and drabs of U.S. technol-ogy. As is the case with the F-16 sale, China will want U.S. strategic concessions in return for concessions of its own.

Which raises the larger issue at stake here. China's argument that missiles and sophisticated strike aircraft are equally dangerous and ought to be jointly controlled—a position that may well be analytically valid—was excluded from the MTCR talks in the interest of simplicity and practicality. In forging a link between its missile sales and the U.S. F-16 sale to Taiwan, Beijing is forcing its broader argument back onto the agenda. To the extent that it succeeds, it will be leaving the realm of rule takers and entering the world of rule makers.

The United States has been willing to see China help write rules that play to U.S. interests, like the Chemical Weapons Convention. But is it ready for such help on subjects dear to its heart? Is it ready to curb its own arms sales, now far and away the world's largest and a key sources of income for the shrinking U.S. defense industrial base, in return for curbs on China's? Is it ready to limit the size, type, or operational freedom of its own forces in East Asia in return for limits on China's force modernization? These questions are far fetched now, but perhaps not for long.

## RULES OR POWER?

Obviously ambitious strategic agreements are worse than useless if Beijing cannot be trusted to keep its word. But that argument goes both ways. China's leaders regard the U.S. F-16 sale to Taiwan as a violation of the 1982 U.S.–China Communiqué on Taiwan, by which Beijing thought it had gained limits on such sales. In fact, the United States has consistently reinterpreted the Communiqué to suit the needs of Taiwan's defense, hungry U.S. defense firms, or presidents campaigning for reelection. A recent Senate move to elevate the Taiwan Relations Act above the Communiqué, virtually nullifying the latter, was softened only by last-minute executive branch lobbying. Surely if the United States can tailor its understanding of signed agreements to its loyalty to an old ally, Beijing can tailor its reading of the MTCR to its continued support to Pakistan?

Despite expressions of outrage over the F-16 sale, China's leaders were not surprised by the move. Strong states, they know, do what they will, while weak states do what they must. Behind moralizing U.S. rhetoric they see a state that does what it will, fashioning agreements to suit its interests and reinterpreting them when convenient. China's leaders take a realpolitik view of the world. No doubt they will "do what they will" if and as their country grows more powerful. Meanwhile, they have every incentive to justify their own arbitrariness by referring to U.S. behavior.

Again, the immediate issue is Taiwan; China's continued growth will make it increasingly difficult for the United States to sustain the studied ambiguities of its policies toward Taiwan and the People's Republic. And the general point applies across the range of activities where U.S. and Chinese interests potentially collide. If U.S. officials want to ground U.S. relations with China in rules—whether tacit or codified in elaborate agreements—they are going to have to abide more honestly by rules themselves. Beijing will happily be a mirror, reflecting U.S. misbehavior in its actions, with penalties that grow as China grows.

## BALANCING AND BARGAINING

China may misbehave anyway; treating it more equitably only maximizes the prospects that it will not. Thus until we know a great deal more about China than we do today, the complement to a more equitable U.S. approach to the country will be continued U.S. strategic engagement in East Asia and vigilance over China's actions. Whether China chooses to become the expansionist dragon some expect or instead seeks the cooperative relationship with the United States that China's leaders say they want, the currency of the relationship will be power, and that means the United States had best keep a good deal of it on hand. If China's leaders conclude that the U.S. military is leaving East Asia in any case, why should they take the United States any more seriously than the United States now takes them?

Ironically, if the challenge to Americans today is merely to think of China as a potential equal, should China actually exploit its raw potential, Americans will find themselves challenged merely to maintain equality! That day may never come (perhaps the sheer enormity of the prospect helps explain why many Americans hope it does not). But economic growth and changed strategic circumstances have already made China's increasing power a potential threat to U.S. interests. It is time Americans began to adjust their policies, and more importantly their perspectives, to prepare for the possibility of a China stronger than any they have seen before.

## NOTES

Thomas L. McNaugher, "A Strong China: Is the United States Ready?" *Brookings Review,* Fall 1994. © Brookings Institution, 1994.

Thomas L. McNaugher, senior fellow, Brookings Institution; currently director of the Arroyo Center, Rand Corporation

# The Growth and Role of the Chinese Military

## Senate testimony by Arthur Waldron

**Mr. Waldron** [*witness, prepared statement*]: Numbering approximately three million men, China's military is the largest in the world. It embraces strategic nuclear missile forces, a land army equipped with roughly eight thousand tanks, a navy having more than fifty submarines and fifty-five major surface combatants, and an air force with four thousand fighters and about five hundred bombers. Most of this equipment is obsolescent or obsolete, but the coming years will witness some modernization: acquisition has already begun of advanced systems such as the Kilo-class submarine and the SU-27 fighter, both purchased from Russia, while others, such as the F-10 fighter being developed by Israel, are on order. . . .

The core of my argument is this: Chinese military activities in East Asia—such as those against the Philippines, Taiwan, and Japan . . . —will pose increasingly difficult challenges to the United States and its friends and allies in the years ahead, with potential for creating economic and political instability, and even conflict, in Asia. This will be the case even though China's military will continue to lag technically. The lesson of the past year for China is that limited force and intimidation operations work, despite technical inferiority.

Both the extent and the limitations of the current Chinese military buildup are well-known. Purchases of advanced equipment from overseas and transfers of technology are proceeding apace, although it is important not to overestimate their effect. Except for its nuclear missile forces, which are high-quality and self-sufficient, little of China's military is close to current standards of modernity. Developing indigenous production capacity for modern systems is an expensive and long-term task. What we are seeing now is not so much that as an attempt to plug gaps, make some upgrades, and acquire a few excellent systems, with a view toward rapidly creating a more intimidating force—albeit one lacking depth.

In other words China looks to be building a classic "risk" force—like the "risk" fleet built by Imperial Germany against Britain in the early years of this century. That is to say, its purpose is as much psychological as military. I have two sets of concerns about it. One is that provocative use of the Chinese military, such as we have seen this year, is already fueling arms races in Asia and may lead—through miscalculation—to actual and even escalating conflict. It has already led to some economic uncertainty, and that could become more serious. The second is that an unexpected and humiliating setback to this "risk" force—the sinking of a Chinese naval patrol in the Spratlys, or the downing of fighters over Taiwan, for example—might trigger a domestic crisis in China.

This second concern reflects the crucial role of the military in domestic Chinese politics. China today is an unstable country in the midst of a massive transition: economic, demographic, and, although this is sometimes not recognized, political as well. A sharp setback for the current forward military policy could displace the fragile political status quo, and lead to reckless escalation—or to mutinies, a *coup d'etat,* or internal conflict. Any of these would have severe spill-over effects, economic and political, on the rest of Asia.

China's existing autocratic system is in any case structurally inadequate to the needs of a modernizing society, and it is furthermore deeply corrupt. At some point in the years ahead it will change. In 1989, it should be recalled, only military intervention saved the Communist regime from popular unrest. Today the grievances that fueled the democracy movement of the 1980s still exist, while the government in Beijing has grown weaker. Possibilities for the future include everything from evolution toward legality and constitutionalism to regional division, domestic unrest, and even civil war. Since 1911, the military has always played a crucial role in regime change in China and no doubt will do so again in the future. For the moment in Beijing, however, President Jiang Zemin and Prime Minister Li Peng—both relatively mediocre and unpopular figures—are working hard to make the military one of the bulwarks of their control.

Appeals to patriotic and national feeling are playing an increasingly conspicuous role in this attempt. Instead of communism, the government now stresses nationalism as its legitimator. The transformation is striking: in place of pictures of communist leaders and slogans about revolution, one now finds symbols such as dragons or the Great Wall. Much of this is welcome: the Chinese people are being allowed to embrace, once again, their magnificent traditional culture.

But the government's purpose is to use nationalism to distract the population from discontent and domestic agendas of reform and democratization. Hence the change has a threatening side as well. Nationalism includes the "recovery" of territory, by military means if necessary. A series of incidents over the past year gives some clue to the problems we may face in Asia if China's domestic problems are not solved, and conflict continues to be displaced outward.

The Chinese seizure of the contested Mischief Reef in the Spratly Islands in February of this year was a tremendous shock to Asia, for it confirmed that China would not simply talk, but would also use its military. The Chinese successfully targeted the Philippines, whose military and alliances are weak, and succeeded: the occupation is now a *fiat accompli*. But the story probably does not end here. Few in Asia doubt that having succeeded once, China will try again. Chinese claims to and occupations of various reefs and islets may well become a pattern.

This brings me to the part of my testimony upon which I would like to lay the most stress. It is true that in the next decade or so, we will not face an all-round military challenge from the Chinese. We will, however, likely have to deal with a series of military and diplomatic incidents of the type I have already mentioned.

The events of this past summer show that intimidation works. I can imagine no negotiation that would have permitted the PRC to establish a position on Mischief Reef, but military force secured it. The same is true for the threatening of Taiwan through missile firings in August. The sense of crisis, and subsequent reported American concessions, could probably not have been achieved otherwise. If such patterns of Chinese behavior continue undeterred, the danger will exist of conflict, possibly escalating.

Thus, we may ask: What will be the United States response if the People's Republic seizes and fortifies another island in the Spratly archipelago? If we do nothing, this will reduce our credibility, worry our allies, and open the way for

more Chinese probing. But what exactly can we do? Do we protest diplomatically? Insist that the Chinese leave the island? Doe the United States Navy, perhaps in association with allies, intervene? That too is an unattractive alternative.
Understandably, everyone hopes that China can be persuaded not to take such
action, but aircraft purchases and airfield construction suggest an ongoing
Chinese military program aimed at the South China Sea.

Much the same can be said about Taiwan. The missile firings last summer
violated the most basic understandings about the non-use of force that were
key to the China policy initiated more than twenty years ago by Richard Nixon.
If the People's Republic should continue attempts at military intimidation of
the island, and we do nothing, then the risk grows that China will be tempted
to push too far. The result would be a very dangerous conflict, into which we
would almost certainly be drawn.

Many other possible flash-points exist: China has territorial disputes with
most of her neighbors, including Vietnam, Russia, Japan, and India. The danger in every case is that deterrence fails and Chinese miscalculation triggers a
conflict which then escalates. My own view is that the sort of challenge to
international security that I have described in connection with China in Asia is
best dealt with early. Otherwise they tend to grow more serious and difficult
to handle.

How the United States responds to such possible challenges will determine
whether we secure our own interests by continuing as a credible player in Asia.
Japan, and other allies and friends, are watching closely. The Japanese–U.S.
relationship is fundamental to the peace of Asia, and Tokyo has been increasingly worried by China's recent activities. Without a strong American role,
peace in Asia will be difficult to keep.

Let me conclude with a comparison to Europe. The international situation
in Asia concerning China is not unlike that in Europe between 1860 and 1914,
when a unified Germany took its place as a major power. During his thirty years
in power, Bismarck managed that emergence rather as Zhou Enlai and Deng
Xiaoping managed China's: in a way that avoided major or escalating conflict.
But after Bismarck's departure in 1890 the new German leaders adopted a policy of territorial and diplomatic assertiveness. An influential role was played by
the military, which built up its armaments and overestimated its own capabilities while failing to discount the possibility that other states would actually
enter a conflict. The result, triggered by a crisis in a small state, was the First
World War.

If we do not want China to play that German role in Asia, we must ensure
that our policies are clear, that our alliances are strong, and that in a context of
diplomatic exchange and economic engagement, deterrence is nevertheless
maintained by demonstrative action if necessary.

**NOTES**

Senate Committee on Foreign Relations Subcommittee on East Asian and Pacific Affairs, "The Growth and Role of the Chinese Military," 104th Congress, 1st sess., October 12, 1995. Testimony by Arthur Waldron.

Arthur Waldron, professor of strategy and policy, Naval War College, Providence, Rhode Island; later professor at the University of Pennsylvania and director of Asian studies at the American Enterprise Institute

# Why We Must Contain China

## *Charles Krauthammer*

If an ambassador is an honest man sent abroad to lie for his country, a statesman is a man who lies from the comfort of home. Regarding China, American statesmen abound. Assistant Secretary of State Winston Lord denies vehemently that America is trying to contain China as it once did the Soviet Union. Our policy is one of engagement not containment, he insists. And Newt Gingrich says on *Face the Nation* that we should help the Chinese people undermine the Chinese government, then spends the next five minutes explaining that he did not really mean undermining at all.

Why are these diplomatic fibs? Because any rational policy toward a rising, threatening China would have exactly these two components: 1) containing China as it tries relentlessly to expand its reach, and 2) undermining its pseudo-Marxist but still ruthless dictatorship. Responsible statesmen are not allowed to say such things. Essayists are.

Does containment mean cold war II, with China playing the part of the old Soviet Union? Not quite. There is no ideological component to this struggle. Until late in life, the Soviet Union had ideological appeal, with sympathizers around the globe. Today's China, unlike Mao's, has no such appeal. China is more an old-style dictatorship, not on a messianic mission, just out for power. It is much more like late 19th century Germany, a country growing too big and too strong for the continent it finds itself on.

Its neighbors are beginning to feel the pressure. China is extending its reach deep into the South China Sea, claiming islets hundreds of miles from China, near four of its neighbors but within the reach of its rapidly growing military. Indeed, while defense spending in Russia and the West has declined, China's is rising dramatically, doubling in the past 10 years. Those dollars are going to intercontinental rocketry, a modernized army and a blue-water navy.

Nor is China deploying its new might just locally. It is sending missile and nuclear technology to such places as Pakistan and Iran. The Pakistan connection represents a flanking maneuver against China's traditional enemy, India; Iran, a leapfrog to make trouble for that old imperial master, the West.

Containment of such a bully must begin early in its career. That means building relations with China's neighbors, starting with Vietnam. For all the emotion surrounding our decision to normalize relations with Vietnam, its significance is coldly geopolitical: Vietnam is China's traditional enemy (they fought a brief war in 1979). We must therefore make it our friend.

A map tells you the rest of a containment strategy: 1) a new security relationship with democratic India, now freed from its odd, cold war alliance with the Soviets; 2) renewing the U.S.–Japan alliance, now threatened by a U.S. Administration so hell-bent on selling carburetors in Kyoto that it is blithely jeopardizing the keystone of our Pacific security; and 3) cozying up to the Russians, who, however ornery elsewhere, have a common interest in boxing in China.

Containment is not a cold war invention. It is a principle of power politics going back centuries. After the Napoleonic wars, the Congress of Vienna created a system of alliances designed to contain a too dynamic France. In our time the Atlantic Alliance contained an aggressive Soviet Union. In between, the West failed to contain an emergent Germany. The result was two world wars. We cannot let that happen with the emerging giant of the 21st century.

But containing China is not enough. Even more important is what Gingrich found himself unable to advocate clearly: undermining its aggressively dictatorial regime.

Undermining begins with unwavering support of such dissidents as Harry Wu, now imprisoned in China on charges of espionage for his human-rights work. The moral reasons are obvious. But beyond the moral is the political. America contained the Soviet Union, but it was dissidents like Solzhenitsyn, Sharansky and Sakharov who brought down the Soviet system from within. Wu and the unnamed thousands he speaks for represent the ultimate threat to the Chinese dictatorship, which is why it reacts to him with ultimate ferocity. And why we need to stand by him steadfastly.

Economic sanctions will not work. They would be even more useless against China's robust economy than they once were against the weaker Soviet economy. Better to wage the human-rights fight in the public arena. Denying Beijing the 2000 Olympics was a serious blow. So is keeping China from joining the World Trade Organization on the terms it desires. Next, Hillary Clinton should respond to the pleas of Wu's wife and lead an ostentatious U.S. boycott of the U.N.'s World Conference on Women, scheduled for Beijing in September. Regimes like China's crave the legitimacy such events confer. Denying them sends a serious message: Liberalize or be ostracized. It should be a lodestar of our policy to grant such public perks only in exchange for signs of toleration and democratization.

Containment aims to prevent war. But a change in regime to a tolerant, democratic China is the better guarantee of peace. Time to apply the pressure and keep it on.

## NOTES

Charles Krauthammer, "Why We Must Contain China," *Time,* Vol. 146, No. 5 (July 31, 1995), p. 72. © 1995 Time Inc., reprinted by permission.

Charles Krauthammer, syndicated columnist

# PART V

# MOUNTING WORRIES OVER CHINA
# (1996–2000)

This mid-1998 cartoon by Mike Peters highlights China's human rights problems by sarcastically suggesting that President Clinton's fortune cookie was made by a prison laborer. Reprinted with permission of Tribune Media Services, Inc. All rights reserved.

# Competing (and Cooperating) Strategies

*Several actions by China in the early to mid-1990s raised concerns in the American policy community. Among them were that China continued nuclear tests following an announced moratorium by the other declared nuclear states; in October 1994, China reportedly threatened to shoot down American military jets that had approached China's territorial waters in the Yellow Sea; and in February 1995, China forcibly occupied a reef in a part of the South China Sea claimed by itself and the Philippines. Most significant were its actions over Taiwan. In May 1995, President Clinton, under pressure from Congress, decided to grant Taiwanese president Lee Teng-hui a visa so that he could visit his alma mater, Cornell University. The decision enraged Chinese officials, who had previously been told no such approval would be forthcoming. In response, the People's Republic of China (PRC) recalled its ambassador from Washington and in July 1995 conducted military exercises in waters near Taiwan. In February and March 1996, on the eve of Taiwan's first direct presidential election, the PRC conducted even larger exercises and test fired missiles that flew close to the island. The United States first warned the PRC of "grave consequences" if it were to take any actual military action against Taiwan and then sent two aircraft carrier battle groups to the vicinity, further signaling its opposition to the PRC's attempts to intimidate Taiwan.*

*A conflict was averted, and the crisis prompted American and Chinese officials to address the deterioration in relations. As a consequence, the Chinese leadership and the Clinton administration intensified efforts to stabilize and broaden the official relationship. The key symbols of these efforts were the summit meetings held between Presidents Clinton and Jiang Zemin in Washington in October 1997 and in Beijing in June 1998. Commentary on President Clinton's strategy fell roughly into three camps: those who praised his actions but called for even further efforts to institutionalize cooperation, those who suggested that the United States should hedge its bets by mixing elements of cooperation with deterrence and pressure in the event China became more aggressive, and those who counseled a pure policy of containment.*

# Remarks to the Asia Society and the United States–China Education Foundation Board

## William J. Clinton

. . . Next week, when President Jiang Zemin comes to Washington, it will be the first state visit by a Chinese leader to the United States for more than a decade. The visit gives us the opportunity and the responsibility to chart a course for the future that is more positive and more stable and hopefully more productive than our relations have been for the last few years.

China is a great country with a rich and proud history and a strong future. It will, for good or ill, play a very large role in shaping the 21st century in which the children in this audience today, children all across our country, all across China, and indeed all across the world, will live.

At the dawn of the new century, China stands at a crossroads. The direction China takes toward cooperation or conflict will profoundly affect Asia, America, and the world for decades. The emergence of a China as a power that is stable, open, and nonaggressive, that embraces free markets, political pluralism, and the rule of law, that works with us to build a secure international order, that kind of China, rather than a China turned inward and confrontational, is deeply in the interests of the American people.

Of course, China will choose its own destiny. Yet by working with China and expanding areas of cooperation, dealing forthrightly with our differences, we can advance fundamental American interests and values.

First, the United States has a profound interest in promoting a peaceful, prosperous, and stable world. Our task will be much easier if China is a part of that process, not only playing by the rules of international behavior but helping to write and enforce them.

China is a permanent member of the United Nations Security Council. Its support was crucial for peacekeeping efforts in Cambodia and building international mandates to reverse Iraq's aggression against Kuwait and restore democracy to Haiti. As a neighbor of India and Pakistan, China will influence whether these great democracies move toward responsible cooperation both with each other and with China.

From the Persian Gulf to the Caspian Sea, China's need for a reliable and efficient supply of energy to fuel its growth can make it a force for stability in these strategically critical regions. Next week, President Jiang and I will discuss our visions of the future and the kind of strategic relationship we must have to promote cooperation, not conflict.

Second, the United States has a profound interest in peace and stability in Asia. Three times this century, Americans have fought and died in Asian wars;

37,000 Americans still patrol the cold war's last frontier, on the Korean DMZ. Territorial disputes that could flare into crises affecting America require us to maintain a strong American security presence in Asia. We want China to be a powerful force for security and cooperation there.

China has helped us convince North Korea to freeze and ultimately end its dangerous nuclear program. Just imagine how much more dangerous that volatile peninsula would be today if North Korea, reeling from food shortages, with a million soldiers encamped 27 miles from Seoul, had continued this nuclear program.

China also agreed to take part in the four-party peace talks that President Kim and I proposed with North Korea, the only realistic avenue to a lasting peace. And China is playing an increasingly constructive role in Southeast Asia by working with us and the members of ASEAN to advance our shared interests in economic and political security.

Next week I'll discuss with President Jiang the steps we can take together to advance the peace process in Korea. We'll look at ways to strengthen our military-to-military contacts, decreasing the chances of miscalculation and broadening America's contacts with the next generation of China's military leaders. And I will reiterate to President Jiang America's continuing support for our "one China" policy, which has allowed democracy to flourish in Taiwan and Taiwan's relationship with the PRC to grow more stable and prosperous. The Taiwan question can only be settled by the Chinese themselves peacefully.

Third, the United States has a profound interest in keeping weapons of mass destruction and other sophisticated weaponry out of unstable regions and away from rogue states and terrorists. In the 21st century, many of the threats to our security will come not from great power conflict but from states that defy the international community and violent groups seeking to undermine peace, stability, and democracy. China is already a nuclear power with increasingly sophisticated industrial and technological capabilities. We need its help to prevent dangerous weapons from falling into the wrong hands.

For years, China stood outside the major international arms control regimes. Over the past decade, it has made important and welcome decisions to join the Nuclear Non-Proliferation Treaty, the Chemical Weapons Convention, the Biological Weapons Convention, and to respect key provisions of the Missile Technology Control Regime. Last year at the United Nations, I was proud to be the first world leader to sign the Comprehensive Test Ban Treaty. China's Foreign Minister was the second leader to do so.

China has lived up to its pledge not to assist unsafeguarded nuclear facilities in third countries, and it is developing a system of export controls to prevent the transfer or sale of technology for weapons of mass destruction.

But China still maintains some troubling weapons supply relationships. At the summit, I will discuss with President Jiang further steps we hope China will take to end or limit some of these supply relationships and to strengthen and broaden its export control system. And I will make the case to him that these steps are, first and foremost, in China's interest because the spread of dangerous weapons and technology would increase instability near China's own borders.

Fourth, the United States has a profound interest in fighting drug trafficking and international organized crime. Increasingly, smugglers and criminals are taking advantage of China's vast territory and its borders with 15 nations to move drugs and weapons, aliens, and the proceeds of illegal activities from one point in Asia to another or from Asia to Europe.

China and the United States already are co-operating closely on alien smuggling, and China has taken a tough line against narcotrafficking, a threat to its children as well as our own. Next week I will propose to President Jiang that our law enforcement communities intensify their efforts together.

Fifth, the United States has a profound interest in making global trade and investment as free, fair, and open as possible. Over the past 5 years, trade has produced more than one-third of America's economic growth. If we are to continue generating good jobs and higher incomes in our country when we are just 4 percent of the world's population, we must continue to sell more to the other 96 percent. One of the best ways to do that is to bring China more fully into the world's trading system. With a quarter of the world's population and its fastest growing economy, China could and should be a magnet for our goods and services.

Even though American exports to China now are at an all-time high, so, too, is our trade deficit. In part, this is due to the strength of the American economy and to the fact that many products we used to buy in other Asian countries now are manufactured in China. But clearly, an important part of the problem remains lack of access to China's markets. We strongly support China's admission into the World Trade Organization. But in turn, China must dramatically improve access for foreign goods and services. We should be able to compete fully and fairly in China's marketplace, just as China competes in our own.

Tearing down trade barriers also is good for China and for the growth of China's neighbors and, therefore, for the stability and future of Asia. Next week, President Jiang and I will discuss steps China must take to join the WTO and assume its rightful place in the world economy.

Finally, the United States has a profound interest in ensuring that today's progress does not come at tomorrow's expense. Greenhouse gas emissions are leading to climate change. China is the fastest growing contributor to greenhouse gas emissions, and we are the biggest greenhouse gas emitter. Soon, however, China will overtake the United States and become the largest contributor. Already, pollution has made respiratory disease the number one health problem for China's people. Last March, when he visited China, Vice President Gore launched a joint forum with the Chinese on the environment and development so that we can work with China to pursue growth and protect the environment at the same time.

China has taken some important steps to deal with its need for more energy and cleaner air. Next week, President Jiang and I will talk about the next steps China can take to combat climate change. It is a global problem that must have a global solution that cannot come without China's participation as well. We also will talk about what American companies and technology can do to support China in its efforts to reduce air pollution and increase clean energy production.

Progress in each of these areas will draw China into the institutions and arrangements that are setting the ground rules for the 21st century: the security partnerships, the open trade arrangements, the arms control regime, the multinational coalitions against terrorism, crime, and drugs, the commitments to preserve the environment and to uphold human rights. This is our best hope to secure our own interests and values and to advance China's in the historic transformation that began 25 years ago when China reopened to the world.

As we all know, the transformation already has produced truly impressive results. Twenty-five years ago, China stood apart from and closed to the international community. Now, China is a member of more than 1,000 international organizations, from the International Civil Aviation Organization to the International Fund for Agricultural Development. It has moved from the 22d largest trading nation to the 11th. It is projected to become the second largest trader, after the United States, by 2020. And today, 40,000 young Chinese are studying here in the United States, with hundreds of thousands more living and learning in Europe, Asia, Africa, and Latin America. . . .

As China has opened its economy, its people have enjoyed greater freedom of movement and choice of employment, better schools and housing. Today, most Chinese enjoy a higher standard of living than at any time in China's modern history. But as China has opened economically, political reform has lagged behind.

Frustration in the West turned into condemnation after the terrible events in Tiananmen Square. Now, nearly a decade later, one of the great questions before the community of democracies is how to pursue the broad and complex range of our interests with China while urging and supporting China to move politically as well as economically into the 21st century. The great question for China is how to preserve stability, promote growth, and increase its influence in the world, while making room for the debate and the dissent that are a part of the fabric of all truly free and vibrant societies. The answer to those questions must begin with an understanding of the crossroads China has reached.

As China discards its old economic order, the scope and sweep of change has rekindled historic fears of chaos and disintegration. In return, Chinese leaders have worked hard to mobilize support, legitimize power, and hold the country together, which they see is essential to restoring the greatness of their nation and its rightful influence in the world. In the process, however, they have stifled political dissent to a degree and in ways that we believe are fundamentally wrong, even as freedom from want, freedom of movement, and local elections have increased.

This approach has caused problems within China and in its relationship to the United States. Chinese leaders believe it is necessary to hold the nation together, to keep it growing, to keep moving toward its destiny. But it will become increasingly difficult to maintain the closed political system in an ever more open economy and society.

China's economic growth has made it more and more dependent on the outside world for investment, markets, and energy. Last year it was the second largest recipient of foreign direct investment in the world. These linkages bring with them powerful forces for change. Computers and the Internet, fax machines and photocopiers, modems and satellites all increase the exposure to people, ideas, and the world beyond China's borders. The effect is only just beginning to be felt. . . .

The more ideas and information spread, the more people will expect to think for themselves, express their own opinions, and participate. And the more that happens, the harder it will be for their government to stand in their way.

Indeed, greater openness is profoundly in China's own interest. If welcomed, it will speed economic growth, enhance the world influence of China, and stabilize society. Without the full freedom to think, question, to create, China will be at a distinct disadvantage, competing with fully open societies in the information age where the greatest source of national wealth is what resides in the human mind. . . .

Our belief that, over time, growing interdependence would have a liberalizing effect in China does not mean in the meantime we should or we can ignore abuses in China of human rights or religious freedom. Nor does it mean that there is nothing we can do to speed the process of liberalization. . . .

Over the past year, our State Department's annual human rights report again pulled no punches on China. We cosponsored a resolution critical of China's human rights record in Geneva, even though many of our allies had abandoned the effort. We continue to speak against the arrest of dissidents and for a resumed dialog with the Dalai Lama, on behalf of the people and the distinct culture and unique identity of the people of Tibet, not their political independence but their uniqueness.

We established Radio Free Asia. We are working with Congress to expand its broadcast and to support civil society and the rule of law programs in China. We continue to pursue the problem of prison labor, and we regularly raise human rights in all our high-level meetings with the Chinese.

We do this in the hope of a dialog. And in dialog, we must also admit that we in America are not blameless in our social fabric: Our crime rate is too high; too many of our children are still killed with guns; too many of our streets are still riddled with drugs. We have things to learn from other societies as well and problems we have to solve. And if we expect other people to listen to us about the problems they have, we must be prepared to listen to them about the problems we have.

This pragmatic policy of engagement, of expanding our areas of cooperation with China while confronting our differences openly and respectfully, this is the best way to advance our fundamental interests and our values and to promote a more open and free China.

I know there are those who disagree. They insist that China's interests and America's are inexorably in conflict. They do not believe the Chinese system will continue to evolve in a way that elevates not only the human material condition but the human spirit. They, therefore, believe we should be working harder to contain or even to confront China before it becomes even stronger.

I believe this view is wrong. Isolation of China is unworkable, counterproductive, and potentially dangerous. Military, political, and economic measures to do such a thing would find little support among our allies around the world and, more importantly, even among Chinese themselves working for greater liberty. Isolation would encourage the Chinese to become hostile and to adopt policies of conflict with our own interests and values. It will eliminate, not facilitate, cooperation on weapons proliferation. It would hinder, not help, our efforts to foster stability in Asia. It would exacerbate, not ameliorate, the plight of dissidents. It would close off, not open up, one of the world's most important markets. It would make China less, not more, likely to play by the rules of international conduct and to be a part of an emerging international consensus.

As always, America must be prepared to live and flourish in a world in which we are at odds with China. But that is not the world we want. Our objective is not containment and conflict, it is cooperation. We will far better serve our interests and our principles if we work with a China that shares that objective with us.

Thirty years ago, President Richard Nixon, then a citizen campaigning for the job I now hold, called for a strategic change in our policy toward China. Taking the long view, he said, we simply cannot afford to leave China forever outside the family of nations. There is no place on this small planet for a billion of its potentially most able people to live in angry isolation.

Almost two decades ago, President Carter normalized relations with China, recognizing the wisdom of that statement. And over the past two and a half decades, as China has emerged from isolation, tensions with the West have decreased; cooperation has increased; prosperity has spread to more of China's people. The progress was a result of China's decision to play a more constructive role in the world and to open its economy. It was supported by a farsighted

American policy that made clear to China we welcome its emergence as a great nation.

Now, America must stay on that course of engagement. By working with China and making our differences clear where necessary, we can advance our interests and our values and China's historic transformation into a nation whose greatness is defined as much by its future as its past.

Change may not come as quickly as we would like, but as our interests are long-term, so must our policies be. We have an opportunity to build a new century in which China takes its rightful place as a full and strong partner in the community of nations, working with the United States to advance peace and prosperity, freedom and security for both our people and for all the world. We have to take that chance. . . .

## NOTES

William J. Clinton, "Remarks to the Asia Society and the United States–China Education Foundation Board," October 24, 1997, *Public Papers of the Presidents of the United States: William J. Clinton 1997, Book II* (Washington, DC: U.S. Government Printing Office, 1999), pp. 1424–1429.

William J. Clinton, 42nd president of the United States (1993–2001)

# The Clinton–Jiang Summits: An American Perspective

## *Harry Harding*

The United States and China experienced considerable tension throughout much of the 1990s—perhaps the greatest tension since they established diplomatic relations in late 1978. As a result of the Tiananmen Crisis of 1989, the Bush administration reduced the level and frequency of official U.S. contact with China, and the Clinton administration threatened to terminate China's most-favored-nation (MFN) status unless its human-rights record improved. The collapse of the Soviet Union in 1991 meant that the two countries no longer faced a common enemy, and no longer had an obvious strategic rationale for their relationship. The growing trade imbalance made the economic relationship between the two countries a cause of contention, rather than a basis for cooperation. The U.S. sale of F-16s to Taiwan in 1992, and, especially, the permission for Lee Teng-hui to visit Cornell University in 1995, led Chinese to suspect that the United States was tolerating, if not actively promoting, pro-independence tendencies on Taiwan. A large number of difficult issues burdened the bilateral agenda between the two countries, without much common ground to buffer the controversies.

**Pat Oliphant's May 1999 cartoon depicts the confusion and difficulty of dealing with the aftermath of the bombing of China's embassy in the former Yugoslavia. Oliphant © 1999 Universal Press Syndicate. Reprinted with permission.**

In 1994, the Clinton administration backed away from its threat to cancel China's most-favored-nation status, and announced a policy of "comprehensive engagement" with Beijing. However, the U.S.–China relationship remained strained. There was still little dialogue between Chinese and U.S. leaders at the highest level. The two governments focused on their differences, and found it difficult explicitly to identify their common interests. They made little progress in addressing controversial bilateral issues. No shared framework shaped the future of China–U.S. relations.

By 1996–1997, the relationship between the two countries had reached a low ebb. Public opinion on both sides was inflamed, as reflected in the United States by more frequent calls for the containment of China, economically and strategically, and in the P.R.C. by a growing perception of the United States as China's next enemy and by support for the idea that China should "say no" to U.S. pressure on trade, human rights, and non-proliferation. Most dangerous of all, Chinese military exercises in the Taiwan Straits in 1995–1996, and the dispatch of two carrier-battle groups by the United States off the coast of Taiwan in response, showed that the two countries could conceivably engage in a military confrontation over the Taiwan issue.

Somewhat paradoxically, these escalating tensions broke the logjam in China–U.S. relations. In relatively short order, the two countries agreed to restore normal bilateral dialogue at the highest level—a dialogue that had been suspended ever since the Tiananmen Crisis of 1989. Specifically, they agreed to an exchange of state visits: the first by Jiang Zemin to the United States in 1997, to be followed by a reciprocal visit to China by Bill Clinton at some later date. . . .

How can we assess the outcomes of the two summits? It is tempting to say that they have fully stabilized the China–U.S. relationship, eliminated the misperceptions and misgivings on each side, and guaranteed that the two countries can build a "constructive strategic partnership" for the 21st Century. However, such an assessment would be far too optimistic.

To be sure, U.S.–China relations now seem far more stable than they were only a few years ago in the aftermath of the Taiwan Straits Crisis of 1995–1996:

- The two countries have established a new framework for their relationship, regarding themselves neither as allies nor as adversaries, but as partners in addressing international issues.
- At the first summit, the two countries identified their common interests, and agreed that they are more important than their differences. At the second summit, they began to show that they could work together openly to advance their common interests on both global and regional issues.
- The two countries have reached an impressive number of agreements on bilateral issues: 24 such agreements in Washington, and another 47 in Beijing. These agreements deal with issues ranging from trade to human rights and from the environment to security, and provide cooperative programs on a wide range of matters related to China's economic and political reforms.
- The two leaders—Bill Clinton and Jian Zemin—have built what appears to be a warm personal relationship. They (and their top foreign-affairs officials) have also established the precedent of direct communication by telephone—something that was not possible with previous generations of Chinese leaders.

In spite of these accomplishments, however, the political base for this new relationship remains shallow in both countries. Although the critics may be less vocal now than they were a year ago, they have not disappeared. . . .

. . . [T]he remaining mutual suspicion reflects the fact that the summits did not remove the underlying structural problems in China–U.S. relations. First, the rapid growth of the Chinese economy, and the slower, but steady, rise of Chinese military power, is shifting the relative balance of power between China and the United States. This shift in relative power is not being moderated by a common enemy, common ethnic ties, or common ideology. In spite of the agreements on military-to-military exchanges reached at the two sum-

mits, confidence-building measures between the two countries' military estab-
lishments remain rudimentary, and China still shows limited willingness to
make its deployments, budgets, and doctrines more transparent.

Second, China's trade surplus with the United States continues to grow, at a
time when protectionist sentiments remain strong in the United States—in
spite of the vitality of the U.S. economy. At neither summit were the two countries able to reach an agreement on China's membership in the WTO—the
strategy that the United States has chosen as the most effective way of addressing bilateral-trade issues.

Third, although China has shown a gratifying willingness to sign the major
international covenants on human rights and to restore both official and unofficial dialogue with the United States on human-rights issues, the process of
political reform in China remains slow. Indeed, events surrounding the second
summit gave critics of China's human-rights record further evidence to support
their case. These events included Beijing's refusal to grant visas to the corre-
spondents of Radio Free Asia who had planned to accompany the President,
and the detention of dissidents in several Chinese cities to prevent them from
contacting U.S. officials or journalists during the President's visit. Moreover,
slow growth and rising unemployment are producing growing social tension in
China. If that tension results in political protest that is repressed by force, then
the human-rights issue in U.S.–China relations could again become explosive.

Finally, the United States retains a residual security commitment to Taiwan,
during a period when the mood on the island seems to be shifting away from
reunification, toward at least *de facto* independence, and toward a more visible
and active role in international affairs. The upcoming legislative and presidential elections on the island could bring into power the principal opposition
party, the Democratic Progressive Party (DPP), many of whose leaders have
previously favored an overt declaration of independence. This could set the
stage for another crisis in the Taiwan Straits.

Thus, more work needs to be undertaken to continue the process of stabilizing China–U.S. relations and of building toward a constructive strategic
partnership. This task is complicated by the fact that Americans and Chinese
build relationships in different ways. Americans think that mutual confidence
comes from concrete progress in managing specific issues; Chinese believe
that mutual confidence comes from agreement on basic principles. Chinese,
therefore, think that trust enables cooperation, whereas Americans are convinced that cooperation builds trust.

Fortunately, these two approaches, while certainly different, are not contradictory. They suggest that we need to take a multi-track approach to the
problem. On the one hand, through both words and deeds, we must reassure
each other that we wish each other well. The United States needs to confirm
that it wishes China every success in its historic drive for modernization and

reform, that it welcomes China's rise as a major power, and that it does not seek either to weaken China or to contain its influence. Conversely, the P.R.C. needs to reassure the United States that it welcomes a continued American role in the Asia–Pacific region, that it seeks the United States as a valued partner in China's efforts at modernization and reform, and that it does not seek to exclude the United States from the region. These kinds of reassurances help to establish the good mutual intentions that are so important to Chinese.

On the other hand, we also need to make measurable progress in narrowing our differences, to achieve visible cooperation in advancing our common objectives, and, above all, to implement, with sincerity and goodwill, the agreements we already have reached. This will help produce the sense of concrete achievement that is so important to Americans. At this point, moreover, the two sides need to redouble their efforts to reach agreements on the two important issues not resolved at the two summits: China's membership in the WTO, and its accession to the MTCR. Similarly, Washington and Beijing need to demonstrate that they are working together regularly and cooperatively to address new international issues as they arise.

Beyond this, several other steps would be helpful:

- The two countries need to schedule another round of summits, this time to involve Vice President Gore and Premier Zhu Rongji—despite the premiers's preoccupation with China's domestic economic reform and the vice-president's preoccupation with his presidential-election bid. At the same time, the two presidents need to continue to build their personal relationship, through bilateral meetings at such fora as the meeting of APEC economic leaders.
- The American press must continue to give extensive and balanced coverage of developments in China, building on the stories published and broadcast around the second summit. More Americans—particularly U.S. political leaders—should travel to China to see those developments first hand.
- The situation in the Taiwan Straits should be further stabilized through the restoration of cross-Straits dialogue and the expansion of cross-Straits economic ties. The objective should be to reach a *modus vivendi* under which neither side will attempt to impose its will unilaterally on the other.
- It would be highly desirable if the Chinese government could expand its program of gradual political reform, featuring elections at the basic levels, the development of the legal system, more active provincial and national legislatures, a freer press, and a more highly developed civil society. To the extent that these positive developments continue, they should be fully reported in the American press.

- The two sides need to prevent developments that could destabilize their relationship—dramatic repression of dissent in China, Chinese exports of weapons of mass destruction, a surge in China's trade surplus with the United States, or a unilateral declaration of independence by Taiwan. If such events cannot be avoided, the two sides must show that they can work cooperatively to restrict their extent and limit their consequences.

Successfully building a constructive strategic partnership between China and the United States will not be an easy task. What happens if we do not succeed?

One possibility is an adversarial relationship, in which the two countries' ties are dominated by their conflicting interests, values, and perspectives. This is conceivable, but unlikely. Our common interests—if only our common interest in avoiding military confrontation and in maintaining our economic ties—will most likely be strong enough to prevent us from devolving into a cold war, let alone a hot one.

The most likely alternative is not confrontation but competition—a relationship in which the two countries constantly seek advantage over one another, viewing their relationship primarily as a zero-sum game in which one loses to the extent that the other gains. A competitive relationship is far short of an adversarial one. Competitors do not wish to destroy their opponents, only to defeat them. Competition is normally conducted within rules, and within reason. Often competitors can work together to maintain the broader economic and strategic environment that supports their competition, and sometimes to turn away new rivals who wish to enter it.

However, a competitive relationship would entail far more friction, and far less cooperation, than a constructive partnership. There would be more differences on bilateral, regional, and global issues. Trust would be minimal. Goodwill would not be assumed. Cooperation in pursuing common interests and in narrowing differences, therefore, would be limited, and would occur only after protracted and contentious bargaining.

Thus, a constructive partnership is vastly preferable to a competitive relationship. Yet, it will take considerable effort for us to achieve that objective. That is the deeper challenge of the continued engagement between our leaders and our societies that will follow the two summits.

## NOTES

Harry Harding, "The Clinton–Jiang Summits: An American Perspective," in Peter Koehn and Joseph Y. S. Cheng (eds.), *The Outlook for U.S.–China Relations Following the 1997–98 Summits: Chinese and American Perspectives on Security, Trade and Cultural Exchange* (Hong Kong: Chinese University Press, 1999), pp. 29–48. Reprinted by permission from the Chinese University Press.

Harry Harding, professor of international affairs and political science and dean of the Elliott School of International Affairs, George Washington University; previously a professor at Swarthmore College and Stanford University and a senior fellow at the Brookings Institution (1983–1994)

# Dealing with a Resurgent China

## *Ted Galen Carpenter*

Relations between the United States and the People's Republic of China have become increasingly testy in recent years, with acrimonious disputes over a variety of issues, including human rights, trade, and the status of Taiwan. There is growing sentiment in Congress and elsewhere for a more hard-line U.S. policy toward Beijing. In its extreme form, that sentiment favors the adoption of a full-blown containment policy, treating China as the Soviet Union was treated during the Cold War.

It would be a mistake for the United States to embrace a containment policy. Such an approach could produce a self-fulfilling prophecy, as a cornered China lashed out against its superpower adversary, thereby becoming the aggressor that the containment policy was designed to prevent.

One cannot ignore, however, the fact that some of Beijing's actions are cause for concern. From the standpoint of American interests, the PRC's casual export of nuclear and ballistic missile technology to Iran and other countries ruled by unpredictable, unsavory, and rabidly anti-American regimes is troubling. That action clearly does not improve the global security environment. Similarly, Beijing's belligerent behavior toward Taiwan and other neighbors in East Asia raises serious questions about what kind of great power China intends to be.

The challenge for an effective U.S. policy toward the PRC is to avoid either provoking needless confrontations or allowing to develop a strategic environment in which Beijing can threaten important American interests. That goal requires Washington to establish clear priorities in its China policy—something that the Clinton administration has generally failed to do.

## TRADE ISSUES

U.S. policymakers need to understand that no country, even one as powerful as the United States, can dictate to other great powers. Washington's relations with China in recent years, however, seem to consist of a lengthy series of demands with little hope that Beijing will respond positively to any of them.

Perhaps the least constructive aspect of the relationship has been the annual controversy about whether the United States should extend China's most-favored-nation (MFN) trade status for another year. Beijing's critics in Congress and elsewhere use the recertification requirement to mount campaigns to condition extension on improvements in the PRC's human rights record, reductions in the multi-billion-dollar bilateral trade deficit, greater protection for the intellectual property rights of American firms, and a host of other issues.

The annual spectacle does little except cause needless friction in U.S.–Chinese relations. The temptation to link trade and human rights is understandable, since Beijing's systematic brutality toward political dissidents offends anyone who values individual freedom. Such repression is all too common in the world, however, and the United States cannot allow moral outrage to govern its trade relations with foreign countries. Moreover, . . . the freedom to buy or sell products and services without arbitrary government interference is itself an important human right—for Americans as well as Chinese.

## BEIJING'S SECURITY BEHAVIOR

While Washington should defuse the confrontation over trade issues, U.S. officials need to express greater concern about other aspects of Beijing's behavior. For example, the PRC has increasingly exported sophisticated weapons, ballistic missile components, and even nuclear-related technology to a number of countries, including states with virulently anti-American agendas, most notably Iran. . . . If the sales were made with the approval of the civilian leadership, Washington should clearly express its view that such actions are destabilizing and could pose a threat to America's security. If the PLA is operating on its own, there are even more serious concerns.

Another troubling aspect to Beijing's political and military behavior is its increasingly aggressive conduct toward its neighbors. Beijing's belligerent actions toward Taiwan in late 1995 and early 1996 received a considerable amount of attention in the United States, but the PRC has also engaged in a distressing amount of saber rattling on other issues during the past two years. It has shown a willingness to use its growing naval power to press territorial claims to the Spratly Islands in the South China Sea, which led to a serious confrontation with the Philippines, another claimant, in 1995. More recently, the PRC made threatening statements and gestures (including military exercises) toward Japan in the territorial dispute between the two countries over eight islands—known as the Diaoyu islands in China and the Senkaku islands in Japan.

The point in not that the United States has important interests at stake in such disputes. Whose claim to islands in the South China Sea is most valid ought to be a matter of indifference to Washington, and under no circumstances should the United States allow itself to be drawn into that multisided dispute if armed conflict erupts. Similarly, whether China or Japan has the better claim to the Diaoyu (Senkaku) islands should have no relevance to the United States. (Unfortunately, because of America's alliance with Japan, this country could become entangled in such a petty squabble—yet another reason to terminate the U.S.–Japanese security treaty.) Even Taiwan's continued de facto independence, while certainly desirable, does not constitute an interest sufficient to justify America's willingness to risk war. . . .

The dilemma facing the United States is how to avoid becoming embroiled in China's disputes with its neighbors without having a power vacuum develop in East Asia that might prove irresistibly tempting to Beijing. The latter development could lead to China's domination of the region and the emergence of a serious security threat to the United States. . . .

## AMERICA AS EAST ASIA'S LONE RANGER

America's dominant position in East Asia has contributed to the region's stability, but the tensions between the PRC and Taiwan in late 1995 and early 1996 demonstrated that the policy has an alarming drawback. In essence, the United States has volunteered to be on the front line of every regional military crisis. That is an exceedingly dangerous strategy.

Although the most recent PRC–Taiwan crisis has receded, there is a high probability of similar imbroglios in the coming years. Not only could the United States find itself entangled in a perilous military confrontation, it might have to wage the ensuing struggle virtually alone. Taiwan would undoubtedly contribute to its own defense, but the reaction in various East Asian capitals to Beijing's menacing behavior indicated that assistance from Washington's other "friends" would be problematic, at best.

Indeed, virtually all of the East Asian governments made a concerted effort to distance their policies from that of the United States as the Clinton administration dispatched two aircraft carriers to the western Pacific to demonstrate concern about the rising tensions in the Taiwan Strait. . . .

That glaring lack of support demonstrates that Washington's encouragement of dependency on the part of the noncommunist East Asian countries has created a most unhealthy situation. Those nations seek the best of both worlds: they want the United States to protect them from Chinese aggression, if that problem should arise, but they do not want to incur Beijing's wrath (or even jeopardize their commerce with China) by allying themselves with a hard-line U.S. policy. That may be a good, albeit cynical, deal for them, but it puts the United States in a terrible position. If China does make a bid for regional hegemony at some point, there is literally no power other than the United States that is positioned to block that bid. That is a blueprint for a U.S.–Chinese war in which China's neighbors conveniently remain on the sidelines.

Instead of continuing to foster the dependence of Japan, South Korea, and other East Asian nations, U.S. policymakers should make clear that American will not risk its very survival to defend them and preserve the stability of their region. Since they have far more important interests at stake than we do, they ought to incur the costs and risks of that mission. Washington's goal should be the emergence of a reasonably stable balance of power in East Asia. China might well be the single most powerful nation in that setting, but Japan and an assortment of midsized powers would have the capability—and the incentive—to counterbalance China and put a limit on its ambitions. The United States should play the role of balancer of last resort in the unlikely event that the PRC or some other country disrupted the regional balance of power and achieved a "breakout" that threatened vital American security interests.

Such a policy would materially reduce the likelihood of a military collision between the United States and China. It would even reduce the number of occasions on which contentious issues between the two countries were likely to arise, thereby maximizing the chances of a cordial bilateral relationship. Eliminating some of those sources of friction would clear the path for continued economic and cultural engagement, a strategy that is most likely to promote the evolution of a more tolerant and democratic China.

## NOTES

Ted Galen Carpenter, "Dealing with a Resurgent China," *Cato Handbook for Congress: 105th Congress* (Washington, DC: Cato Institute, 1997). Reprinted by permission from the Cato Institute.

Ted Galen Carpenter, vice president for defense and foreign policy at the Cato Institute

# Speak Plainly to the Paper Tiger

## *Gerald Segal*

On 3–4 April 1998 something unique in diplomacy happened—the leaders of Asia came to Europe. But the Asia-Europe Meeting (ASEM) in London was the second time these leaders had met—the first having been in Bangkok in March 1996. Bangkok??? What happened to the greatest Asian power—China? In fact, China's back seat at both ASEM meetings is a sign of the times. China is not a terribly important country. It is a country that appears to punch so far above its real weight that it is best described as a virtual power.

This may seem a strange argument to hear from one of those piranha who swim in the threat-rich waters of a strategic studies think tank, and even more odd from someone who began his career in the China-watching business. Surely a country with a permanent seat on the United Nations Security Council and arguably the world's most glorious continuous civilization must be ranked among the world's greatest powers. Listen to the piranha from [one] of the American think tanks and you would believe that China is a "near peer competitor" of the United States getting reading for "the coming war."

Forget it . . . at least for a decade or two. China is a fragile state, in some sense a mirror of Japan, that quintessential power that punches well below its weight. Consider the three main features of modern power and China's ranking. In military power, China is mostly a paper tiger. It has lost or drawn virtually every war it has fought since 1960. Since it failed to "teach Vietnam a lesson" in 1979, it has understood the need to modernize its peasant army from the deepest of its grassroots. But by doing so with paltry resources it has made little headway. China is a second-rate (albeit not third-rate) military power.

China can seize rocky reefs from "great powers" such as the Philippines but when a great power says "boo," the Chinese blink. In recent years China has backed away from confrontation with Japan over the Senkaku islands. When rabid nationalism got the better of their senses in 1966 and China threatened Taiwan with missiles, the United States scared the living daylights out of China by wiggling the radars and cruise missiles in its high-tech navy. China watched in horror when the United States implemented some of its "revolution in military affairs" in Iraq in 1991 and destroyed massed armour (including hundreds of Iraqi tanks bought from China). China may be a power when it picks on its smaller neighbours, but it is no match for any real great power.

In terms of international political power, China is an even punier pygmy. This country exerts no ideological pull on anyone; it cannot even nudge North Korea to pursue China-like market reforms. Beijing's remnant of a Communist Party is headed for the dustbin of history and the only interesting ideological question is whether its Communist play-actors can re-make themselves into capitalists fast enough to survive the tides of history. When President Clinton lectured visiting President Jiang Zemin in 1997 about being "on the wrong side of history," he was stating a fact, not even hazarding a guess about China's future. It will not be long before Chinese start asking that most fundamental of questions—was the 1949 Communist revolution really necessary. If there is a contribution that Chinese people will make to the world's test-bed of ideas it will come from Taiwan—the place that held the first free presidential election in the history of Chinese civilization.

China is one of those hobbled powers (like Japan) that has no real friends (Japan at least has formal allies). Its sense of nationhood even exerts little appeal for wealthy ethnic Chinese who live in Asia and around the world. The ethnic Chinese like the opportunity to make money out of China, but few would contemplate living in a decaying Communist regime. China's current flirtation with 19th century nationalism makes it increasingly out of step with a world that is becoming interdependent and open. China's leaders still believe they can manage the power of the information age and can produce an innovation economy in an authoritarian state. This is a country whose leaders look backwards even as they speak vacuously of the coming century belonging to them. China takes pride in its creeping experimentation with village-level democracy which, however admirable, will merely make the country ready for the late 20th century when its competitors in Asia and the developed world will have sped into the information and innovation age. Without a much deeper democracy and more open economy and society, China is ill placed to produce the next Microsoft or even Intel.

The picture of China is only marginally more impressive in economic terms. The truth is that China could disappear off the map of the world economy and one would hardly notice. It accounts for less of world trade that the Asian countries that melted down in the recent crisis, and the impact of the Asian crisis on European and American prosperity has been negligible. China is a smaller export market for developed countries than the Netherlands. Americans invest more in Colombia than in China. As was the case at the end of the previous century, Western business leaders dream of the China boom that supposedly lies just around the next bend; the reality is nearly every non-ethnic Chinese investor in China loses money. The power of the myth of the China market is the only sensible explanation for the fact that China regularly comes high on the table of foreigners expectations of future returns on investment, and yet near the bottom of the table of actual returns. A remarkably persistent triumph of hope over experience!

The story is unlikely to improve for some time, if only because of the depths of China's current economic woes. One might think it odd to describe an economy with an official growth rate of 8% as woeful, but numbers, especially Chinese numbers, are deceptive. The growth in the Chinese labour force of just over 3% a year requires a growth rate of the same size just to stand still. A further 3% of China's growth rate is useless production by state owned industries (SOEs) producing the un-saleable that piles up in rusting inventories. Even official figures say that 43% of China's SOEs were unprofitable in 1995. An 8% growth rate soon seems to be less impressive, especially with inflation below zero and deflation taking its toll.

The problems of the Chinese economy can be described as those associated with a transition from a planned to market economy. SOEs are the remnants of an old economic philosophy of controlling the commanding heights. In that ancient and now literally bankrupt model, SOEs were not just supposed to be producing the industrial base of Chinese power, they were the providers of welfare. Come down from the commanding heights and you need to build a welfare system. But building welfare systems and coping with large numbers of unemployed requires money and China's financial system has dire problems. Put off providing a welfare system and the more than 120 million unemployed migrants will swell, bringing serious risks of social unrest. Even Chinese officials admit that its banking system is bankrupt; bad loans are 30% of GDP, twice the level of the Southeast Asian countries that crashed and called in the IMF. Some 90% of Chinese bank loans are to these SOE dinosaurs that often use the funds simply to pay wages arrears.

So on comes the Great Reformer—the new Prime Minister Zhu Rongji—to break through into a more market economy. To her the adulation for Zhu at the ASEM summit in London, one would think that "one-chop Zhu" as he likes to be known can put his chop to a decree for reform of the SOEs and all will be well. But we have heard this before. Zhu was supposed to have got a grip on uppity provinces and township enterprises that were rejecting central control of the economy, but the reality has been that Zhu chose discretion over valour and came to terms with powerful regional forces running a much more decentralized economy. The result, among other things, has been the banking crisis. Although Zhu is no Gorbachev, he is like the ill-fated but still necessary Soviet leader in talking seriously about reform and probably forcing a process that will end up somewhere very different than first planned.

It is hard to be sure where Zhu Rongji thinks he is taking the Chinese economy, and without such certainty, it is impossible to be optimistic about his chances for success. His reformist circles have spoken of the Korean Chaebols as a model for reformed SOEs and a new-fangled banking sector. God help China! South Korea's recent economic crash has led to a hasty re-think but the result seems to be something pretty similar to Chaebols-with-Chinese characteristics. One could be more optimistic about the Chinese economy if one thought that China had learned the lessons of Asia's recent crash. What is more likely is that China will learn the wrong lessons. It will slow up China's opening to the outside world for fear of being swamped by the hurricanes of an open global economy. You can certainly forget about the convertibility of the Chinese currency any time soon. Neither will China hurry to make market-opening concessions to gain WTO entry.

One can have some sympathy for the new Chinese caution. It was China's close analysis of Asia's earlier economic success through an embrace of the global market that first stimulated China's own reforms in the early 1980s, and so setbacks in Pacific Asia will naturally make China think twice. China will have seen a regional economy devoid of indigenous leadership and at the mercy of American-organised, Western institutions such as the IMF and private banks. China will have also seen the death of "Asian Values" and the notion that there is a distinctive form of Asian capitalism. A China that until recently used to crow about the fading of American power and the creeping decrepitude of the West, has now gone silent. The proud boasts of quickly overtaking the U.S. in GDP are gone. Some Westerners talk about how China "had a good crisis" because it did not devalue its currency and has sounded supportive of its neighbours and even the IMF. But China has merely demonstrated the power of the passive—a promise not to fail or foul-up the plans of others is not active leadership that shapes, let alone re-shapes the region. Once again, China gets inordinate credit for doing something ordinary.

Of course China in not necessarily crippled for all time. Sustained reforms can gradually bring the reality of Chinese power up to something like its reputation. But the power gap will be with us for at least a generation and in the meantime there are clear implications for the world beyond the great walls of China. The first challenge is to learn how to treat China in a realistic fashion. If this really is a fragile and flawed power, then we need be less neuralgic in the way we tiptoe around the country "for fear of waking the sleeping giant." Speak plainly to China. Tell them what is in our interest and what we feel about them. Tell them they are on the wrong side of history. Speak plainly about human rights.

It is also safe to engage more closely with this country. Encourage people-to-people contacts. Contaminate the Communist regime with *Baywatch* and Mickey Mouse. Help their middle classes aspire to the wealthy life of their fellow ethnic Chinese in Hong Kong, Taiwan or Singapore. Explain how Asians grow rich in a more democratic Korea, Japan and especially Taiwan.

But it is also safe to temper engagement with constraint of unwanted action—a policy of constrainment rather than simple-minded containment or engagement. If you don't want China to capture Taiwan, then send in the American fleet. If you do not want to lose your islands in the South China Sea, then ask the Americans and other allies to help. If China sells component of weapons of mass destruction to Pakistan, Iran or Iraq, then punish their companies and withhold the sale of our high technology.

In short, treat China with a view towards how you want it to behave. It is in our interest that China becomes rich and interdependent with us all, but only if it plays by the rules and is constrained from using force. Yes, this is a Western agenda, but China would expect us to have nothing less. By pretending that modern China is strong we do ourselves, and the Chinese people, a serious and potentially dangerous injustice.

## NOTES

Gerald Segal, "Speak Plainly to the Paper Tiger," *New Statesman*, April 17, 1998. Reprinted by permission from the *New Statesman*.

Gerald Segal, director of studies at the International Institute for Strategic Studies
and director of the ESRC's Pacific Asia Programme of the Economic and Social
Research Council

# Challenges Facing the Next U.S. Ambassador
# to the People's Republic of China

### Senate testimony by Winston Lord

**Ambassador Lord** [*witness, prepared statement*]: . . . My name is Lord, and I
will now proclaim ten commandments for dealing with China. I trust you will
engrave these in stone.

*The first commandment. Thou shalt not demonize China.* It is not the Soviet
Union. It does not claim or seek a global mandate for its system or its ideology.
It does not support foreign Communist movements or proclaim a Brezhnev
doctrine or station troops overseas.

It confronts enormous economic problems, including increasingly difficult
reforms, the pressures of globalization, and awesome environmental damage.
Its military strength is exaggerated, lagging further and further behind the
United States in most categories. It is surrounded not by weak or vassal states
but rather a string of substantial powers, many of whom it has recently fought—
Russia, Japan, India, Vietnam.

Beijing faces severe domestic risks to stability and unity, including huge economic disparities, systemic corruption, social unrest, a spiritual vacuum, and a
longing for greater freedom.

It has been moving toward a market economy and bettered the material lives
of many citizens. It does allow greater freedom for travel, work, and grumbling
in private. It is behaving more responsibly on nuclear nonproliferation, and is
helpful on several regional and global issues. It seeks positive relations with the
United States in its own self-interest.

In short, in our national debate, we should reject the views of the apocalypse
camp.

*The second commandment. Thou shalt not sanitize China.* As we head
toward the twenty-first century, China represents our greatest international
challenge. It is the world's fastest-growing economic power. Its military
strength is advancing in selective areas and could threaten our friends and our
overseas forces. Its past aggressiveness includes for example, Tibet in the
1950s, India in the 1960s, Vietnam in the 1970s. It now pressures Taiwan,
trawls the South China Sea, and flexes its missiles.

China opposes the United States on many key security problems, such as Iraq and Kosovo, and it is friendly with rogue states. It behaves suspiciously on missile proliferation. It is brutal in its repression of dissidents, political and religious freedom, ethnic minorities and Tibet.

Beijing increasingly resorts to nationalism to maintain political control, and its government media is highly abusive of the United States. It seeks to reduce American power in the Asia-Pacific region and envisages a world in which China is once again the Middle Kingdom.

In short, in our national debate on China, we should reject the views of the apologists.

*The third commandment. Thou shalt not contain China.* This is the prescription of the apocalypse camp. It is neither necessary, desirable, nor possible. To treat China as an enemy would be a self-fulfilling prophecy when the jury is out on its future course.

We would forfeit cooperation in areas where our interests overlap, and we would exacerbate tensions elsewhere. We would divert military, diplomatic, and financial resources from other tasks. Unlike the Cold War coalition for containment against the Soviets, here we would be alone. While many countries are apprehensive about China, they do not wish confrontation. We could, in short, complicate China's emergence as a power, but we couldn't control it.

If instead we attempt first to forge positive ties with China and fail, then we would have demonstrated to our friends and to our domestic public that containment was forced upon us.

*The fourth commandment. Thou shalt not roll over for China.* This is the prescription, however denied or disguised or unintentional, of the apologist camp. While we should not regard China as an enemy, neither should we assume it will be a friend. China—as it should, and we should—will act in its own hardheaded self-interest. It will respect us and be more cooperative if we act firmly and without illusions. We should avoid excessive *mea culpas*. Often when there are frictions in our bilateral relations, it is *China's* fault, and not ours.

We should negotiate hard on issues and strictly enforce agreements, with sanctions if necessary. We should scrupulously control the export of sensitive technology. We should clearly oppose Chinese threats against Taiwan. While adhering to a one China policy we should fulfill our security commitments, including the Taiwan Relations Act and arms sales. We should proceed with regional and national missile defense, keyed in part to China's own actions. We should continue to press Beijing publicly and privately on human rights and democracy, the issues of Tibet, the rule of law. We should strongly support the Voice of America and Radio Free Asia. In so doing we reject the rationalization that Chinese history or Asian values or "stability" justifies repress.

*The fifth commandment. Thou shalt erase the phrase "strategic partnership."* To be sure, the Administration says that this is a goal, not reality. But inevitably the distinction is lost. It tags the United States as naive, complacent, overeager. It undercuts domestic and congressional support for clear-eyed engagement. So let us stop using the phrase in the same breath with China and save it for our allies.

Our relationship with China blends cooperation, competition, and conflict. We should treat it with respect, reciprocity, and resolve.

*The sixth commandment. Thou shalt recall that China covets America.* I need not elaborate why China is crucial to American security, economic and diplomatic concerns. But it is important, especially at times of tension, that we remember that China needs us at least as much as we need China.

There are the obvious economic incentives. We take a third of their exports and run a $60 billion deficit. Beijing sorely needs our investment and technology. Less obvious, but equally significant, is the geopolitical factor. The Soviet threat has disappeared and China is more ambivalent about our Asian presence. But for several decades, China will bank on the United States to provide balance in a neighborhood filled with historical rivals.

Finally, of course, China must deal with us because we are the world's superpower.

*The seventh commandment. Thou shalt pursue a positive agenda.* Too often the debate on China in this country dissolves to trade versus human rights, money versus morality, commerce versus conscience. The fact is that *both* should be pursued. Each builds on the other.

More fundamentally there is an expansive agenda of other issues where we and China can cooperate or at least pursue parallel policies. These have been addressed but receive little attention.

Let me just list some examples in staccato form. They include wrestling with challenges of regional security—Korea, South Asia, the Persian Gulf, Central Asia; tackling global problems—the environment energy, crime, terrorism, drugs; and strengthening international institutions—the UN, WTO, APEC, regional security dialogues and arms control regimes.

We should encourage China's active participation in global and regional organizations with a view to taming Chinese adventurist impulses through interdependence.

The Administration has been pursuing dialogue and exchanges on some of these topics. We need to work at this agenda more systematically and publicize it so as to clarify the national debate and bolster the case for engagement. To this end, there should be routine summit meetings with China in good times and bad.

*The eighth commandment. Thou shalt keep thy powder dry.* As we address this extensive agenda, we must also shore up indispensable foundations. We should maintain our alliances and our forward military presence. We should be prepared to use our assets if necessary, as we did near the Taiwan Straits in 1996. We should build positive relations with China's neighbors as ends in themselves, but also to hedge against future Chinese behavior.

*The ninth commandment. Thou shalt encourage freedom.* Promoting democracy and human rights cannot be our only goal in China, but it must be high on the agenda. It supports our other objectives. It is necessary for domestic and congressional support. It reflects the American tradition of melding pragmatism and principles. Moreover, it serves our national security as well. A China that is more open, humane, and lawful will be less aggressive and more cooperative on the world stage.

This is not a matter of seeking arrogantly to impose our values on China. It is an appeal to China's self-interest. A freer China would burnish its international image and its relations with the United States. A freer China is essential for future economic development in the age of information. A freer China is needed for political stability—if Beijing continues to shut off the safety valves of peaceful assembly, expression and dissent, it will sow the very chaos it fears.

*The tenth commandment. Thou shalt proclaim these principles from the mountaintop.* The commandments I have sketched envisage a nuanced, multilayered, strenuous, lengthy engagement with China. Domestic backing will require persistent mountaintop, presidential attention, articulation, and leadership.

Mr. Chairman, I believe a policy that embodies these ten commandants will curb both hostility and indulgence toward Beijing. If we honor these principles with steadiness and stamina, we will promote both our interests and our values, and we will preserve the support of the American people.

## NOTES

Senate Committee on Foreign Relations, "Challenges Facing the Next U.S. Ambassador to the People's Republic of China—(Includes Nomination Hearing of Adm. Joseph W. Prueher)," 106th Congress, 1st sess., October 27, 1999. Testimony by Winston Lord.

Winston Lord, former assistant secretary of state for Asian and Pacific affairs during the Clinton administration (1993–1997); staff member of the National Security Council during the Nixon administration (1969–1973); former U.S. ambassador to China (1985–1989)

# The China Threat

## *Bill Gertz*

The People's Republic of China is the most serious national security threat the United States faces at present and will remain so into the foreseeable future. This grave strategic threat includes the disruption of vital U.S. interests in the

Pacific region and even the possibility of a nuclear war that could cost millions of American lives.

Yet under the "engagement" policy of President Clinton and his advisers, the China threat has been wished away with meaningless platitudes and unrealistic expectations that China will somehow evolve peacefully into a benign democracy. It is a policy of weakness and passivity that ill serves America's national interests.

In stark contrast, China's hard-eyed communist rulers have set out on a coolly pragmatic course of strategic deception that masks their true goals: undermining the United States around the world and raising China to a position of dominant international political and military power. They seek to push the United States out of the vital Pacific region and achieve virtual Chinese hegemony in Asia. In a world growing more interdependent by the hour, China's ambitions cannot be shrugged off.

The reason Americans should take the threat from China so seriously is that it puts at risk the very national existence of the United States. And the reason the world should take the China threat so seriously is that our country, by virtue of its wealth and power, is the leading force for freedom and democracy everywhere. Without this leadership, there is little hope of a better life for all mankind.

The China threat demands a strategic response from the United States, not ad hoc policies that have failed to promote real change within the dictatorial government in Beijing. Under the Clinton-Gore administration, China was dismissed as a threat or even a potential threat. The apparent reason for what amounted to a policy of appeasement was trade and business interests, combined with the compromising of Bill Clinton by Chinese interests that contributed heavily to his campaign funds. But there is also a more sinister reason: an ideological affinity for China's supposedly "progressive" brand of communism among top White House advisers and even the president himself. Going beyond the Left's long-standing and relatively harmless "anti-anticommunist" infatuation, this blinkered view sees China as the last best hope for the triumph of Marxist ideas.

These wishful thinkers desperately want China and its communist rulers to prosper, in hopes that the misguided idealism of their college days will thereby survive the universal discrediting of communism in the past decade.

U.S. intelligence officials have made it clear that the failure of the Clinton-Gore administration to understand the China threat and do something about it started at the top. A White House list of intelligence priorities of interest to the president and his national security advisers did not even include China as a principal target. The list was sent to the Central Intelligence Agency and heavily influenced how senior intelligence officials gathered, analyzed, and reported secret intelligence to the policymakers. The absence of China from the target list demonstrated that Bill Clinton did not want to know what China was really doing.

To address the China threat adequately, U.S. leaders must first understand the threat, then develop and implement a strategic plan to eliminate the threat. Such a plan must include at least the following elements:

- **Launch a major intelligence "blitz" against China:** U.S. intelligence agencies today have very limited capabilities for gathering strategic intelligence information from China. The small number of China specialists within the U.S. intelligence community must be augmented with as many as 2,500 to 3,000 China specialists. The CIA and the Defense Intelligence Agency must devote most of their resources to developing networks of agents inside China's Communist Party, the government, the People's Liberation Army, and related organizations. China's more open economic situation has created tremendous espionage opportunities. Electronically, the National Security Agency must be tasked to build up its eavesdropping targeted at China. The National Reconnaissance Office, in charge of spy-photographic satellites, should be tasked to develop greater surveillance, reconnaissance, and intelligence-gathering capabilities directed at the difficult target of Chinese government and military activities. Analytically, the orthodox notion of a nonthreatening China should be replaced with a hardheaded realism based on American national interest: Without knowing and understanding both the threats and the opportunities presented by China's communist regime, American leaders will be unable to formulate strategic policies. A massive intelligence collection effort is needed.
- **Develop a strategic plan:** The United States needs to carry out a comprehensive effort to analyze and formulate strategic policies for dealing with the China threat, both short-term and long-term. The starting point is to recognize that, despite the Clinton administration's policies—and partly because of them—the communist regime in Beijing is not evolving in a democratic, nonthreatening direction. Instead, it is becoming more threatening. China's communist government has realized that the economic precepts of Marxism-Leninism do not bring prosperity. But it obviously has not considered the real problem: its brutal communist dictatorship. It has modified its economics without recognizing that its guiding ideology is fundamentally flawed and would have to be discarded to truly bring about reform. An American strategic plan must begin with a solution that includes a democratic alternative. The Communist government must be replaced and a process of "de-communization," similar to de-Nazification following World War II, must be adopted.
- **Strenthen alliances in Asia:** The United States should seek to develop a strategic alliance as part of a larger policy of pressuring China into adopting noncommunist democratic reform. The United States must play

the leading role in Asia, acting as a force for freedom and democracy. The alliance must be aboveboard in frankly identifying China as the major threat to peace, stability, and freedom in Asia. The alliance should include Japan and South Korea in Northeast Asia, the Philippines and other friends in Southeast Asia, and India in Southwest Asia. India's turn toward reliance on nuclear weapons is a direct result of the pro-China policies adopted by the Clinton administration. The result has been greater instability in Southwest Asia, with India and Pakistan engaging in a nuclear standoff. To the north, the United States must do everything possible to end the emerging anti–U.S. alliance between Russia and China. More must be done to help Russia democratize, and U.S. benefits should be used as leverage to prevent its alliance with Beijing. The policy can be likened to "containment" of China in the same way the West contained the Soviet Union during the Cold War. The United States needs to appeal directly to the Chinese people, just as it appealed to the people in the Soviet bloc, to reject communism. The Chinese people need symbols and hope, not a U.S. government that kowtows to unelected dictators. They need to know that the United States will be a beacon of hope for them, helping them to be not only prosperous but also free and governed democratically. The People's Republic of China should be admitted to the fraternity of free nations only when it becomes free.

- **Bolster American military forces:** The foundation for a strategic policy toward China is a strong United States military and an effective national security posture in the Pacific. The Clinton administration has systematically weakened the nation's capabilities across the board. Under Clinton, the military became a social experimentation laboratory for liberal attacks on a fundamentally conservative institution. Budget cuts combined with expanded nonmilitary missions have devastated military preparedness and morale. The unprecedented disarmament since the collapse of the Soviet Union in 1991 must be halted. Military alliances in Asia must be reestablished along with diplomatic alliances. Because China is sharply building up its missile forces, a U.S. national missile defense directed at countering China must be deployed as soon as possible. China has shown no willingness to curb its buildup of short-, medium-, and long-range missiles, and the development and deployment of a U.S. missile defense to counter them must be speeded up. The missile defenses will neutralize the key element of China's program of power: nuclear missiles, both intercontinental and regional.

- **Create a pro-democracy Pacific community:** A key strength of America is its diversity, and Asian-Americans have played one of the most important roles in our society. The Beijing government regards all Chinese living abroad as its citizens, based on common ethnicity. The

Americans among the so-called overseas Chinese must take the lead in forming a new Pacific community that will promote American values of democracy and freedom. The ultimate goal would be to work together with all people in the Pacific community of nations—including those in North and South America—to bring about the peaceful replacement of the communist government in China with a democratic alternative. A fundamental element of this community would be the clear announcement that the United States will never abandon the people of Taiwan and that Taiwan will never be traded away into the slavery of communist rule.

The United States today is a Pacific and therefore Asian power, as much as it is an Atlantic and European power. As such, we have a great stake in the freedom and prosperity of the region. Failure to promote democracy and freedom will leave Asia in the hands of a Chinese dictatorship that within three decades could become the region's—if not the world's—dominant power.

## NOTES

Bill Gertz, *The China Threat: How the People's Republic Targets America* (Washington, DC: Regnery, 2000), pp. 199–203. Copyright by Henry Regnery Publishing. All rights reserved. Reprinted by special permission of Regnery Publishing, Inc., Washington, D.C.

Bill Gertz, defense and national security reporter for the *Washington Times*

# Assessing China's Military

*As concern over China's security behavior rose, analysts stepped up efforts to understand China's military capabilities and intentions. Wide differences of opinion reflect different assumptions and yardsticks, but they also suggest the significant obstacles observers face due to the lack of transparency of the PRC's military.*

## China's Hollow Military

### Bates Gill and Michael O'Hanlon

How good is China's military, and how much should the United States care? There are ample grounds for addressing these questions. In 1995, and then again in 1996, the People's Republic of China (PRC) splashed missiles off the Taiwanese coast. It also reinforced military facilities on the Spratly Islands, which China claims although they are hundreds of miles from its shores. More recently, the PRC has undertaken a steady build-up of short-range missiles opposite Taiwan—hardly, it seems, a benign development, particularly when considered alongside President Jiang Zemin's presumed goal of reuniting Taiwan with the Chinese mainland during his tenure in office. And now these questions have been given a new urgency by the espionage allegations contained in the Cox report.

The PRC, then, has demonstrated a number of intentions and aims that warrant close American attention. The ongoing dispute over Taiwan, for example, is ripe for troublesome misperception. Chinese ambitions toward the Spratly Islands do not converge with U.S. interests or, for that matter, with those of nearby countries. The PRC continues to criticize harshly America's global alliance system and its assertive foreign policy. More generally, Beijing appears poised to translate its growing economic power into greater military strength and geopolitical weight, as indeed a Chinese defense white paper acknowledged last year.

Despite all of the above, we believe that the recent clamor over China's strategic ambitions is greatly overblown. Most of the Chinese aims that turn counter to U.S. interests are in fact not global or ideological but territorial in nature, and confined primarily to the islands and waterways to China's south and southeast. In addition, Beijing has recently taken a number of steps to cooperate with the United Sates on security matters: signing the Chemical Weapons Convention and nuclear test ban treaty, terminating its assistance to nuclear facilities in Pakistan, pledging to cut off ballistic missile transfers to Pakistan as well as nuclear and anti-ship cruise missile trade with Iran, and quietly restraining the North Koreans. Moreover, China is plagued by enormous socioeconomic problems, whose solution requires maintaining good relations with the world's major economic powers—and with the United States in particular.

That said, our main focus in this article is less on the PRC's intentions, always subject to change in any event, than on its military capabilities. An enormous gap separates China's military capabilities from its aspirations. The PRC's armed forces are not very good, and not getting better very fast. Whatever China's concerns and intentions, its capacity to act upon them in ways inimical to U.S. interests is severely limited, and will remain so for many years.

To begin with, consider some basic facts: China remains a developing country, with per capita income levels—even after twenty years' growth of historic proportions—only about one-tenth those of the West. China's living standards trail even those of American adversaries such as Iran, Yugoslavia and pre-Desert Storm Iraq. It faces enormous challenges in its agricultural, environmental and banking sectors, which its arteriosclerotic central government is ill-equipped to address.

Looking at these facts, the new commander-in-chief of U.S. Pacific forces, Admiral Dennis Blair, has declared that China will not represent a serious strategic threat to the United States for at least twenty years. In almost every respect, China's armed forces lag behind the U.S. military by at least a couple of decades; in many areas they even compare poorly with the "hollow force" that the United States fielded in the immediate wake of the war in Vietnam. And on matters ranging from the professionalism of its officer corps and troop morale to training and logistics, China's military is in even worse shape than that.

## AN EMPTY THREAT

China wields by far the world's largest military, with 2.8 million soldiers, sailors and airmen—twice the American number. (The United States is number two;

the only other countries with more than a million active duty troops are China's neighbors—Russia, India and North Korea.) Yet China's military was a full million people stronger in the 1980s—before PRC leaders recognized that its size actually worked against their aim of developing a modern force. Raw size is deceptive. Two million of China's soldiers serve in the ground forces, where their primary responsibilities are to ensure domestic order and protect borders—not to project power. Then, too, the Pentagon estimates that only about 20 percent of those ground forces are even equipped to move about within China. A still smaller number possess the trucks, repair facilities, construction and engineering units, and other mobile assets needed to project power abroad.[1]

In China's ever expanding defense budget, which has grown by more than 50 percent in real terms over the course of the 1990s and is to increase 15 percent this year, there is also less than meets the eye. Much of this year's increase represents compensation to the Chinese armed forces for divesting themselves of their many business operations, which sapped China's military readiness. Even with these increases, China's announced defense budget will still only total about $12 billion, less that 5 percent of the U.S. figure.

Of course, that $12 billion figure does not capture all Chinese military spending. It does not include spending on foreign arms purchases, nuclear weapons development, most of China's military research and local militias. Nor does it account for subsidies to China's ailing defense industries, or administrative costs such as demobilization and pensions. Taking these additions into account, and adjusting for purchasing-power parity effects—admittedly a difficult and imprecise business—China's actual defense expenditures are generally estimated at somewhere between $35 billion and $65 billion a year. But these are still modest numbers—especially for such a huge military. Even at the higher estimates, China spends less than 25 percent of what the United States spends on defense, while supporting a force twice as large.

This basic disparity will not change anytime soon. First, as noted, China faces enormous economic challenges that limit its ability to fund a military expansion. Second, even if China begins to close the gap with the United States, it starts from a position of marked inferiority. The United States owns a "capital stock" of modern military equipment valued at close to $1 trillion; China's corresponding figure is well under $100 billion. As such, one can see why a recent study concluded that the Chinese military would have to increase spending on hardware by $22–39 billion annually for ten years to wield a force capable of significant power projection. Further, this estimate does not take into account the additional investments that would be required to man, train, deploy and sustain such a modern force. China is in no position even to attempt this scale of effort.

## WEAPONS AND TRAINING

As congressman Barney Frank has sardonically observed, China did recently acquire its first aircraft carrier. But it then immediately anchored it in Macao and transformed it into a recreation center. So much for the next great hegemon's efforts to launch a blue-water fleet by the turn of the century.

More detailed assessments of Chinese military capability and readiness tell a similar story. Consider China's combat air force. Though roughly equaling the aggregate air power numbers of the United States, China's air forces include only a few dozen so-called "fourth generation" combat aircraft and only a couple hundred "third generation" aircraft. The rest rely on 1960s or even older technology. By contrast, all of the U.S. Air Force, Navy and Marines' 3,000-plus fighters are fourth generation models. China's projected fourth generation arsenal in the year 2005 is expected to include perhaps 150 fighters—by which point the United States will have purchased 300 "fifth generation" aircraft.

Two additional factors render an even bleaker assessment: supporting equipment and overall military readiness. First, as a recent Pentagon report observed, the PRC's air forces possess minimal aerial refueling capabilities, poor surveillance aircraft and a behind-schedule program to acquire airborne warning and control planes.[2] Second, and as another Pentagon report describes, the electronic warfare capabilities of the PRC air force are "extremely limited by western standards."[3] Programs are underway in China to improve certain specialized capabilities, such as the use of space, long-range precision strike, and other "strategic dimensions of warfare."[4] But the PRC continues to have trouble modernizing its forces. What passes in the literature as "capabilities" are often better understood as long-term aspirations.

As for the caliber of China's military manpower, it is hard to be more damning than the Pentagon's most recent report on PRC military capabilities. It acknowledges that Chinese troops are generally patriotic, fit and good at basic infantry fighting skills, but then goes on to say:

> Ground force leadership, training in combined operations, and morale are poor. The PLA is still a party army with nepotism and political/family connections continuing to predominate in officer appointment and advancement. The soldiers, for the most part, are semi-literate rural peasants; there is no professional NCO (non-commissioned officer) corps, per se. Military service, with it low remuneration and family disruption is increasingly seen as a poor alternative to work in the private sector.[5]

China's military training is elsewhere assessed as getting better, though still weak, particularly as concerns joint service operations.

With respect to the hardware on which those troops rely, the Defense Intelligence Agency expects that, by 2010 or so, perhaps 10 percent of China's overall military will have acquired "late Cold War equivalent" heavy equipment and become reasonably proficient in employing it. Even that will leave them twenty years behind the American curve—and the remaining 90 percent of the force more obsolescent yet.

## PROJECTING POWER

So much for an assessment of China's overall military readiness. Some would argue that this type of analysis misses the point in any case. Many American analysts contend that while the United States should not fret too much about China's traditional military power, it should recognize that Beijing, having watched the Gulf War on CNN, might utilize "asymmetric warfare" to threaten American interest in the Taiwan Straits and the South China Sea. By employing advanced cruise missiles, sea mines, submarines, imaging satellites, anti-satellite weapons, computer viruses and other specialized weaponry, China would wage "local war under high-tech conditions" in a manner that exploits American vulnerabilities.

There is a kernel of truth in this concern—militaries, after all, routinely seek to exploit the weaknesses of their adversaries. But it is a only kernel. To defeat Taiwan, for instance, China would need to land enough troops on the island to overcome Taiwan's quarter million-strong ground forces (plus some fraction of its 1.5 million man reserve force). But currently China cannot even move a quarter million soldiers overland into Mongolia or Vietnam. What is more, this type of power projection is precisely the type of operation that future military technology may render even more difficult.

The sum total of China's amphibious transport capacity (about 70 ships) can move 10,000 to 15,000 troops. Its airborne transport may carry 6,000 more.[6] True, China could utilize fishing vessels and cargo ships, and tap its civilian air fleet, for an operation against Taiwan. But all of these vessels, military and civilian, would be fiercely attacked before they reached the island. Making matters worse for China is the fact that there are only a few suitable beachheads on Taiwan where PRC forces could land.

Even if only half of Taiwan's fleet of nearly 500 combat aircraft survived an initial Chinese assault with missiles and fighters, the remaining aircraft could wreak enormous damage on an amphibious armada. The surviving planes would carry enough weapons that in theory they could sink almost the entire amphibious armada in a single sortie. Although Taiwan's air force may not yet have large numbers of anti-ship missiles like the U.S. Harpoon in its arsenal, it could inflict a fair amount of damage with its own Hsiung Feng 2 anti-ship weapons—and would probably be provided with weapons like the Harpoon fairly quickly. Taiwan also possesses highly effective air-to-air missiles, which would pose a serious threat to Chinese troop transport aircraft.

Things get even worse from the Chinese standpoint. To quote the Pentagon again, "China's C41 [command, control, communications, computers and intelligence] infrastructure cannot support large scale, joint force projection operations at any significant distance from the country's borders." Granted, Taiwan is only about one hundred kilometers from the mainland (though many PRC aircraft would have to operate from several hundred kilometers' distance, given constraints on the capacity of individual airfields). But even if the distances involved are not great, the operation would be enormously complex, as China would need to destroy Taiwan's air force, sink its fleet, deceive its ground forces about the armada's primary objective—and do all of these things after Taiwan was fully aware that hostilities were imminent, since a major and largely visible build-up of Chinese forces would already have taken place. Nor could China rule out the participation of American forces. Even if the United States did not put its combat assets in harm's way, it could provide Taiwan all-weather day-night reconnaissance and targeting data from spy satellites and aircraft.

Bizarrely, after making many of these arguments in its own report, and further concluding that Beijing is making few efforts to improve its lift capacity, the Pentagon's 1999 report on the PRC–Taiwan military balance concludes that, absent third-party intervention, China could probably carry out a successful amphibious assault by 2005. The basis for reaching this conclusion, however, is either unstated or unpersuasive.

China could plausibly *blockade* Taiwan—at least well enough to cut commerce severely and extract a steep economic price from Taipei. Here, the same technical realities and trends working against a Chinese amphibious invasion of Taiwan might actually work in the PRC's favor. Surface vessels in confined waters are already quite vulnerable. If anything, they are becoming more so—and China has in recent years vastly improved the quality of its anti-ship cruise missiles.

China has a large navy, too, one that boasts some 60 submarines, 50 large surface combatants and hundreds of smaller ships. Of the submarines, three are high-quality Kilo-class vessels purchased from Russia; another five are indigenously produced Han nuclear-powered attack submarines. They do not carry anti-ship missiles at present, but may soon. China's stock of torpedoes and mines, too, is well suited for blockade-style operations. But recall, this is a navy for which a three-ship crossing of the Pacific for its first ever visit to a mainland U.S. port—San Diego in March 1997—proved a huge undertaking. Even so, as Taiwan's navy has only 4 submarines, 36 major surface combatants and about 100 smaller surface combat ships, it might well find itself outmatched by the PRC navy. Or at least that is the conclusion of the Pentagon.

In any cross-strait blockade or naval conflict, Taiwan's main advantage would be air cover, especially if it reacted to a PRC blockade by shutting down its ports that face China and routing ships to its less vulnerable eastern harbors.

China, however, could pursue Taiwanese-flagged vessels beyond the range of Taiwan's aircover. Even if the PRC navy suffered huge losses, it could effectively discourage merchant shipping and shut down much of Taiwan's export economy.

These options would not be available to China if the United States intervened. Deploying two carriers several hundred miles east of Taiwan, the United States could, with the assistance of the Taiwanese air force, clear the seas of Chinese warships. U.S. airpower, to use a well-coined phrase, can "do" open water much better that it can ferret Serbian tanks and troops out of Kosovo's woods. American anti-submarine warfare capabilities would be challenged only against China's best submarines, of which the PRC only has a handful. At most a few merchant or naval vessels would be lost on the U.S./Taiwan side before the Chinese threat was eliminated.

On the matter of asymmetric Chinese approaches to defeating the U.S. military during a conflict over Taiwan, it is especially important to distinguish China's aspirations from its capabilities. It is true that Chinese writers intend to utilize information warfare and other concepts derived from what American analysts often term the revolution in military affairs (RMA). This approach to countering America's edge in traditional military capabilities undoubtedly has particular allure in a nation that gave the world Sun Tzu. But the fact that Chinese military writers can blend ancient maxims with concepts borrowed from the U.S. RMA debate does not mean they will be able to exploit its principles and technology during a conflict in the Straits. And even if China succeeds in developing one type of asymmetric weapon (e.g., a laser anti-satellite weapon), we will retain other systems that will not be threatened (e.g., radar satellites and surveillance aircraft). . . .

Today, both China and Taiwan are modernizing their forces. But Taiwan will surely do so much faster, especially given its high-tech economy, its willingness to purchase weapons abroad, and a modernization agenda that emphasizes capabilities such as precision strike, maritime reconnaissance and integrated air defense. China's armed forces talk a good high-tech game, but possess few of the requisite assets and are redressing their weaknesses at a very slow pace.

As for the Spratly Islands, where China has been constructing facilities of late, Beijing seems mostly interested in the economic potential of the surrounding waters and seabeds. Fortunately for it, the countries nearest to the Spratlys—the Philippines and Vietnam—possess little military wherewithal to challenge its claim to the islands. Hence, China's decision to claim sovereignty over the Spratly Islands, while hardly justifiable in law, is not entirely surprising.

Still, given China's inability to project substantial power very far beyond its borders, the PRC will be able to assert and maintain control over the Spratlys now and in the foreseeable future only if the United States allows it to do so. Washington may in fact decide on such a course, even if diplomatic skirmishes over the islands continue to pit China against formal U.S. allies like the Philippines—provided, that is, that China does not attempt to control the adjacent sea lanes. But the Spratlys could prove a costly prize for Beijing. The modest economic benefits accruing would probably be more than balanced by strong political resentment from neighboring states. In that event, the United States might be granted land bases in countries like the Philippines, from which it could patrol and expand its own influence in the region.

## THE SCANDALS

For all of the fear and suspicion aroused by illicit transfers of U.S. military technology, they have not fundamentally shifted the strategic balance between China, Taiwan and the United States. While their impact will not be trivial, neither will it be catastrophic.

Consider first the question of nuclear espionage. A native Taiwanese scientist, Wen Ho Lee, allegedly provided China with information on the Trident III missile warhead, known as the W-88; he may have also leaked computer codes mimicking the behavior of that and other warheads. . . . Warheads of that power formerly weighed well over 1,000 pounds; the W-88 warhead reportedly weighs hundreds. With this powerful lightweight warhead, China could place several warheads on missiles that currently carry only one.

That would not change China's ability to threaten the continental United States, which it has been able to do for almost two decades. Beijing at present has about 20 ICBMs that can reach the U.S. mainland. In addition, it has a nuclear-armed submarine, though the vessel is barely seaworthy and would need to approach within about 1,000 miles of the U.S. coast to launch its weapons successfully. China also possesses some 300 nuclear warheads it could use against U.S. or allied forces in Asia. . . .

The Hughes/Loral scandal may be the most significant of the recent cases. As part of their work in launching satellites on Chinese carrier vehicles, these companies may have helped China correct a problem in its guidance systems for their strategic rockets. Any technology transfer that increases the accuracy and reliability of China's rockets and missiles will surely aid its ICBM force and its efforts to place military satellites in space. Here too, though, we must be cautious in our conclusions. After all, we still do not know exactly what information was transferred; the former U.S. commander of Pacific forces, Admiral Joseph Prueher, for one, appears not to believe the data was of great import. Even if China's launch capabilities do improve slightly as a result of the transfer, its fledgling satellite program is rudimentary and will likely remain so for years to come. . . .

China's military is simply not very good. The majority of its members serve in the ground forces, but so lack in transport and mobile logistics assets that they are more aptly described as internal security personnel. Their training ranges from spotty to poor. Moreover, the armed forces remain plagued by poor pay, nepotism and party favoritism, and attract few of China's brightest citizens.

The PRC's power projection capabilities, too, are constrained by huge weaknesses—especially in areas such as aerial refueling, electronic warfare, command and control, and amphibious and air assault assets. China owns considerably less top-level military equipment than medium military powers like Japan and Britain; it owns even less than smaller powers such as Italy, South Korea or the Netherlands. Nor has it embarked on a concerted effort to purchase sophisticated new weapons. Though some analysts estimate China's military budget to be as high as $65 billion a year in purchasing power terms, the resources it devotes to acquiring modern weaponry are akin to those of countries spending $10–20 billion a year on defense.

The numerous defects of its military establishment notwithstanding, China is a rising power that could one day significantly challenge the United States and its allies in East Asia. But that day will not come anytime soon; it will be at least twenty years before China can pose such a threat. Why it would wish to do so, even with a strong military, remains an open question.

## NOTES

Bates Gill and Michael O'Hanlon, "China's Hollow Military," *The National Interest*, No. 56 (Summer 1999), pp. 55–62. Reprinted with permission. © *The National Interest*, No. 56, Summer 1999, Washington, D.C.

Bates Gill, senior fellow and director of the Center on Northeast Asia Policy Studies at the Brookings Institution; Michael O'Hanlon, senior fellow at the Brookings Institution

1. William S. Cohen, "The Security Situation in the Taiwan Strait," Report to Congress pursuant to the FY99 Appropriations Bill (Washington, DC: Department of Defense), p. 11.

2. Cohen, "The Security Situation in the Taiwan Strait," pp. 6, 13.

3. William S. Cohen, "Future Military Capabilities and Strategy of the People's Republic of China," Report to Congress pursuant to the FY98 National Defense Authorization Act (Washington, DC: Department of Defense, 1998), p. 8.

4. See Mark Stokes, *China's Strategic Modernization: Implications for U.S. National Security* (Colorado Springs, CO: Institute for National Security Studies, October 1997).

5. Cohen, "The Security Situation in the Taiwan Strait," p. 11.

6. Cohen, "The Security Situation in the Taiwan Strait," p. 9; and "Future Military Capabilities and Strategy," pp. 15–16.

# China's Military: A Second Opinion

## James Lilley and Carl Ford

In their recent article in the pages of *The National Interest* ("China's Hollow Military," Summer 1999), Bates Gill and Michael O'Hanlon write that "China's military is simply not very good." We think they got that half right. China is no military superpower and will not acquire that status for some years to come. But measured in term of its capacity to challenge key U.S. allies in East Asia, China's capabilities have grown exponentially. That is the point; the authors miss it.

Gill and O'Hanlon assert that because China presently has a limited capacity to attack, say, Manhattan, it is therefore "severely limited" in its ability to act upon its "concerns and intentions." But in setting up such a straw man, it is the authors' arguments, not the capabilities of the People's Liberation Army (PLA), that are severely limited. It is China's burgeoning ability to challenge U.S. interests in East Asia, not the danger it poses to the continental United States, that threatens to draw America into a military confrontation in the years ahead. Indeed, one need only look back three years to the Taiwan Strait crisis of 1996—when thousands of U.S. military personnel stood minutes from military confrontation with communist Chinese naval forces—for a preview of what may lie in the future.

Recently, others have observed that, "Increasingly, political pressures are pushing the U.S. toward a self-fulfilling prophesy: Treat China as if it is inevitably hostile and dangerous, and it is more likely to become hostile and dangerous."[1] Gill and O'Hanlon harbor a similar fear, and it is one that we share. But we believe that understating the potential threat China poses to American interests, as the authors have done, is just as wrong as exaggerating it. Sound policy formulation starts with solid assessments, not false assumptions.

By emphasizing direct comparisons between the defense capabilities of the United States and the PRC, the authors create an artificial and misleading construct. Such comparisons distort more than they enlighten. Few imagine that the People's Republic of China (PRC), either now or in the foreseeable future, could best the United States in an all-out war. Though comforting in the abstract, that reality is not terribly relevant to the challenges at hand. What the Jiang regime gives every indication of striving for is sufficient military clout to achieve its aims in Asia. In the short term, it wishes to intimidate Taiwan sufficiently to bring about unification on Beijing's terms. Accomplishing that entails limiting or closing off entirely Washington's ability to intervene early and with enough force to prevent Taiwan from being overwhelmed. Looking further ahead, the PRC seeks to cow its neighbors and diminish American influence in the region. For these purposes, the PLA is close to being good enough today—and even better tomorrow.

## TRENDS COUNT

First, it makes a big difference where you fight a war. Beijing would be no match for the United States in the Persian Gulf or off the beaches of Waikiki, but a battle fought in Sichuan province would be a very different matter. The same applies to the Taiwan Strait. Anyone who believes that such a confrontation would be a walkover for American forces misunderstands the challenges the PLA would pose to U.S. operations near China's shores, and how difficult it would be even for the United States to operate on a major scale so far from home. That Beijing does not presently seek to provoke a military confrontation with the United States, and is deterred for now from lesser military actions in the Taiwan Strait, should not delude anyone into believing that China would not be a formidable opponent on its own turf, or that the PLA is as "hollow" as the authors would have readers believe.

Further, any comparison that depends merely on counting up all our military assets or raw defense expenditures for its persuasive power is almost always wrong. Consider, to begin with, Beijing's defense budget. The government has agreed to increase military spending by almost 13 percent next year. Apologists both inside and outside China downplay that boost by claiming that it still leaves the PLA's level of expenditures far short of the Pentagon's. They also argue that most of the increase goes for improving "living standards" and is therefore not very important. Such statements make for good sound bites, but are seriously misleading. Even those who minimize China's military heft admit that defense spending overall "has grown by more than 50 percent in real terms over the course of the 1990s," as Gill and O'Hanlon state. The authors' protestations to the contrary notwithstanding, these trends are important.

Trends provide a good indication of intentions. Investments of the sort Beiing is making can mean only one thing: China is determined to improve the PLA's fighting capability. While most nations are reducing defense expenditures in the post–Cold War era, China is one of the few doing the opposite. We see the same trend in the PLA's training activities, the theoretical work being churned out by its think tanks and educational institutions, and, most important, in its buildup opposite Taiwan.[2]

Analysts of the Gill-O'Hanlon school typically claim that these increases in military spending are largely benign, going mostly to meet personnel costs. They argue in this vein knowing full well that personnel and related costs take up the bulk of military budgets in any army. What they neglect to mention is that many of the uses for which these expenditures are intended—the PLA's modernization drive and its stepped-up training activities, for example—will have considerable impact on China's military capabilities.[3] Across the board, the PLA is engaged in a major spending effort to upgrade weapons and equipment and improve its operational capabilities. According to the Pentagon, these efforts have already enhanced China's ability to project military power. One important example is China's growing stock of ballistic missiles aimed at Taiwan. The quick-srtike capability these missiles provide China will only increase between now and 2005.

It is also important to recognize that China never tells the truth about its defense spending. For years experts have considered the publicly released figures to be only the tip of the iceberg. While no one can be certain, since much of the funding is hidden, many estimate that the unclassified budget probably understates real spending by at least a third. In fact most Western estimates put China's annual military expenditure between 28 and 50 billion U.S. dollars—that is, 4 to 7 times the official figure. Moreover, it is precisely in the areas of weapons acquisition and training—both of which the PLA finances with profits from its sale of missiles and other weapons to rogue nations such as Iraq, Iran, Libya and Syria—that the Chinese are most secretive.

We can, however, observe in general terms China's broad interest in military research and acquisitions. The PLA's programs run the gamut of leading-edge military technology. From multiple missile warheads to stealth technology and the neutron bomb, the PLA is investing considerable amounts of time and money to improve its arsenal and its ability to project power. Obtaining air refueling platforms and airborne early warning aircraft remains high on the PLA's priority list, and it will likely acquire both in the near future. China has also show considerable interest in improving its naval aviation assets and has discussed the need for aircraft carriers.[4] And despite its strident protests over U.S. theater missile defense plans, China has long been working to improve its own missiles defense capabilities. As Paul Bracken points out, "Ballistic missiles break down the entire strategy of forward engagement from fixed bases. They are directed at the key vulnerability that Western powers in Asia always faced but that until recently Asian nations could not exploit."[5] Indeed, it is difficult to identify a weapons system or new technology that China is *not* hoping to acquire.

Also absent from Gill and O'Hanlon's comparison of U.S. and PRC defense spending is any recognition of the costs and restraints associated with Washington's status as a superpower. Our global military responsibilities have always come at considerable cost. Much of our defense spending, dating back to the Cold War, goes toward maintaining nuclear deterrence for ourselves and our allies. While the end of the arms race brought reduced requirements, we still maintain a massive nuclear capability and the ability to retaliate anywhere in the world. China, by contrast, channels its defense expenditures to much narrower uses.

## APPLES AND ORANGES

Gill and O'Hanlon suggest that China's antiquated logistics system would severely limit the PLA's ability to fight a real war, especially one outside its borders. Again the naysayers have it half right. China's logistics system is not very modern, and it cannot supply large amounts of cargo by air or support troops fighting far from home. Then again, it was not designed with such purposes in mind. For that, China would need to add new capabilities on top of its existing system.

In China's far western areas, such as Xinjiang, that is, on a small scale, exactly what the PLA seems to be doing. Worried about the activities of Americans and others in the former Soviet states bordering China, and lacking an adequate road and rail network in the area, the PLA has begun improving its logistics system in the region. While these efforts are just beginning, they could serve as a model for similar operations elsewhere in China.

In any case, the appellation "old" does not always mean "bad," and for the PLA's logistics system "tried and true" offers a more apt description than "outmoded" or "ineffective." Chinese forces depend on an elaborate network of existing supply and support facilities all over China, connected primarily by road and rail. The network can sustain the PLA in combat for extended periods of time over vast geographic areas. While the PLA's logistics infrastructure is best suited for protracted defense of its homeland, it can be adapted to support modest forays outside China. For example, the well-timed 1974 seizure of the Paracel Islands from South Vietnam involved successful amphibious tactics against a weaker enemy, executed with dispatch and overwhelming force.

China's continental approach to logistics differs sharply from the American system of power projection. Comparing the two obscures more than it clarifies. For our system, as it developed during the Cold War, depends on creating sea and air links to anywhere in the world on short notice. While each new crisis poses different challenges for the United States, all, except for those of a minor nature, require forward bases to channel supplies into theaters of operation. Without forward bases, severe limits exist on the size of the force we can deploy and how long our naval air units can remain engaged. China, by contrast, is its own forward base.

Just as "old" is not always "bad," so the PLA's large size, which many point to as proof of its technological shortcomings, is not necessarily a drawback. There are times when bigger is better. For one thing, the PLA's size enables it to mount a defense in depth, a classical continental strategy, and the opposite of the essentially linear defense adopted by NATO during the Cold War. China's strategy substitutes successive lines of forces prepositioned in the most defensible terrain for the qualities of mobility and lethality favored by NATO. True, this puts a premium on maintaining large numbers of troops and requires a sizable land mass. But with each success, an invader—much as Napoleon or Hitler in Russia, or the Japanese in China—will find his logistics tail increasingly vulnerable. There is no reason why a continental defense strategy such as this would not prove effective for the Chinese under modern battlefield conditions. It would be at least good enough to deter the United States or some other would-be aggressor from waging a ground war on the Asian mainland. And in the absence of such a threat, it is hard to image subduing China with air power alone.

## THE NUCLEAR DIMENSION

We looked in vain for any treatment by the authors of the nuclear dimension in a confrontation with China. Yet any discussion of China's military capabilities is incomplete without it. Not since the Cuban Missile Crisis has the United States come up directly against another nuclear-armed power. Neither for that matter have any of our opponents been able to bring the fight to the U.S. mainland. While we have proved adept at bringing war to the other side almost without limits, our rear areas and support bases have gone untouched. Not so in the case of a confrontation with Beijing. Were one to commence, we would have to be mindful of the PLA's nuclear capability, regardless of how unlikely its use might be.

Small by U.S. and Russian standards, China's mostly land-based missile force can strike the continental United States from fixed silos in western China. Both the 2nd Artillery (China's Strategic Rocket Force) and the navy field less reliable systems—at least at present. But that is about to change. Two new missiles, the DF-31 and DF-41, are modern solid fuel missiles probably with multiple warheads, and are far more mobile than previous Chinese systems.[6] Both can reach the United States. The DF-31 was successfully tested on August 2 of this year, a launch with a message for both Taiwan and the United States. The JL-II, another new missile under development, has submarine applications, and should be tested this year as well.[7] China's submarine force is still mostly a threat in East Asia, but sudden submarine attacks on Taiwan's shipping could prove devastating, as Taiwanese forces lack a modern and effective anti-submarine warfare capability. Nevertheless, the mobility inherent in each of these new systems make them highly survivable even against our latest and best high-tech surveillance systems.

## CHINA'S ABILITY TO TAKE TAIWAN BY FORCE

The authors are nowhere more off base than on their assessment of the military threat China poses to Taiwan. Since they wish to conclude that the PLA is a "hollow military" and that "an enormous gap separates China's military capabilities from its aspirations," they make two important assumptions: first, that the FY99 Department of Defense military balance report to Congress is seriously wrong; and second, that the United States would intervene to protect Taiwan.

Let us take a closer look at what the Department of Defense has to say in its report to Congress that Gill and O'Hanlon find so bizarre. They seem to have several passages in mind.

On China's defense strategy and force planning:

In recent years, there has been growing evidence that China's force developments strategy is being influenced, in part, by its focus on preparing for military contingencies along its southeastern flank, especially in the Taiwan Strait and the South China Sea.

On a PRC blockade of Taiwan:

Barring third party intervention, the PLAN's quantitative advantage over Taiwan's Navy in surface and sub-surface assets would probably prove overwhelming over time. Taiwan's military forces probably would not be able to keep the island's key ports and SLOCs open in the face of concerted Chinese military action. Taiwan's small surface fleet and four submarines are numerically insufficient to counter China's major surface combatant force and its ASW assets likely would have difficulty defeating a blockade supported by China's large submarine force.

On missile strikes:

Within the next several years, the size of China' SRBM force is expected to grow substantially. An expanded arsenal of conventional SRBMs and LACMs targeted against critical facilities, such as key airfields and C41 nodes, will complicate Taiwan's ability to conduct military operations.

On PLA air superiority:

while the majority of the mainland's air fleet will still be composed of second and third generation aircraft, the sheer numerical advantage of older platforms augmented by some fourth generation aircraft could attrit [sic] Taiwan's air defenses sufficiently over time to achieve air superiority.

On conducting an amphibious invasion:

The PLA likely would encounter great difficulty conducting such a sophisticated campaign by 2005. Nevertheless, the campaign likely would succeed—barring third party intervention—if Beijing were willing to accept the almost certain political, economic, diplomatic, and military costs that such a course of action would produce.

None of the Pentagon's findings strike us as being out of line. All, except for the implications of the recent missile deployments near Taiwan, have been known and widely accepted by intelligence analysts for many years. Indeed, while Gill and O'Hanlon disagree with the Pentagon's most important conclusions, they cite approvingly those portions of the report that have negative things to say about the PLA.

As the report suggests, Taiwan would face an enormous challenge in defending itself against a determined PRC attack. The island is too close to the mainland and the mismatch in force levels too great for Taipei to hold out indefinitely. Although Taiwan's technological advantages, higher levels of training and adequate preparations would prolong the struggle, defeating China is simply too tall an order for Taipei so long as the mainland is prepared to suffer huge casualties and bear the condemnation of the international community. Obviously, costly mistakes by either side or just sheer luck could change the equation, but in terms of raw capability China emerges triumphant under nearly all plausible scenarios.

The name of the game for Taiwan, then, is deterrence. Taipei's best chance for survival lies in convincing Beijing that the costs of an invasion are prohibitive, and that the island can hold out long enough for the international community, and especially the United States, to come to its rescue. In the first instance, this means maintaining a qualitative edge over the PRC. Here perception is almost as important as reality. Without ready access to high-technology weapons systems, which come almost exclusively from the United States, Taiwan cannot sustain the confidence of its troops or its population. On the other hand, any slippage in quality might persuade Beijing that the military balance had shifted in its favor, or that international support for Taiwan is eroding. In either case, Beijing would be emboldened.

Unless Taipei can prolong the conflict beyond a few weeks, the likelihood that the United States, or anyone else, will intervene declines sharply. Give the United States enough time and it can go anywhere and fight anyone with a high probability of success. Rob us of that opportunity, however, and we will be put at a disadvantage, especially if the scene of the combat is far away and our access to bases is limited. Take the case of North Korea. By any measure that nation is no match for either the United States or South Korea. But U.S. and South Korean military officials alike worry mightily about what could happen between the Demilitarized Zone and Seoul during the first few days of any war, or the consequences such a conflict might have if it should commence when the United States is tied down somewhere else. Thus, the North Koreans, with possibly one or two nuclear weapons against America's estimated six thousand, have been able to blackmail the United States for billions of dollars of aid.

Taiwan, like South Korea, must maintain forces sufficient to convince planners in Beijing that they cannot achieve their military objectives quickly. The PRC's new missile deployments opposite Taiwan make this task increasingly difficult. China's General Staff seems to have recognized that its threats of a blockade, an air war or an amphibious assault have become less and less credible, because such time-consuming operations would provide outsiders an opportunity to weigh in on Taiwan's side. The missile threat bears directly on this question, as any rocket attack would come as a rapid *blitzkrieg*-like bombardment.

Which is exactly why missile defense figures so prominently in Taiwan's current thinking. Now that the PLA has placed a greater emphasis on conventional ballistic and cruise missiles in its deployments opposite Taiwan, Taipei is reconsidering its need for THAAD and AEGIS missile defense systems. Both will likely receive a higher priority in future arms sales discussions between Taiwan and the United States, and for good reason.

China, and those in the United States who take its side in its dispute with Taiwan, would argue, of course, that there is a much easier and safer alternative to Taiwan's growing insecurity—concede China's claim of sovereignty over the island. Since Taiwan is a democracy and an overwhelming number of its citizens reject that option, this would only happen if Taiwan's population is sufficiently intimidated or otherwise coerced into doing so. Obviously, the American response to China's strong-arm tactics is crucial. Any lack of resolve on our part sends dangerous signals to both Taiwan and the mainland. Fortunately, President Clinton's deployment of aircraft carriers in response to the 1996 missile firing incident does not appear to have been an aberration, but rather evidence of a new American consensus in support of Taiwan having a say in its future.

This does not mean that Americans want to go to war with China, and we think the authors too quickly count the United States into the military equation. Under any circumstances, becoming caught in a conflict with the PRC is the last thing we want to do. Granted the introduction of U.S. forces changes the equation dramatically and would prove an almost insurmountable obstacle for the PLA. Much, however, depends on the amount of time it takes us to react and on what forces we commit to the conflict. Then, too, there is the nuclear dimension to think about. In fact, Taiwan depending on the United States so heavily for its defense seems to be the most risky option for everyone.

Better that the island, as envisaged in the Taiwan Relations Act, maintain "a sufficient self-defense capability," and reserve for the United States an important, but secondary, role in its defense. Such a course is the most stable and the least susceptible to miscalculation on Beijing's part. Let the PLA General Staff make its calculations of peace or war based primarily on what it confronts immediately across the Taiwan Strait, rather than considerations of what might be available by way of the United States.

This approach has the virtue of putting the PRC at the center of decision-making concerning Taiwan's defense preparations, but in the right way. The consistent message America would be sending to China is: "It is up to you. Strong-arm tactics will not work. Military build-ups and other provocative actions, contrary to promoting your interests, will only accelerate and intensify

Taiwan's defense effort, its arms purchases from the United States, and sympathy for its cause."

# NOTES

James Lilley and Carl Ford, "China's Military: A Second Opinion," *The National
Interest*, No. 57 (Fall 1999), pp. 71–77. Reprinted with permission. © *The National
Interest*, No. 57, Fall 1999, Washington, D.C.

James Lilley, resident fellow at the American Enterprise Institute and former U.S.
ambassador to China (1989–1991); Carl Ford, president of Ford and Associates, an
international consulting firm specializing in Asian military issues

1. Gerald F. Seib, "Another Threat Looms: China As New Demon," *Wall Street
Journal*, May 26, 1999.

2. William S. Cohen, "The Security Situation in the Taiwan Strait," Report to
Congress pursuant to the FY99 Appropriations Bill (Washington, D.C.: Department of
Defense, 1999).

3. Ibid.

4. Shen Zhongchang, et al., "21st-Century Naval Warfare," in *Chinese Views of
Future Warfare*, ed. Michael Pillsbury (Washington, D.C.: National Defense University
Press, 1998), pp. 261–74.

5. Bracken, *Fire in the East* (New York: Harper Collins, 1999), p. 48.

6. Richard D. Fisher, Jr., "China Increases Its Missile Forces While Opposing U.S.
Missile Defense," *Heritage Foundation Backgrounder*, No. 1268, April 7, 1999.

7. James Kynge and Stephen Fidler, "China's Submarine-Launched Missile to Be
Tested," *Financial Times*, June 3, 1999.

# 16

# Taiwan: Between Reassurance and Deterrence

*The question of Taiwan's relationship with the PRC has remained the most vexing issue in U.S.–China relations. In addition to differing judgments about the cross-strait military balance, addressed in the previous chapter, the policy community in the late 1990s debated to what extent Beijing and/or Taipei should be deterred from taking actions that would lead to war or should be reassured that the United States did not maintain policies contrary to their interests. Although these issues arose in the late 1970s and early 1980s, Taiwan's democratization and the emergence of Taiwanese nationalism altered the context in which such debates occurred. In July 1999, Taiwan's president Lee Teng-hui told a reporter that Taiwan and the PRC had "special state-to-state relations," and in March 2000, Chen Shui-bian, of the historically pro-independence Democratic Progressive Party, was elected president.*

## U.S.–Taiwan Relations

### House testimony by Susan L. Shirk

**Dr. Shirk** [*witness*]: . . . Thank you for the opportunity to speak with you today about one of the U.S.'s most important and unique relationships in the Asia-Pacific region: our relationship with Taiwan.

I know that people in the Congress and elsewhere have questions about the state of U.S.–Taiwan relations during this period when the United States is developing its relations with the PRC through Presidential summits. I welcome this opportunity to clarify any misperceptions that may exist about the Administration's policy toward Taiwan.

I will not read my entire testimony; we have submitted it to you. But I do want to begin by highlighting the vibrancy of our economic relationship—Taiwan is the seventh largest market for U.S. exports—as well as the affinity that the United States and Taiwan have for each other as competitive democracies.

I also want to highlight the strength of our unofficial relationship, particularly since the Taiwan policy review of 1994. I am particularly proud of our bilateral "Open Skies" Agreement to expand opportunities for U.S. airlines going to Taiwan and the rest of Asia, which was signed this past spring.

Another very significant achievement was helping Taiwan move toward membership in the World Trade Organization by concluding a bilateral market access agreement this past February.

Let me concentrate in my oral remarks, however, on the ways our policy contributes to Taiwan's security, and thereby to the broader peace and stability of the Asia Pacific region.

First, our policy insists that the resolution of the relations between the PRC and Taiwan must be peaceful, and urges direct dialog between the two sides as the best hope for peaceful resolution.

Second, we remain firmly committed to fulfilling the security and arms transfer responsibilities of the Taiwan Relations Act, which gives Taiwan the ability to defend itself.

And third, U.S. forward-deployed forces play a critically important role, as President Clinton's deployment of two carrier groups to the waters near Taiwan in March 1996 demonstrated.

We believe that by maintaining continuity and stability in these three policies, we have created a good environment for the PRC and Taiwan to take steps toward rapprochement. Over the past decade, the trade, investment, and travel flows between the two sides have increased dramatically, to the point at which the PRC is now Taiwan's third largest trading partner, and it has over $30 billion of Taiwan investment.

This is a very positive trend because Taiwan's security depends on more than military factors. Ultimately, stability in the Strait depends upon the ability of the two sides to come to terms with each other. For this reason, the Administration has encouraged Taipei and Beijing to reopen the dialog that Beijing broke off in 1995. We do not pressure either side, nor do we want to mediate. But we do tell both sides the same thing, emphatically and repeatedly; namely, that we hope they will resume dialog because dialog is the best way to diffuse tensions and build confidence.

We are encouraged by recent signs of a willingness of the two sides to resume their dialog. Last month, there was a meeting between the Straits Exchange Foundation and the Association for Relations Across the Taiwan Strait, the two unofficial or quasi-official organizations which carry out direct contacts between Beijing and Taipei. We hope to see additional meetings in the near future.

I am struck by the fact that these moves toward cross-Strait rapprochement and dialog are occurring at the same time as we are having summits with the PRC. It illustrates the fact that U.S.–PRC–Taiwan relations are not a zero-sum game.

We are strengthening our engagement with the PRC because we are working toward the goal of a China that is stable and peaceful; that tolerates different views and adheres to international rules of conduct; and that cooperates with us to build a secure regional and international order. But our progress in working with the PRC has not come at Taiwan's expense. We remain resolutely committed to our unofficial relations with Taiwan, in accordance with the Taiwan Relations Act and the three joint communiqués. There will be no fourth communiqué; nor will our relationship with Taiwan be diluted or sacrificed in any way. Our efforts to improve relations with the PRC are intended to strengthen peace and stability in East Asia, and in that sense will benefit the region as a whole, including Taiwan.

I am proud of the way in which we have maintained frequent and frank communications with the Taiwan authorities through AIT [American Institute in Taiwan] and TECRO [Taipei Economic and Cultural Representative Office] before and after the summits with the PRC; this communication plays an essential function in reassuring Taiwan that our policies toward Taiwan are unshakeable, and that our relations with the PRC and Taiwan are not zero-sum, but instead are mutually reinforcing.

As recent moves to resume cross-Strait dialog are demonstrating, strong U.S.–PRC relations are conductive to the improvement of Tapei-Beijing relations.

Let me conclude by addressing the question of whether the United States should assume a direct role in resolving Taiwan's future. This Administration, like the five Republican and Democratic Administrations before it, firmly believes that the future of Taiwan is a matter for the Chinese people on both sides of the Strait to resolve themselves. No Administration has taken the position on how or when they should do so; what we have said, and what I am repeating today, is that the United States has an abiding interest that any resolution be peaceful.

In accordance with our commitments, we are continuing to pursue our traditional "one-China" policy. Consistent with this policy, we do not support "two Chinas" or "one China," "one Taiwan," Taiwan independence, or Taiwan's membership in the United Nations.

While only the Chinese on both sides of the Strait can determine their future, the United States must continue to play a role in ensuring the peace and stability of the region. Only within such a stable environment can the two sides return to a regular and fruitful cross-Strait dialog, and we believe that this dialog has the potential to address the larger issues.

Our engagement with the PRC adds to this regional stability and this kind of environment, and therefore, is of direct benefit to the people on Taiwan. Just as regional stability contributes to cross-Strait communication, so, too, does cross-Strait communication enhance regional stability. Such dialog is, thus, in all parties' interests, including those of the United States.

Our policy, Mr. Chairman, remains firm. It is up to the two sides to resolve their differences directly and peacefully. We should stay out of the middle. But this does not mean that we will be inactive. We will work hard to expand the strong web of unofficial relations which binds us to the people on Taiwan, and we will work equally hard to improve our relations with Beijing. We will at the same time encourage Taipei and Beijing to return to an active and direct dialog. All three sides of the triangle can and will reinforce each other, and the result will be beneficial to all of us, as well as to others in the Asia-Pacific region.

## NOTES

House Committee on International Relations, "U.S.–Taiwan Relations," 105th Congress, 2nd sess., May 20, 1998. Testimony of Susan L. Shirk.

Susan L. Shirk, deputy assistant secretary of state for China, Taiwan, and Hong Kong during the Clinton administration (1997–2000); previously and since professor of political science at the University of California, San Diego

# The Administration's Position on Taiwan

## Senate floor remarks by Frank Murkowski

. . . During the President's trip to China last month, President Clinton clarified his policy toward Taiwan. He indicated while in Beijing—that the United States, in agreeing to the One China policy, had agreed with China that reunification would be peaceful. Further, while in Shanghai, he went a step further and, for the first time, uttered that the United States supports the "Three Noes" long advocated by the government of the People's Republic of China. That is the United States does not support one Taiwan, one China; the United States doe not support Taiwan independence; and the United States does not support Taiwan's membership in nation-state based international organizations.

To understand why this concerns me, Mr. President, one needs to understand the nuances of our federal law and policy toward Taiwan. It is in the Taiwan Relations Act, which was passed by Congress and signed into law by the President in 1979—back when the United States officially broke off relations with the Republic of China on Taiwan in favor of the People's Republic of China (PRC), Section 2(b) (3) states that ". . . the future of Taiwan will be determined by peaceful means." We have also signed Three Joint Communiqués with the PRC which address the Taiwan question. While they all speak to the peaceful resolution of the Taiwan question, none goes so far [as] to speak to the question of reunification.

Up to now, the saving grace of American policy toward China and Taiwan, if there were any grace to it, was the ambiguity. China did not know what the United States would do if Taiwan declared independence; or if China attacked. They thought they found out in 1996, when the President rightly sent two aircraft carriers to the Taiwan Straits to show our strength and resolve—while the Chinese conducted missile tests aimed at influencing the national presidential elections in Taiwan. But we have a whole new ballgame, now Mr. President. What a difference a day makes.

Incredible, Mr. President. The Administration then feigns innocence and insists that the President's remarks did not constitute a policy change and that our policy on Taiwan has not changed since 1979—that it is the same now as it was then. I'm sorry, but I have to expose this for what it is—a world of make believe. If you repeat something enough times, eventually people will take it as the gospel. Well not this time.

This is a policy change, and a serious one at that. Considered collectively, which I know the Chinese government is doing, it appears to be a major concession by the United States on the issue of Taiwan. . . .

In agreeing to the "Three Noes," President Clinton has effectively stated that the United States will not support Taiwan independence even if Beijing agrees to it. Is this the message that was intended to be delivered? Think about it—the United States used to maintain the line that peaceful resolution was all that mattered because this in itself protected the rights of the 21 million people in Taiwan. If they could cut a deal with Beijing that allowed the two to go their separate ways, presumably our earlier policy would be fine with that. Personally, as the PRC becomes more open, I wouldn't rule out the possibility that an agreement could be reached. But President Clinton's remarks have ruled this possibility out—because the United States will not support an independent Taiwan. President Clinton just told the Chinese that they don't need to negotiate with Taiwan because so far as we are concerned an independent Taiwan is not an option. . . .

## NOTES

Frank Murkowski, "The Administration's Position on Taiwan," remarks on the Senate floor, July 17, 1998.

Frank Murkowski, Senator (R-Alaska)

"If we dig deep enough, they say, we can go all the way to China or Hong Kong but not, at this point, to Taiwan."

**Alluding to the story often told to American children, that if you dig far enough you'll reach China, Jack Ziegler's cartoon argues that the U.S. and Taiwan are unable to have close relations because of the P.R.C.'s "one China" policy. © 2002 The New Yorker Collection from cartoonbank. com. All rights reserved.**

# Why Taiwan's Security Needs to Be Enhanced

## Stephen J. Yates

Congress passed the 1979 Taiwan Relations Act (TRA) to ensure that Taiwan's security would not be compromised as a result of the termination of diplomatic relations between China and the United States. Since then, the United States has continued to sell defensive arms to Taiwan. Nevertheless, this democratic state's security is still threatened by China's escalating military modernization and buildup across the Strait. Today, Taiwan suffers from the inability to participate in (or even observe) advanced joint military exercises. And the United States is failing to faithfully implement the legislative intent of the TRA.

To address thee concerns, Senators Jesse Helms (R-NC) and Robert Torricelli (D-NJ) cosponsored S. 693, the Taiwan Security Enhancement Act (TSEA), to bridge the gap between the legislative intent of the TRA and the implementation of its key provisions. The measure calls on the U.S. government to recognize Taiwan's changing defense needs in light of the Mainland's determined military modernization and the more general revolution in military affairs from which Taiwan is diplomatically isolated. The bill's complement in the House, H.R. 1838, has a long and impressive bipartisan list of cosponsors. Yet the Clinton Administration is opposed to the bill, and supporters fear they may not be able to secure the two-thirds majority necessary to override a veto.

## THE TRA'S INTENT

Section 3(a) of the TRA instructs the U.S. government to make available "defense articles and services" to Taiwan, and "in such quantity as may be necessary to enable Taiwan to maintain a sufficient self-defense capability." Sections 3(b) notes that, "The President and the Congress shall determine the nature and quantity of such defense articles and services based solely on their judgment of the needs of Taiwan."

The legislative history of the TRA makes clear that these two provisions were intended to ensure that Taiwan was not relegated to using second-class military hardware and technology, that its defense needs would be determined without regard to the views of the Mainland, and that the President would at least consult with Congress in making this determination.

## TAIWAN'S MILITARY DISADVANTAGE

Taiwan clearly is at a disadvantage *vis à vis* China. Today, the People's Republic of China has a 65 to 4 advantage in submarines and a 4,500 to 400 numerical advantage in aircraft, an edge increased by its acquisition of advanced foreign technology primarily from Russia, but also from Israel and the United States. According to a February 1999 Department of Defense report, China's buildup means that, "By 2005, the PLA will possess the capability to attack Taiwan with air and missile strikes which would degrade key military facilities and damage the island's economic infrastructure."

## WHAT THE TSEA WOULD DO

The TSEA would re-establish congressional oversight of arms sales to Taiwan and empower the President to make available to Taiwan advanced defensive weapons systems and training. In the end, it aims to improve Taiwan's self-defense capability.

To address Taiwan's hardware needs, the TSEA would increase the technical staff of the American Institute in Taiwan, and it would require the Administration to report on Taiwan's requests for defense articles. In addition, it would authorize, but not mandate, the sale of satellite early warning data, missile defense systems, modern air defense equipment, and naval defense systems (including submarines).

To address Taiwan's software needs, the TSEA instructs the Secretary of Defense to devise a plan to enhance programs with Taiwan's military "for operational training and exchanges of personnel for work in threat analysis, doctrine, force planning, operational methods, and other areas."

These provisions are consistent with U.S. obligations under the Taiwan Relations Act, and they are clearly appropriate, given the Mainland's changing military posture. But the TSEA is meeting strong resistance from the Administration and even some Members of Congress.

## SECURITY PROMOTES PEACE

Taiwan will never be China's military equal. But parity with China is not Taiwan's objective, and it should not be the objective of the United States. Nevertheless, the United States remains obliged under the Taiwan Relations Act to sell Taiwan defense articles and systems based solely on Taiwan's defense needs. Taiwan's defense needs require an increasing reliance on advanced military software (technology, training, and strategy) in order to counter the Mainland's overwhelming hardware advantage.

To promote U.S. interests by deterring aggression and promoting freedom in the Taiwan Strait, the United States should:

- Faithfully implement Section 3 of the Taiwan Relations Act. Congress should exercise its legal right to participate in the determination of Taiwan's defense needs, and ensure that consideration of the Mainland's views does not hinder Taiwan's self-defense capability.
- Improve Taiwan's self-defense capability. Given Beijing's overwhelming hardware advantage, emphasis on missile modernization, and willingness to use missiles to intimidate Taiwan, Taiwan needs to increase it reliance on high technology—including missile defense. The alternative is near total vulnerability or total reliance on U.S. intervention.

Policymakers should discount arguments that warn that enhancing Taiwan's security will encourage "moves toward independence" and a regional arms race. Such alarmist views ignore the history of cross-Strait dialogue, which progresses when Taiwan feels secure. For example, productive talks took place in 1993, after the 1992 F-16 sales and in 1998, after the 1996 U. S. aircraft carrier deployment.

Given the Administration's opposition to the TSEA, enhancing Taiwan's security will be an uphill battle for Congress. Nevertheless, the people of Taiwan demand that their government use every reasonable means at its disposal to protect them from an attack or coercion by the Mainland. For America, enhancing Taiwan's security, rather than increasing its vulnerability, is most conducive to peace and stability as well as freedom and prosperity for both sides of the Strait.

## NOTES

Stephen J. Yates, "Why Taiwan's Security Needs to Be Enhanced," *Heritage Foundation Executive Memorandum,* No. 632 (October 25, 1999). Reprinted by permission from the Heritage Foundation.

Stephen J. Yates, senior policy analyst in the Asian Studies Center at the Heritage Foundation (1999); joined the staff of Vice President Dick Cheney in 2001

# The Taiwan Security Reduction Act

## David M. Lampton

The most dangerous piece of foreign policy legislation in memory is moving through Congress. It is titled the Taiwan Security Enhancement Act. Introduced in the Senate by Jessse Helms (R-N.C.) and Robert Torricelli (D-N.J.) and in the House by Rep. Tom DeLay, it ought to be called the Taiwan Security Reduction Act.

If enacted, the legislation would diminish Taiwan's security, alarm friends and allies and greatly increase the chances of armed conflict between America and China. Though a watered-down version of the act probably soon will pass the House, its future is less certain in the Senate. If the bill passes the Senate too, the president must (and I believe will) veto it. If the president rolls over, the American people can expect renewed military tension in the Taiwan Strait. Taiwan citizens will risk falling markets, fleeing capital and diminished security. Washington can forget Sino-American cooperation on major issues. And East Asia can prepare for an arms race.

That the bill is moving through the legislative process now is due, in part, to a Taiwan lobbying effort fueled by money given to politicians, Washington think tanks and law and public relations firms though a variety of probably legal channels. This river of money makes the alleged illegal campaign contributions from the People's Republic of China (PRC) look like chump change.

Beyond money, the legislation draws life from a genuine problem. Over the past two decades, Washington has negotiated complex arrangements with Beijing governing ties with the PRC and Taiwan. These agreements, along with the 1979 Taiwan Relations Act, create ambiguities about the circumstances under which Washington would respond to violence in the Taiwan Strait.

Generally, such ambiguity is undesirable, because uncertainty can foster dangerous miscalculations. In this case, however, if Washington makes it clear that it will support Taipei militarily no matter what it does, we inadvertently encourage unnecessarily provocative behavior by Taiwan that might draw the United States into bloody conflict with Beijing. Conversely, were Washington too timid in deterring Beijing from resorting to force in the Taiwan Strait, we could jeopardize Taiwan's security by leading the PRC to think we might not respond. Some ambiguity is the most prudent middle course.

And in fact there isn't that much ambiguity in the current situation, if Taiwan is not provocative. After all, President Clinton sent a 16-ship flotilla, with two aircraft carriers, to the waters off Taiwan in 1996 when Beijing fired missiles in the island's direction. Further, form 1994 to 1996 Taipei was the fourth largest recipient of U.S. arms, with the pace of deliveries jumping dramatically in 1997, largely because of the sale of F-16s. Taiwan buys so much weaponry that it has had difficulty absorbing, maintaining and operating the equipment. In 1997 the United States sold 8.5 times the value of weapons to Taiwan (in constant dollars) than it did in 1981.

The U.S. legislation is doubly provocative because it both inflames Chinese nationalism and strengthens the PRC military's claims for more weapons and money, on the one hand, and reinforces those in Taiwan who think they can manipulate the U.S. political systems at will, on the other. Further, the act perpetuates the myth in Taiwan's presidential palace that with 1.3 billion people only 95 miles away, Taiwan's security can be principally secured by military means.

If this legislation emerges from Congress in anything like the Senate version, it deserves a presidential veto for five reasons:

- It is unnecessary. The president already has the legal authority to sell Taiwan the weapons it needs.
- The framework by which U.S.–PRC–Taiwan relations have been managed for the past 20 years has permitted Taiwan to make dramatic economic and political progress. If the current framework "ain't broke, don't fix it."
- The legislation directs the executive branch to establish direct military communications, training and other relationships with the Taiwan armed forces, which amounts to a functional reestablishment of the 1955 Mutual Defense Treaty with the island. This would run counter to the terms on which diplomatic relations between Washington and Beijing were established in 1979.
- The bill encourages the transfer of upper-tier antimissile defenses to Taiwan that do not yet exist and which the United States may eventually wish to keep under its own control. Such a declaration would fuel a PRC missile buildup now, while an easily overpowered defense for Taiwan is years away.

- The U.S.–China relationship has enough problems now without saddling this administration with still more—or a new administration with a deteriorating security environment.

## NOTES

David M. Lampton, "The Taiwan Security Reduction Act," *Washington Post*, October 31, 1999, p. B7. Reprinted by permission from David M. Lampton.

David M. Lampton, director of China studies at the Johns Hopkins University School of Advanced International Studies; former professor of political science at Ohio State University; president of the National Committee on U.S.–China Relations (1988–1997)

# 17

# Weapons In, Weapons Out

*In 1999, multiple charges surfaced that China had stolen nuclear secrets from the United States. That March, American scientist Wen Ho Lee, who was born in Taiwan, was arrested for transferring classified data on to unsecured computers with the supposed intent of passing the information to the PRC. Then in May 1999, the House Select Committee on U.S. National Security and Military/Commercial Concerns with the PRC issued a report (the "Cox Report," named after the committee's chairman, Christopher Cox, R-CA) alleging that China had stolen U.S. nuclear secrets over a prolonged period, allowing it to quickly modernize its nuclear forces. Lee himself was released in September 2000 after pleading guilty to one charge of mishandling nuclear secrets. At the final hearing, the presiding judge demonstrated that he was unconvinced of the government's accusations. However, the clear weaknesses in security at the Los Alamos nuclear facility and the ambiguity of what China obtained through Lee or through other means provided ample room for disagreement about the consequences for U.S. security. At the same time, there was additional evidence in the late 1990s of continued missile proliferation by China. However, there was still no agreement on whether China's actions had violated existing agreements or whether the United States should use sanctions to punish China for its behavior.*

## Chinese Takeout

### Henry Sokolski

For nearly a year now, the media have detailed how China has been stealing America's best strategic technology. Last week, though, the *New York Times* dropped a bombshell. Wen Ho Lee, the Los Alamos National Laboratory scientist already suspected of handing China information about a U.S. nuclear warhead, known as the W-88, may have compromised every nuclear weapons design in America's arsenal.

Unlike previous stories of Chinese thefts instigated in the Carter and Reagan years, this news immediately put President Clinton in the penalty box. In mid-March, the president insisted he had not been told of any espionage that had occurred on his watch. Wen Ho Lee, however, transferred the bulk of several thousand secret nuclear weapons files in 1994 and 1995. Worse yet, White House officials, including the president, had reason to know.

In fact, the FBI began a formal criminal investigation of Lee in 1996. On at least three separate occasions, the FBI subsequently briefed the president's national security adviser on the Lee case and the "acute threat" of Chinese nuclear computer espionage at the laboratories. The last briefing, in November 1998, detailed more examples of spying at the laboratories. Finally, early in January, Congress sent the president an additional written warning.

And the White House's response? Wen Ho Lee was allowed continued access to all of Los Alamos's most sensitive weapons information until late last year and was only fired on March 8. As for highly visible corrective actions, the Department of Energy did—regrettably—take one step: It removed its security chief, an official known for persistently criticizing the department's lax security procedures.

Now, no fewer than nine congressional committees are investigating. So far, their aim has been to prevent anything like this from happening again. And in this they can't help but succeed: After what Wen Ho Lee stole from the laboratories, there are hardly any nuclear weapons design secrets left to protect. So, what did he lift? Two kinds of nuclear weapons design information: the national laboratories' "legacy code" and their input data. The legacy code is a computer file containing all the information scientists have gleaned from over four decades of U.S. nuclear testing. It's designed to predict how nuclear weapons will perform. What it won't tell you are the key aspects of any given warhead design. That is largely captured by input data. Put the two together and you not only can project a weapon design's likely performance, you can generate a blueprint of the weapon itself.

Before he was fired, Wen Ho Lee was updating these codes and, from the FBI's investigation of what he downloaded onto his home computer, it looks as though he pretty much stole everything Los Alamos had. Intelligence officials recently established that someone accessed his home computer. They even have documents proving that China secured exact data on at least a half-dozen of America's most advanced weapons. What they lack is legal proof that Lee passed this information on to China.

Still, given Lee's known communications with convicted Chinese spies and his effort to hide evidence (he tried to erase between 1,000 and 2,000 of the stolen files after his last interview with investigators), it's reasonable to assume the worst.

China currently has a relatively small strategic stockpile: 20 ponderous intercontinental-range nuclear rockets and about 400 nuclear weapons that can threaten its Asian neighbors. The systems that can reach the United States, because of their crudity and enormous size, are vulnerable on the ground and would be relatively easy to deflect with missile defenses.

In the next decade, expect all of this to change. China, ever eager to increase its production of nuclear weapons materials, recently acquired the latest in uranium enrichment technology from Russia. With the new, highly efficient nuclear designs it has stolen, though, it will require only a fraction of what it previously needed to modernize its arsenal. Not 20, then, but hundreds of weapons could before long be trained at the United States; and thousands more deployed to face down our Asian allies.

These new systems, moreover, would be small enough to be placed on hard-to-target mobile launchers (which China is developing) and could be clustered on their intercontinental rockets in numbers sufficient to challenge planned U.S. national missile defenses. Larger in number, smaller in size, higher in accuracy, and with faster reentry speeds, these new Chinese warheads are guaranteed to complicate development of U.S. missile defenses for Asia.

Finally, because of the codes it has stolen and the advanced U.S. computer technology our government has allowed to be transferred, China will be able to build this force without the warning afforded by nuclear testing. The White House may still argue that ratifying the Comprehensive Test Ban Treaty is our best hope to prevent further nuclear proliferation. But China—which signed the treaty only months after Wen Ho Lee downloaded the last of Los Alamos's nuclear weapons codes—knows better.

Whether Beijing will actually build up its nuclear forces and spread the strategic technology it has gained to others remains to be seen. If the United States and its allies can close ranks and convince Beijing that such moves would be self-defeating, China may well decide to restrain itself. This prospect, however, will depend far more on what Congress and the White House do now to strengthen U.S. and Asian security than on anything they might belatedly attempt concerning the security of our national laboratories.

## NOTES

Henry Sokolski, "Chinese Takeout," *The Weekly Standard,* May 17, 1999, pp. 14–15. Reprinted with permission of *The Weekly Standard,* May 17, 1999, Copyright News America Corporation.

Henry Sokolski, director of the Nonproliferation Policy Education Center

# The Cox Report and the Threat from China

## Joseph Cirincione

Everyone who wants to talk about Chinese nuclear forces will have to start for at least the next year with a discussion of the Cox Report. In brief, the *Cox Committee report*, like the Rumsfeld Commission before it, has taken a real problem and hyper-inflated it for political purposes.

I had the privilege of serving on the professional national security staff of the House of Representative for over nine years. I know congressional reports. I have written congressional reports. This is no congressional report. It is a propaganda piece. With its unprecedented, expensive, glossy publication style it is much more like the "Soviet Military Power" series produced by the Reagan Administration than it is like any other committee report.

It compares unfavorably, for example, with the sober, serious, balanced report from the Senate Select Committee on Intelligence, on the same subject, released a few weeks before the Cox report. This is what a congressional report should be. The Shelby report is hard-hitting and critical of the Administration. But it is not hysterical and not, as Cox Committee member Congressman Norm Dicks admitted about his report, a "worst case assessment."

Turning to the substance, House Majority Leader Dick Armey summarizes the report for us when he says, "It's very scary, and basically what it says is the Chinese now have the capability of threatening us with our own nuclear technology."

He gets that information directly from the Report's overview, which states:

- "These thefts of nuclear secrets from our national weapons laboratories enabled the PRC to design, develop and successfully test modern strategic nuclear weapons sooner than would otherwise have been possible."
- "The stolen U.S. nuclear secrets give the PRC design information on thermonuclear weapons on a par with our own . . . the stolen information includes classified information on seven U.S. thermonuclear warheads."
- Then, later on p. 60 of Volume I of the report, "The stolen U.S. secrets have helped the PRC fabricate and successfully test modern strategic thermonuclear weapons."

These are dramatic statements. They are also not true, at least according to the combined judgement of all of our national intelligence agencies and an *independent review* panel led by Adm. David Jeremiah and including Brent

Scowcroft. It is understandable that the Cox Committee made mistakes. After all, according to Committee Member John Spratt, they only turned to the matter of Chinese espionage on October 21 [1998], and concluded taking testimony on the issue on November 15 and filed their report Jan. 3 [1999].

The Committee had spent most of its time in 1998 investigating charges that critical technology was transferred to the PRC by major U.S. corporations while using Chinese rockets to launch American satellites. Many in the Republican leadership had hoped this investigation would lead to impeachment charges against the President. A number of Republican leaders went to the floor of the House and Senate and accused the President of treason for allegedly facilitating this transfer of information. These charges could not be substantiated. The Cox Committee then hurriedly took testimony from only three witnesses on the nuclear weapons security issue: DOE intelligence official Notra Trulock, a CIA analyst, and a Los Alamos employee. The Cox report basically presents the Notra Trulock view of China, unchallenged and unbalanced.

## CHINA'S CHANGING NUCLEAR POSTURE

Let's take a step back and review what China's nuclear capabilities are.

Deep in China's Henan province, a hundred miles from the ancient city of Xi'an, China has deployed in silos and in caves about 20 Dong Feng-5 missiles. They are deployed with their liquid fuel tanks empty and with their 4- and 5- megaton nuclear warheads detached and stored separately. Though each has enough explosive power to vaporize an average city, the force pales in comparison to the 5,500 warheads the United States deploys on its modern, highly accurate missiles, or even the 144 warheads the United Kingdom carries on its Trident sea-launched ballistic missiles.

Of the five recognized nuclear powers (the United States, Russia, Britain, France and China), China has the oldest, least capable, and most stable nuclear deterrent force. China deployed the first Dong Feng-5 (or "East Wind") in 1981. Slowly, over the years, the numbers have grown to the current 20 missiles deployed. For two decades, this atomic arsenal, along with dozens of intermediate- and short-range nuclear missiles and air-dropped bombs, has served China's strategic interests.

China has plans to modernize the missile force, and actually has been trying to implement those plans for well over a decade. . . . Like the other powers, China uses a variety of methods to acquire the information it needs to develop its weaponry, including espionage.

Earlier this year, the Cox committee report—then classified—recommended that the Executive branch conduct a comprehensive damage assessment on the implications of China's acquisition of U.S. nuclear weapons information. The

Administration did so, forming a team of officials from the CIA, DIA, DOD, NSA, INR, FBI, and other agencies and the nuclear laboratories. An independent panel of nuclear experts, Chaired by Admiral David Jeremiah and including General Brent Scowcroft, Dr. John Foster and others then reviewed their damage assessment. In April, they issued their report. This net assessment has been lost in the political firestorm generated by recent congressional hearings and reports. It deserves to be read carefully. They reached two critical conclusions.

The Damage Assessment team concluded:

China's technical advances have been make on the basis of classified and unclassified information derived from espionage, contact with U.S. and other countries' scientists, conferences and publications, unauthorized media disclosure, declassified U.S. weapons information, and Chinese indigenous development. The relative contribution of each cannot be determined.

This means that we do not know, and may never know, whether the Chinese got most of their information from spying or from the Internet.

The tip-off that China had at least some classified information on U.S. weapons designs came from an unusual 1995 incident. In an apparent attempt to establish a double-agent, a Chinese national walked into a U.S. office in Asia with an armful of top-secret Chinese documents. One of these was a paper dated 1988 listing the characteristics of a number of deployed U.S. nuclear weapons. While much of this information, such as yield, weight, and accuracy was readily available, one tidbit was not—the radius of the primary stage of the W-88 warhead. This sent alarm bells ringing, and it is the basis for the charge that China has design information on all our current nuclear warheads. But the suspect nature of this double agent and the documents he produced make it difficult to evaluate the seriousness of the situation.

The discovery this March that critical nuclear design data was illegally moved from a classified to an unclassified computer at Los Alamos National Laboratory is much more serious. Even here, it is still not known if any of the information actually reached China.

We do know, however, that whatever information China accessed has had little impact on their nuclear weapons. The Damage Assessment panel concluded:

Significant deficiencies remain in the Chinese weapons program. . . . To date, the aggressive Chinese collection effort has not resulted in any apparent modernization of their deployed strategic force or any new nuclear weapons deployment.

China has had the technical capability to develop a multiple independently targetable reenty vehicle (MIRV) system for its large, currently deployed ICBM for many years, but has not done so.

This assessment directly contradicts the central message of the Cox report. China will modernize its nuclear forces and its conventional military forces. But it is so far behind the United States and our allies that America's military leaders conclude unanimously, as Commander-in-Chief of the Pacific Command Admiral Dennis Blair testified this year, "China would not represent a serious military threat to the U.S. for at least 20 years."

Director of the Defense Intelligence Agency General Patrick Hughes concludes bluntly in his annual threat assessment, "There is no indication that China will field the much larger number of missiles necessary to shift from a minimalist, retaliation strategy to a first-strike strategy.". . .

This DIA assessment is consistent with the policy of a minimum deterrence force that China has pursued since it first began its nuclear weapons program. China has never had any intention of making the same mistake the Soviet Union and the United States made during the Cold War: engaging in an expensive race that produce over 125,000 nuclear weapons (at the cost on the U.S. side alone of over $5 trillion). China has sought a minimum force, adequate to deter a nuclear adversary from attacking first, knowing that there would be a nuclear launch in response. . . .

Obviously, China's plans could accelerate. If the United States and Japan increase their military presence on China's borders by deploying missile defenses, if the U.S. enters into a de facto military alliance with Taiwan over missile defenses, or if India were to deploy nuclear-armed missiles in significant numbers, China's military could well demand and get a greater share of China's scarce resources.

The overall Chinese strategic vision remains the same: China wants 20 to 30 years of international peace and stability in order to modernize its economy and raise the standard of living for its population. Only then would true military modernization be possible. During this economic modernization process much could change in China, including the very nature of the regime. In fact, some would say that democratization is essential for China's sustained economic growth.

Much depends on how America handles this critical relationship. Campaign agendas or political hyperbole should not overrule the sound judgements of our military leadership nor stampede us into reckless confrontations or expensive new military programs.

## NOTES

Joseph Cirincione, "The Cox Report and the Threat from China," presentation to the Cato Institute, Washington, DC, June 7, 1999. Reprinted by permission from Joseph Cirincione.

Joseph Cirincione, director of the Non-Proliferation Project, Carnegie Endowment for International Peace

# United States Policy Regarding
# the Export of Satellites to China

*House testimony by Gary Milhollin*

## FAILURE TO APPLY SANCTIONS LAW

**Mr. Milhollin** [*witness, prepared statement*]: . . . China's exports remain the most serious proliferation threat in the world. Since 1980, China has supplied billions of dollars worth of nuclear weapon, chemical weapon and missile technology to South Asia, South Africa, South America and the Middle East. It has done so despite U.S. protests, and despite repeated promises to stop. The exports are still going on, and while they do, they make it impossible for the United States and its allies to halt the spread of weapons of mass destruction. . . .

In the early 1990s, Chinese companies were caught selling Pakistan M-11 missile components. The M-11 is an accurate, solid-fuel missile that can carry a nuclear warhead about 300 kilometers. In June 1991, the Bush administration sanctioned the two offending Chinese sellers. The sanctions were supposed to last for at least two years, but they were waived less than a year later, in March 1992, when China promised to abide by the guidelines of the Missile Technology Control Regime.

But by December 1992, in violation of its promise, China had shipped 34 M-11 missiles to Pakistan. Waiving the sanctions was a mistake.

In August 1993, the Clinton administration applied sanctions for two years, after determining that China had violated the U.S. missile sanctions law a second time. Then in October 1994, the United States lifted the sanctions early again, when China pledged once more to stop its missile sales and comply with the MTCR.

Since late 1994, the stream of missile exports has continued. U.S. officials say that China's missile exports have continued up until the present moment, unabated. These exports include the sale of missile-related guidance and control equipment to Iran as well as Pakistan.

In fact, our officials have learned that they were duped in 1992 and 1994. China was not promising what we thought it was. Our officials now realize that China interprets its promises in 1992 and 1994 so narrowly as to make them practically meaningless. It is clear that China has not complied with the MTCR in the past, that it is not complying now, and that it probably never will comply unless something happens to change China's attitude on this question.

In its latest venture, China is helping to build a plant to produce M-11 missiles in Pakistan. U.S. officials say that activity at the plant is "very high." If the

Chinese continue to help at their present rate, the plant could be ready for missile production within a year.

By the autumn of 1996, the intelligence community had completed an airtight finding of fact on China's missile transfers to Pakistan. There was clear proof that the transfers had happened. All the factual analysis necessary to apply sanctions had been finished. A similar finding on China's missile exports to Iran had also been made.

And roughly one year earlier, an important legal analysis had been completed. The legal analysis established that sanctions could be applied where a foreign person "conspires to or attempts to engage in" the export of any MTCR equipment or technology. Thus, sanctions could be applied *without* a finding that hardware or technology had actually been exported. A conspiracy or even an attempt to transfer such items would be enough. One did not need a photograph of a missile with "made in China" written on the side.

The findings of fact and the legal analysis showed clearly that China should be sanctioned. Both the findings and the analysis had been circulated to the relevant agencies by autumn of 1996. Both Pakistan and Iran were covered. The process, however, was short-circuited at that point.

The next step would have been for the National Security Council to call a meeting at which each agency could submit for the record its views on whether sanctions should be imposed. The NSC would then forward these views to the Department of State, which would prepare a decision memorandum for the Under Secretary, who has the legal authority to impose sanctions.

But none of these steps were ever taken. The State Department simply chose not to complete the administrative process. Thus, the sanctions law is not being implemented as Congress intended and, in fact, is being circumvented. It is obvious that the law can never take effect unless the administrative process is completed, so the failure to complete it is manifestly illegal.

. . . The State Department is no longer saying that there is "not enough evidence" to apply sanctions to China. It is now saying that it has "not yet made a determination" to apply sanctions, which is quite different. In effect, the State Department is saying that it has not applied sanctions because it has not chosen to complete the administrative process. I recommend that Congress take steps to see that the law is enforced.

Now that Pakistan has demonstrated its nuclear weapon capability, and announced that it will mount nuclear warheads on missiles, this matter has become urgent. The Chinese-supplied M-11s will actually carry nuclear weapons. President Clinton has said that the world should try to prevent India and Pakistan from putting warheads on missiles, but his Administration refuses to apply a U.S. law designed to prevent Pakistan from acquiring missiles in the first place. . . .

## CHINA IN THE MTCR?

This past March, the Administration invited China to join the Missile Technology Control Regime. In a memorandum dated March 12, White House staff member Gary Samore stated the reasons for making the offer. Sanctions figured prominently among them. If China joined, the memo stated, China could expect "substantial protection from future U.S. missile sanctions."

Mr. Samore could have said "complete protection." Under Section 73 of the Arms Export Control Act, sanctions would not apply to a Chinese company if China joined the MTCR even if the company transferred complete missiles to Iran or Pakistan. Sanctions would be avoided if the sale were legal under Chinese law, or if China took action against the company, or if China found the company to be innocent. In effect, the Administration offered China a complete shield against U.S. sanctions law.

The Administration was also offering China a second benefit. As things stand now, if a U.S. exporter gets an order from a known missile maker in China, the exporter cannot make the sale without notifying the government and getting an export license. This is required by Section 6 of the Export Administration Act. If China were to join the MTCR, however, no license would be required for such a sale. U.S. firms could deliberately outfit Chinese missile manufacturing sites without telling anyone.

It is difficult to see how such an offer is prudent. China has repeatedly failed to comply with MTCR guidelines since promising to do so in 1992 and 1994. There is no real evidence that China has changed its ways. Thus, the offer seems to be yet another effort to insulate Chinese aerospace companies from U.S. sanctions laws so that satellite launches can continue.

## CONCLUSION

When we look at the history of U.S. sanctions policy, we see a willingness to sanction China for missile proliferation in both the Bush Administration, which applied sanctions in 1991, and in the Clinton Administration, which applied sanctions in 1993. But in 1995, the Clinton Administration policy changed. China supplied the C-802s to Iran in 1995; China supplied other missile components to Iran and Pakistan in 1995 and has continued to supply up to the present time. And in 1996, the Administration refused to act on explicit findings by the intelligence community that the transfer occurred. Also in 1996, the Administration started transferring control over satellites exports from the State to the Commerce Department, insulating them from the application of missile sanction laws in the future. For some reason, the Administration decided in either 1995 or 1996 that missile sanctions would no longer be part of U.S. policy in dealing with China.

Why did U.S. policy change? I don't know the answer to that question, but I urge the Committees to look into it.

We do know the result of the policy change. It gave China a green light to proliferate. Our government's policy on sanctions has enabled Chinese satellite launch companies to sell missiles and missile components to Iran and Pakistan without fear of punishment. Thus, it may be that we are asking the wrong question about how our satellite export policy affects missile proliferation.

Whether or not our satellite exports caused U.S. missile technology to go to China, they have made it easier for Chinese missile technology to go to Pakistan.

India, of course, has watched this happen. India watched China help Pakistan make not only missiles but the nuclear warheads to go on them. India also watched the United States invent every excuse possible not to do anything about it. America asked the Indians to show restraint in nuclear testing, but America was unwilling to put restraints on its own satellite companies by sanctioning China. The Indians no doubt concluded that Uncle Sam was against the spread of the bomb unless it might cost him something. It should not surprise us if our non-proliferation policy lacks credibility.

### NOTES

House Committees on National Security and International Relations, "United States Policy Regarding the Export of Satellites to China," 105th Congress, 2nd sess., June 17, 1998. Testimony by Gary Milhollin.

Gary Milhollin, director, Wisconsin Project on Nuclear Arms Control

# Don't Push China on Proliferation

## Phillip C. Saunders and Evan S. Medeiros

The Senate's rejection of the Comprehensive Test Ban Treaty dealt a damaging blow to U.S. nonproliferation policy. Now the Clinton administration and Congress must reconsider how to address one of the biggest challenges to U.S. security: proliferation of weapons of mass destruction and their delivery systems.

A National Intelligence Council report in September [1999] publicly stated—for the first time—that China has transferred M-11 missiles to Pakistan. This unequivocal statement presents the administration with a dilemma. Under U.S. law, transfers of missiles or related technology exceeding Missile Technology Control Regime, or MTCR, parameters—the ability to deliver a 1,100-pound payload over 186 miles—trigger sanctions. The administration can either impose sanctions and provoke a crisis in relations with China or circumvent the law by ignoring convincing evidence of missile transfers that occurred in 1991–92.

The challenge for the Clinton administration is to resolve this dilemma while advancing the goals of combating proliferation and improving relations with China.

The intent behind the 1990 Missile Control Act mandating sanctions is to punish current missile exporters and to deter future sales. With respect to China, able diplomacy by the Bush and Clinton administrations has largely accomplished this goal. Bilateral negotiations from 1990 to 1994 persuaded China to reduce and then to halt transfers of M-series ballistic missiles to Syria, Iran, and Pakistan.

In the case of Syria, U.S. diplomats persuaded China to cancel a contract for M-9 missiles, even though the Syrians had already paid. The U.S. imposed limited economic sanctions on China in 1991 and 1993 over transfers of M-11 components to Pakistan. By 1994, this pressure resulted in China freezing the deal and strengthening its initially limited commitment to adhere to the MTCR. In October 1997, China even agreed to stop selling to Iran C-801 and C-802 cruise missiles, which are not covered by any accord.

China's recent record on missile proliferation is by no means perfect. It is not a full MTCR member and does not have export laws covering MTCR-controlled items. The U.S. continues to have concerns about transfers of dual-use technology not covered in China's nonproliferation commitments and about unauthorized exports by Chinese companies. Yet compared with a decade ago, when China openly sold intermediate range missiles to Saudi Arabia, the scope of China's missile proliferation activities have declined dramatically.

The recent intelligence report does not involve a new transfer of M-11 missiles to Pakistan. China already has been sanctioned twice for these activities. Additional sanctions now are unlikely to advance U.S. nonproliferation goals.

Internal Chinese debates on issues such as MTCR membership and the test ban treaty ratification are at a crucial stage. China likely would respond to sanctions by limiting future cooperation on these issues and might even backtrack on its exiting commitments. Moreover, the Senate rejection of the CTBT is causing even U.S. friends and allies to question U.S. commitment to international arms control and nonproliferation agreements. China is likely to conclude that the U.S. only supports arms control when it is convenient.

Sanctions would deal another blow to strained relations only beginning to improve after the Chinese Embassy bombing in Belgrade. Our conversations with Chinese foreign ministry officials and army officers indicate that many Chinese view the months leading up to Taiwan's March presidential elections as a dangerous time. They worry that, as anti-China sentiments in the U.S.

grow, Lee Teng-hui will be emboldened to make further moves toward independence, and China will be compelled to respond with force.

This adds up to an overwhelming case for waiving sanctions on the grounds of U.S. national security interests. The Clinton administration should admit that China transferred the missiles to Pakistan in the early 1990s, but it should decline to impose sanctions because they would not advance U.S. nonproliferation objectives.

We do not mean to suggest that the issue of nonproliferation is unimportant. Rather, the issue is so important that policymakers must concentrate on policies that work.

The administration and Congress should focus on the fundamental question of what measures will persuade China to behave in a manner consistent with international norms on nonproliferation, arms control and international trade. Sanctions are one tool, but in this case, mechanical imposition of sanctions will at best be ineffective and at worst counter-productive.

## NOTES

Phillip C. Saunders and Evan S. Medeiros, "Don't Push China on Proliferation," *Los Angeles Times*, November 18, 1999, p. B11. Reprinted by permission from Phillip C. Saunders and Evan S. Medeiros.

Phillip C. Saunders, director of the East Asia Nonproliferation Project of the Center for Nonproliferation Studies at the Monterey Institute of International Studies; Evan S. Medeiros, senior research associate at the Center for Nonproliferation Studies at the Monterey Institute of International Studies

# 18

# Permanent MFN: Trade and Human Rights

*In 2000, the U.S. Congress considered whether to provide China permanent most-favored-nation status (also known by then as permanent normal trade relations [PNTR]). The debate contained many of the same arguments from the hearings held in 1979 and in the 1990s over the annual extension of MFN. However, the 2000 deliberations took on added significance because if granted permanent MFN, this potential carrot (or stick) would no longer be available to U.S. policymakers. That year, Congress passed legislature that was then signed by President Clinton to grant China permanent MFN upon its entry into the World Trade Organization, which occurred in late 2001.*

## Giving the People's Republic of China Permanent MFN: Implications for U.S. Policy

### Senate testimony by Greg Mastel

#### THE WTO ACCESSION AGREEMENT

**Mr. Mastel** [*witness, prepared statement*]: . . . Trade agreements are by their nature compromises. As a result, they are normally not "perfect" from any individual perspective. The agreement with China is no exception. Unquestionably, a number of provisions could be improved. Chinese tariffs could be lowered beyond the 17 percent China has agreed to. Foreign telecommunications firms and banks could be granted more leeway to operate in China. It is possible that subsequent negotiations between China and other WTO members may improve the terms on these or other issues.

On paper, however, the "deal" negotiated between Washington and Beijing has a good deal to commend it. China does agree to substantial tariff cuts.

China does commit to substantial new market access for agricultural products. U.S. banks and insurance firms are promised substantially increased access to Chinese consumers.

Unfortunately, the problem in negotiating trade agreements with China in recent years has not been convincing China to promise improvements, it has been getting China to fulfill its promises. Already, Chinese press reports indicate that China does not plan to rigorously fulfill the agricultural provisions in the WTO accession agreement.

A careful examination of the four recent major trade agreements the United States has struck with China strongly suggests that compliance problems have been serious.

## INTELLECTUAL PROPERTY—1992

One of the best-known agreements between the United States and China involves protection of intellectual property—patented, copyrighted, and trademarked material. The United States has sought improved protection of intellectual property from China for many years.

After the threat of sanctions, the Bush administration convinced China to undertake a sweeping update of its laws protecting intellectual property. China brought its intellectual property protection regime largely into compliance with accepted western norms.

Unfortunately, these legal changes had little discernible impact on the ground. Chinese piracy of music recording, computer programs, and films grew at an alarming rate at least through the mid-1990s. Movies and computer programs made by Chinese pirates turned up as far away as Canada and Eastern Europe.

After trying to address matters through quiet consultations, the Clinton administration threatened to impose trade sanctions in 1995 unless the situation improved. As the deadline for sanctions approached, China agreed to step up enforcement efforts.

A year later, however, it was apparent that China's promises had resulted in little improvement. Once again, the Clinton administration threatened sanctions. After much complaint, the Chinese agreed to a much more specific enforcement regime.

With consistent pressure from the United States, China has regularly produced records of pirate operations shut down and held press demonstrations with steamrollers crushing pirated CDs. Although these demonstrations do show at least some ongoing effort to attack the problem of piracy, they also demonstrate that piracy continues at a high level. Although it is difficult to precisely measure, U.S. pressure has won some results, but the U.S. industry estimates that losses to piracy today are greater than they were when the topic of enforcement was raised in 1995. . . .

In many ways, the efforts made to enforce the agreement on piracy of intellectual property are unique. Both the private sector and the Clinton administration have made enforcement of this agreement a priority for the better part of a decade. Still, glaring enforcement problems remain. If it had not been for the ongoing, high-level enforcement efforts by the United States, there is no reason to believe that China would have made a serious effort to fulfill the promises made in 1992.

## MARKET ACCESS—1992

Unfortunately, the high level commitment made to enforce the intellectual property agreement has not been repeated on other agreements. A sweeping agreement struck with China in 1992 on market access issues is a case in point.

Through the early 1990s, China followed an unabashedly protectionist trade policy excluding many foreign products with a number of trade barriers. Under threat of sanctions similar to those used on intellectual property, the Bush administration successfully negotiated a sweeping market access agreement with China aimed at lowering trade barriers and creating new opportunities for U.S. exports.

In its latest reports on the subject, the Clinton administration states that China has "generally" fulfilled its commitments. On some of the easily verifiable matters covered by the agreement, like elimination of formal barriers and lowering tariffs, China does seem to have implemented the agreement. In a number of other areas, however, there have been glaring and obvious problems. . . .

First, China agreed in 1992 to eliminate all import substitution policies—policies that aim to substitute domestic production for imports. In formal state plans on automobiles and pharmaceuticals approved by Chinese economic policy makers at the highest levels, import substitution requirements were specifically included. Similar policies are included in lower level Ministry directives on a number of products, including power generation equipment and electronic products.

Import substitution is perhaps the most direct form of protectionism possible and it was officially renounced in 1992. Still, time and time again the Chinese government has ignored this commitment.

China also agreed to phase out an entire class of barriers, import licenses, and not raise new barriers. Shortly, after import licenses were phased out, however, China announced a suspiciously similar set of import registration requirements for many of the products previously covered by import licenses. A number of new trade barriers on products ranging from electricity generating equipment to pharmaceuticals have also sprung up.

Finally, China agreed to make all laws and regulations relevant to foreign trade public—a major change in a country where many regulations and policies are not made part of the public record. Many such directives are now publicly available. Yet, this seemingly elementary provision has also not been implemented in a number of areas, including government procurement regulations.

Taken separately, it is difficult to estimate the economic importance of each of these violations. It is clear, however, that they are clear, unambiguous examples of the Chinese government directly violating the terms of the 1992 market access agreement. These charges have been officially made for a number of years, and the Chinese government has offered no denial or explanation. . . .

## TEXTILE TRANSSHIPMENT

For decades, trade in textiles and apparel has been governed by a special trading arrangement known as the Multi Fiber Agreement (MFA). Under the MFA, importers and exporters of textiles negotiate what amount to specific quotas on textile imports on a bilateral basis. As the world's largest textile exporter and the world's largest importer, China and the United States, respectively, both participate in the MFA and concluded a parallel bilateral agreement in 1994.

For some years, there have been persistent reports of transshipment of textiles and apparel by Chinese entities to avoid MFA limits. In essence, transshipment involves Chinese companies labeling textiles made in China as having originated elsewhere, usually Hong Kong or Macao, to avoid MFA limits. Given the illegal nature of transshipment, accurate figures are not available on the scope of the problem. A past U.S. Customs Commissioner estimated that transshipment from China into the U.S. market amounted to about $2 billion worth of imports annually. A more recent Customs study noted that as much as $10 billion in Chinese textile exports were not officially accounted for—much of this undoubtedly found its way into the U.S. market.

This issue deserves particular attention in connection with any discussion on the size of the U.S. trade deficit with China. A number of individuals, I believe incorrectly, argue that the size of the U.S. trade deficit with China is greatly exaggerated. Invariably, the analysts that take this position simply ignore the issue of textile transshipment. If the findings of the U.S. Customs Service are correct with regard to transshipment, it means that official U.S. statistics on the trade deficit with China actually underestimate the deficit by several billion dollars per year because they overlook Chinese textile exports illegally transshipment through Hong Kong and Macao.

The Customs Service has undertaken a number of enforcement efforts to address transshipment over the years, including reducing China's official MFA quotas as a penalty for transshipment. In 1997, China and the U.S. reached a four-year Textile Trade Agreement that, among other things, reduced quotas in fourteen apparel and fabric categories where there were repeated instances of transshipment and strengthened penalties for transshipment. Nevertheless, in May 1998, USTR and Customs brought action against China for violation of the agreement, imposing $5 million in charges on textiles illegally transshipped.

Each year, a list of Chinese, Macao and Hong Kong companies involved in transshipment is also released. On the most recent list, 23 of the 26 companies assessed penalties for illegal transshipment were from China, Hong Kong or Macao, and 27 of the 32 companies under investigation were from China, Hong Kong or Macao. Despite these efforts, the problem of transshipment unquestionably continues.

Whatever one's views on the desirability of the MFA, China's record of tolerating massive transshipment of textiles and apparel to avoid MFA quotas is hardly an encouraging example of China's record of trade agreement compliance.

## PRISON LABOR

Similar problems have been identified with regard to China's exports of goods made with prison labor. China has an extensive system of prison work camps that produce products ranging from apparel to tools and machinery. Often, prison work forces are leased to private sector firms to assemble or manufacture various products. Under a 1930s U.S. law, it is illegal to import into the United States products made with prison or forced labor.

Over the years, there have been persistent allegations that a number of imports from China violated this law. In 1992, the Bush administration concluded a bilateral agreement to halt the export of forced labor goods to the United States and to hold periodic consultations between Customs officials from both countries.

Despite the agreement, advocacy groups interested in the topic of prison labor have produced evidence that various Chinese companies exporting to the United States are involved in prison labor commerce, found evidence that various products made with prison labor have been imported into the United States, and done hidden camera investigations in China indicating that Chinese companies are prepared to export prison labor products to the United States.

Because it is very hard to distinguish prison labor goods from other goods in commerce, it is impossible to make a credible estimate of the size of the problem. However, the State Department's 1998 report on Human Rights Practices in China found that Chinese cooperation under the 1992 agreement had been "inadequate" and that when complaints were brought by the U.S., "the Ministry of Justice refused the request, ignored it, or simply denied the allegations made without further elaboration." The report also notes that Chinese officials have attempted to unilaterally define Chinese work camps as not covered by the 1992 agreement—an interpretation that renders the agreement virtually meaningless.

## CAN CHINA BE TRUSTED?

After reviewing the available evidence, it is clear that there have been serious enforcement/compliance issues involving every recent trade agreement concluded with China. In some cases, it can be credibly argued that the agreement still resulted in an on-balance improvement in the relevant Chinese trade practices. That said, China's implementation fell far short of fulfilling the letter and spirit of all trade agreements. Without an extensive U.S. enforcement effort on intellectual property, most of the progress that has been made would likely never have come about.

China's defenders often claim that China's record is no worse that that of other countries. Without question, it is true that a number of U.S. trading partners appear to have cheated on trade agreements over the years. Japan is most often cited as an example. . . .

The problem of poor enforcement/implementation of trade agreements in China appears to go beyond a simple matter of countries ignoring provisions of trade agreements so as not to offend important domestic constituencies. As many Chinese leaders have conceded China lacks a reliable rule of law. In the trade arena, this means that it is difficult or impossible for any entity in the Beijing government to direct policy changes that bind China's diverse collection of Ministries, State Owned Enterprises, and provincial governments.

Unfortunately, although international pressure may at times be helpful, the WTO is not a magical solution to this problem. The WTO is the ultimate in an international, rule-of-law based institution. It is unclear that it will be able to police a country that operates without a rule-of-law. Trade policies in China are often made in secret without a paper trail. It may well be impossible to even document the existence of objectionable Chinese trade practices much less win a WTO dispute settlement panel against them.

To some, problems of enforcement may seem to be a rather trivial concern. These critics should keep in mind that none of the benefits ascribed to a WTO agreement with China will be achieved without enforcement. In fact, if China simply ignores the terms of the WTO as it has other agreements the benefits could be quite limited; the damage done to the credibility of the WTO under this scenario, however, could be lasting and serious.

Critics would also do well to keep in mind that there is no guarantee that the current relatively reform minded leaders in Beijing will prevail. Given the uncertainties of Chinese politics, it is certainly possible to imagine a much less reform oriented regime, perhaps one led by the military or hard line elements, emerging in China. Instead of using the WTO as a springboard for domestic reform, such a regime could us the WTO as a shield to block foreign sanctions against their policies. Such a regime would pose enormous WTO enforcement problems as well as challenges on may other fronts.

In fact, membership in the WTO will only help Chinese reformers, like Zhu Rongji, reform China's economy if it is enforced. Viewed from this perspective, a vigorous, ongoing effort to enforce the WTO in China may be the best thing the United States could do to further the cause of reform in China.

Unfortunately, as the above examples demonstrate, the record of the United States in carrying out such enforcement efforts is far from reassuring. Historically, efforts to enforce trade agreements have been transient and unpredictable, often blocked by other government priorities or concerns of some U.S. companies that tough enforcement actions might compromise their specific interests.

In light of this record on enforcement and China's weak compliance record, the Congress would do the United States and, ultimately, Chinese reformers a favor by creating vigorous enforcement procedures as a quid pro quo for approving permanent MFN for China. This could take the form of annual reviews, in which the Congress has a direct role, backed up by the promise of trade action to ensure that enforcement of the WTO remains a priority of the United States.

. . . China's membership in the WTO seems likely this year, but the task of bringing China into compliance with the WTO's provisions will likely take decades. A successful effort will take the ongoing effort of Congresses and administrations that will not be elected for years to come. If this Congress and this administration can build an ongoing framework to ensure attention to these important issues, they will do the future Congressmen, future Presidents, the cause of reform in China, and America as a whole a great service.

## NOTES

Senate Committee on Foreign Relations, "Giving the People's Republic of China Permanent MFN: Implications for U.S. Policy," 106th Congress, 2nd sess., April 11, 2000. Testimony by Greg Mastel.

Greg Mastel, director, Global Economic Policy Project, New America Foundation

# Permanent Normal Trade Relations for China

## *Nicholas R. Lardy*

### CHINA'S DOMESTIC ECONOMIC CHALLENGES

China faces a major challenge in sustaining the rapid economic growth that since 1978 has characterized its transition from a planned economy to a market economy. Economic growth, according to official data, was 7.1 percent in 1999, the seventh consecutive year in which growth was slower than in the previous year. The official Chinese government forecast for 2000 is 7.0 percent, which would continue the growth slowdown yet one more year.

The challenge the leadership faces is actually much greater than these numbers suggest. The official data overstate the pace of economic expansion and the gains in real economic welfare, if for no other reason then the fact that there has been an extraordinary build up of unsold and unsaleable inventories over the past decade. . . . While some increase in inventories is needed to support higher levels of output, the disproportionately large inventory build up in China reflects the continued production of low quality goods for which there is little or no demand. Chinese society would have been much better off if the goods had never been produced. China's Premier, Zhu Rongji, in his annual address to the National People's Congress in March, acknowledged that inventory build up was an ongoing problem and that China must "limit the production of non-marketable products." Of course, if China's banks were operating on a commercial basis, they would have cut off additional working capital loans to foundering companies, automatically limiting the build up of inventories.

Whatever the precise rate of real economic growth, there is little doubt that the Chinese economy has slowed significantly in recent years, despite a massive program of increased government expenditures and lending by state-owned banks through which the leadership has sought to prop up economic growth via increased outlays for investment.

In addition to the growth slowdown, there are several other indicators of the challenges China's leadership faces in the wake of the Asian financial crisis. Export growth has slowed dramatically since 1997. Between 1987 and 1997 Chinese exports surged from less than US$40 billion to $183 billion, an average annual rate of expansion of 16.5 percent. But in the past two years, export growth has been far more modest, averaging only a little over 3 percent annually.

Similarly, after watching foreign direct investment inflows soar from US$3–4 billion annually in the late 1980s to $45 billion in 1997, the leadership saw foreign direct investment growth evaporate in 1998 and then witnessed a significant decline to US$40 billion in 1999. This shrinkage in foreign direct investment is the first ever in the reform period.

Similarly, year after year foreign banks were willing to extend larger and larger amounts of foreign currency loans to China. But in 1998 foreign lending to China began to decline and after January 1999, when the Guangdong International Trust and Investment Company declared bankruptcy, loans declined sharply for the first time in more than a decade. By the end of the third quarter of 1999, total foreign currency lending to China by banks was down by US$20 billion, or about one-fourth, compared to year-end 1997.

Finally, for the first time in three decades China's leadership is grappling with the problem of price deflation. The underlying problem has been over-investment in many sectors, leading to excess capacity and a tendency for manufacturers to cut prices in an effort to sell enough product to cover the cost of their labor and other variable inputs. Thus, price deflation in China for some critical products, such as steel, long predates the Asian financial crisis. But that crisis significantly deepened the deflationary trend since China's fixed exchange rate against the U.S. dollar meant that deflation elsewhere in the region was imported into China. While deflation is over in most of Asia because of a brisk recovery, deflation in China not only persists but accelerated in 1999.

## THE SEARCH FOR A NEW GROWTH PARADIGM

China's sweeping bilateral agreement with the United States on the terms of its membership in the World Trade Organization, concluded last fall, reflects the search by the Chinese leadership for a new growth paradigm. There is widespread recognition that repeated short-term fiscal stimuli, which have been used to shore up growth since 1997, are no more than a temporary expedient. These short-term measures may prevent a complete collapse of economic growth, but they cannot generate sustained economic growth in the long run. The leadership has concluded that sustaining growth in the long run depends critically on allocating resources more efficiently rather than simply maintaining the highest rate of overall investment in the world. The leadership believes it can achieve increased efficiency by reducing the restrictions that have previously constrained the private sector of the economy and by bolstering competition, which will follow from opening up China more fully to the global economy.

To increase competition and stimulate productivity gains, the leadership has agreed to continue to reduce both tariff and nontariff barriers. More importantly, it has agreed to more fully open its service sector to increased foreign ownership. Financial services, telecommunications, and distribution (including wholesaling and retailing) are the most important areas where foreign firms will have significant new opportunities. All these steps will increase competition, thus placing significant additional pressure on domestic firms to lower their cost structures in order to survive. China's reformist leadership, in effect, is using the membership requirements of the World Trade Organization as a lever to achieve fundamental changes in state-owned enterprises and state-owned banks that they have long sought but which have been somewhat elusive.

There can be little doubt that the leadership fully appreciates the risks of the course on which they have embarked. Already tens of millions of urban workers have lost their jobs in state and collective factories as China accelerates domestic economic restructuring in preparation for increased international competition that inevitably will follow its membership in the World Trade Organization. Many of those who have been laid-off have found new jobs in the competitive portions of the economy—the rapidly growing private, foreign-funded, and export-oriented sectors. But those who lack the skills, or live in cities long dominated by state-owned factories, have little prospect for finding new jobs locally. Rising levels of urban unemployment, compounded by delays in the distribution of living allowances due laid-off workers and pensions due those already retired from failing state-owned companies, have led to widespread urban violence. In rural areas, too, the prospect is for substantial dislocation as China reduces its subsidies for basic staple commodities, such as wheat and corn, again in anticipation of increased inflows of lower-priced foreign products.

The willingness of the leadership to incur these substantial short-term economic and political costs in the pursuit of long-term economic gains is a measure of the depth of their commitment to further reforms.

## U.S. INTERESTS

Granting PNTR to China is strongly in the U.S. national interest for several reasons. First, denying China PNTR would require the United States to invoke Article XIII of the Final Act of the Uruguay Round, meaning that we would not apply the World Trade Organization Agreement with respect to China, even after it became a member of the organization. The notice to non-apply would have to be delivered prior to the time the General Council of the World Trade Organization meets to approve the terms and conditions of China's membership, probably sometime in the second half of 2000.

China, in turn, would then almost certainly invoke Article XIII with respect to the United States, meaning that U.S. firms would not benefit from most of the sweeping market opening measures to which China agreed in the November 1999 bilateral agreement. Under the terms of an existing bilateral trade agreement, U.S. firms could expect their products to face lower import tariffs in China. But they would not be eligible to participate in the liberalization China has promised in financial services, telecommunications (including the internet), and distribution. And the United States would not be able to utilize the World Trade Organization's multilateral process to resolve trade disputes with China. Although the United States could subsequently reverse its non-application, during the intervening period firms from Europe, Japan, Canada, Australia, and elsewhere would gain a decisive advantage over U.S. firms, particularly in the service sectors that China has agreed to open more fully.

Second, and even more importantly, the failure of the U.S. Congress to grant PNTR to China would undermine the position of reformers in China. They have overcome intense domestic opposition to membership in the World Trade Organization, in part by arguing that such membership is the only means of avoiding the process of annual renewal of normal trade relations in their largest export market—the United States.

The United States should embrace the commitment of the Chinese leadership to integrate China more fully in the world economy, rely more heavily on market forces to allocate resources within China, liberalize further the flow of information on which the market depends, expand the role of the private sector, and provide greater protection to intellectual property.

Over a period of time these commitments will have profoundly transforming effects within China as well as expanding trade and investment relations with the rest of the world. The most effective way for the U.S. Congress to signal support for these developments is to pass legislation authorizing the president to extend PNTR status to China when it enters the World Trade Organization. Failure to do so plays into the hands of conservative elements in China that seek to constrain the role of the private sector, limit the role of the market, restrict the development of the internet, and generally control more tightly the flow of information.

Finally, the failure of the U.S. Congress to grant permanent normal trade relations to China would significantly undermine the position of our negotiators in the final stage of China's entry to the World Trade Organization—the drafting of the protocol of accession and the report of the working party. These two documents, which will be negotiated in a multilateral setting in Geneva after China has concluded all of its bilateral negotiations, will spell out in detail China's commitments on all WTO rules. While some of these already have been specified in the November 1999 bilateral agreement between China and the United States, several critical commitments remain to be set forth and clarified at the multilateral stage.

While not all of these remaining issues have been publicly identified, at a minimum they include the details of China's commitment to eliminate agricultural export subsidies, which are not set forth in the bilateral agreement between China and the United States; China's commitment to comply with both the Uruguay Round Agreement on Technical Barriers to Trade and the

Understanding on the Interpretation of Article XVII of GATT 1994, which covers the activities of state trading enterprises; and the details of the trade policy review process that will track China's compliance with its terms of accession once it has become a WTO member.

Given the importance of the issues that remain to be addressed, it is strongly in our interest that the voice of U.S. negotiators be just as strong in the multilateral negotiations as it was in the bilateral negotiations that led to the November 1999 agreement. The best way to assure this is for the U.S. Congress to provide the President with the authority to extend permanent normal trade relations to China.

## NOTES

Nicholas R. Lardy, "Permanent Normal Trade Relations for China," *Brookings Policy Brief,* No. 58 (May 2000). Reprinted by permission from the Brookings Institution Press.

Nicholas R. Lardy, senior fellow, Brookings Institution

# Complete and Utter Nonsense

## *Thomas L. Friedman*

During a visit to Shanghai last year my *Times* colleague Seth Faison and I interviewed the top managers of one of China's largest food companies, which had been partially privatized. While Seth interviewed the Chinese executives in Chinese, I leafed through the company's annual report. On the first page there were four pictures: the chairman, the vice chairman, the general manager and "the Communist Party representative" to the company. At one point I interrupted Seth's interview, pointed to the picture of the Communist Party rep and asked our Chinese hosts: "Say, what does this guy do?" They waved at the picture with disdain, as if to say: "He doesn't do anything. Just ignore him."

That encounter always stuck in my mind because it illustrated one of the political implications of the rise of the private, free-market economy in China. When managers and workers, students and intellectuals are no longer totally dependent on the state or the Communist Party for jobs, they are much more likely to speak their own mind and act on their own interests. That is a fact worth remembering as the U.S. Congress now debates whether to grant China permanent normal trade relations with America.

To be sure, the claims by some Clintonites or business types that trade will lead inexorably to democracy in China are exaggerated and too deterministic.

But even more ridiculous is the claim by John Sweeney, head of the A.F.L.-C.I.O., that "there is no information showing that China is improving its human rights situation or workers rights situation," and thus no reason to support permanent normalized trade ties with China.

As any regular visitor to China can see (unfortunately the U.S. unions have been discouraging members of Congress from visiting China and seeing for themselves), there is ample evidence that the strengthening of private enterprises and free markets in China, and the surge in Internet usage there, is creating the space and private incomes for more Chinese to live independent of the government and thereby expand their personal freedoms. And the more Chinese can live without the state, the more the democrats among them can afford to speak their minds and the more other Chinese can afford to listen.

Read Elisabeth Rosenthal's May 8 [2000] front-page piece from Beijing in this newspaper. It details the messy reality of today's China, where the leadership, terrified about the political fallout from China's joining the World Trade Organization, is cracking down—and will continue to do so—at the same time that Chinese liberals are becoming more self-confident and willing to challenge the state.

"In the China of today," writes Ms. Rosenthal, a *Times* Beijing reporter, "threats from the central authorities have diminished influence. Bookstores are still filled with provocative books. And people fired from government institutes can now often find a way to make a living in the expanding private sector. . . . Even as Chinese intellectuals bemoan the current climate, they feel more inconvenienced than terrified by the government's wrath. 'The methods are pretty much the same as in Deng Xiaoping's and even Mao's time,' [a] professor said. 'What's different is that nobody pays attention anymore. . . . Intellectuals don't feel that much pressure.'"

Ms. Rosenthal also notes that several recent devastating critiques of China's rulers, and disclosures about corruption in the Communist Party, have been circulated first on the Internet in China, and the Chinese leadership has been powerless to stop it. The China trade pact Congress is currently debating greatly enhances the ability of U.S. companies to invest in Internet development in China.

The truth is the A.F.L.-C.I.O. couldn't care less about political change in China. That is just a cover for their head-in-the-sand protectionism. China could become a democratic paradise tomorrow and Mr. Sweeney and his union would still oppose this trade bill, because they see it (wrongly) as just a vehicle to move U.S. manufacturing jobs to China.

The A.F.L.-C.I.O. is free to argue that this bill will hurt U.S. workers. Republican hard-liners are free to argue that China's entry into the W.T.O. will make it a more formidable geopolitical rival to the U.S. But for either of them to say that this bill will hurt the cause of democratization in China, or that it won't help create more islands from which Chinese democrats can operate and more tools by which they can communicate, is to speak utter nonsense, and, one hopes, a majority of Congress will see it as such.

## NOTES

Thomas L. Friedman, "Complete and Utter Nonsense," *New York Times*, May 16, 2000, p. A23.

Thomas L. Friedman, foreign affairs correspondent for the *New York Times*

# Statement against Granting China Permanent Most-Favored-Nation Status

## *House floor remarks by David E. Bonior*

It's almost sunrise in Guangdong Province in China. Soon, the 1,000 workers at the Qin Shi factory will be getting ready to go to work.

Most of them are young people—some even 16 years old. They work 14-hour shifts, seven days a week. They're housed in cramped dormitories that resemble prisons.

And their average pay is 3 cents an hour.

They make handbags for export here to America. We're told we need this trade deal to open vast new markets for American goods. But these Chinese workers can't even afford to buy the products they make themselves.

How are they going to buy our cars . . . our cell phones . . . our computers?

You can't have free markets without free people.

We should have learned the lessons of NAFTA.

Jobs lost in food processing. In consumer products. In high-tech. 100,000 auto industry jobs lost—forever. Where are those men and women today? Oh, they're working—making a fraction of what they used to earn. And the jobs they used to have? They're now performed by workers making pennies on the dollar in Mexico's economic free-fire zone called the *maquiladora*.

But as harsh as life can be in Mexico, China is far worse. It is a police state. A nation where injustice is law and brutality is order.

Alexis de Tocqueville once wrote that if people are to become or remain civilized, "the act of associating together must grow and improve in the same ratio in which the equality of conditions is increased." That's what enabled America to become the most prosperous nation in the world.

**John Spencer's 1997 cartoon suggests big business interests dominate American policy toward China and support the political status quo there. Reprinted by permission from John Spencer.**

It wasn't the forces of world commerce that enabled coalminers and steelworkers and auto workers to take their place in the American middle class. No. It was leaders like Walter Reuther. And it was other Americans exercising the right to form unions. To create political parties. To build women's organizations. To organize churches and civic groups. That's what the Progressive Movement was all about.

Democracy is something that grows from the ground up. Theodore Roosevelt understood that long before any of us.

It wasn't global trade that created our national parks—or the laws that protect our air and water—it was the environmental movement. And it wasn't free trade that won women the right to vote or beat Jim Crow. It was the commitment and the sacrifice of the suffragettes and civil rights leaders. It was the Elizabeth Cady Stantons. The A. Philip Randolphs. The Martin Luther Kings. And our colleague John Lewis.

The advocates of this trade deal tell us that prosperity is a precondition for democracy. They're wrong—they have to grow together.

While trade may make a handful of investors wealthy, democracy is what makes a nation prosperous.

Americans value trade, but we're not willing to trade in our values.

We understand that this approach to trade is really the past masquerading as the future.

It's turning back the clock on a hundred years of progress.

Some oppose this trade deal because of its impact on the environment. Still others out of concern for national security. And others still out of a deep commitment to religious liberty and human rights. But while we sometimes speak with different voices, we each share the same vision. It's de Tocqueville's vision of a civilized society.

And it's a vision of a new kind of global economy: an economy where people matter as much as profits.

It's almost sunrise in Guangdong Province. Soon the workers at the Qin Shi Handbag Factory will begin another workday.

Today we can send them a message of hope.

A message that the global economy we want isn't one where working families in China and Mexico and America compete in a hopeless race to the bottom.

We have a better vision than that.

It's a vision of a global economy where all of us have a seat at the table.

It's a vision of a new global economy where none of us are on the outside looking in.

At the beginning of the last century, the Progressive Movement began a struggle that made the promise of democracy and prosperity real for millions of Americans.

Now, from this House of Representatives, we carry on that struggle for human dignity into a new century. For families here in America—and throughout the world.

We have just begun.

## NOTES

David E. Bonior, "Statement against Granting China Permanent Most-Favored-Nation Status," remarks on the House floor, May 24, 2000.

David E. Bonior, congressman (D-MI)

# 19

# China Hands or China's Hands?

*In the late 1990s, accusations intensified that those Americans involved with China had a conflict of interest in being proponents of good Sino–U.S. relations. Most of the charges, such as those contained in the following article by John Judis, were leveled at former government officials who had become consultants for foreign businesses operating in China. Henry Kissinger was the most common object of attention because of his supposed unequaled influence on American policy. Though not presented here, similar accusations have also been made against American scholars, who purportedly have limited their criticism of the Chinese government in order to maintain their access to China.*

## Chinatown

### *John B. Judis*

#### HOW CHINA BOUGHT THE ESTABLISHMENT

"Much of the American foreign policy establishment, including three former secretaries of state and other former senior officials of both parties, turned a collective thumbs down yesterday on the Clinton administration's policy of linking trade with China to Beijing's human rights performance," the *Washington Post* reported on March 16, 1994. Anyone who read the *Post*'s account, which described a Council on Foreign Relations meeting chaired by former Secretaries of State Henry Kissinger, Cyrus Vance and Lawrence Eagleburger, would have come away knowing that a quorum of foreign policy luminaries had offered a grave indictment of U.S. China policy. What they wouldn't know was one particularly relevant fact about those luminaries: namely, that Kissinger, Vance and Eagleburger each have business ties to China. Kissinger is the founder of a firm, Kissinger Associates, which helps its corporate clients secure business in China; Vance is a corporate lawyer who chaperones clients seeking outlets in China; and Eagleburger, once the president of Kissinger Associates, now works for a Washington law firm where he has also helped businessmen secure contracts in China.

Yet this gathering was not in the least unusual. Increasingly, many of our most distinguished and, in theory, disinterested, experts on U.S. China policy are selling their reputations and knowledge to clients with very particular business interests in China. Almost every prominent former government official who speaks out on this subject has direct or indirect financial ties to China. Most of them are Republicans, because a Republican administration first reestablished ties with China in 1972, and because Republicans controlled the White House for most of the next twenty years. Besides Kissinger and Eagleburger, they include: former Secretaries of State Alexander Haig and George Shultz, former Secretary of Defense Dick Cheney, former National Security Adviser Brent Scowcroft, former U.S. Trade Representatives Carla Hills and Bill Brock, and former Senate Majority Leader Howard Baker. But Democrats have also gotten in on the China game. Besides Vance, there is, for example, former Secretaries of State Edmund Muskie and Warren Christopher, former Ambassador to China Leonard Woodcock, former U.S. Trade Representative Robert Strauss and former Senator Gary Hart.

Unlike the ex-officials who have lobbied for Japan and Japanese corporations, these former officials don't work directly for China or for Chinese businesses, and most have no personal investment in China. The relationship is more subtle and indirect. They are employed by, or serve as, lawyers, advisers or consultants to American companies that have invested, or want to invest, in China. Some, like Kissinger, Hills, Scowcroft and Haig, are high-priced consultants who run their own firms. Others, like Cheney, formerly a director of Morgan Stanley and now the chairman of Halliburton Oil, and Shultz, a director of Bechtel, work for the businesses they seek to help. And still others, like Vance and Howard Baker, are senior or managing partners in law firms that represent companies with an interest in China. What all of them have to offer is not so much knowledge of China as clout with its government—clout based in part on the statements they have made about U.S. policy toward China.

American businesses use these former officials to gain access to high Chinese officials who would otherwise be reluctant to entertain visits from businessmen or bankers. Explains Roger Sullivan, the former president of the National Council for U.S.–China Trade, "The Chinese have all the traditional views toward business. It's crass, lower-class. Higher-level officials don't like businessmen that much. You have to have someone else with you if you want to see them." James Lilley, who was ambassador to China in the Bush administration and is now a professor at the University of Maryland, concurs. "There is a standard procedure that, if you want to do business in China and get the con-

tracts, you have to have someone to open doors, and people who were in prominent positions are often very good door openers."

But having been friendly toward China while in office is not enough to guarantee access, even for the most exalted former officials. They must also be seen
as ongoing friends and defenders of China's rulers. Explains Lilley, "If you want
to deal in China, you will sing their tune. This can take a number of forms. It
can take the form of bringing congressional visitors over, it can take the form of
an op-ed piece in the *New York Times*, it can take the form of a speech, it can
take the form of lobbying Congress. There are many, many ways you can influence things."

The pressure to make favorable statements about China mounts as a visit
nears, or as contracts are under consideration. Even when a delegation arrives, the Chinese will often keep them in suspense about how high-
ranking an official they'll get to see. Says Sullivan, "It is always put to you
that here is your schedule, and at such and such a date you are going to see
a high-level official, but they won't tell you who it is going to be." When a
former American official—whatever his motive—gives a speech denouncing
those who want to tie trade with China to human rights, he is enhancing his
ability to open doors at the highest levels in China. If he gives a speech
denouncing Chinese policies, he is likely to find himself shunted off to the
provinces, taking tea with some minor functionary.

The classic new China hand is, of course, Kissinger. Kissinger has won access
to China's markets for a number of his firm's clients. In 1995, for instance, he
helped GTE sign a memorandum with China's United Telecommunications
Corporation to jointly develop China's massive telecommunications system. At
the same time, he is the Chinese government's most prestigious defender. In
1987, at the behest of China's ambassador to the U.S., Kissinger even founded his
own lobby, the American China Society, which he ran out of Kissinger Associates.
Most recently, he is credited with weaning House Speaker Newt Gingrich from
his support for Taiwan—in July 1995, Kissinger called Gingrich after the Speaker
advocated recognizing Taiwan as an independent nation—and with persuading
the Clinton administration to decouple trade from human rights.

Other former statesmen have followed closely in his footsteps. The most
egregious example is probably Haig, who was Kissinger's aide during the open-
ing of China in 1971–72. After resigning from the Reagan administration as
Secretary of State in 1982, Haig established Worldwide Associates, a
Washington consulting group. One of his main clients has been United
Technologies, of which he is a former chief operating officer and president.
Haig has helped the Connecticut conglomerate win billions of dollars in con-
tracts in China for everything from airplanes to air conditioners.

Haig has maintained his access to high Chinese officials through unflagging
defense of their actions. Sullivan call him the "classic patsy of the Chinese." In

October 1989, for instance, four months after Chinese troops crushed pro-democracy demonstrators, Haig was the only prominent American to join Deng Xiaoping in Tiananmen Square for the celebration of the fortieth anniversary of the People's Republic. Lilley and the ambassadors from Japan and Western Europe boycotted the celebration, as did American businessmen. Afterwards, Deng praised Haig for his "courage." Haig has also consistently opposed any American policy that displeases the Chinese. Last year, he even criticized then-U.S. Trade Representative Mickey Kantor for trying to crack down on Chinese software piracy. "I think Mr. Kantor lets domestic American politics play too heavy a sway in his outspoken criticism of our trading partners, whether it be in Tokyo or Beijing," Haig declared.

Haig has also done his bit in Washington. Last year, he called Representative Christopher Cox and other Republican congressmen to demand they back Most Favored Nation trading status (MFN) for China. Haig berated Cox for opposing MFN and championing Taiwan, prompting Cox to inquire with the House office whether Haig was a registered lobbyist. He's not. When I interviewed Haig, I wanted to ask him why, but I never got that far. My first question—whether there was any problem with having business interests in China while making public pronouncements on U.S. China policy—made him too indignant. "I don't see any conflict there at all. I have business dealings all over the world, including my own country, and I don't think that deprives me of the ability to make judgments on international affairs, which I spent a good part of my life involved in. Who has planted these nasty questions in your craw?" When I tried to rephrase the question, he hung up on me.

Haig is revered by China's leaders, but disliked and even scorned in Washington, particularly by Republicans who remember his trying to take charge after the Reagan assassination attempt. Scowcroft, by contrast, is widely respected in both Beijing and Washington, though the former national security adviser has mixed public policy pronouncements on China with private business just as freely.

Scowcroft, like Eagleburger, also served as president of Kissinger Associates before joining the Bush administration. After leaving the White House, he founded the Scowcroft Group, to consult for businesses, and a nonprofit policy group, the Forum for International Policy, which operates out of the same suite of K Street offices. Like Haig and Kissinger, he helped clients win contracts in China. Last October, for instance, he helped secure a meeting between Chinese Premier Li Peng and Dean O'Hare, the chairman of the Chubb insurance company.

And Scowcroft, too, defends China against its critics. Last year, he gave speeches and briefings on China and MFN at the Heritage Foundation for Republican House members. His Forum for International Policy faxed "issue briefs" on China to congressional offices. Some of these briefs seemed to betray the same sort of "blame America first" logic that old Leftists used to resort to when they spoke of the Soviet Union. In one, published on June 12 last year, Scowcroft and former Bush State Department official Arnold Kanter blamed the U.S. for Chinese sales of nuclear technology to Pakistan, arguing that "an accretion of non-proliferation legislation" had led us into strategic blunders.

Though other members of the informal China lobby are more discreet than Kissinger, Haig and Scowcroft, they, too, get themselves into situations in which they appear to be abusing their roles as members of the foreign policy establishment. One such incident involving former Defense Secretary Cheney stirred the wrath of some of his fellow Republicans on Capitol Hill. In February 1995, the Chinese Navy entered the waters around the disputed Spratly Islands and erected structures on Mischief Reef, which is also claimed by the Philippines. Philippine President Fidel Ramos ordered the Philippine Navy to the area, and the Philippine ambassador complained to Washington.

In March, Cheney, who had joined the board of directors of Morgan Stanley, visited China with representatives from the bank and secured meetings with high-ranking Chinese officials, including Defense Minister Chi Haotian. In Beijing on March 10, after three days of meetings, Cheney told Xinhua News Agency, "I do not really perceive any threat from China to the world or to the region." After leaving China, Cheney attended a business meeting in Singapore, where he made further public statements suggesting that he believed the Philippines had no cause for concern. According to Reuters, Cheney said he did not think China had embarked upon a "hostile course" in the area. Afterwards, one Republican China expert on Capitol Hill told me, "Cheney's statement [on Mischief Reef] was very mischievous. Saying China is not a threat sent a message to Southeast Asian countries who were backing the Philippines that major parts of the U.S. establishment weren't going along." In the months after Cheney's visit, the People's Construction Bank of China, a joint venture between the government and Morgan Stanley, announced a major expansion of its services.

Kissinger, Haig, Scowcroft, Cheney, Hills, Vance and Shultz stand atop a pyramid of numerous former officials who are involved in U.S. China policy and who share the same conflict of interest. Kanter and former NSC staff member Eric Melby work for Scowcroft. Former USTR official Erin Endean works for Carla Hills at Hills & Co. in Washington, D.C., where she advises firms about investing in China. In January 1996, former Clinton Commerce Department official David Rothkopf joined Kissinger Associates as its managing director. As Ron Brown's deputy undersecretary for international trade, Rothkopf had supervised Deputy Assistant Secretary John Huang.

These lower-ranking officials don't have the same influence on Capitol Hill as Kissinger or Scowcroft, but they can function more plausibly as impartial experts, particularly for the media. The same reporters who would hesitate before quoting Kissinger or Haig as impartial experts on China are happy to rely on Rothkopf or Kanter. Last November, for example, *Business Week* blithely invoked Rothkopf's expert opinion about the "importance of cultivating the relationship with China." In August, Reuters, citing Rothkopf's opinion that China should be made "a full member of the global trading system," left out his affiliation with Kissinger Associates, identifying him only as a former Commerce Department official.

Rothkopf or Kanter can argue that their opinions are independent of their employers, but the Chinese don't see it that way. The Chinese government closely monitors what researchers and policy wonks in this country say and write about China. One head of a policy group, who didn't want his name or organization revealed for fear of further reprisal, told me what happened when one of his researchers, writing in an obscure academic journal, described China's trade policy as "mercantilist." The Chinese Embassy in Washington immediately protested to the businesses that funded the policy group.

Until now, the new China hands and their minions have had the best of both worlds. Not only have they gained contracts for their clients; they have shaped opinion in Washington, too. Says one aide to a Republican congressman, "They are respected voices on foreign affairs. Congress is especially susceptible to authoritative statements from Kissinger and Vance because so few members have any experience or knowledge about foreign affairs. Between [Richard] Armey, [Thomas] Delay and [John] Boehner, you've got zero knowledge of foreign affairs." A Senate Republican aide who has advocated a harder line toward China told a similar story. "I can deal with the Motorolas of the world," he said. "The problem I have is the George Shultzes, where these guys show up and they are not directly on the payroll. You get overwhelmed as a staff guy. You get a discussion going, and then someone gets a call from Scowcroft and he is off the reservation again."

And the work of the former officials nicely complements that of the corporate lobbyists. While the lobbyists appeal to the politicians' instincts for electoral survival, the former officials seem to offer an intellectual rationale for obeying those instincts. Explained one House aide, "I have been in meetings and heard members say that they have to vote for MFN, but they need some way to cover their own rear ends. That just tells me right there, they are not making the vote on any intellectual or moral grounds. They are making the vote because of their campaigns. The role of Scowcroft or Kissinger is to provide cover."

But in the long run, the new China hands' success may prove to be the country's failure. Some of the policies they promote may have been justifiable on their merits. It made a certain sense for the Clinton administration not to base its trade negotiations on China's human rights record. But many of the former officials have not simply argued for pursuing negotiations on different tracks, but for virtually abandoning any effort to influence either China's highly protectionist trade policies—at the root of last year's record $39.5 billion deficit—or its support for tyranny at home and abroad. They identify the interests of American corporations abroad with the interests of Americans at home, many of whom could see their jobs shifted from Seattle to Shanghai. They overlook the fact that China could pose a far greater threat to international security than rogue states like North Korea or Iraq. And, as they did in Iran, they cast America's lot with an unpopular autocracy.

Perhaps more important, the new China hands could have a corrosive effect on American democracy. In foreign policy debates, average Americans, as well as many of their political representatives, often defer to prominent former officials whom they believe speak disinterestedly for the national interest. When the public becomes aware that they are also speaking for the interest of their business clients, the cynicism about how important policy decisions are made will deepen. This, together with revelations about the Clinton Commerce Department and presidential campaign, and a growing anxiety about the role of money, especially foreign money, in American politics, could precipitate a crisis of political confidence as profound as that caused by Watergate. Those who understand what has happened to the foreign policy establishment can't conceal their concern. Says Lilley, "Who are the real objective observers? It's like Diogenes looking for an honest man. It is very, very hard to find one."

## NOTES

John B. Judis, "Chinatown," *The New Republic,* Vol. 216, No. 10 (March 10, 1997), pp. 17–20. Reprinted by permission of *The New Republic,* © 1997, The New Republic, Inc.

John B. Judis, writer for *The New Republic*

# Why Our China Policy?

## *William F. Buckley Jr.*

The mists of conspiracy have been floating over the discussion of the United States' China policy, but it wasn't until last week that one heard it said out loud. It was spoken by Arianna Huffington at a debate (*Firing Line*) on the question of trading with China. We have had month after month of public hearings having to do with the financing of the Democratic campaign of 1996, and the stress has been on the Asian presence. All that money directed to the campaign asking for—what?

Mrs. Huffington says it's obvious. Her debate partners (Sen. Tim Hutchinson of Arkansas, former Gov. Jerry Brown of California, Gary Bauer of the Family

Research Council) seated beside her, she suggested that what had been bought was the President of the United States and the Congress. Bought to do what? Bought to ignore the human-rights report of the State Department and to continue trading with China under the Most Favored Nation clause.

Now Mrs. Huffington had intimated her approach early in the two-hour debate by making a most extraordinary accusation. It is that Henry Kissinger argues in favor of continuing trade because his consulting firm does business in China. She cited the Disney Corporation, which retained Kissinger Associates a fortnight ago, allegedly to guide Disney through the Chinese flak over the forthcoming movie *Kundun*, which dramatizes the Communists' genocidal assault on the Tibet of the Dalai Lama.

Dr. Kissinger was floored by the charge and groped unsuccessfully for appropriate words to meet it in the minute or so left to him in that segment of the debate. He managed to say that a mere 3 per cent of the business done by Kissinger Associates relates to China, but Mrs. Huffington then charged that Kissinger was slow to react to the Tiananmen Square massacre of 1989 because of his commercial predilections with regard to China.

Dr. Kissinger did say, in the final few seconds, that he thought it wrong to impute greed after forty years of policy analysis under academic and public scrutiny. But the audience (of seven thousand) roared with excitement at the drama—the striking Greek-American writer/activist charging the former Secretary of State with selling out to Mammon.

Dr. Kissinger, for all his skills as a diplomat, is inexpert at crowd control in public debates. He might have turned to Mrs. Huffington and said: If I reasoned about you as you reason about me, wouldn't I venture that the only reason you married that mindless California millionaire was to latch onto his money, which you did, and then divorce him, which you have done? But I am prepared to assume you had other motives in marrying him. On Tiananmen Square, you are correct that I did not react to the military seizure with astonished indignation. What astonished me wasn't that the army moved into the Square, it was that the protestors were permitted for so long to preside over the Square—China is not a free society. When I recommend policies on China you should be prepared to assume I recommend them as what I consider to be in the best interests of the United States. If I were a doctor doing an appendectomy I wouldn't start out by cursing the appendix.

That might have slowed Mrs. Huffington down, though she was on a tear. Sen. Trent Lott on the affirmative team asked her whether she really believed that the congressional vote in favor of continuing trade was the result of political money coming in from China. Her answer? "Absolutely."

What hovered over the scene at the University of Mississippi was the question: Is it conceivable that the deployment of Chinese money is responsible for the dispensation under which our trade policies with China are operating? My own reaction is: Sure; and Vincent Foster did not commit suicide, Lee Harvey Oswald was only one of the assassins and Oliver Stone is right, the lid on the true story was put down with the cooperation of the FBI, the CIA, President Johnson, and the Supreme Court; and yes, Robert Welch was actually correct, President Eisenhower was a clandestine Communist.

The investigating committees have clearly demonstrated that there were a lot of funny-money machinations in the 1996 campaign and that Asian and Asian-related agents were very active. But to suggest that our policy—to continue to trade with China—is dictated by commercial greed and Chinese manipulation staggers the mind. We are talking about a policy endorsed by every living ex-President, every living ex-Secretary of State, every living ex-National Security Advisor. To suggest that Henry Kissinger would counsel policy contrary to the interests of his country as he understands them leaves the observer speechless. How to explain such a charge? In the Huffington epistemology, one would have to find a commercial reason for it.

## NOTES

William F. Buckley Jr., "Why Our China Policy?" *National Review,* November 24, 1997, pp. 66–69. Taken from the On The Right column by William F. Buckley Jr. © 1997, distributed by Universal Press Syndicate. Reprinted with permission. All rights reserved.

William F. Buckley Jr., syndicated columnist and founder of the *National Review*

# PART VI

# CHINA: A STRATEGIC COMPETITOR? (2001)

**Steven Breen's April 2001 cartoon reflects a common sentiment in the United States that China was unfairly holding an American surveillance plane and its crew. Reprinted by permission from Copley News Service.**

# Redefining the Relationship, Again

*In a pattern similar to that of earlier presidents, George W. Bush campaigned for the presidency and began his tenure in the White House with the stated intention of being firmer with China than his predecessor, yet he eventually moderated his stance. Early crises over the plane collision incident and the announcement of the sale of advanced weapons to Taiwan in the spring of 2001 suggested a tougher approach. However, by that summer and certainly after the September 11 terrorist attacks, the earlier rhetoric defining China as a "strategic competitor" fell out of favor and was no longer uttered by administration officials. Just prior to the APEC summit held in Shanghai in October 2001, where President Bush met with Chinese president Jiang Zemin, Secretary of State Colin Powell gave the clearest sign that the administration would not entirely abandon the Clinton administration's approach toward the PRC.*

## A Distinctly American Internationalism

### *George W. Bush*

... The Eurasian landmass, in our century, has seen the indignities of colonialism and the excesses of nationalism. Its people have been sacrificed to brutal wars and totalitarian ambitions. America has discovered, again and again, that our history is inseparable from their tragedy. And we are rediscovering that our interests are served by their success. In this immense region, we are guided, not by an ambition, but by a vision. A vision in which no great power, or coalition of great powers, dominates or endangers our friends. In which America encourages stability from a position of strength. A vision in which people and capital and information can move freely, creating bonds of progress, ties of culture and momentum toward democracy.

This is different from the trumpet call of the Cold War. We are no longer fighting a great enemy, we are asserting a great principle: that the talents and dreams of average people—their warm human hopes and loves—should be rewarded by freedom and protected by peace. We are defending the nobility of normal lives, lived in obedience to God and conscience, not to government.

The challenge comes because two of Eurasia's greatest powers—China and Russia—are powers in transition. And it is difficult to know their intentions when they do not know their own futures. If they become America's friends, that friendship will steady the world. But if not, the peace we seek may not be found.

China, in particular, has taken different shapes in different eyes at different times. An empire to be divided. A door to be opened. A model of collective conformity. A diplomatic card to be played. One year, it is said to be run by "the butchers of Beijing." A few years later, the same administration pronounces it a "strategic partner." We must see China clearly—not through the filters of posturing and partisanship. China is rising, and that is inevitable. Here, our interests are plain: We welcome a free and prosperous China. We predict no conflict. We intend no threat. And there are areas where we must try to cooperate: preventing the spread of weapons of mass destruction—attaining peace on the Korean peninsula.

Yet the conduct of China's government can be alarming abroad, and appalling at home. Beijing has been investing its growing wealth in strategic nuclear weapons . . . new ballistic missiles—a blue-water navy and a long-range air force. It is an espionage threat to our country. Meanwhile, the State Department has reported that "all public dissent against the party and government [has been] effectively silenced"—a tragic achievement in a nation of 1.2 billion people. China's government is an enemy of religious freedom and a sponsor of forced abortion—policies without reason and without mercy. All of these facts must be squarely faced. China is a competitor, not a strategic partner. We must deal with China without ill-will—but without illusions. By the same token, that regime must have no illusion about American power and purpose.

As Dean Rusk observed during the Cold War, "It is not healthy for a regime . . . to incur, by their lawlessness and aggressive conduct, the implacable opposition of the American people." We must show American power and purpose in strong support for our Asian friends and allies—for democratic South Korea across the Yellow Sea . . . for democratic Japan and the Philippines across the China seas . . . for democratic Australia and Thailand. This means keeping our pledge to deter aggression against the Republic of Korea, and strengthening security ties with Japan. This means expanding theater missile defenses among our allies. And this means honoring our promises to the people of Taiwan. We do not deny there is one China. But we deny the right of Beijing to impose their rule on a free people. As I've said before, we will help Taiwan to defend itself. The greatest threats to peace come when democratic forces are weak and disunited. Right now, America has many important bilateral alliances in Asia. We should work toward a day when the fellowship of free Pacific nations is as strong and united as our Atlantic Partnership. If I am president, China will find itself respected as a great power, but in a region of strong democratic alliances. It will be unthreatened, but not unchecked. China will find in America a confident and willing trade partner. And with trade comes our standing invitation into the world of economic freedom. China's entry into the World Trade Organization is welcome, and this should open the door for Taiwan as well. But given China's poor record in honoring agreements, it will take a strong administration to hold them to their word.

If I am president, China will know that America's values are always part of America's agenda. Our advocacy of human freedom is not a formality of diplomacy, it is a fundamental commitment of our country. It is the source of our confidence that communism, in every form, has seen its day. And I view free trade as an important ally in what Ronald Reagan called "a forward strategy for freedom." The case for trade is not just monetary, but moral. Economic freedom creates habits of liberty. And habits of liberty create expectations of democracy. There are no guarantees, but there are good examples, from Chile to Taiwan. Trade freely with China, and time is on our side. . . .

## NOTES

George W. Bush, "A Distinctly American Internationalism," speech at the Ronald Reagan Presidential Library, Simi Valley, California, November 19, 1999.

George W. Bush, governor of Texas and Republican candidate for president of the United States; 43rd president of the United States (2001– )

# Remarks at Business Event

## Colin L. Powell

. . . I am pleased to be here as sort of the advance guard for President Bush. He is winging his way here as we sit, and I know that everybody's looking forward to seeing him as he makes his first visit to Asia as President.

For me to be back in Shanghai is a very exciting experience. I first came to this city in 1973. I was a young lieutenant colonel in the United States Army. It was a few months after President Nixon had made his historic visit to China and I was one of the first Army officers of the United States Armed Forces who was allowed back into China. There were six military officers in my group—three Army, three Air Force—and we were something of a curiosity in China at that time as you can well imagine, and we were very well escorted, I might also say, at that time (Laughter). But to come back now and to land as I did last night and to drive into the city and to see what has happened, not in the past 28 to 29 years, but really just in the last 12 or 13 years, is absolutely remarkable. To think back to 1973 as a young lieutenant colonel and talking to many Chinese citizens who we had some access to and asking them what their greatest ambition was, what their aspiration was for their families, for their children, for their future, and they said, a sewing machine, a bicycle, and an AM radio. That was it. They were all on bicycles.

I remember going up into the mountains way north of here and meeting with a group of villagers who were taking this terraced hill and fixing it, just terracing it, so they could grow a little bit of rice. The rains would come unexpectedly and wash it all back down, and the next day they would start up again, just stacking rocks one on top of the other. And then going on the other side of the mountain and bringing soil over to this side of the mountain. This driving spirit that was there and has been in this country for so many, many years, waiting to be released, waiting to be turned loose, waiting for the opportunities to do great things for this country. And to come back here some almost 30 years later—I've only been back once in those intervening 30 years—to come back here this long time later and to see what's been accomplished is just remarkable.

It has been accomplished by enlightened political leadership. It has been accomplished by enlightened economic policy. It has been accomplished by the driving spirit of the Chinese people. It has been accomplished by leaders such as you. Business leaders such as you, who are willing to come here and to see the possibilities, see the prospects, see the opportunities, and invest. It was also accomplished, never let us forget, by American consumers. American consumers who need the products that come from China. American consumers who are not in the upper salary levels, but who are making 20, 25, 30 thousand dollars a year and go into . . . stores that cater to them and will sell them products that they can afford that will help them make their ends meet. And so it works both ways.

This city has been built by Chinese labor and Chinese creativity and Chinese energy, but also because lines of trade and lines of communication and this economic openness existed between our two nations which allowed American consumers and consumers elsewhere in the world to benefit from what is happening here in Shanghai and in so many other parts of China, as well. It benefits all of us, and it has to be pressed and pursued and continued in every possible way to make sure that the wealth we see in Shanghai and some of the other cities in China is expanded throughout the society.

The Chinese leadership cannot rest and we cannot rest along with them until what we see here really is reflected throughout the entire society of 1.2 or

[1.3] billion people. What they have learned, and what we have known all along, is that when you generate wealth, when you create wealth, that wealth can be used not only to build great cities, but to provide an education for rural children, to provide a roof over someone's head, a school, a well, an opportunity to perhaps put in a more efficient crop or rotate crops. All kinds of things can happen but only if you have the wealth that will allow you to do that.

So I congratulate you for what you have done, and I certainly congratulate the Chinese leadership for what they have accomplished in these years. We have an excellent relationship with China right now and I think as a result of President Bush's visit the relationship will grow and improve and thrive. He is very much looking forward to meeting with President Jiang Zemin tomorrow.

People have tried to capture this relationship in one or two specific terms. Are they an enemy to be? Are they a strategic competitor? And what I discovered early on in my tenure as Secretary of State, I think all of us in the Administration now understand that the relationship is much too complex to try to capture in a single term or slogan that everybody can use, say, "aha, that's it." No, that is not it. Much too complex. The basis of the relationship, I think, is increasingly of an economic nature. When people say to me, what is the most important thing going on with China right now—40 percent of their exports are coming through the United States of America. That is something that they will think twice about with respect to putting that at risk. Does that mean that all is well, that we share all their values, and we have no disagreements with them? Of course not. It means that two strong, powerful nations, both of which have a place in this world, both of which are Asia-Pacific nations, can talk to one another, and if there is a basis of trust, if there is a common understanding of each other's interests, we can pursue those areas where we aren't in agreement and make good things happen. And when we disagree we can disagree openly and candidly, face-to-face.

So we are not reluctant to say to the Chinese government that we have concerns about human rights issues in China. We will always express those concerns to you because that is part of our value system and we would not be Americans if we did not try to convey to you what we feel strongly about, what our value system's about. We also are going to talk to you about issues having to do with proliferation of certains kinds of materials or weapons to other nations where we think this is not in the best interest of our relationship, not in the best interest of the world community. It would be irresponsible of us to be reluctant to speak to you candidly about that if we are going to have the kind of relationship that allows us to move forward as two responsible nations moving forward.

So there is no reason for us to become enemies. The United States is not looking for enemies. We don't want any enemies, don't need any enemies. By heavens when they show up we will protect ourselves and we will defend ourselves and we will defeat our enemies. . . .

We want to see China and Taiwan enter the World Trade Organization. We need to see the next round get started or launched. We need to keep moving forward. We need to restore confidence in the world's economies, but especially in the American economy. We have a strong economy; it will come back. It may take a little bit of time, but it will come back. It will come back because of who we are. People who believe in themselves, people who believe in the promise of democracy and the free enterprise system, and believe in the fundamental values of human rights and human dignity. A value system that is increasingly being copied by nations around the world, at their own pace and in their own manner, and consistent with their own history and culture over time.

China has seen what can happen when you start to move in this direction. I am one of those who firmly believe the more they see of it, the more they will gain an appreciation for the rule of law and fundamental human rights for all citizens, and they will be encouraged to continue moving in that direction. The nations of the world that adopt these values, consistent with their own history and culture, respecting the rights of their people, taking care of their people, investing in their people, getting ready for this twenty first century world, those nations will progress and move forward. Those that do not, the Iraqs of the world, the North Koreas of the world, remaining transfixed in some past life, will find themselves being left further and further behind. . . .

### NOTES

Colin L. Powell, "Remarks at Business Event," Shanghai, China, October 18, 2001.

Colin L. Powell, secretary of state during the George W. Bush administration (2001– ); chairman of the Joint Chiefs of Staff (1989–1993)

# Looking to a Non-Ally in China

## Richard Fisher

While the United States is correct to seek China's assistance in what will be a long war against terrorism, it should harbor no illusions that China will share all of the same goals in this fight, or that China will cease being a longer term adversary.

Yes, Chinese President Jiang Zemin was swift to condemn the Sept. 11 terrorist attacks in the United States, and China has shared some counterterrorism intelligence. And it would be welcome to have Beijing's full cooperation for the many battles ahead. But as he meets Jiang Zemin in Shanghai, President Bush should be mindful that any future Chinese assistance in the war on terror can only be effective if China reverses the aid that it has given to a number of rogue states.

For example, should Osama bin Laden or his allies obtain a nuclear weapon in the future, it is likely that many of its components will come via Pakistan or Iran, and could very well carry the stamp "Made in China." China's assistance to Pakistan's nuclear weapons program dates back to the mid-1970s and includes the training of engineers, provision of nuclear-fuel-reprocessing components, and perhaps even the plans to make nuclear weapons. China has sold Pakistan more than 30 of the 180-mile range M-11 ballistic missiles. China has also sold Pakistan the means to build solid-fuel 450-mile-range Shaheen-1 and 1,200-mile-range Shaheen-II missiles.

China has sold Iran nuclear-reactor and nuclear-fuel-reprocessing components and cruise missiles that could conceivably carry a small nuclear device.

For more than a decade the United States has been "engaging" Chinese officials in a repetitive pattern of U.S. complaints, Chinese denials and promises not to proliferate, occasional U.S. slap-on-the-wrist sanctions, but with no definitive cessation of Chinese proliferation. So far, Beijing is correct to question U.S. resolve. It took the Bush administration until August this year to impose some sanctions on Chinese companies selling Shaheen missile parts to Pakistan, a program that likely began early in the Clinton administration, which produced no Shaheen-related sanctions during its two terms.

This failure to stop Chinese proliferation helped fuel the nuclear missile race between India and Pakistan. And as the latter weakens under pressure from radical pro-Taliban forces, the danger increases that nuclear weapon technology could fall into the hands of terrorist groups like bin Laden's. But rather than isolate radical Islamic regimes that harbor or aid terrorists, Beijing engages them, too. In recent months, China has been caught red handed helping Saddam Hussein to build new fiber-optic communications networks that will enable his missiles to better shoot down U.S. aircraft. Beginning in late 1998, according to some reports, after they gave Beijing some unexploded U.S. Tomahawk cruise missiles, the Taliban began receiving economic and military aid from China.

The more important subtext is that China engages these regimes because it shares their goal of cutting down U.S. power. And, incredibly, China may be attracted to using their methods as well. Bin Laden himself has a fan club in some quarters of China's People's Liberation Army (PLA). In their 1999 book *Unrestricted Warfare*, two PLA political commissars offer praise for the tactics of bin Laden. They note that bin Laden's tactics are as legitimate as the tactics that Gen. Norman Schwartzkopf used in the Persian Gulf war. Of bin Laden, they state that the "American military is inadequately prepared to deal with this type of enemy."

While some U.S. analysts downplay *Unrestricted Warfare* as written by officers with no operational authority, it is well known that the PLA is preparing to wage unconventional warfare, especially cyber warfare. Should China attack Taiwan, the PLA would want to shut down the U.S. air transport system. The

PLA now knows this can be done with four groups of terrorists, or perhaps by computer hackers that can enter the U.S. air traffic control system and cause four major airline collisions.

So to qualify as a U.S. ally in the war on terrorism, China must stop lying about its nuclear and missile technology proliferation and prevent states like Pakistan and Iran from fielding nuclear missiles. Also, China must end its economic and military commerce with regimes that assist terrorists, like the Taliban and Iraq. In addition, China must halt its preparations for a war against Taiwan, a war that will very likely involve U.S. forces.

In this regard, it is not time to end Tiananmen massacre sanctions on arms sales to China, such as allowing the sale of spare parts for U.S.–made Blackhawk helicopters. The administration is considering this move to reward China and to allow it to rescue U.S. pilots that may be downed over Afghanistan. China has plenty of good Russian helicopters to do that job, and it makes no sense to revive military technology sales to China as it still prepares for war against Taiwan.

In his Sept. 20 speech, Mr. Bush correctly declared that "any nation that continues to harbor or support terrorism will be regarded by the United States as a hostile regime." China's aid to the Taliban and its continued nuclear proliferation are not friendly actions. The United States should press China to undo all it has done to strengthen the sources of terrorism.

## NOTES

Richard Fisher, "Looking to a Non-Ally in China," *Washington Times,* October 21, 2001. Copyright © 2001 News World Communications, Inc. Reprinted by permission from the *Washington Times.*

Richard Fisher, senior fellow, the Jamestown Foundation

# The Mixed Messages of the Bush–Jiang Meeting

## Susan L. Shirk

The Shanghai meeting between President George W. Bush and President Jiang Zemin restored the positive tone of U.S.–China relations, which had been disrupted by the April collision of military planes off the South China coast and the early Bush administration labeling of China as a "strategic competitor." Their common interest in combating terrorism caused the Presidents to play down the perennial contentious issues of human rights, non-proliferation, and Taiwan, as well as the issue of missile defense. It would be premature, however, to conclude that this positive tack represents a new course for U.S.–China relations.

The headline of the Bush-Jiang meeting, especially in China, was the return to an optimistic label for the relationship. Jiang expressed China's desire to develop a "constructive and cooperative relationship" with the United States. Bush said that the United States seeks a relationship with China that is "candid constructive, and cooperative." The words "constructive" and "cooperative" used in the same sentence were China's number one objective for the meeting. The Chinese put as much weight on words as on actions. They needed the reassurance of a public commitment from President Bush that while he had abandoned Clinton's goal of a "constructive, strategic partnership," he did not view China as an adversary.

The other positive message was that the two countries were cooperating in the war against terrorism. The Chinese turned over the agenda of the Shanghai APEC meeting, originally designed to showcase China's economic miracle, to the U.S.–led war against terrorism. President Bush emphasized how much he appreciated that China's supportive response to 11 September came "immediately," and with "no hesitation" and "no doubt." China's insecure leaders are genuinely fearful that terror attacks by Uighur Islamic extremists in the northwestern province of Xinjiang could destabilize other parts of China, even though most analysts believe that the number of Uighurs trained in Al Qaeda camps is quite small. The Chinese also are eager to show the Americans that they are a responsible, civilized power, not a big rogue state.

Do the words of reassurance and common focus on terrorism mean that the meeting was a turning point in U.S.–China relations, averting the trend toward confrontation? The threat of terrorism provides a new strategic focus for Sino-American relations, something that has been lacking since the disappearance of the Soviet threat a decade ago. Without such a strategic focus, domestic critics in both countries exercise greater influence over their nations' policies toward one another. The critics are in the governments as well as in the societies. A popular consensus in the United States that terrorism is a much greater threat than a "rising China" and a popular consensus in China that terrorism is a much greater threat than "American hegemonism," would enable foreign policy makers in both countries to quiet the critics and pursue cooperation.

The subtext of the Bush-Jiang meeting, however, is that popular threat perceptions have not yet been transformed. Both Presidents used their public remarks to signal to domestic audiences that they will stick to their principles and not "appease" one another:

- President Bush said that he sought a relationship with China that was "candid" as well as "constructive" and "cooperative."
- President Jiang declined to endorse the U.S. military action in Afghanistan and warned that anti-terrorist actions should have "clearly defined targets," should "hit accurately," and "avoid innocent casualties."

- President Bush, in a reference to Chinese repression of Uighur separatists in Xinjiang, made the human rights point that "the war on terrorism must never be an excuse to persecute minorities."
- President Jiang emphasized the importance of the Taiwan question, but President Bush would only go so far as to state the long-held U.S. policy of "one China" in a pre-departure Washington press conference and in the private meeting, but not in his public remarks in China.
- President Bush mentioned the "need to combat the proliferation of weapons of mass destruction and missile technology," but the Chinese rejected American efforts to resolve an ongoing dispute over Beijing's sales of missile technology to Pakistan before the meeting. The United States has lifted related sanctions against Pakistan but not against China.
- Both Presidents, and the American officials who provided background for the press, referred openly to the continuing differences between the two governments.

The common threat of terrorism opens new possibilities for U.S.–China cooperation. But the mixed messages of the Bush-Jiang meeting make clear that the Presidents will have to work harder to make the case to their governments and their publics. Ordinary Chinese feel the threat of terrorism less directly than do ordinary Americans. The issues of human rights and Taiwan that divide the two societies will not go away, and new differences are likely to arise if the United States pursues a long war in Afghanistan, which is uncomfortably close to China.

## NOTES

Susan L. Shirk, "The Mixed Messages of the Bush–Jiang Meeting," National Committee on U.S.–China Relations, October 22, 2001. Reprinted by permission from the National Committee on United States–China Relations.

Susan L. Shirk, professor of political science at the University of California, San Diego; deputy assistant secretary of state for China, Taiwan, and Hong Kong during the Clinton administration (1997–2000)

# The Plane Collision

*On April 1, 2001, an American Navy EP-3 electronic surveillance plane collided with a Chinese military jet over the South China Sea. The Chinese aircraft crashed into the water, and its pilot was killed, but the U.S. plane was able to safely land at a military airfield on the Chinese island province of Hainan. Accusing the U.S. plane of intentionally crashing into the Chinese jet, violating Chinese airspace, and landing without permission, China detained the 24-member crew for 11 days and released them only after the United States issued a letter of regret over the incident. That summer the plane was disassembled and returned to the United States on a chartered Russian cargo plane. The various reactions to the incident demonstrated how emotionally charged the debate over China policy had become.*

## U.S. Letter to Chinese Foreign Minister Tang Jiaxuan

### Joseph W. Prueher

Dear Mr. Minister:

On behalf of the United States Government, I now outline steps to resolve this issue.

Both President Bush and Secretary of State Powell have expressed their sincere regret over your missing pilot and aircraft. Please convey to the Chinese people and to the family of pilot Wang Wei that we are very sorry for their loss.

Although the full picture of what transpired is still unclear, according to our information, our severely crippled aircraft made an emergency landing after following international emergency procedures. We are very sorry the entering of China's airspace and the landing did not have verbal clearance, but very pleased the crew landed safely. We appreciate China's efforts to see to the well-being of our crew.

In view of the tragic incident and based on my discussion with your representative, we have agreed to the following actions:

- Both sides agree to hold a meeting to discuss the incident. My government understands and expects that our aircrew will be permitted to depart China as soon as possible.
- The meeting would start April 18, 2001.
- The meeting agenda would include discussion of the causes of the incident, possible recommendations whereby such collisions could be avoided in the future, development of a plan for prompt return of the EP-3 aircraft, and other related issues. We acknowledge your government's intention to raise U.S. reconnaissance missions near China in the meeting.

Sincerely,
Joseph W. Prueher

## NOTES

Joseph W. Prueher, "U.S. Letter to Chinese Foreign Minister Tang Jiaxuan," April 11, 2001.

Joseph W. Prueher, U.S. ambassador to China (1999–2001); former commander in chief of the U.S. Pacific Command (1996–1999)

# Chinese Twins

## William Saletan

Every time the United States negotiates with China, a war of words breaks out. On one side are Americans who demand a "principled" hard line against China's aggression. On the other side are Americans who advocate "constructive engagement" to coax China toward economic and political freedom. In the spy plane standoff that ended this morning, the hawks and engagers were at each other's throats again. But their enmity was, as always, dishonest. They need each other. Without the hawks, the engagers would have no sticks to wave at China. And without the engagers, the hawks would have no carrots to withdraw.

The latest charade began Friday, when the *Weekly Standard* editorial, co-authored by editor Bill Kristol, denounced "the profound national humiliation that President Bush has brought upon the United States" by expressing his regret at the death of a Chinese pilot in the spy plane incident. Calling advocates of engagement "appeasers," the editorial assailed Bush's "weakness," "fear," and "capitula-

**The cartoon portrays the holding of an American surveillance plane in April 2001 as another insidious attempt by the Chinese to obtain advanced U.S. military technology. Reprinted by permission from Mike Thompson, the *Detroit Free Press*, and Copley News Service.**

tion." On the weekend talk shows, the engagers fired back. Vice President Dick Cheney and Secretary of State Colin Powell excoriated the *Standard* editorial. Cheney called it "one of the more disreputable commentaries I've seen in a long time" and warned that such rhetoric might "inflame" the U.S.–China standoff.

It's true that Bush's advisers didn't enjoy being accused of weakness. And it's true that they didn't want to let emotions in both countries spin out of control. But that didn't deter them from putting the *Standard*'s tirade to good use. In every TV interview, administration officials tried to scare China by playing up outrage on the right, in Congress, and among the American public. The message to Beijing was: If you don't release our crew, you'll empower the anti-China hard-liners we've been restraining.

The telling pattern in the comments of U.S. officials throughout the standoff was their indirection. Rather than criticize China, American politicians professed sad concern that other politicians and constituencies, furious at China's behavior, might force the United States to retaliate. Administration officials warned of what Congress might do. Members of Congress warned of what their colleagues might do. Constructive engagers, alluding to polls, warned that their pragmatism might be overwhelmed by American nationalism. Powell's hand-wringing performance on *Face the Nation* was worthy of an Oscar:

> Congressional delegations are canceling their trips to China. . . . They're also say-ing, "You know, Secretary Powell, you'll have a much more difficult time with, say, getting another permanent normal trading relations bill through." . . . When they do come back [from recess], if this has not been resolved . . . there will be action. There will be a great sense of outrage. . . . It's affecting the environment that we will be facing when we take the [Taiwan arms] sale up on Capitol Hill, if there is a perception that China is not acting in a responsible and reasonable manner. So even though we're keeping it separate, I can't help but say to the Chinese that it could become linked in the overall political climate.

To what extent were Powell's engagers and Kristol's hawks sincere in their quarrel? Certainly less than they conveyed on the Sunday morning shows, which they knew the Chinese would watch closely. The day afterward, at an American Enterprise Institute forum, Kristol conceded that his editorial might help Powell and Cheney:

> It strengthens them diplomatically, because now they can go to the Chinese gov-ernment and say, "Hey, if you guys don't come through with these people very, very soon, we have all these insane right-wingers out there frothing at the mouth, wanting to arm Taiwan and launch a trade war, and these guys represent millions of infuriated Americans who are about to take to the streets and call their con-gressmen." Would that it were so. But if the Bush administration wants to say that in their private diplomacy with the Chinese government, that's fine, too.

Former Defense Department official Richard Perle, who associated himself with Powell's side of the debate, endorsed Kristol's theory. "I like to think that the Chinese in Beijing, trying to figure out what we're doing, have decided that the president . . . can't hold Bill Kristol off much longer. And so maybe that will accelerate the process." Kristol and Perle were joking about the *Standard's* prestige. But they weren't joking about using indignation on the American right to scare China.

If the engagers need the hawks in this way, it's just as true that the hawks need the engagers. Look at the sanctions the hawks propose to apply to China. "It is essential that the Chinese be made to pay a price for their actions, huffs the *Standard*. "The United States must respond in ways that directly affect China's interests. Congress can do its part easily: by rejecting China's most-favored-nation trade status when it comes up for renewal later this spring." On the *Today* show, Kristol elaborated: "We have a huge amount of leverage over Beijing. They desperately want the president to go there in October. They des-perately want to have the Olympics. They desperately want to continue with most favored nation status. . . . We have a host of relationships with them that can begin to be cut back."

Yes, we do. But the only reason those relationships can be cut back is that we built them in the first place. If the *Standard* had gotten its way, there would be no MFN trade status to retract. If Bush had ruled out a trip to China and had committed the United States to oppose China's bid for the Olympics, none of that "leverage" would exist. Yes, we could have told the Chinese that if they didn't release our crew, they'd be even less likely to get a trade agreement or a presidential visit or the Olympics. But withholding a favor you're already withholding doesn't pack the same punch as taking back a favor that has been offered or has come to be expected.

To the hawks, Sino-American relations are about addiction. "The Chinese believe, with good reason, that the American business community has a hammerlock on American policy toward China, and that Congress will never dare cut off American business's access to the Chinese market," the *Standard* charged Friday. "Congress has a chance to prove that . . . the United States can break this addiction." Five days later, the American crew is coming home, thanks to Chinese anxiety that the impasse might have jeopardized China's blossoming economic and political relations with the United States. Addiction, it turns out, is a two-way street.

## NOTES

William Saletan, "Chinese Twins," *Slate* (www.slate.msn.com), April 12, 2001. Slate © UFS. Reprinted by permission.

William Saletan, senior writer with *Slate*

# U.S. Is Sorry—For Giving China MFN

## Letter to the editor of the Richmond Times-Dispatch

Editor, *Times-Dispatch*:

Here's our apology to China in the Hainan incident.

Dear China: We're sorry that you don't train your fighter pilots better. As a token of our apology, here's a copy of Microsoft Flight Simulator 2000. We're sorry that your front-line fighter planes can't outmaneuver a 35-year-old prop-driven airliner. Perhaps you'd like to consider purchasing some surplus 1950s' era Lockheed Starfighters from Taiwan (which just replaced all its with shiny new F-16s).

We're sorry you believe your territorial waters extend all the way to Australia. For future reference, here's an American 6th grade geography textbook. (Please take note of the copyright information printed inside the cover.)

**Drew Sheneman's cartoon captures the emotions of many Americans who believed that instead of the U.S. owing China an apology for the April 2001 plane collision incident, it was China that deserved condemnation. Reprinted with permission of Tribune Media Services, Inc. All rights reserved.**

We're sorry you can't seem to see your part of this incident. We know that it may seem easier to blame others than to take responsibility.

Consider this while we build several new Aegis destroyers for our friends in the Republic of China (Taiwan). We're especially sorry for treating you with such respect for the past 20 years. We'll definitely rethink this policy, and will probably go back to treating you like a common untrustworthy street gang very soon. We're very sorry for ever granting you Most-Favored-Nation trading status. This will be rectified at the earliest opportunity.

## NOTE

Letter to the Editor, "U.S. Is Sorry—For Giving China MFN," *Richmond Times-Dispatch,* April 24, 2001, p. A12. Reprinted by permission from the *Richmond Times-Dispatch.*

# China's Bid for the 2008 Olympics

*After sitting out a round, in 2001 Beijing was once again a finalist to host the summer Olympics. Although Congress did not pass a resolution in 2001, debate in the United States raged again over whether China should be encouraged or stopped from hosting the games. The arguments raised in 2001 were similar to those raised eight years earlier, but the atmosphere was more charged because of the various crises that had occurred during that time span. On this occasion, Beijing easily won the support of the International Olympics Committee (IOC), beating out its closest challenger, Toronto, in the second round of voting, 56 to 22.*

## Do Not Award China the 2008 Olympics

### *Editors of the* Detroit News

Advocates of economic and diplomatic engagement with China argue correctly that this policy will give the United States—and the rest of the world—valuable tools to prod the country toward democracy and freedom. But allowing China to host the 2008 Olympics will serve mostly to legitimize its repressive government—not these broader policy objectives.

The International Olympic Committee, which is scheduled to vote on the venue for the games Friday, ought to reject Beijing's bid.

The Bush administration has decided to neither oppose nor support China's longstanding ambition to play host. The administration argues that it has no leverage to influence the outcome of the vote—which appears to be veering strongly in China's favor—because the U.S. government does not have a seat on the committee. Moreover, it notes, the prospect of hosting the games will force China to postpone at least for nine years any designs to militarily take over Taiwan. For this reason, Taiwan has been among the staunchest supporters of China's bid.

These are not irrelevant concerns. Yet the Olympics are not an entitlement to which all nations can lay equal claim; they are a privilege that ought to be reserved for states that adhere to minimum principles of justice and human rights. But Beijing's autocrats have not paid so much as lip service to these principles. Instead, even while pushing their bid for the Olympics, they have used crushing force against peaceful demands for more freedom of religion by groups such as the Falun Gong, intensified their crackdown on domestic dissidents and arrested U.S. citizens traveling in China on trumped up charges of spying.

There would be an argument to turn a blind eye to these transgressions if—as with trade and diplomacy—the Olympics resulted in a net transfer of power from the Communist Party to the Chinese people. But the arrangements for the Olympics are made not by private entities but by the host government. Thus, the games inevitably become a tool for showcasing the achievements of the ruling regime—at the people's expense.

It is true that most Chinese are as eager as their government to host the Olympics as a way of restoring a national pride wounded by centuries of subjugation by outside powers. Some fear that a failure to land the games yet another time may well lead to a resurgence of nationalism and slow liberalization efforts in China.

But the Chinese people also abhor the repressive tactics of their Maoist rulers. It ought to be possible for the Olympic committee to refuse Beijing's autocrats the prize they seek while recognizing the legitimate aspirations of the Chinese people.

The Olympic committee claims that it will not allow ideology or politics to interfere with its choice of venue. But such phony even-handedness produced the sordid spectacle of Adolf Hitler presiding over the games in 1936. The committee should not allow that spectacle to be repeated.

### NOTE

Editorial, "Do Not Award China the 2008 Olympics," *Detroit News*, July 12, 2001, p. 10. Reprinted with permission from *The Detroit News*.

# Yes, Award Olympic Games to a Changing China

## *David Shambaugh*

If the International Olympic Committee makes the bold and momentous decision this Friday to award the 2008 Games to Beijing, it will recognize the reality that China has arrived as a major power in Asia and the world.

That includes sport. At the past three Summer Games, Chinese athletes have become prominent in swimming, badminton, table tennis, gymnastics, volleyball, long-distance running and rifle shooting.

As in the human rights and political domain surrounding China's bid, this sporting success has not come without controversy. Some athletes have been found guilty of illegal doping, and others have been suspected. Stories of inhumane training regimens have come to light. Yet, as in other areas, China is making progress. Its Olympic officials have strengthened national drug testing programs. They have cracked down on coaches and the system borrowed from the former East Germany that perpetuated such abuses.

The IOC will base any choice of Beijing as the 2008 host primarily on the city's merits and abilities to put on a first-rate set of Games. This would be a gamble because Beijing's current condition does not warrant such a selection. The transportation and lodging infrastructure is quite inadequate, the city is blanketed by pollution and snarled by traffic, and many other aspects of daily life in the Chinese capital require improvement.

Preparing for the 2008 Games might be just the incentive to the local and national governments, as well as Beijing's citizens, to clean up the city. The government has promised to invest billions in such preparations. Given China's record of accomplishment when it puts its mind to something, it is reasonable to assume that it could all be achieved in time. The net result would be a far more habitable city after the Games close.

Being awarded the Olympics would be an immense source of national pride for the 1.3 billion Chinese, and could satiate the legitimate patriotic yearnings of the public. It would simultaneously stimulate nationalism, particularly during the Games themselves. This could bare the ugly side of Chinese nationalism, xenophobia. In the past two decades there have been nasty incidents of Chinese fans attacking foreigners during and after matches lost by China.

Still, awarding Beijing the 2008 Games would be a signal to the Chinese people and the world that China is not a pariah state.

There are valid concerns about China's bad human rights record. The IOC has to wrestle with these. But transgressions in this area are insufficient to deny the Games to China. South Korea's record under a series of military juntas was hardly stellar when it hosted the 1988 Summer Games. Hosting the Olympics proved to be an important step forward in South Korea's political maturity and its progress toward full democracy.

One should not be naive about the political nature of the Chinese regime, and piously expect democracy to blossom after 2008. But it can be expected that the Olympics would provide important impetus to political reforms under the so-called fourth generation of leaders who will come to power in October next year.

Many Chinese now recognize and speak clearly about the need to open up the political system. The Olympics might help.

Certainly hosting the Olympics would be a powerful disincentive for the government to undertake draconian domestic crackdowns or aggressive actions abroad, notably against Taiwan, during the intervening period. The Games would offer strong positive incentives for responsible behavior.

Taiwan, recognizing this, has supported Beijing's Olympic bid. Indeed, it is quite likely that some of the sporting competition would be held in Taiwan.

Getting the Games would confirm China's status as a leading diplomatic power. Not only is it a member of the United Nations Security Council, its international diplomacy has become very active. Its leaders now travel all over the world, and the government is increasingly involved in affairs outside its own region.

China belongs to virtually every major international organization. Its expected accession to the World Trade Organization later this year will be the capstone on the lengthy process of integrating China back into the institutional family of nations.

Above all, awarding China the 2008 Olympics would be a recognition of the tremendous economic advances that the country has made since the death of Mao in 1976. GNP has more than quadrupled, and the standard of living for all classes has shown marked improvement.

This is even the case deep in the countryside. There are severe and stubborn economic and social problems in China, many caused by the reforms themselves, but the overall progress made in merely two decades is nothing short of stunning.

No country in history has come as far as China in such a short period and on such a mammoth scale. This reality deserves global recognition.

## NOTES

David Shambaugh, "Yes, Award Olympic Games to a Changing China," *International Herald Tribune,* July 13, 2001, p. 10. Reprinted by permission from the *International Herald Tribune.*

David Shambaugh, professor of international affairs and political science and director of the China Policy Center at George Washington University and nonresident fellow at the Brookings Institution; former editor of *The China Quarterly*

# PART VII

# CHINESE REACTIONS TO THE AMERICAN DEBATE

# Debating China Policy in the United States:
## A Chinese Perspective

## WU XINBO

China policy has been a constant subject of debate in the United States, particularly since Tiananmen and the end of the Cold War. Such debate has reflected the changing perceptions of and shifting policy preferences toward China. The Chinese always watch the debate carefully and jump in sometimes by either rebutting one argument or endorsing another. This chapter examines some of the major debates since normalization and provides a Chinese perspective on the exchanges of gunfire.

In the 1980s, a major debate of U.S. China policy centered on the Taiwan issue and particularly the Sino–U.S. Communiqué of August 17, 1982, regarding U.S. arms sales to Taiwan. Opponents argued that since China needs trade with the United States, Beijing would not risk relations with Washington for the sake of Taiwan and the United States did not have to yield to the Chinese demands on the issue.[1] This argument is very problematic. It is true that Beijing values trade and economic ties with the United States, but this does not mean that the Taiwan issue is unimportant to China. The unification of Taiwan with the mainland, along with economic modernization and promoting world peace, were set as the three priorities on China's national agenda in the 1980s. In the eyes of Beijing, the Taiwan issue is at least as important as economic growth and could be even be more so, given its impact on China's national security and the legitimacy of the Chinese Communist Party. As we know now, Deng had decided that China would degrade relations with the United States should Washington reject making a reasonable concession on the issue of U.S. arms sales to Taiwan. Therefore, contrary to this argument, there did exist a real danger that U.S.–China ties might be jeopardized because of the Reagan administration's initial stance on the issue. Critics also complained that the August 17 Communiqué compromised Taiwan's security, and this is again not true. On the contrary, the compromise between Beijing and Washington provided a stable framework for Sino–U.S. relations as well as Beijing–Taipei–Washington relations; and Taiwan's security was thus enhanced. As John Holdridge convincingly argued, "Because of the improved relations between China and the United

States, Taiwan has never been more secure."² As long as the United States practices significant restraint on its arms sales to Taiwan, Beijing would feel more confident about the prospect of peaceful solution of the Taiwan issue, and Taiwan need not worry about its security.

In the wake of the Tiananmen Incident, the China debate in the United States revolved around alternative approaches to China. The hard-liners opposed President Bush's dispatches of two missions to Beijing and the extension of most-favored-nation (MFN) status for China, while the soft-liners, like the Bush administration, wanted to avoid the temptation to be excessively punitive on China, especially in ways that harm U.S. interests. Here the hard-liners were flawed, as they failed to differentiate the short-term response from the long-term policy toward China. In the short term, the United States understandably needed to express its strong disapproval of what occurred in Tiananmen, and in this regard, the Bush administration had taken measures, such as suspending arms exports and high-level government exchanges and seeking postponement of multilateral development bank loans beyond those for basic human needs. American policy toward China, however, should by no means stand there, and it should adopt a long-term perspective—how to bring Sino–U.S. ties back to a normal track since the United States has developed profound interests in this bilateral relationship and how to promote China's economic openness and political freedom. After Tiananmen, if the Chinese leadership showed no interest in improving relations with Washington and was intent on rolling back the policy of opening up and reform, then the hard-line approach might have been justified. Yet Deng was in fact not only eager to see the renormalization of ties with the United States but also determined to continue the course of opening up and reform, and this attested to the wisdom and vision of the soft-line approach. Richard Solomon was correct when he argued that extending MFN for China serves U.S. interests in promoting U.S. objectives of reform, modernization, and the advancement of human rights; of maintaining productive official contacts; of protecting American interests and American consumers; and in working to maintain stability and prosperity.³

Since the 1990s, the debate on China has revolved around the following topics: how to view the reemergence of China as a world power, how to cope with a rising China, and how to define the nature of Sino–U.S. relations in a changing context.

In the 1980s, the U.S. political elite stated that a strong China would help promote regional stability and serve U.S. interests—in their understanding, a more powerful China would contribute to U.S. efforts to contain the Soviet Union. With the end of the Cold War, U.S. policymakers no longer publicly claimed that they would like to see the emergence of a strong China. In fact, as Thomas McNaugher observed, the United States, despite its own strength, "has been consistently uncomfortable with the prospect of a strong China."⁴ Many in the United States worry that a strong China would undermine the paramount position of the United States in East Asia and pose a challenge to U.S. interests in the region. The alarmists, like Charles Krauthammer and Arthur Waldron, exaggerated the "China threat" by comparing China to Germany before World War I.[5] From a Chinese perspective, such a concern is unwarranted and reflects a selfish, parochial view. To put the issue of a rising China in the right perspective, the U.S. political elite should first and foremost acknowledge that a stronger China will benefit the Chinese people. Having suffered from poverty, backwardness, and weakness in their modern history, the Chinese people are eager to make their country wealthy and strong, and there is nothing wrong in their genuine wishes of this sort. Moreover, a strong China will also help promote regional stability. The past has shown that when China was poor and weak, East Asia would invite major power competition, and chaos and turmoil prevailed in the midst of their efforts to build their respective spheres of influence. The historic analogy of China to late-19th-century Germany—"a country growing too big and too strong for the continent it finds itself on"—reflects a misreading of today's China. As Chas Freeman convincingly argued, "China is not Germany, Japan, the USSR, or even the United States. China does not seek lebensraum; is not pursuing its manifest destiny; does not want to incorporate additional non-Han peoples into its territory; has no ideology to export; and is certainly not a colonizer and does not station any troops overseas."[6] In other words, because of the different cultural and historical background, various rising powers behave differently, and not every rising power is doomed to become an evil empire—some may be, some may not. China, because of its tradition of seeking cultural superiority rather than political-military conquest and its experience of being humiliated in its modern history, is highly unlikely to behave like prewar Japan or Germany, or the Soviet Union during the Cold War. Most important, the reemergence of China as a major power coincides with China's integration into the world community, which means that as China grows up materially, it is also learning to become a responsible power. While Waldron pointed to the territorial disputes between China and its neighbors, such as Vietnam, Russia, India, and Japan, as evidence of China being a source of threat in Asia, the fact is that Beijing, over the past several years, has successfully resolved most border problems with Russia, reached an agreement with Vietnam on the demarcation of the land border, and stabilized the line of actual control with India. This confirmed McNaugher's observation that "far from being a threat, today's China would seem to confirm liberal claims that economic growth and interdependence encourage cooperation and conflict resolution."[7]

On the related issue of how to deal with a rising China, the debate in the U.S. policy and intellectual community proceeds roughly along two lines: containment and engagement. The containment argument is flawed, first because it misjudged China by describing it as an evil power, like pre–World War I Germany or the Soviet Union, and, in fact, China is not. Second, a U.S. policy of containment against China is unlikely to be supported by its Asian allies and friends. While harboring some concern about a rising China, these countries generally believe that the right way is to bring China into the international community and encourage it to become a responsible power. Having important stakes in normal Sino–U.S. ties, most Asian countries would shun away from a U.S. initiative that will turn China into an enemy. Krauthammer suggested that Washington contain China by "building relations with China's neighbors, starting with Vietnam."[8] Wishful thinking. Although Hanoi may harbor some concern over a stronger China, it is no longer in a mood to join hands with another superpower to confront China, as it did in the late 1970s by tilting toward Moscow against Beijing. For the sake of Vietnam's national interests, it needs to maintain normal relations with both China and the United States, and, in fact, Sino–Vietnam ties today are in better shape than U.S.–Vietnam relations. Most important, any U.S. attempt to isolate China economically will not work in a time of globalization, interdependence, and China's opening up. Given the fact that the bulk of China's trade and investment is within Asia, a U.S. policy of containment against China will not achieve the same results as in the case of the Soviet Union during the Cold War.

The Clinton administration's China policy, as it turned out, was a mixture of engagement and prevention. Although it is understandable that the United States needs to prepare for worst-case scenarios while engaging China, it is always a challenge not to turn preventive actions into preemptive ones, which are more containment oriented. Theoretically, there is a line between these two; in practice, however, it is very difficult not to cross the line. As a result, some measures that Washington may deem as preventive means against a rising China ended up being regarded by Beijing as containment. On the security front, for instance, the United States has been paying more attention to China's defense modernization and is trying to frustrate Chinese efforts to procure advanced defense technology and weapons systems from others. American security arrangements in the region, like the redefinition of the U.S.–Japan alliance, U.S. security linkages to Southeast Asian countries, and so on, manifest a strong rationale to check China. In the opinions of many America watchers in China, if Washington has not yet started to contain China, it certainly has acted to guard against and constrict China.[9] Therefore, the question of how to prevent a policy drift from engagement to containment is yet to be addressed by the liberal school in the U.S. political and academic community.

Aside from the containment–engagement nexus, a fundamental problem with the U.S. attitude toward a rising China is whether Washington is willing (or ready) to accommodate legitimate Chinese concerns. Washington should not just call on China to conform to the rules and practices that the United

States has developed over the post–World War II period; it should also think about revising or altering some of the rules and practices that China reasonably views as unfair and/or threatening to China's national interests. As McNaugher asked, "Is it [the United States] ready to curb its own arms sales, now far and away the world's largest and a key source of income for the shrinking U.S. defense industrial base, in return for the curbs on China? Is it ready to limit the size, type, or operational freedom of its own forces in East Asia in return for limits on China's force modernization?"[10] The midair collision between a Chinese jet fighter and a U.S. spy plane in April 2001 suggests that as China gets stronger, it will become less tolerant with the excessive and aggressive espionage by the United States. Washington may take for granted such intelligence activities against China and others since it has been accustomed to this kind of behavior, but China will be more and more inclined to regard this as a provocation rather than a norm in international relations.

The third question is the definition of U.S. relations with China. For some time after the end of the Cold War, the United States encountered trouble in understanding the nature of Sino–U.S. ties. In 1997, during Chinese president Jiang Zemin's visit to the United States, both countries agreed to "build toward a constructive strategic partnership." However, it drew a lot of criticism from both within and outside the Clinton administration. The critics complained that it is neither appropriate nor realistic to view China as a "strategic partner," even a potential one. During the 2000 presidential campaign, Republican candidate George W. Bush painted China as a "strategic competitor." While the Clinton administration avoided setting a tone about the current status of relations with China, it took a forward-looking and positive gesture. The Bush administration, however, seemed to paint the present and future of Sino–U.S. ties with a gloomy color. Things began to change quickly, however. During a short visit to Beijing in July 2001, Secretary of State Colin Powell suggested that the United States seeks to develop a "constructive and cooperative" relationship with China, and he would discard the phrase "strategic competitor" to describe Beijing, a position confirmed by President Bush himself when he traveled to China in October 2001 for the APEC meeting in Shanghai. Whether this marks a substantive change in thinking or only a superficial one in rhetoric, however, remains to be seen.

From a Chinese perspective, a proper description of bilateral ties is not unimportant. The way you define your relations with another country reflects your basic attitude toward bilateral ties, and in this sense, a positive and constructive disposition by both sides is crucial to the healthy development of Sino–American relations. It is true that China–U.S. relations are complex and multifaceted, difficult to describe by a single word or phrase. However, a positive definition would deliver goodwill and express a good intention, set up a positive target for both sides to endeavor to achieve, and help create political willingness in both capitals to solve differences and expand cooperation. On the contrary, a negative tone would evoke suspicion from one side about the other, poison the atmosphere of bilateral ties, and cause both sides to formulate policies that drive bilateral relations in a negative direction. The reality is that, currently, China and the United States are both partners and competitors. Looking into the future, however, efforts should be geared toward narrowing differences and expanding cooperation. The evolving international context, the changes occurring in China, and the constant self-adjustments in U.S. foreign policy will make possible a "constructive and cooperative relationship" between the two major Pacific powers.

## NOTES

1. Senate Foreign Relations Committee, "U.S. Policy toward China and Taiwan," 97th Congress, 2nd. sess., August 17, 1982. See chapter 4 of this volume.

2. Ibid.

3. House Committee on Foreign Affairs Subcommittees on Human Rights and International Organizations, Asian and Pacific Affairs, and on International Economic Policy and Trade, "Most-Favored-Nation Status for the People's Republic of China," 101st Congress, 2nd sess., May 24, 1990. See chapter 10 of this volume.

4. Thomas McNaugher, "A Strong China: Is the United States Ready?" *Brookings Review,* Fall 1994. See chapter 13 of this volume.

5. For example, Charles Krauthammer, "Why We Must Contain China," *Time,* July 31, 1995. See chapter 13 of this volume.

6. Chas W. Freeman Jr., "An Interest-Based China Policy," in Hans Binnendijk and Ronald N. Montaperto (eds.), *Strategic Trends in China* (Washington, DC: National Defense University, 1998), pp. 123–124.

7. McNaugher, "A Strong China."

8. Krauthammer, "Why We Must Contain China."

9. Wu Xinbo, "U.S. Security Policy in Asia: Implications for China–U.S. Relations," *Contemporary Southeast Asia,* Vol. 22, No. 3 (December 2000), p. 488.

10. McNaugher, "A Strong China."

# The American Debate over China Policy:
# A Chinese View

## ZHU FENG

Chinese people find it difficult to understand how China policy has been debated in the United States over the past three decades in the midst of a dramatically changing relationship. It is not only the substance of the debate but the process by which the debate has unfolded that perplexes Chinese. However, it is not only helpful but also necessary for Chinese to understand all aspects of the American debate in order to enhance our two countries' mutual understanding and find a better way to carry out ties today.

Four broad conclusions can be made about the American debate. First, China has examined the debate largely through the lens of China's own customs, values, and identity. Most Chinese do not know how American political and social institutions operate because we live in a completely different system that has been shaped by a different political culture. China has lacked the public space for the kind of debate that readily occurs in America. The policy debate in China is quite political and less scholarly. In the United States, although the policy debate has visible political elements, it is at least full of independent and diverse viewpoints. As a result, many Chinese review American writings on China policy in a common way.

Second, Chinese believe that Americans' self-interest, individual and national, affects their policy proposals. Thus, many Chinese are deeply skeptical of the real intentions behind America's China policy. Some Chinese have gone too far, arguing that the United States has been trying to fragment, weaken, and Westernize China in order to inhibit China from becoming powerful and beyond America's control. In the worst-case scenario, they suggest that the United States might choose to contain China with its military might.

Third, the majority of Chinese equate American global leadership with an American-manufactured hegemonic order and accordingly perceive American hegemonism as a major threat to China. Such hegemony implies not only domination of interstate relations but also the spread of a common ideology and political system. Many Chinese thus believe that the sharp distinction between the two countries' ideologies and political systems will almost inevitably result in some sort of conflict. This would explain, in their eyes, why the United States has taken steps to maintain its superiority over China and has taken desperate steps such as supporting Taiwan's separatist movement, launching human rights attacks, and even silently circling China with military force. Therefore, anti-hegemonism has been perceived by many Chinese as China's leading task if it is to create a more secure and prosperous world for itself.

Finally, since many Chinese believe that China has been demonized in the American debate, this has negatively affected how Chinese feel about the United States. Looking back at the trajectory of Sino–American relations over the past 10 years, what is most painful might not be the embassy bombing in 1999 or the plane collision in 2001 but rather the increasingly repulsive emotions each side has developed toward the other. The feelings of inevitable conflict, lack of trust, and destructive growth of interference by domestic politics in both countries might be more dangerous than individual events and create the basis for inciting future tensions. The growing emotional nature of ties has inhibited the possibility of finding a way to accommodate each other, eroding the political resources to resolve disputes in a conciliatory manner.

## DEFINING THE RELATIONSHIP

To determine the responsibility for the mutually growing sense of conflict, we must first look at the shifting general definitions each side has used as a foundation of the bilateral relationship. On the American side, President Nixon confessed that China was one of the most important states in the world in 1969. Under such strategic thinking, China's strategic weight could not be neglected. Thus, the United States courted China in order to restructure the global balance of power and sided with China against their common adversary—the Soviet Union. Then Nixon visited China in 1972 and took the initial steps toward the normalization of bilateral relations. The Nixon–Kissinger approach defined U.S.–China ties completely on the basis of the classical theory of power politics, interpreting China's value exclusively from its international "weight," with no care about China's domestic politics.

However, this definition of relations did not work well after the Tiananmen Incident and the end of the Cold War. Relations between the United States and China were deeply affected by the growing American emphasis on human rights and the movement from a bipolar to a unipolar world system in the 1990s. In 1992, Democratic presidential candidate Bill Clinton criticized the Chinese government as a "rogue state." Such words showed that the United States was frustrated by China sticking to its authoritarian system. Though the Clinton administration finally came up with the term "engagement" to define its China policy, the American debate was tangibly haunted by disputes over a rising China and the "China Threat." China's military warning to Taiwanese separatists through the use of missile tests in 1996 directed American attention toward China's military intentions, and the debate turned toward the question of what policy the United States should adopt if the engagement strategy was not sufficient to counter China.

In the early 1990s (and in his selection in this book), Harry Harding suggested that the United States and China were neither friends nor foes.[1] Such a formulation is very helpful in terms of recognizing the changed reality of U.S.–China relations with the end of the Cold War and the disappearance of the strategic triangle traditionally pulling the United States and China together. But this "neither friend nor foe" description cannot be the basis for how China and the United States can benefit and complement each other. Nor does it provide much guidance for specific policy suggestions at the practical level. Nothing is more important than the term developed in the early 1990s to reconceptualize the changed nature of U.S.–China relations because it indicates that the traditional source that allowed U.S. and Chinese "gears" to mesh—China as a balancer against the Soviets—had disappeared, and in its absence, China became the major target of human rights critics. In particular, the Tiananmen Incident deeply and decisively affected Americans' stance toward China and the Chinese government.

Unfortunately, when America changed its perception of China, China did not follow step at the same pace. China naïvely and stubbornly held to the view that the United States would be a reliable political partner as it had been from the Nixon administration to the first Bush one, who China perceived as all situated within the American political mainstream. Inadequate attention was given to the altered strategic focus and interests of the United States and to the sharply increased negative American sentiments against an authoritarian government in China. At the same time, in order to consolidate and enhance its domestic political authority, China had to fight back against U.S.-based human rights attacks and spread the allegation of a Western conspiracy to subvert China's Communist system through "peaceful evolution." There was a clear contradiction between China's goal to stabilize and improve Sino–American relations and its utilitarian need to put down domestic opposition and strengthen national solidarity. However, this was an understandable choice since Deng Xiaoping and Jiang Zemin were reformers, not revolutionaries; or, as we say, neither was a "Chinese Gorbachev."

Deng Xiaoping quickly moved China forward after nearly 15 years of reform and opening up, but he could not make China discard all the historical, cultural, and institutional relics accumulated by the 30 years of Maoist rule. China decided to keep moving in ways consistent with its own reality and possibilities. China refused to follow the Russian model by undertaking democratization overnight. The Chinese Communist Party and the people learned a great lesson from the demise of the former Soviet Union, contending that the Soviet collapse led to an impoverished and fragmented new state; such change was not only costly but also completely unsuitable to China. Undoubtedly, the demise of the Soviet Union and the triumph of Western democracy and freedom around the world brought much pressure to bear on China in world affairs, but it also helped Chinese leaders appeal to new sources of support to more persuasively enhance its political legitimacy in China than it had ever done before. The awareness of preventing China from experiencing "Soviet Union-ization" definitely promoted the Chinese government's capabilities and determination to stand firm against American-sponsored democratization and not "dance to the American tune."

However, China's leaders have maintained a strong willingness to accelerate China's ongoing incorporation into the world community and have firmly kept China on the course of reform and opening up. Apart from the political system, extensive and profound changes continue to take place in China, some of them visible and others seemingly invisible. There is no doubt that such a willingness to continue reforms and credible policy choices will lead to the formation of a "new China," even with its own limits and gradual progress. When viewed from many angles, China is in a dynamic phase, and it will play a positive and constructive role at both the regional and the global level. The United States must welcome, encourage, and advocate China's changes and development. Even though it will never fully pass the American test, China is destined to become an American partner to create a more secure, prosperous, and liberal world. Therefore, the American debate over China policy needs to be less ideological and take a more sympathetic posture toward China. China is the world's most populous country and represents the hopes for a high quality of life for one-fifth of the world's population, which is no easy task for anyone.

## THE RISE OF CHINESE NATIONALISM

The American debate has contained dramatically different arguments and policy suggestions over the past three decades. Quite a number of American experts and specialists, based on their own value system, have focused on China's stubborn unwillingness to further political reform and its hesitation to fairly treat its citizens. Some of them overestimate China's growing military might and economic strength. And in recent years, many have made the "China Threat" the foundation for how they study China. This debate and the long list of disputes in the bilateral relationship have left the Chinese people frustrated over the past decade.

Many have remarked that the United States and China have a "love–hate" relationship. On the love side, Chinese admit that the United States is the most important country on earth and that China cannot afford to lose the cooperation and support of America. Furthermore, no one in China would deny the benefits of sound and healthy ties between the two countries for China's drive to achieve modernization. However, on the hate side, Chinese dislike America's hegemonic arrogance and hate to be frustrated and even humiliated by America's human rights attacks, their blocking of China's bid to host the 2000 Olympic Games, and its support for Taiwan's growing separatist movement. It seems that this side of Chinese people's views has grown in recent years. Many Chinese believe that the embassy bombing in Belgrade on May 8, 1999, was intentional and not a "tragic mistake." Many Chinese shouted anti-American slogans on websites and complained that the government acted softly after the EP-3 reconnaissance plane crashed into a Chinese naval jet on April 1, 2001. They were two appalling days as well as appalling signals if used to measure Sino–American ties. The two events were not only crises in the bilateral relations but also a deep warning that anti-Americanism in China is looming over the relationship.

Many in the American debate believe that the Jiang Zemin administration has intentionally cultivated nationalism as the new ideological glue to hold China together in ways that has bred anti-Americanism. Such views are also portrayed as an official tool to counter American pressure to divert domestic opposition. To be honest, these sentiments have largely not been the product of a government plot to stoke nationalistic sentiment but have been the natural reflection of the Chinese people's increased feelings of disgust toward the United States. I remember a conversation about Sino–American relations I had in the summer of 2001 with a young American at Peking University. He told me that China deserved the frustration and even humiliation it has experienced because China has not yet conformed to international standards. I confessed that China really needs to do more to polish its global image but that nothing could justify attempts to humiliate China when it is sincerely engaged in opening up to the outside world and striving for deeper interdependence. Chinese have long held these feelings, which are a foundation for the growing sense of nationalism in the country.

On the other hand, like in most developing countries, Chinese views toward the United States and the rest of world are quite varied and reflect China's social structure. Based on this author's own recent research, the more marginalized a Chinese person is in the changing social order, the more likely he or she is to be in favor of anti-American policies. Therefore, anti-Americanism is often connected with opposition to the Chinese government and with complaints against its current policies.

The Jiang Zemin administration has been trying to arbitrate and even repress nationalistic feelings against the United States since growing nationalism is a double-edged sword. Anti-Americanism helps the Chinese government bargain firmly on some disputes. But it will eventually damage the government's efforts to promptly escape the shadows cast by any thorny crises between the two countries, and it will likely devastate Jiang's political resources to seek stability and development of Sino–American relations in the long run. Thus, in recent years the Jiang Zemin administration has had to struggle to control anti-Americanism in China.

Actually, it is desirable for every government to nurture and make good use of nationalistic sentiments as a coherent tool to reinforce their political appeal. China is no exception. Anti-Americanism comes partly from the deeper social changes referred to previously and partly from Chinese traditional pride and self-recognition as a large power. As long as China has conflicts with the United States, it will be hard to erase anti-Americanism altogether. However, even if such feelings were expressed on websites after the terrorist attacks in September 2001, such anti-Americanism is not in the mainstream. Americans may have felt pained after they found out that some Chinese were cheerful after the World Trade Center towers collapsed, but this is not a complete picture of China. Most Chinese were saddened and heartily agreed to closely side with the United States in the international campaign against terrorism.

## THE "CHINA THREAT" AND REALPOLITIK

The view of a "China Threat" exhibited in the American debate is perceived by the Chinese people as an indication that some Americans have panicked. Many Chinese wonder why China suffered a great deal at the hands of foreigners when it was so poor and backward yet still suffers from the distorted pictures like the "China Threat" when it began to be powerful. In their view, the "China Threat" is a conspiracy aimed at blocking China's rise by exaggerating China's military modernization and setting up barriers for its economic advancement.

In academia, the "China Threat" has been represented in three ways. One is that China is building up its military and will expand its influence via force. The second is that China's fast economic growth rate will inevitably lead to a transition of power between it and the world's strongest country, jeopardizing American dominance over the world. (Particularly since it has kept its Communist system and ideology, a rising China must be a large concern to the West.) The third is that China has refused to give up the right to use force as a solution to the Taiwan issue. China's military solution toward the Taiwan issue signifies to some China's willingness to expand militarily. The Cox Report's description of China peeping at America's top nuclear secrets seems to have partially reinforced these views.

However, this theory is totally groundless; reality has proven and will continue to prove that such worries are childish. Today's world politics have changed much since before World War II and are not dominated any longer by the "rules of the jungle." History has demonstrated that military expansion leads directly to the exhaustion of power. I am sure that the Chinese government clearly understands this, and that is why it has stressed since the early 1980s that military modernization must be subject to national economic construction and development. No military officers have been among China's top political leaders for nearly 10 years, and as Gill and O'Hanlon show in their article, most of China's weaponry is outdated. China will obviously be militarily strong and economically powerful someday, but this will take a long time to achieve. Over the near term, China will not match or even substantially be able to challenge the United States.

In addition, the general theory of a power transition between rising and falling powers, rooted in realpolitik, does not apply to China's case. China's territorial claims will not bring about any profits that could be valuable to China and inspire military expansion. Moreover, contemporary international relations will not allow China to pursue its interests via military means. China's military threat to Taiwan is often cited as a manifestation that China is prone to using force. But Taiwan is a special case. China's claim over Taiwan and its strong wish to have Taiwan completely return to its sovereignty derive from its historic mission and the people's desire to maintain China's national integrity; it is unrelated to any military expansion. One can be confident in predicting that China will not resort to military force unless Taiwan declares independence. In that regard, military force is a last resort, while mainland China has never excluded the possibility of using other means to solve this problem.

Some have argued that as a country going through such a massive transition, there is a great deal of uncertainty about its domestic policies, something that could make China's foreign policy orientation equally difficult to predict. However, as a great country, China surely knows what its goals are and behaves as a "rational actor." Cost-benefit analysis is leading China to follow the major global trends. As such, China could become an increasingly "benign" authoritarian regime and evolve in new ways, something that empirical studies show is aided through the development of a market economy.

With its entry into the World Trade Organization and its successful bid to host the 2008 Olympic Games, China is going to continue to press to be incorporated into the world community. The more open China becomes, the more cooperative it will be with others and the more it will adapt its relationship with the West. China's moderate reactions to the Bush administration's pullout from the ABM Treaty in December 2001 and its virtual silence in response to reports in January 2002 of 27 bugging devices having been found on Jiang Zemin's newly delivered Boeing 767 both demonstrate China's increasing maturity in its dealings with sudden events that could hurt relations.

China is becoming more open, more tolerant, and more important. The aftermath of the terrorist attacks underscores precisely the useful role China can play when the United States and China cooperate. The ongoing war against terrorism around the world also has created an opportunity to put the relationship on a more solid footing. But the problem is that plenty of disputes will not disappear even with more intense cooperation in this area, and such disputes will trouble ties from time to time. Personally, I fondly hope that American academia, the public, and policy circles would notice the new signals coming from China and carry the debate to a new level: be less skeptical based on self-interest and an orientation toward democracy and be more understanding, sympathetic, and tolerant based on a respect for China's different culture and policy practices. Regardless of whether China has made enough progress already politically, my country is heading in the direction of providing greater protection of individual freedom and the prosperity of a market economy. It is an unstoppable trend and will probably be accelerated after the post-Jiang era arrives. Since Jiang Zemin will retire from his key posts in the fall of 2002, China is currently going through the difficulties of a succession of power. Yet whoever comes to power in Zhongnanhai, China's White House, will no doubt continue to cement a better Sino–American relationship. Thus, the American debate over China policy should be sensitive to these trends and in the post–terrorist attack era provide China with greater reassurance: the United States is China's friend and has no intention of hurting China and containing its development. In return, China should quickly move to echo the American appeal of its own intentions.

It is likely that both the Chinese and the American side will try to steer their debates in new directions. While these debates may be controversial and heighten mutual suspicion and even hostility, it is hoped that they will be full of passion and emphasize friendship and interdependence, which will necessarily facilitate the further exploration and building of cooperative ties rooted in strong institutions and trust. If China and the United States can do that, the peoples of both countries would be overwhelmingly satisfied.

## NOTE

1. Harry Harding, *A Fragile Relationship: The United States and China since 1972* (Washington, DC: Brookings Institution, 1992). Also see chapter 14 of this volume.

# Further Reading

The literature on U.S. policy toward China is massive. No bibliographic essay can entirely do justice to the full range of issues covered and cite all those individuals who have made valuable contributions. The following is an eclectic sample of useful works that complement the selections in this book.

The normalization announcement was analyzed from different perspectives in two edited volumes. Contributors to John Tierney Jr., *About Face: The China Decision and Its Consequences* (New Rochelle, NY: Arlington House, 1979), were relatively more critical than those found in Harry Harding (ed.), *China and the U.S.: Normalization and Beyond* (New York: China Council of the Asian Society, 1979). Critical commentaries published right after the announcement include "The China Card," *The New Republic,* January 6, 1979, pp. 5–6; Mike Lavelle, "Blue-Collar Views—China Is a Threat to U.S. Labor," *Chicago Tribune,* January 9, 1979, sec. 3, p. 3; and William Safire, "Reading Teng's Mind," *New York Times,* December 21, 1978, p. A25. Edward Friedman was more sympathetic in his "Reality on China," *New York Times,* December 17, 1978, sec. 4, p. 21.

The debate following normalization about the efficacy of a military relationship with China was awkward. While opponents of sales were outspoken, defenders were publicly less vocal. The most important and clearest public defense of strategic ties with China came before restoration of diplomatic relations, in 1975, with Michael Pillsbury's, "U.S.–Chinese Military Ties?" *Foreign Policy,* No. 20 (Fall 1975), pp. 50–64.

The enthusiasm for good relations with China that President Reagan displayed during his 1984 summit were echoed in numerous media commentaries and reports of the time that China was quickly moving toward capitalism, which would benefit the U.S. economy and perhaps its security. Among these optimistic pieces were William Safire, "Greatest Leap Forward," *New York Times,* December 10, 1984, p. A23; Dorothy E. Jones et al., "Capitalism in China," *Business Week,* January 14, 1985, p. 53; and Warren Christopher, "China Is Likely to Stay Independent," *Newsday,* December 16, 1985, p. 49. Scholar

Michel Oksenberg stresses the benefits to the United States of a stable and prosperous China in his "The United States' Interest in China," in Robert F. Dernberger et al. (eds.), *The Chinese: Adapting the Past, Building the Future* (Ann Arbor: University of Michigan Center for Chinese Studies, 1986), pp. 691–703. A critique of Reagan's 1984 visit to China is found in the editorial, "China Card Shuffle," *The New Republic*, May 14, 1984, pp. 4–6. Gerald Segal shows his skepticism about the benefits to the United States of a strong China in "As China Grows Strong," *International Affairs*, Spring 1988, pp. 217–231. A good overview of China's human rights situation as of the mid-1980s that is critical of the Reagan administration's apparent neglect of the issue is Roberta Cohen, "People's Republic of China: The Human Rights Exception," *Human Rights Quarterly*, Vol. 9, No. 4 (November 1987), pp. 447–549.

In late 1989, there were a large number of commentaries written denouncing President Bush's dispatch of Scowcroft and Eagleburger to Beijing. These include Richard Cohen, "It Was Burlesque," *Washington Post*, December 13, 1989, p. A25; Jim Hoagland, "The Descent of American Diplomacy," *Washington Post*, December 17, 1989, p. B7; Li Lu, "In China, I'd Be Dead," *New York Times*, December 24, 1989, sec. 4, p. 11; and Patrick J. Buchanan, "U.S. Crawls Back to Toast Butchers of Beijing," *Human Events*, December 30, 1989, p. 10. Nien Cheng, famous for her *Life and Death in Shanghai* (New York: Penguin, 1986), a penetrating autobiography of her travails in Mao China, defended the December mission in "A Distasteful but Necessary Mission," *Washington Post*, December 15, 1989, p. A25.

Those searching for broad overviews of Sino–U.S. relations since the mid-1990s that suggest a cooperative approach would be well served by the following works: A. Doak Barnett, "U.S.–China Relations: Time for a New Beginning—Again," The James and Margaret Loe Memorial Lecture, The Paul H. Nitze School of Advanced International Studies, April 14, 1994; Thomas J. Christensen, "Chinese Realpolitik," *Foreign Affairs*, Vol. 75, No. 5 (September–October 1996), pp. 37–52; Audrey Kurth Cronin and Patrick M. Cronin, "The Realistic Engagement of China," *Washington Quarterly*, Vol. 19, No. 1 (Winter 1996), pp. 141–169; Thomas L. Friedman, "The New China Consensus," *New York Times*, May 26, 1996, sec. 4, p. 11; Kenneth Lieberthal, "A New China Strategy," *Foreign Affairs*, Vol. 74, No. 6 (November–December 1995), pp. 35–49; Joseph S. Nye Jr., "The Case for Deep Engagement," *Foreign Affairs*, Vol. 74, No. 4 (July–August 1995), pp. 90–102; Michel Oksenberg and Elizabeth Economy, *Shaping U.S.–China Relations: A Long-Term Strategy* (New York: Council on Foreign Relations, 1997); Jonathan Rauch, "Go Ahead and Appease China—It's the Right Thing to Do," *National Journal*, Vol. 31, No. 49 (December 4, 1999), pp. 3447–3448; Robert S. Ross, "Beijing as a Conservative Power," *Foreign Affairs*, Vol. 76, No. 2 (March–April 1997), pp. 33–44; Robert Lee Suettinger, "The United States and China: Tough

Engagement," in Richard N. Haass and Meghan L. O'Sullivan (eds.), *Honey and Vinegar: Incentives, Sanctions, and Foreign Policy* (Washington, DC: Brookings Institution Press, 2000), pp. 12–32; David Shambaugh, "Containment or Engagement of China? Calculating Beijing's Responses," *International Security*, Vol. 21, No. 2 (Fall 1996), pp. 180–209; David Shambaugh, "Facing Reality in China Policy," *Foreign Affairs*, Vol. 80, No. 1 (January–February 2001), pp. 50–64; and Ezra F. Vogel, *Living with China: U.S.–China Relations in the Twenty-first Century* (New York: Norton, 1997). A wide-ranging comparison of China's engagement with several countries and regimes that ultimately stresses the benefits of liberal strategies of integrating China in the international system and democratization is Alastair Iain Johnston and Robert S. Ross (eds.), *Engaging China: The Management of an Emerging Power* (London: Routledge, 1999).

Several articles and books that advocate various hedging strategies that mix elements of cooperation and contention are Zbigniew Brzezinski, "Living with China," *The National Interest*, No. 59 (Spring 2000), pp. 5–21; Ted Galen Carpenter and James A. Dorn, *China's Future: Constructive Partner or Emerging Threat?* (Washington, DC: Cato Institute, 2000); James A. Gregor, "Qualified Engagement: U.S. China Policy and Security Concerns," *Naval War College Review* (Spring 1999), pp. 69–88; Zalmay Khalilzad, "Congage China," *RAND Issue Paper*, No. IP-187 (Santa Monica, CA: Rand, 1999); James J. Przystup, "A Commonsense Strategy toward China," *Heritage Foundation Committee Brief*, No. 28 (April 23, 1997); Gerald Segal, "Does China Matter?" *Foreign Affairs*, Vol. 78, No. 5 (September/October 1999), pp. 24–36; James Shinn (ed.), *Weaving the Net: Conditional Engagement with China* (New York: Council on Foreign Relations Press, 1996); and Ross Terrill, "Policy Tip: Just Let China Be China," *Newsday*, June 10, 1994, p. A61.

Some of the most notable works that attack President Clinton's engagement strategy and urge a policy of pressure or containment are Richard Bernstein and Ross H. Munro, *The Coming Conflict with China* (New York: Vintage, 1997); Robert Kagan, "What China Knows That We Don't: The Case for a New Strategy of Containment," *Weekly Standard*, January 20, 1997, pp. 22–27; Steven W. Mosher, *Hegemon: China's Plan to Dominate Asia and the World* (San Francisco: Encounter Books, 2000); Gideon Rachman, "Containing China," *Washington Quarterly*, Vol. 19, No. 1 (Winter 1996), pp. 129–139; and Arthur Waldron, "Deterring China," *Commentary*, Vol. 100, No. 4 (October 1995), pp. 17–21. William Safire's cautiously optimistic 1984 column should be contrasted with his pessimistic "Great Leap Backward," *New York Times*, February 28, 2000, p. A19. Two articles notable for their similar titles and conclusions yet that come from publications with historically conflicting ideologies are The Editors, "Sell Out," *New Republic*, December 16, 1996, p. 7, and David Tell, "Selling Out to China," *Weekly Standard*, December 23, 1996, pp. 9–10.

Several studies published since the mid-1990s that stress the limits of China's military capabilities are Kenneth W. Allen, Glenn Krumel, and Jonathan Pollack, *China's Air Force Enters the 21st Century* (Santa Monica, CA: Rand, 1995); Karl W. Eikenberry, "Does China Threaten Asia-Pacific Regional Stability?" *Parameters* (Spring 1995); Paul H. B. Godwin, "China's Defense Modernization: Aspirations and Capabilities," *Asian Perspectives on the Challenges of China* (Washington, DC: National Defense University Press, 2001), pp. 15–28; Ron Montaperto, "China as a Military Power," *Strategic Forum*, No. 56 (December 1995); Rick Reece, "On the Myth of Chinese Power Projection Capabilities," *Breakthroughs* (Spring 1998); and Michael D. Swaine and Ashley J. Tellis, *Interpreting China's Grand Strategy: Past, Present, and Future* (Santa Monica, CA: Rand, 2000).

In contrast, works that find China's military modernization more successful—and threatening to the United States—include Chong-Pin Lin, "Red Army," *The New Republic,* Vol. 213, No. 21 (November 20, 1995), p. 27; Bill Gertz, *Betrayal: How the Clinton Administration Undermined American Security* (Washington, DC: Regnery, 1999); Mark A. Stokes, *China's Strategic Modernization: Implications for the United States* (Carlisle, PA: Army War College Strategic Studies Institute, September 1999); Edward Timperlake and William C. Triplett II, *Red Dragon Rising: Communist China's Military Threat to America* (Washington, DC: Regnery, 1999); and Larry Wortzel, "Why Caution Is Needed in Military Contacts with China," *Heritage Foundation Backgrounder,* No. 1340 (December 2, 1999). A novel based on this premise is Chuck Devore and Steven W. Mosher, *China Attacks* (Buy Books on the web.com, 2000).

Two sets of exchanges concerning Chinese power are Arthur Waldron, "Why China Could Be Dangerous," and Karl Zinsmeister, "Why China Doesn't Scare Me," *The American Enterprise* (July/August 1998), and Aaron L. Friedberg, "The Struggle for Mastery in Asia," *Commentary*, November 2000, pp. 17–26, and Aaron L. Friedberg and Critics, "Facing China," *Commentary*, February 2001, pp. 16–26. A study that finds both significant strengths and weaknesses in China's military is James R. Lilley and David Shambaugh (eds.), *China's Military Faces the Future* (Armonk, NY: M.E. Sharpe, 1999).

The literature on the U.S.–PRC–Taiwan triangle is voluminous. An excellent historical review of relations is Nancy Bernkopf Tucker's *Taiwan, Hong Kong, and the United States, 1945–1992: Uncertain Friendships* (New York: Twayne Publishers, 1994). The various options for the United States on Taiwan policy are spelled out in her "China–Taiwan: U.S. Debates and Policy Choices, *Survival,* Vol. 40, No. 4 (Winter 1998–1999), pp. 150–167. Representative contributions that stress the need to reassure both the PRC and Taiwan and deter each from taking provocative action are Ralph N. Clough, *Cooperation or Conflict in the Taiwan Strait?* (Lanham, MD: Rowman & Littlefield, 1999); David Shambaugh, "Taiwan's Success Story," *Washington Post,* March 19, 2000, p. B7; and Nancy

Bernkopf Tucker, "War or Peace in the Taiwan Strait?" *Washington Quarterly*, Vol. 19, No. 1 (Winter 1996), pp. 171–187. Pieces that are more sensitive to Taiwan's need for reassurance from the United States include Aaron L. Friedberg, "Will We Abandon Taiwan?" *Commentary*, May 2000; James Lilley and Arthur Waldron, "Taiwan Is a 'State': Get Over It," *Wall Street Journal*, July 14, 1999, p. A22; Andrew J. Nathan, "What's Wrong with American Taiwan Policy," *Washington Quarterly*, Vol. 23, No. 2 (Spring 2000), pp. 93–106; and Stephen J. Yates, "Clinton Statement Undermines Taiwan," *Heritage Foundation Executive Memorandum*, No. 538 (July 10, 1998). Ted Galen Carpenter argues that the United States should aid Taiwan through weapons sales and not a commitment to intervene in a crisis in his "Let Taiwan Defend Itself," *Cato Policy Analysis*, No. 313 (August 24, 1998). And a collection of views from scholars from the United States, the PRC, and Taiwan are contained in Gerrit W. Gong (ed.), *Taiwan Strait Dilemmas: China–Taiwan–U.S. Policies in the New Century* (Washington, DC: CSIS Press, 2000).

The text of the Cox Report is available on-line at hillsource.house.gov/ CoxReport/report/welcome2.html. The most detailed scholarly critique of the report's findings is M. M. May (ed.), *The Cox Committee Report: An Assessment* (Stanford, CA: Center for International Security and Cooperation, Stanford University, December 1999). Briefer interpretations with alternative viewpoints of the Cox Report and charges of Chinese espionage are found in Charles Krauthammer, "The Real China Scandal," *Washington Post*, May 28, 1999, p. A35; Michael Ledeen, "The Administration Quashes Truth Tellers on China," *Wall Street Journal*, June 10, 1999, p. A26; Bill Mesler, "The Spy Who Wasn't," *The Nation*, August 9/16, 1999; and Jonathan D. Pollack, "The Cox Report's 'Dirty Little Secret,'" *Arms Control Today* (April/May 1999), pp. 26–27, 34–35.

Opinion pieces that stress the benefits of trade with China are "Keeping China's Door Open," *Boston Globe*, May 15, 1990, p. 14; Nick Liang, "MFN Looks Good to Tiananmen Leader," *Christian Science Monitor*, June 16, 1997, p. 19; Richard Lowry, "China Trade—Without Guilt," *National Review*, May 14, 2001, pp. 39–41; and Stephen J. Yates, "U.S. to China: Join the WTO, but Real Work Lies Ahead," *Heritage Foundation Executive Memorandum*, No. 638 (December 9, 1999). An informative edited volume that makes the case for permanent MFN for China is James R. Lilley and Wendell L. Wilkie II (eds.), *Beyond MFN: Trade with China and American Interests* (Washington, DC: AEI Press, 1994). The opposing side is forcefully argued in "The Bamboo Gulag," *Richmond Times-Dispatch*, June 3, 1990, p. G6; Liu Binyan, "Bush's Policy on China Repeats Old U.S. Errors," *Newsday*, June 25, 1990, p. 47; Robert L. Bernstein and Fang Lizhi, "America's Must Be One of the Voices," *Los Angeles Times*, November 5, 1991, p. B7; A. M. Rosenthal, "Who Pays China's Army?" *New York Times*, August 5, 1994, p. A25; Michael A. Ledeen, "No Tyrants Allowed," *Weekly Standard*, Vol. 2, No. 23 (February 24, 1997), p. 28; and Wei

Jingsheng, "Free Trade with China? No, It Will Subsidize Tyranny," *Wall Street Journal,* May 18, 2000, p. A26. A study that argues that China should be allowed entry into the World Trade Organization only if it creates the proper domestic legal institutions beforehand is Mark A. Groombridge and Claude E. Barfield, *Tiger by the Tail: China and the World Trade Organization* (Washington, DC: AEI Press, 1999).

Many of the previously mentioned general treatments of relations and those dealing with MFN discuss human rights policy. Three nongovernmental organizations that regularly publish reports on China's human rights situation and have consistently been critical of American policy are Amnesty International (www.amnesty.org), Human Rights Watch (www.hrw.org), and Laogai Research Foundation (www.laogai.org). Works that challenge some of the findings of Harry Wu of the Laogai Foundation is Robert Wright, "The Trouble with Harry," *The New Republic,* July 31, 1995, p. 6, and James D. Seymour and Richard Anderson, *New Ghosts, Old Ghosts: Prisons and Labor Reform Camps in China* (Armonk, NY: M. E. Sharpe, 1998). Suggestions for how the United States could promote a human rights agenda with China that stresses cooperative solutions is Harry Harding, "Breaking the Impasse over Human Rights," in Vogel, *Living with China,* pp. 165–184. A creative essay that argues that the United States and others would more successfully engage China's leaders on human rights issues if they emphasized how China's current situation compares with earlier periods in Chinese history rather than with contemporary Western standards is Jeffrey N. Wasserstrom's "Beyond Ping-Pong Diplomacy: China and Human Rights," *World Policy Journal,* Winter 2000–2001, pp. 61–66.

Works since 1990 that argue American businessmen, current and former government officials, and/or academics have had a conflict of interest in advocating good ties with China include Bernstein and Munro, *The Coming Conflict with China,* pp. 105–129; Gao Zhan (as told to Alix Spiegel), "My Ordeal in a Chinese Cell: An American University Scholar's Six Months Behind Bars," *New York Times Magazine,* September 16, 2001, pp. 32–37; Bill Gertz and Rowan Scarborough, "Friend of China," *Washington Times,* January 7, 2000, p. A9; Christopher Hitchens, *The Trial of Henry Kissinger* (London: Verso Books, 2001); John B. Judis, "Sullied Heritage: The Decline of Principled Conservative Hostility to China," *The New Republic,* April 23, 2001; Steven W. Mosher, *China Misperceived: American Illusions and Chinese Reality* (New York: Basic Books, 1990); and Gerald Segal, "Hong Kong, China and the 'Pander Tendency,'" *The World Today,* March 1997. One of the few published responses to these charges by one of the accused of having a conflict of interest is Robert Kapp (the president of the U.S.–China Business Council), "Bookshelf: The Coming Conflict with China," *China Business Review,* Vol. 24, No. 4 (July–August 1997), pp. 44–45.

# Index

*Page numbers appearing in italics refer to political cartoons*

Egypt, U.S. support of, 9–10
electronic warfare capabilities of China, 204
Embassy bombing, Chinese, 242, 305
emigration practices, 15–17, 117
employment: in China, 123; in U.S., 58
Endean, Erin, 265
environmental problems, 92, 174–75
espionage, 208, 231–33
Europe (Western), cooperation in theater nuclear force modernization, 29
"even-handed treatment" policy, 14, 16
Eximbank credits, 16
Export Administration Act, 240
exports from China: average annual growth of, 252; weapons, 82, 166, 174, 184, 238, 279. *See also* sanctions, economic
exports to China: Clinton's comments on, 174; consequences of removal of most-favored-nation status, 127–28; controls for, 22–23, 26; market access issues, 247–48; satellites, 238–41; textiles transshipment, 248–49; viewed as not important, 189; weapons, 27, 28–32
exports to Taiwan, weapons: amount of, 228; as intent of TRA, 225–26; and Joint Communiqué on the Establishment of Diplomatic Relations, 35–37; and normalization negotiations, 40–41; while exporting to China, 29

*Face the Nation*, 165, 286
Faison, Seth, 256
Falun Gong, 290
Fang Lizhi, 140–42
*Far Eastern Economic Review*, 151
Final Act of the Uruguay Round, 254
financial condition of China. *See* economic condition of China
Fisher, Richard, 278–80

Fitzgerald, F. Scott, 119
footwear industry, 22–23
forced labor, 249–50
Ford, Carl, 210–18
Ford, Gerald, 7
Forum for International Policy, 264–65
Foster, John, 236
Frank, Barney, 204
"free enterprise" in China, 123
Freeman, Chas, 297
Friedman, Thomas L., 256–58
Fulbright program, 115
Fulbright scholars, 96
FY99 military balance report, 209, 215

gas emissions, greenhouse, 174–75
Germany, comparison/contrast of China with, 150, 290, 297
Gertz, Bill, xxiv, xxv, 195–99
Gill, Bates, 201–9, 307
Gingrich, Newt, 165, 166, 263
Glenn, John, 38, 42, 83
global climate change, 175
Gorbachev, Mikhail S., 102, 106
Gore, Al, 174–75, 182
Graybow, Charles, 149–51
Gregor, A. James, 69–73
growth of China's power: arms agreements, 160; Chinese military, 161–64; containment by U.S. as response to, 165–67; effect on regional stability, 156; history of U.S. reaction toward, 156–57; involvement in arms control, 158–59; stress on nationalism instead of communism, 163; U.S. conditional help with, 157
GTE Corporation, 263
Guangdong International Trust and Investment Company, 253

Haig, Alexander Jr., 25, 27, 99, 262, 263–64
Halliburton Oil, 262

Hamilton, Lee H., xv

Hansen-Sturm, Cord, 19–20

Harding, Harry, 178–84

Hart, Gary, 262

Havel, Vaclav, 129

Hayakawa, S. I., 38–39

hegemony, Soviet, 7, 12, 29–30, 69–70

Helms, Jesse, 145–47, 224, 227

Herblock, *139*

Hills, Carla, 262, 265

Hitchcock, David, 155

Holdridge, John H.: House testimony by, 25–28; Senate testimony by, 39–41, 42; on strategic relations with China, 30; on Taiwan issue, 295–96

Hong Kong, emigration to, 17

House Select Committee on U.S. National Security and Military/Commercial Concerns, 231. *See also* Cox Report

Hua Guofeng (Hua Kuo-feng), 12, 104

Huang, John, 265

Huang Hua, 30

Huffington, Arianna, 267–68

Hughes, Patrick, 237

Hughes/Loral scandal, 208

human rights: Colin Powell's comments on, 276; discussions at Clinton-Jiang summits, 181; and emigration, 15–17; further reading, 314; in history of China, 45, 47; and most-favored-nation (MFN) status, 15–17, 18, 20–21, 138–40, 144, 185; prison labor, 249–50; promotion of, 45, 46–47; reconciling with U.S. security interests in Asia, 43–50; and Tiananmen Square, 90–94, 99, 119; U.S. criticism of China's actions, 176, 303, 305; use in the power play of foreign policy, 138–40, 185

Hussein, Saddam, 279

Hu Yaobang, 31

IAEA (International Atomic Energy Agency), 75, 77, 81, 82

IMF (International Monetary Fund), 71

immigrants, Chinese, 198–99

imperialism of China, 67–69

importation, 22–23, 58, 247–48

income in China and Taiwan. *See* median income

India: building relations with, 166; effect of U.S.–China military relationship, 30–31; and Nuclear Nonproliferation Act, 80; relationship with Soviet Union, 31; reliance on nuclear weapons, 198; trade relationship with U.S., 31; view of U.S. non-proliferation policy, 241

informal news sources, *1*

information warfare, 207

intelligence agencies, U.S., 196–97

internal conflicts, importance of Chinese military in preventing, 162

International Atomic Energy Agency (IAEA), 75, 77, 81, 82

International Monetary Fund (IMF), 71

International Olympic Committee (IOC), 149, 151, 152, 153, 289, 290

international organized crime, 174

International Trade Commission (ITC), 22

Internet use in China, 257

investment in China, 9. *See also* exports to China

IOC (International Olympic Committee), 149, 151, 152, 153, 289, 290

Iran: China's weapons exports to, 82, 238, 242, 279; U.S. and liberalization program, 10

isolation of China. *See* containment policy

Israel, U.S. lack of support of, 9–10

ITC (International Trade Commission), 22

# About the Contributors

**Lee H. Hamilton** has been director of the Woodrow Wilson International Center for Scholars in Washington, D.C., and director of the Center on Congress at Indiana University since 1999. From 1965 to 1999, he served as a U.S. representative from Indiana and became very influential in foreign affairs. He served as a member of the Committee on Foreign Affairs (now the Committee on International Relations) for his entire time in Congress, and he chaired the committee from 1993 to 1995. He also chaired the subcommittee on Europe and the Middle East for more than twenty years. Hamilton also chaired in Congress the Joint Economic Committee, the Permanent Select Committee on Intelligence, the Joint Committee on the Organization of Congress, and the Select Committee to Investigate Covert Arms Transactions with Iran. Hamilton is a graduate of Depauw University and the Indiana University School of Law.

**Scott Kennedy** (Ph.D., political science, George Washington University) is assistant professor of East Asian languages and cultures and adjunct assistant professor of political science at Indiana University. His research interests include political economy, Chinese politics, and U.S.–China relations. His dissertation, "In the Company of Markets: The Transformation of China's Political Economy," examined the growth of business influence on China's public policy process. His articles have appeared in the *China Quarterly, Problems of Post-Communism,* the *Journal of East Asian Affairs,* and the *Asian Wall Street Journal.* From 1993 to 1997, he was a research assistant in the Foreign Policy Studies Program of the Brookings Institution.

**Wu Xinbo** (Ph.D., international relations, Fudan University) is professor at the Center for American Studies at Fudan University, which he joined in 1992. He teaches Sino–U.S. relations and writes widely about China's foreign policy, Sino–American relations, and Asia-Pacific issues. Wu is the author of *Dollar Diplomacy and Major Powers in China, 1909–1913* (Fudan University Press, 1997) , and he has published numerous articles and book chapters in China, the

United States, Japan, Germany, South Korea, Singapore, and India. He has been a visiting scholar at George Washington University, Stanford University, the Henry Stimson Center, and the Brookings Institution.

**Zhu Feng** (Ph.D., international relations, Peking University) is professor and director of the International Security Program at Peking University's School of International Studies. He writes extensively on missile defense, Sino–U.S. relations, and regional security issues in East Asia. His new book is titled *The Ballistic Missile Defense and International Security* (Shanghai People's Press, 2001).